CROSS-BORDER TRANSFER AND COLLATERAL
OF RECEIVABLES

Legal systems around the world vary widely in terms of how they deal with the transfer of and security interests in receivables. The aim of this book is to help international financiers and lawyers in relevant markets in their practice of international receivables financing. Substantively, this book analyses three types of receivables financing transactions, ie outright transfer, security transfer and security interests. This book covers comprehensive comparison and analysis of the laws on the transfer of and security interests in receivables of fifteen major jurisdictions, encompassing common law jurisdictions, Roman–Germanic jurisdictions and French–Napoleonic jurisdictions, as well as relevant EU Directives. To be more specific, this book compares and analyses the relevant legal systems of the US, Canada, New Zealand, Australia, Korea, Japan, France, Belgium, England, Hong Kong, Singapore, China, Germany, Austria and the Netherlands. Furthermore, in order to analyse those legal systems from the international perspective, this book compares relevant international conventions; it also proposes to establish an international registration system for the transfer of and security interests in receivables.

Cross-border Transfer and Collateralisation of Receivables

A Comparative Analysis of Multiple Legal Systems

Woo-jung Jon

·HART·
OXFORD · LONDON · NEW YORK · NEW DELHI · SYDNEY

HART PUBLISHING
Bloomsbury Publishing Plc
Kemp House, Chawley Park, Cumnor Hill, Oxford, OX2 9PH, UK

HART PUBLISHING, the Hart/Stag logo, BLOOMSBURY and the Diana logo are
trademarks of Bloomsbury Publishing Plc
First published in Great Britain 2018

First published in hardback, 2018
Paperback edition, 2020

Copyright © Woo-jung Jon 2018

Woo-jung Jon has asserted his right under the Copyright,
Designs and Patents Act 1988 to be identified as Author of this work.

All rights reserved. No part of this publication may be reproduced or transmitted in any form or by
any means, electronic or mechanical, including photocopying, recording, or any information
storage or retrieval system, without prior permission in writing from the publishers.

While every care has been taken to ensure the accuracy of this work, no responsibility for loss
or damage occasioned to any person acting or refraining from action as a result of any statement in it
can be accepted by the authors, editors or publishers.

All UK Government legislation and other public sector information used in the work is Crown
Copyright ©. All House of Lords and House of Commons information used in the work is
Parliamentary Copyright ©. This information is reused under the terms of the Open Government
Licence v3.0 (http://www. nationalarchives.gov.uk/doc/open-government-licence/version/3) except
where otherwise stated.

All Eur-lex material used in the work is © European Union,
http://eur-lex.europa.eu/, 1998–2020.

A catalogue record for this book is available from the British Library.

Library of Congress Cataloging-in-Publication Data

Names: Jon, Woo-Jung, 1976-, author.
Title: Cross-border transfer and collateralisation of receivables : a comparative
analysis of multiple legal systems / Woo-jung Jon.
Description: Portland, Oregon : Hart Publishing, 2018. |
Includes bibliographical references and index.
Identifiers: LCCN 2017045284 (print) | LCCN 2017045673 (ebook) |
ISBN 9781509914364 (Epub) | ISBN 9781509914340 (hardback)
Subjects: LCSH: Transfer (Law). | Conflict of laws—Security. | Accounts receivable. |
Payments. | Negotiable instruments. | Security (Law)
Classification: LCC K7218.T7 (ebook) | LCC K7218.T7 J66 2018 (print) | DDC 343.08/7—dc23
LC record available at https://lccn.loc.gov/2017045284

ISBN: HB: 978-1-50991-434-0
PB: 978-1-50993-826-1
ePDF: 978-1-50991-435-7
ePub: 978-1-50991-436-4

Typeset by Compuscript Ltd, Shannon

To find out more about our authors and books visit www.hartpublishing.co.uk. Here you will find
extracts, author information, details of forthcoming events and the option to sign up for our newsletters.

FOREWORD 1

The importance of receivables financing in the financial world today cannot be underestimated. As payment methods have become more instantaneous and electronic, so the financing of trade and businesses by negotiations of bills of exchange and promissory notes has become less prevalent. Businesses do, however, still sell or provide services on credit, and the financing of the resultant receivables is a critically important way of maintaining cash flow. Moreover, asset-based financing (particularly receivables financing), with the increased comfort for financiers which comes from the focus on the collateral as the source of repayment, is often a much cheaper form of financing than that based on other structures. In the past years, such financing has become much more international, and receivables financing is a major means of global capital flow. It is therefore a most apposite time to consider the law relating to cross-border receivables financing.

This book, which grew out of the author's doctorate at the University of Oxford, for which I was his supervisor, makes two significant contributions to the scholarship in this area. First, it includes a detailed comparative study of the law relating to the transfer of receivables, performed by asking a number of questions and answering them with reference to the law in 15 jurisdictions, including common law and civil law jurisdictions, plus common law jurisdictions which have personal property security legislation in place. Having demonstrated that there are a plethora of different approaches to perfection and priority of receivables transfers, the argument is made that a transnational approach is to be preferred. Thus, the book develops a scheme for an international registry of transfers of receivables, on the lines of the Cape Town Convention on International Interests in Mobile Equipment 2002. Some of the most difficult issues in such a scheme, such as the issue of scope, are tackled ingeniously by limiting the register to receivables transferred or granted by a particular type of SPV: businesses would be incentivised to use such a structure by the cheaper credit available from the use of the register. Not only is the scheme described in detail, the author also provides a draft Convention showing the precise details of how the scheme would work.

This book is worthy of the attention of all those interested in cross-border receivables financing, and also all those interested in transnational commercial law solutions to legal issues thrown up by globalisation and the internationalisation of capital flows. I am delighted that all Woo-jung Jon's hard work while he was a student, and his experience since then, have come to fruition in this book, and I am very honoured to have the opportunity to write this foreword.

Louise Gullifer
Professor of Commercial Law, Oxford University
28th August 2017

FOREWORD 2

Woo-jung Jon has written a fascinating book on the comparative law of receivables transfers and securities. His work embodies a vast amount of careful scholarship, looking not only at familiar comparisons of English common law with French and German laws, or European laws with American, but also taking in lively arenas of common-law experimentation in Far Eastern and Commonwealth jurisdictions, and more rarely still, encompassing the burgeoning legal systems of China, Korea and Japan. The full list of jurisdictions covered comprises the United States, Canada, New Zealand, Australia, Korea, Japan, France, Belgium, England, Singapore, Hong Kong, China, Germany, Austria and the Netherlands. And of course Woo-jung also takes in the international trade and arbitration world as well, studying the UNIDROIT Cape Town Convention for movables alongside the various EU, EBRD, and UN rules covering this vast area of commercial and financial life. So this is a ground-breaking work in global comparative commercial law, showing a linguistic and jurisprudential command of the sources that is truly impressive. It may be that only a lawyer from Korea could have assimilated so much global jurisprudence, with such an open and enquiring mind, and with such sensitivity to the content of varied national laws and an absence of distorting preconceptions. In this fluent and masterly performance, Woo-jung draws on deep practical knowledge of legal and commercial practice, and has also benefited from the doctrinal rigour of law studies at Oxford with leading figures such as Louise Gullifer and Sir Roy Goode who guided his studies. I too was pleased to have a role in the cultivation of Woo-jung's scholarship as one of his supervisors and examiners; this was certainly a case where the pupil taught the teacher.

*

This book is primarily cast in terms of legal doctrine; it is not a work of legal sociology or economics. Doctrine provides a powerful language by which the work of lawyers in very different systems can be understood and compared, but as Woo-jung constantly reminds us, we must still be mindful of the limits of law in setting the terms for practice, and sensitive to local ways of working as transactional technicians that may not be captured in the formal or 'black-letter' concepts we find in the legal sources. Indeed, doctrinalists from different jurisdictions may find great difficulty in even understanding each other's languages; receivables can be described in different places variously as property or obligations, as primary legal debts or secondary equitable claims, as novations, assignments or pledges, or given new legislative denominators. Thorny problems such as perfection of assignments with multiple claimants, or the operation of anti-assignment clauses, permit of no simple answers. We live with a global menagerie of jurisprudential concepts that do not align neatly with the species of transaction that each concept denotes, and this book makes a major contribution in identifying the conceptual issues.

Woo-jung Jon starts with the problem that international and domestic commercial laws, in these inevitable conditions of conceptual complexity, have failed to provide a transparent, well-understood and cost-efficient system for transferring or securing securities in the cross-border flows of finance that are such a feature of today's global world. He argues that receivables remain an important asset class for small and medium businesses as well as large industrial, utility and financial institutions, allowing impersonal and stable finance stream to be won without sacrificing the continued operation of the borrower's business should collateral have to be attached. It is therefore important to design a system that works and works well. He further argues against a trend to walling of national economies as a remedy against financial bubbles and contagion, suggesting (perhaps controversially) that effective cross-border finance can help spread risks and solve cash-flow or liquidity crises by allowing fresh money from one jurisdiction to support systemically distressed debt in another. But Woo-jung is also keenly aware that local legal systems cannot easily sacrifice local methods of conceiving, transferring and securing assets; legal cultures are too entrenched, and legal-political sovereignties are not to be sacrificed too quickly in a world where globalisation provokes increasing anxieties. Woo-jung's resolution of this set of interlocking puzzles is elegant and convincing: his overarching insight is to identify the need for a broadly recognized international system of notice filing registration, modelled on the UNIDROIT Cape Town Convention on interests in movables, that will allow the existence and priority of attached receivables to be set by the time of registration in each relevant jurisdiction, but with the publicity of the register being made available to each jurisdiction to use within its own distinctive legal order, thus preserving subsidiarity.

As a legal historian studying the evolution of commercial life governed by law, I am well aware that great changes may grow from seemingly technical and carefully-defined reforms. Whether the publicity of securities created by the proposed international register would lead to new methods of assessing credit-worthiness and matching the supply of credit to collateral is an intriguing question that lawyers and legislators do not need to answer; they can create promising legal techniques to solve defined problems, and leave commerce to evolve in response. With this in mind, I look forward to following future editions of this path-breaking work, and measuring the impact of Woo-jung's learned and imaginative legal scholarship in the world of international commerce. At the very least Woo-jung has made a case to be answered, and he has prepared an intellectual feast of comparative scholarship for all lawyers interested in questions surrounding the creation, perfection, priority and enforcement of dealings in receivables.

Joshua Getzler
25 Sep 2017

Fellow of St Hugh's College and Professor of Law and Legal History at the University of Oxford, and Conjoint Professor of Law at the University of New South Wales

FOREWORD 3

This book is a comparative research on cross-border transfer and collateralisation of receivables. Receivables are increasingly transferred and collateralised across national borders. Transactions of enormous volume of receivables are being carried out every day, which continues to increase its pace. Disposal of non-performing loans, securitisation and factoring involve the assignment of receivables. Currently, however, the jurisdictions of the world have all sorts of different legal approaches about what financiers have to do to obtain the validity of dealings in receivables, so that the global position is extremely complicated and much of it is out of date or impenetrable.

There is a dearth of textbooks on receivables financing. The last comprehensive text was Fidelis Oditah's *Legal Aspects of Receivables Financing* in 1990. There are parts of other books that cover the issue but not in depth. So in principle there is room for this book.

The author of this book is one of my former students at the Seoul National University Law School, and he and I have enjoyed maintaining correspondence and communications; professional, academic and personal, since 1997. Even when I resided in The Hague, the Netherlands as a judge and president of the International Criminal Court, we continued to discuss his doctoral works closely. I am delighted that Dr Jon's doctoral dissertation is published in book form by a prestigious publisher, Hart Publishing.

This book contains 7 Chapters, namely, apart from an introduction and conclusion, 5 substantive Chapters. Chapters 2, 3 and 4 examine the law in many different jurisdictions and the different registry systems, which I think are the most useful aspect of this book. The author compares 15 major jurisdictions with analyses of legal families generally and the EU financial collateral directives in particular.

Chapters 5 and 6 are devoted to his bold and innovative proposals. He proposes a new international registration system for transfers and security interests over receivables, building upon, but going much further than, the UN Convention on the Assignment of Receivables in International Trade. A proposal for a draft international convention has been made, partly modelled on the Cape Town Convention of 2001 for aircraft. There are many differences between huge tangible aircraft and vast numbers of intangible receivables floating around. However, the author deals with the technical and complicated subject with great aplomb and ingenuity. He has comprehensively covered all the angles that matter and discussed a feasibility of such an international receivables registry.

If the author's original proposal is realised, it would suffice to check the proposed international receivables registry, probably without having to refer to the national systems. It is expected that such an international receivables registry would reduce transaction costs of global receivables financing.

Professor Dr Sang-Hyun Song
President, Korean Committee for UNICEF

ACKNOWLEDGEMENTS

This book is written based upon my doctorate thesis at the University of Oxford, 'Establishing an International Registration System for the Assignment and Security Interest of Receivables'. I would like to express my deep gratitude to the professors, scholars and friends, without whom I could not write this book, whose stimulating advice, considerate guidance and invaluable suggestions helped me in all the time of research for and writing of this book.

I am indeed deeply indebted to my supervisor, Professor Louise Gullifer of the University of Oxford, Faculty of Law, Director of the Secured Transaction Law Reform Project, who, from the beginning, was of the greatest help and gave wonderful teachings, gracious encouragement and full support for me to conduct comparative research on various jurisdictions and to understand complicated legal concepts of English common law and secured transactions.

I am also deeply obliged to Professor Sir Roy Goode for his insightful advice and invaluable comments. As Professor Sir Goode is the father of the Cape Town Convention, I was most privileged to be examined by him for my doctorate degree. I sincerely thank him for sharing his wisdom and precious experiences with me.

I would like to thank especially Professor Joshua Getzler of the University of Oxford, Faculty of Law, for his endless support and encouragement and inspiring advice and comments from the early days when I first arrived in Oxford. It was my pleasure and honour to start and finish my student life in Oxford with him.

I sincerely appreciate Professor Philip Wood's precious inspiring teaching and generous support. I am also very grateful for Professor John Armour of the University of Oxford, Faculty of Law and Professor Wolf-Georg Ringe of the University of Hamburg.

I am very much obliged to Professor Lynn M LoPucki of UCLA School of Law for his graciously sharing his vital knowledge with me. I thank Professor Steven L Schwarcz of Duke University School of Law for his invaluable advice and our discussions. I also thank Professor Lorenzo Stanghellini of the University of Florence in Italy for his kind advice. I sincerely thank Professor Jacob Ziegel of the University of Toronto for his insightful advice about Canadian registration systems of personal property security interests.

Since the ultimate goal of my project is to propose an international convention which could be acceptable globally, I attempted to research as many jurisdictions as possible. My academic odyssey was long, and I met many excellent scholars around the world.

I studied at Seoul National University College of Law in Seoul, Korea, Peking University Law School and Tsinghua University Law School in Beijing, China, Tokyo University Faculty of Law in Tokyo, Japan, and researched at the United Nations Commission on International Trade Law (UNCITRAL) in Vienna, Austria, the International Institute for the Unification of Private Law (UNIDROIT) in Rome, Italy and the Max Planck Institute for Comparative and International Private Law in Hamburg, Germany.

I sincerely thank President SONG Sang-Hyun, who was my supervisor at Seoul National University for his endless support and mentoring. I also thank Professor LEE Ki-Su of Korea University Law School for his inspiration and encouragement. I deeply thank Professor CHAI Lee-Sik of Korea University Law School for his generous support. I also thank Professor KIM Kon Sik of Seoul National University Law School for his invaluable teachings and generous support. I thank Professor CHOI Young-Hong of Korea University Law School for his insightful mentoring and guidance. I thank Professor YOON Nam-Geun of Korea University Law School for his excellent teachings and gracious support. I deeply thank Professor SUK Kwang-Hyun of Seoul National University Law School for his invaluable advice, gracious support and generous encouragement. I thank Professor MYOUNG Soon-Koo of Korea University Law School for his precious lessons and encouragement. I sincerely thank Professor KIM Yong-Jae of Korea University Law School for his excellent teachings and precious mentoring.

I thank Justice KIM Jae-Hyung of the Korea Supreme Court for his invaluable teaching and advice on Korean civil law and the Korean Security Registration Act and endless support. I also thank Professor SONG Ok-Rial of Seoul National University Law School for his gracious encouragement and invaluable advices. I sincerely thank Professor JANG Junhyok of Sungkyunkwan University Law School for his precious teachings on comparative analysis of private international laws with respect to priority of the assignment of receivables. I thank Professor KWON Young-Joon of Seoul National University Law School for his inspiring advice and comments on the issue of notice-filing systems.

I carried out research at Tokyo University Faculty of Law in Japan as a research student. I sincerely thank Professor DOGAUCHI Hiroto for his inspiring perspectives on the assignment of receivables and invaluable information on the Japanese assignment registration system. I also deeply thank Professor KANDA Hideki for his precious advice and guidance on my research of Japanese financial laws.

I would also like to thank Professor Omi HATASHIN of Osaka Jogakuin College for his help in my comparative analysis of Japanese laws.

I also researched at Peking University Law School in China. I deeply thank Professor PENG Bing for his invaluable guidance and teaching. I am sincerely grateful to Professor GUO Li for his precious advice and comments. I thank Professor XU Defeng for his precious guidance and teaching with respect to Chinese insolvency law. I thank Professor LOU Jianbo for his excellent suggestion of a registration system for the assignment of receivables in China. Furthermore, I am deeply indebted to Professor LI Qingchi of the Chinese Academy of Governance for his great support of my research on Chinese financial laws.

At Tsinghua University Law School in China. I thank Professor WANG Chenguang for his gracious support and insightful advice. I sincerely thank Professor TANG Xin for his invaluable teachings and support. I deeply thank Professor Tarrant Mahony for his excellent teachings and advice.

Thanks to the UNIDROIT scholarship, I was able to research at UNIDROIT. I would like to deeply thank UNIDROIT for this support. I had wonderful times in Rome for two months, during which period, I was able to learn about the registration system of the International Registry of Mobile Assets under the Cape Town Convention. I sincerely thank Mr Martin John Stanford for his invaluable support and teachings. I also thank Mr John Atwood for sharing his unique and precious experiences and practical information about the operation of the Cape Town Convention.

I also had a wonderful season at the UNCITRAL in Vienna, Austria. I deeply thank Dr Spiros V Bazinas for his gracious support and encouragement and sharing his comprehensive knowledge and experience with me. I am very much indebted to Mr Jae-Sung LEE for his support, advice and guidance.

Thanks to the Max Planck Society Scholarship, I was able to research at the Max Planck Institute for Comparative and International Private Law in Hamburg, Germany. I sincerely thank Professor Ulrich Drobnig for his invaluable advice and comments on my research project. I also thank Professor Reinhard Zimmermann, Professor Jürgen Basedow and Professor Christian Heinze.

My classmates from the Faculty of Law and friends supported me in my research work. I want to thank Professor Ying-Chieh WU of Singapore Management University for his warm help, support, kind interest and valuable suggestions. I deeply thank Professor Moira Gillis of the University of Oklahoma, who looked closely at the final version of my thesis for English style and grammar, correcting both and offering suggestions for improvement.

I would particularly like to pass on special thanks to the staff of Hart Publishing whose invaluable support and advice enabled me to publish this book.

CONTENTS

Foreword 1 v
Foreword 2 vii
Foreword 3 xi
Acknowledgements xiii
Table of Cases.. xxix
Table of Statutes, Conventions and Model Laws xxxi
Table of Online Registers xlv
List of Tables xlvii

1. Introduction 1
   1-1. Receivables 1
   1-2. Transfers of Receivables 2
        1-2-1. International Transfers of Receivables.................2
        1-2-2. Securitisation..3
        1-2-3. Factoring...4
   1-3. Security Rights in Receivables..4
   1-4. Security Transfer of Receivables 6
   1-5. Transfers Rather than Security Rights 7
   1-6. Proposal of an International Receivables Registry.............8
   1-7. Research Methods..9
   1-8. Overview of this Book 10
2. Security Rights Registries 11
   2-1. Introduction...11
   2-2. Publicity..12
        2-2-1. Methods of Publicity..12
        2-2-2. The Function of Publicity....................................13
               2-2-2-1. Providing Information to the Public.....13
               2-2-2-2. Evidence 14
   2-3. The Security Rights System in Common Law Jurisdictions................14
        2-3-1. Security Rights Registries in English Law 14
               2-3-1-1. English Courts of Equity Allowing
                        Non-possessory Charges..........................14
               2-3-1-2. The Publicity Problem of Non-possessory
                        Charges..15
               2-3-1-3. Registration as an *Ex Ante* Method 16

		2-3-1-4.	The Origin of Security Rights Registries in English Law 16
		2-3-1-5.	The Debtor-Based Indexed Registration System 17
	2-3-2.	Uniform Commercial Code Article 9 of the US 18
		2-3-2-1.	Historical Background 18
		2-3-2-2.	The Notice-Filing System 19
	2-3-3.	The Personal Property Security Acts (PPSAs) 20
2-4.	The Security Rights System in Civil Law Jurisdictions 20
	2-4-1.	The *Numerus Clausus* Principle 20
	2-4-2.	The Fiduciary Transfer of Title for Security Purposes 23
	2-4-3.	Special Registers 24
		2-4-3-1.	Germany 24
		2-4-3-2.	France 24
		2-4-3-3.	China 25
	2-4-4.	The General Security Rights Registry 28
		2-4-4-1.	France 28
		2-4-4-2.	Optional Registration 28
		2-4-4-3.	Japan 29
		2-4-4-4.	Korea 32
2-5.	International Efforts of Harmonisation 37
	2-5-1.	Soft Laws 37
		2-5-1-1.	The EBRD Model Law on Secured Transactions 37
		2-5-1-2.	The OAS Model Inter-American Law on Secured Transactions 38
		2-5-1-3.	The UNCITRAL Model Law on Secured Transactions 39
		2-5-1-4.	The Draft Common Frame of Reference (DCFR) 39
	2-5-2.	International Conventions 40
		2-5-2-1.	The UN Convention on the Transfer of Receivables in International Trade 40
		2-5-2-2.	The Convention on International Interests in Mobile Equipment 41
2-6.	The Pros and Cons of a General Security Rights Registry 42
	2-6-1.	Pros 42
		2-6-1-1.	Using Movable Assets as Security 42
		2-6-1-2.	Civil Law Jurisdiction v Common Law Jurisdiction 42
		2-6-1-3.	The World Bank Report 43
	2-6-2.	Cons 45
		2-6-2-1.	Over-leverage 45
		2-6-2-2.	Secured Creditor v Unsecured Creditor 46
	2-6-3.	Analysis 46

		2-7.	Filing Systems..47
		2-7-1.	Document-Filing System v Notice-Filing System...............47
		2-7-2.	The Effect of Notice-Filing..48
		2-7-3.	Advance Registration of Notice-Filing 50
		2-7-4.	Information Required for Effective Registration 51
			2-7-4-1. UCC Article 9..51
			2-7-4-2. The New Zealand PPSA...52
			2-7-4-3. The Australian PPSA..52
			2-7-4-4. The UNCITRAL Model Law on Secured Transactions..52
			2-7-4-5. UK Register of Company Charges 52
			2-7-4-6. The Korean Security Registration Act.................53
			2-7-4-7. The Japanese Transfer Registration Act.............53
	2-8.	Parties' Reciprocal Confirmation Instead of Registrar's Review.......57
		2-8-1.	Safeguards against Improper Registration under a Notice-Filing System..57
		2-8-2.	Comparative Research...58
			2-8-2-1. Compulsory Notice to the Grantor......................58
			2-8-2-2. Authorisation of the Grantor before or after Registration 59
			2-8-2-3. Consent of the Grantor Required before Registration 62
	2-9.	Search for Registration 65
		2-9-1.	Register of Charges in the UK at Companies House 65
		2-9-2.	UCC Article 9..66
		2-9-3.	The Japanese Transfer Registration Act 66
		2-9-4.	The Cape Town Convention 68
	2-10.	Conclusion 68
3.	Transfers of and Security Rights in Receivables 69
	3-1.	Introduction...69
	3-2.	Comparative Analysis on Priority and Perfection 70
		3-2-1.	The Definition of Perfection 70
		3-2-2.	Case Study...71
		3-2-3.	Six Common Questions 72
		3-2-4.	Table of Preliminary Answers..73
	3-3.	Priority 75
		3-3-1.	Priority of Transfers vis-a-vis Third Parties (Question 3)......75
		3-3-2.	Notification 75
			3-3-2-1. Notice of the Transfer to the Debtor 75
			3-3-2-2. Transferees not Entitled to Give Notice to the Debtor of the Receivable 77
			3-3-2-3. Transferees Entitled to Give Notice to the Debtor of the Receivable..78

		3-3-2-4.	Perfection against the Debtor of the Receivable...... 80
		3-3-2-5.	Set-off..80
	3-3-3.	Registration 81
	3-3-4.	The Time of Creation Doctrine 82
		3-3-4-1.	Neither Notice nor Registration.............................82
		3-3-4-2.	The Delivery of the Transfer Deed (*Bordereau*)...... 84
	3-3-5.	The Priority of Security Rights vis-a-vis Third Parties (Question 4) 86
3-4.	Perfection 88
	3-4-1.	Perfection of Transfers against the Insolvency Administrator (Question 1) 89
	3-4-2.	The Insolvency Administrator as a Transferee.......................90
	3-4-3.	The Insolvency Administrator as a Trustee............................92
		3-4-3-1.	Equitable Assignment under English Law 92
		3-4-3-2.	New Zealand..93
	3-4-4.	Perfection of Security Rights in the Insolvency Procedures of the Grantor (Question 2) 94
3-5.	Check Points 96
	3-5-1.	Priority between Transfers and Security Rights (Question 5) 96
	3-5-2.	The Potential Transferee's Check Points (Question 6) 98
3-6.	Classification of Jurisdictions..99
	3-6-1.	Classification 99
	3-6-2.	The Information Centre...102
3-7.	Answers to the Six Common Questions..103
	3-7-1.	The Six Common Questions 103
	3-7-2.	The US 103
		Qs 1, 2. Perfection...103
		Qs 3, 4, 5. Priority...104
		Q6. The Potential Transferee's Check Points.....................105
	3-7-3.	Canada...105
		Qs 1, 2. Perfection...105
		Qs 3, 4, 5. Priority...106
		Q6. The Potential Transferee's Check Points.....................106
	3-7-4.	New Zealand...106
		Qs 1, 2. Perfection...106
		Qs 3, 4, 5. Priority...107
		Q6. The Intending Transferee's Check Points 108
	3-7-5.	Australia..108
		Qs 1, 2. Perfection...108
		Qs 3, 4, 5. Priority...109
		Q6. The Potential Transferee's Check Points.....................109
	3-7-6.	Korea..109
		Qs 1, 3. Transfers 109

	Qs 2, 4. Security Rights..110
	Q5. Priority between Transfers and Security Rights..........111
	Q6. The Potential Transferee's Check Points.....................112
3-7-7.	Japan..112
	Qs 1, 2, 3, 4. Perfection and Priority...................................112
	Q5. Priority between Transfers and Security Rights..........114
	Q6. Potential Transferee's Check Points 114
3-7-8.	France 114
	Q1. Perfection of Transfers 114
	Q2. Perfection of Security Rights 117
	Q3. Priority of Transfers..117
	Q4. Priority of Security Rights 118
	Q5. Priority between Transfers and Security Rights..........118
	Q6. The Potential Transferee's Check Points.....................118
3-7-9.	Belgium..119
	Q1. Perfection of Transfers 119
	Q2. Perfection of Security Rights 119
	Qs 3, 4, 5. Priority 120
	Q6. The Potential Transferee's Check Points.....................120
3-7-10.	England...120
	Q1. Perfection of Transfers 120
	Q2. Perfection of Security Rights 121
	Q3. Priority of Transfers..121
	Q4. Priority of Security Rights 125
	Q5. Priority between Transfers and Security Rights..........126
	Q6. The Potential Transferee's Check Points.....................126
3-7-11.	China 127
	Q1. Perfection of Transfers 127
	Q2. Perfection of Security Rights 129
	Q3. Priority of Transfers..130
	Q4. Priority of Security Rights 130
	Q5. Priority between Transfers and Security Rights..........130
	Q6. Potential Transferee's Check Points 131
3-7-12.	Germany..131
	Q1. Perfection of Transfers 131
	Q2. Perfection of Security Rights 132
	Q3. Priority of Transfers..133
	Q4. Priority of Security Rights 134
	Q5. Priority between Transfers and Security Rights..........134
	Q6. The Potential Transferee's Check Points.....................134
3-7-13.	Austria 135
	Qs 1, 3. Transfers..135
	Qs 2, 4. Security Rights..135

			Q5. Priority between Transfers and Security Rights..........136
			Q6. The Potential Transferee's Check Points.....................136
		3-7-14.	The Netherlands..136
			Q1. Perfection of Transfers 136
			Q2. Perfection of Security Rights......................................137
			Qs 3, 4, 5. Priority 138
			Q6. The Potential Transferee's Check Points.....................138
		3-7-15.	Singapore...138
			Q1. Perfection of Transfers 138
			Q2. Perfection of Security Rights......................................139
			Q3. Priority of Transfers 139
			Q4. Priority of Security Rights..140
			Q5. Priority between Transfers and Security Rights..........141
			Q6. The Potential Transferee's Check Points.....................142
		3-7-16.	Hong Kong..142
			Q1. Perfection of Transfers 142
			Q2. Perfection of Security Rights......................................143
			Q3. Priority of Transfers 143
			Q4. Priority of Security Rights..144
			Q5. Priority between Transfers and Security Rights..........145
			Q6. The Potential Transferee's Check Points.....................146
	3-8.	The EU Directive on Financial Collateral Arrangements..................146
		3-8-1.	The Parties: Financial Institutions......................................146
		3-8-2.	Financial Collateral..147
			3-8-2-1. Cash and Financial Instruments......................147
			3-8-2-2. Credit Claims..147
		3-8-3.	Perfection 148
		3-8-4.	Priority 148
		3-8-5.	Implementation 148
	3-9.	Conclusion 150
4.	Conflicts of Laws and Technical Issues of the Debtor-Indexed Registration System 152
	4-1.	Introduction..152
	4-2.	The Governing Law 152
		4-2-1.	Transferor and Transferee..153
		4-2-2.	Transferor and Debtor, Transferee and Debtor...................153
		4-2-3.	Insolvency Administrator and Transferee...........................154
		4-2-4.	Attachment Creditor and Transferee 154
		4-2-5.	Transferee 1 and Transferee 2..154
	4-3.	The Governing Law for Priority...155
		4-3-1.	The Rome I Regulation 155
		4-3-2.	Private International Law..156
	4-4.	Perfection Methods and Check Points 159

		4-4-1.	What to Do for Perfection in International Transfers.......159
		4-4-2.	The Potential Transferee's Check Point 162
	4-5.	The Experience of the UN Receivables Convention 163
	4-6.	Registration is the Solution 163
		4-6-1.	Problems of the Notification Requirement........................ 163
			4-6-1-1. Facilitating Transfers of Future Receivables 164
			4-6-1-2. Facilitating Bulk Transfers of Receivables 164
		4-6-2.	Registration or No Publicity 165
		4-6-3.	Problems with No Publicity of Transfers 167
		4-6-4.	Is Registration Necessary? 168
	4-7.	The Double Debtor Problem 170
		4-7-1.	The Systemic Weakness of the Debtor-Indexed Registration System 170
		4-7-2.	English Law 173
			4-7-2-1. The *Nemo Dat Quod Non Habet* Rule................ 173
			4-7-2-2. Bona Fide Purchaser for Value without Notice... 174
		4-7-3.	UCC Article 9 and the PPSAs... 175
			4-7-3-1. Taking Subject to the Perfected Security Right...175
			4-7-3-2. Buyer in the Ordinary Course of Business 176
		4-7-4.	Change of Jurisdiction... 177
	4-8.	Floating Charges 178
		4-8-1.	English Floating Charges... 178
		4-8-2.	Security Rights in After-Acquired Property under the UCC and the PPSAs 179
		4-8-3.	Floating Charges with Negative Pledge 180
	4-9.	Reservation of Title 180
		4-9-1.	Reservation of Title v Transfer.. 180
			4-9-1-1. English Law.. 182
			4-9-1-2. UCC Article 9 and the PPSAs............................... 182
			4-9-1-3. Purchase-Money Security Interest 183
		4-9-2.	Floating Security Rights v Reservation of Title 185
			4-9-2-1. English Floating Charges 186
			4-9-2-2. Security Rights in After-Acquired Property under UCC Article 9 and the PPSAs.................. 186
	4-10.	Conclusion 187
5.	The International Receivables Registry 188
	5-1.	Introduction 188
	5-2.	Scope of the International Receivables Registry............................. 189
		5-2-1.	Translation 189
		5-2-2.	Identification.. 189
		5-2-3.	Separate International Registry for Each Type of Property 190

	5-2-4.	The International Receivables Registry..................................191
	5-2-5.	Receivables 192
	5-2-6.	Transfer 192
	5-2-7.	Security Rights 193
	5-2-8.	An International Receivables Registry Should Cover Both Transfers and Security Rights..194
5-3.	International Receivables Registry Registration............................194	
	5-3-1.	Limitation of Scope of the International Receivables Registry 194
	5-3-2.	Three Approaches to Unify the Laws.....................................196
		5-3-2-1. Compulsory Registration..196
		5-3-2-2. Optional Registration..196
		5-3-2-3. Providing Guides and Models 197
	5-3-3.	The Relationship between the Proposed International Receivables Registry Convention and National Laws..........197
		5-3-3-1. Compulsory or Optional..197
		5-3-3-2. Problems with the Optional Registration System 198
5-4.	The Compulsory Registration System with Limited Scope of Application 200	
	5-4-1.	To Confine the Internationality of the Transfer of Receivables 200
	5-4-2.	To Limit Types of Receivables..202
	5-4-3.	To Limit the Value Amount of Receivables 203
	5-4-4.	To Limit the Parties to be Registered....................................203
5-5.	Restriction of the Scope of Application of the Proposed International Receivables Registry Convention 204	
	5-5-1.	The IRT..204
	5-5-2.	The Transferor or Grantor Needs to be an IRT 205
	5-5-3.	The IRT-Indexed Registry 206
5-6.	Registration of an IRT 207	
	5-6-1.	Public Notification of the List of IRTs...................................207
	5-6-2.	Two Methods to Use the International Receivables Registry 207
		5-6-2-1. Establishing a Separate IRT 207
		5-6-2-2. Registering Itself as an IRT 208
	5-6-3.	Pre-existing Security Rights..209
	5-6-4.	Pre-existing Transfers...210
	5-6-5.	Sanctions for False Registration 212
		5-6-5-1. Fines 212
		5-6-5-2. Disqualification of the IRT 212
		5-6-5-3. Compensatory Damages 212
5-7.	Deregistration of an IRT...213	

		Contents	

	5-8.	The Sphere of Application of the Proposed International Receivables Registry Convention 213
	5-8-1.	Connecting Factors..213
	5-8-2.	Future Receivables 214
	5-8-3.	A Legal Person (Company)................................215
	5-8-4.	Interaction with the Cape Town Convention 217
		5-8-4-1. The Scope of the Cape Town Convention and its Protocols................217
		5-8-4-2. Transfer of Associated Receivables....217
		5-8-4-3. Extension of the Cape Town Convention to the Transfer of Receivables.............................218
	5-8-5.	Contractual Prohibition on the Transfer of Receivables...219
	5-9.	The Operation of the International Receivables Registry................220
	5-9-1.	A Notice-Filing System..220
		5-9-1-1. Why the Proposed International Receivables Registry Should be a Notice-Filing System.......220
		5-9-1-2. The Information Required for International Receivables Registry Registration 221
	5-9-2.	Parties' Reciprocal Confirmation Instead of Registrar's Review 222
	5-9-3.	Email Notification Linked to International Receivables Registry Registration...223
	5-9-4.	Supervisory Authority and Registry....................224
	5-9-5.	International Receivables Registry Online Search 226
	5-10.	Conclusion 226

6.	Priority in the International Receivables Registry 229
	6-1. Introduction..229
	6-2. Perfection 230
	6-3. Priority...230
	6-3-1. Priority by Order of Registration........................230
	6-3-2. Knowledge of an Unregistered Transfer or Security Right 231
	6-3-3. Registration has Nothing to do with Effectiveness against the Debtor..232
	6-3-4. Priority between Registration and Notice to the Debtor.......233
	6-3-5. Priority between Transfers and Security Rights.................234
	6-3-5-1. Prior Security Rights and Subsequent Transfer..............................234
	6-3-5-2. Prior Transfers and Subsequent Security Rights 234
	6-3-6. Double Transfers of a Receivable of an IRT......................235
	6-3-6-1. Double Transfers by an IRT 235

		6-3-6-2.	Double Transfers by an IRT and Subsequent Transfers by the Transferees 236
		6-3-6-3.	Double Transfers by an IRT and Subsequent Security Rights by the Transferees 237
	6-3-7.	Double Security Rights in a Receivable of an IRT 238
		6-3-7-1.	Double Security Rights Created by an IRT 238
		6-3-7-2.	Security Rights by an IRT Followed by Transfers of Secured Creditors 238
		6-3-7-3.	Double Security Rights Created by an IRT Followed by Transfers of Secured Creditors 239
		6-3-7-4.	Security Right Created by an IRT and Subsequent Security Right by the Secured Creditor 240
6-4.	The Double Debtor Problem 240
	6-4-1.	Security Rights and Subsequent Transfers 240
	6-4-2.	International Receivables Registry Jurisdiction 242
		6-4-2-1.	IRT → IRT → Non-IRT 242
		6-4-2-2.	IRT → Non-IRT → Non-IRT 243
		6-4-2-3.	Non-IRT → IRT → Non-IRT 245
	6-4-3.	The Secured Creditor's Rights in Proceeds 245
	6-4-4.	The Consent of Secured Creditors to a Transfer to a Non-IRT 246
6-5.	Floating Security Rights of the International Receivables Registry 247
	6-5-1.	The Fixed Charge and the Floating Charge 247
		6-5-1-1.	The Characteristics of Receivables 247
		6-5-1-2.	The Practice of Financial Institutions 248
		6-5-1-3.	Security Rights 248
	6-5-2.	Two Types of Security Rights over Receivables in the International Receivables Registry 248
	6-5-3.	Floating Security Right v Subsequent Transfer 249
	6-5-4.	Floating Security Right v Subsequent Security Right 249
	6-5-5.	Crystallisation 250
6-6.	Reservation of Title 250
	6-6-1.	Reservation of Title v Transfer 250
	6-6-2.	Floating Security Right v Reservation of Title 251
	6-6-3.	Purchase-Money Security Interests 251
6-7.	Preferential Creditors 252
6-8.	Proceeds 252
	6-8-1.	Proceeds from the Collection and Sale of Receivables 252
	6-8-2.	Proceeds Separated and Reasonably Identifiable 253
	6-8-3.	Dual Security Rights in a Transferred Receivable and Proceeds from Sale 253
	6-8-4.	The Proposed International Receivables Registry Rules on Proceeds 254

    6-9. Bonds 254
        6-9-1. Debt Represented by Bonds 254
        6-9-2. Covered Bonds..254
        6-9-3. Security Rights in the Bond Issuer's Receivables 255
    6-10. Subordination Agreements 256
    6-11. Conclusion 257

7. Conclusion..259

Appendix: Draft Convention on Priority of Transfers of, and Security Rights in, Receivables ('Draft International Receivables Registry Convention')..........263
Article 1 (Definitions)...263
Article 2 (Sphere of Application) 264
Article 3 (Registration of the IRT) 265
Article 4 (Deregistration of the IRT)...265
Article 5 (Priority)...265
Article 6 (Perfection)...266
Article 7 (Proceeds)...266
Article 8 (Transfer of a Security Right)...267
Article 9 (Floating Security Right) 267
Article 10 (Rights Having Priority without Registration)......................267
Article 11 (International Receivables Registry) 268
Article 12 (The Supervisory Authority and the Registrar).....................268
Article 13 (Information Required to Effect Registration)......................269
Article 14 (Registration, Amendment and Discharge)...........................269
Article 15 (Transferees Entitled to Give Notice to the Debtor)..............270
Article 16 (International Receivables Registry Jurisdiction).................270
Article 17 (Consent of Secured Creditors to Transfer to a Non-IRT) 271
Article 18 (Sanction for False Registration)...271
Article 19 (Search)...271
Article 20 (Contractual Prohibition on Transfers of Receivables) 272

Bibliography 273
Index 277

TABLE OF CASES

France

Cass Com. 5 July 1994, RTD com. 1995, 172 117
Cass Com. 4 July 1995, Bull civ IV, No 203; D 1996, Som, 208 116
Cass Com. 13 February 1996, Banque 1996, No. 569, 91 118
Cass Com. 12 January 1999, D Aff 1999, 336 117

Germany

BGH 20 June 1990, BGHZ 111, 376 157
BGH 26 November 1990, NJW 1991, 1414 157

The Netherlands

Sogelease case, HR 19 May 1995, NJ 1996, 119 137

Privy Council

Vandepitte v Preferred Accident Insurance Corporation of New York [1933]
   AC 70 (PC) 219

United Kingdom

Agnew v Commissioner of Inland Revenue [2001] UKPC 28, [2001] AC 710 (PC) 179
Banco Central SA v Lingos & Falce Ltd (The Raven) [1980] 2 Lloyd's Rep 266 81
Barbados Trust Co Ltd v Bank of Zambia [2007] EWCA Civ 148, (2007)
   9 ITELR 689 (CA) 219
Bim Kemi AB v Blackburn Chemicals Ltd (No 1) [2001] EWCA Civ 457; [2001]
   2 Lloyd's Rep 93 81
Carreras Rothmans Ltd v Freeman Mathews Treasure Ltd [1985] Ch 207 (Ch) 14
Compaq Computer Ltd v Abercorn Group Ltd [1993] BCLC 602 (Ch)..........124, 182, 186
Dearle v Hall (1828) 3 Russ 1 .... 18, 76–77, 87, 96, 106–07, 121–26, 139–46,
                                                                         173–74, 179, 182, 186, 237, 247
Ellerman Lines Ltd v Lancaster Maritime Co Ltd [1980] 2 Lloyd's
   Rep 497 (QB) 125, 141, 145
English and Scottish Mercantile Investment Co v Brunton [1892] 2 QB 700..................186
E. Pfeiffer Weinkellerei-Weineinkauf GmbH & Co v Arbuthnot Factors Ltd [1987]
   BCLC 522, [1988] 1 WLR 150 (QB) 124, 182, 186
Evans v Rival Granite Quarries Ltd [1910] 2 KB 979 (CA) 178–79
G & T Earle Ltd v Hemsworth (1928) 44 TLR 605 186
Gorringe v Irwell India Rubber and Gutta Percha Works (1886) LR 34
   Ch D 128 (CA) 120, 138, 142

Heath v Crealock (1874) LR 10 Ch App 22 174
Joseph v Lyons (1884) 15 QBD 280 (CA)...174
Hallas v Robinson (1885) 15 QBD 288 (CA) 174
Holt v Heatherfield Trust Ltd [1942] 2 KB 1 ....92–93, 120, 139, 142
Mangles v Dixon (1852) 3 HLC 702, 10 ER 278 (PC) 80
Taylor v London and County Banking Company [1901] 2 Ch 231 (CA) 174
Three Rivers District Council v Governor and Company of the Bank of
    England [1996] QB 292, 298, 308–09 (CA) 92
Phillips v Lovegrove (1873) LR 16 Eq 80 80
Pilcher v Rawlins (1872) LR 7 Ch App 259 174
Raiffeisen Zentralbank Osterreich AG v Five Star General Trading LLC [2000]
    EWCA Civ 68, [2001] QB 825 (CA) 154
Re Diplock [1948] Ch 465 (CA) 174
Re Connolly Bros Ltd (No 2) [1912] 2 Ch 25 (CA)...185
Re Pinto Leite and Nephews [1929] 1 Ch 221 (CA) 81
Re Queensland Mercantile and Agency Co [1892] 1 Ch 219 (CA)..................................157
Re Spectrum Plus Ltd [2005] UKHL 41, [2005] 2 AC 680 (HL) 42, 179
Re Yorkshire Woolcombers Association Ltd [1903] 2 Ch 284 (CA) 179
Roxburghe v Cox (1881) 17 Ch D 520 (CA) 81
Shea v Moore [1894] IR 158 (CA) 15
Siebe Gorman & Co Ltd v Barclays Bank Ltd [1979] 2 Lloyd's Rep 142 186
Standard Rotary Machine Co Ltd (1906) 95 LT 829 186
Twyne [1558–1774] All ER Rep 303; 3 Co Rep 80 b; Moore KB 638; 76 ER 809
    (Court of Star Chamber) 15–16
Wilson v Kelland [1910] 2 Ch 306...186
R (on the Application of Cukurova Finance International Limited) v Her Majesty's
    Treasury [2008] EWHC 2567 (Admin) 149

United States

Corn Exchange National Bank v Klauder 63 S Ct 679, 318 US 434 (1943) 18

TABLE OF STATUTES, CONVENTIONS AND MODEL LAWS

Australia

Personal Property Securities Act 2009 ....20, 54–5, 81, 87, 91, 94, 108, 214, 245, 251

http://www.comlaw.gov.au/Details/C2011C00388
- s 12(3)(a) 108
- s 18(2) 179
- s 18(3) 179
- s 20(2)(b) 179
- s 33(2) 183
- s 40(3)(b) 178
- s 46(1) 176–77, 180
- s 55(2) 109
- s 55(3) 109
- s 55(4) 109
- s 55(5)(a) 109
- s 62 184
- s 64(1) 185
- s 76(2)(b) 179
- s 77(1) 158
- s 77(2) 156, 158
- s 150(2) 59
- s 153(1) 52
- s 157(1)(b) 58
- s 157(4) 59
- s 178(1) 59
- s 182(1) 59
- s 182(4)(a) 59
- s 239(2) 156
- s 267 ....82, 108
- s 267A 82, 108

Austria

Civil Code (Allgemeines bürgerliches Gesetzbuch)
- s 427 135
- s 452 135
- s 1392 135
- s 1394 135

Federal Law Implementing the Federal Law Governing Safety in Financial Markets
(Financial Markets Safety Act—FinSG) and Modifying the Private International Law
Act (Bundesgesetz, mit den ein Bundesgesetz über Sichereiten auf den Finanzmärkten
(FINSG) erlassen wird und das Bundesgsetz über das internatoinale Privaterecht
geändert wird) 150
Financial Collateral Act (Finanzsicherheiten-Gesetz) 149, 150

Belgium

Civil Code
http://burgerlijkwetboek.be
http://www.droitbelge.be/codes.asp#civ
    art 1690(1)..120
    art 2075...119
    art 2076 119
Private International Law 156
    art 87(3)...157

Canada

Ontario Personal Property Security Act 1990 ....185, 245
http://www.e-laws.gov.on.ca/html/statutes/english/elaws_statutes_90p10_e.htm
    s 1(1)..105
    s 7(1)(a)(i)...156
    s 12...179
    s 20(1)(b)..105
    s 25(4)...183
    s 28(1)..176–77, 180
    s 30(1)1...82, 106
    s 30(1)4..106
    s 33...184
    s 45(3)...106
    s 46(6)...58
    s 49..59
    s 56(2.1)...59
    s 56(5)(b)(i)...59
Saskatchewan Personal Property Security Act 1993 ....58, 106, 185, 245
http://www.qp.gov.sk.ca/documents/English/Statutes/Statutes/P6-2.pdf
    s 2(1)(q)...59
    s 2(1)(qq)(ii)(A) 105
    s 7(2)(a)(i)...156
    s 7(3)...178
    s 13..179
    s 20(2)...105
    s 28(3)...183
    s 30(2)..176–77, 180
    s 34..184
    s 34(6)...185
    s 35(2)..82, 106
    s 43(4)...106

Table of Statutes, Conventions and Model Laws

s 43(12) 58
s 50(3) 59
s 50(4) 59
s 50(5) 59
s 50(7) 59

China

Contract Law (合同法) 127–28
    art 80 .... 27, 130
Insolvency Law (企业破产法)
    art 31(2) 127, 169
Property Law (物权法) 23
    art 223(6) 27, 87, 129
    art 228 .... 23, 87, 129
Law of the Application of Law for Foreign-Related Civil Relations
    (涉外民事关系法律适用法) 157
Measures for the Registration of Pledge of Receivables
    (应收账款质押登记办法) 27–8, 31, 36, 130
Order of the People's Bank of China No4 (2007) 27, 128–130
http://www.gov.cn/gongbao/content/2008/content_970304.htm
    art 2 130
    art 4 36
Administrative Measures for the Securitisation of Credit Assets (AMSCA) 128–29
Announcement of the People's Bank of China and China Banking Regulatory
    (信贷资产证券化试点管理办法)
Commission No 7 (2005) 128
http://vip.chinalawinfo.com/newlaw2002/slc/slc.asp?gid=57934
    art 1 129
    art 6 128
    art 12 128
Supreme People's Court Provisions Regarding Several Issues on Examining Applicable
    Laws Concerning Financial Asset Management Company's Acquisition, Management
    and Disposal of Non-performing Loan Asset of State-Owned Bank Cases
(SPC Provisions on Disposal of NPLs) 128–29
(最高人民法院关于审理涉及金融资产管理公司收购、管理、处置国有
    银行不良贷款形成的资产的案件适用法律若干问题的规定)
Judicial Interpretation No 12 (2001) 128
http://www.law-lib.com/law/law_view.asp?id=15250
    art 6 128

European Bank for Reconstruction and Development (EBRD)

EBRD Model Law on Secured Transactions 37–8
http://www.ebrd.com/downloads/research/guides/secured.pdf
    art 6(1) 38
Publicity of Security Rights—Guiding Principles for the Development of a Charges
    Registry 37, 102, 197
http://www.ebrd.com/downloads/legal/secured/pubsec.pdf

EU

1980 Rome Convention on the law applicable to contractual obligations
('Rome Convention')
http://eur-lex.europa.eu/LexUriServ/LexUriServ.do?uri=CELEX:41998A0126(02):
EN:NOT
- art 3(1) 159
- art 12(1) 157, 159
- art 12(2) 157

Regulation (EC) No 593/2008 of the European Parliament and of the Council of 17 June 2008 on the law applicable to contractual obligations (Rome I) [2008] OJ L 177/6 153
http://eur-lex.europa.eu/LexUriServ/LexUriServ.do?uri=CELEX:32008R0593:EN:NOT
- art 14(1) 153
- art 14(2) 153

Proposal for a Regulation of the European Parliament and the Council on the law applicable to contractual obligations (Rome I)
http://eur-lex.europa.eu/LexUriServ/LexUriServ.do?uri=CELEX:52005PC0650:EN:NOT
- art 13(3) 155

Regulation (EC) No 864/2007 of the European Parliament and of the Council of 11 July 2007 on the law applicable to non-contractual obligations (Rome II) [2007] OJ L199/40
http://eur-lex.europa.eu/LexUriServ/LexUriServ.do?uri=OJ:L:2007:199:0040:01:EN:HTML
- art 10 153
- art 10(3) 155

Directive 2002/47/EC of the European Parliament and of the Council of 6 June 2002 on financial collateral arrangements [2002] OJ L168/43 .... 146–50, 165–66
http://eur-lex.europa.eu/LexUriServ/LexUriServ.do?uri=CELEX:32002L0047:EN:NOT
- recital 10 147
- art 1(2) 147
- art 1(4)(a) 147
- art 2(1)(b) 147
- art 6 147
- art 8(1) 148
- art 8(2) 148

Directive 2009/44/EC of the European Parliament and of the Council of 6 May 2009 amending Directive 98/26/EC on settlement finality in payment and securities settlement systems and Directive 2002/47/EC on financial collateral arrangements as regards linked systems and credit claims [2009] OJ L146/37 .... 149–50, 165–66
http://eur-lex.europa.eu/LexUriServ/LexUriServ.do?uri=CELEX:32009L0044:EN:NOT
- art 2(4)(a) 146
- art 2(4)(b) 146
- art 2(4)(c) 147
- art 2(5)(a)(ii) 147
- art 2(6)(a) 148

France

Civil Code (Code civil)
http://www.legifrance.gouv.fr/Traductions/en-English/Legifrance-translations
    art 1690 .... 76, 79, 114–15, 165
    art 1691 79
    art 2337 .... 28, 117
    art 2338 28
    art 2340 28
    art 2351 24
    art 2356 5
    art 2361 117
Civil Aviation Code (Code de l'aviation civile)
http://www.legifrance.gouv.fr/affichCode.do?cidTexte=LEGITEXT000006074234
    art 121-2 24
    art 122-7 24
Commercial Code (Code de commerce)
http://www.legifrance.gouv.fr/Traductions/en-English/Legifrance-translations
    art L142-5 24
    arts L142-1–L143-23 24
    arts L523-1–L523-15 24
    arts L524-1–L524-21 24
    arts L525-1–L525-20 24
Industrial Cinema Code (Code de l'industrie cinématographique)
http://www.legifrance.gouv.fr/affichCode.do?cidTexte=LEGITEXT000006070882&
    dateTexte=20080505
    art 33 24
Intellectual Property Code (Code de la Propriété Intellectuelle)
http://www.legifrance.gouv.fr/Traductions/en-English/Legifrance-translations
    art L132-34 24
    art L613-9 24
    art L714-7 24
Monetary and Financial Code (Code Monétaire et Financier) 85, 88, 116, 118, 166
http://www.legifrance.gouv.fr/Traductions/en-English/Legifrance-translations
    arts L133-7–L133-11 24
    art L211-20 24
    arts L211-36–L211-40 148
    arts L214-43–L214-49 116
    art L214-43 116
    arts L313-23–L313-34 .... 84, 115
    art L313-23 .... 84, 115
    art L313-25 115
    art L313-26 115
    art L313-27 .... 117, 158
Décret n° 2004-1255 du 24 novembre 2004 pris en application des articles L. 214-5 et L.
    214-43 à L. 214-49 du code monétaire et financier et relatif aux fonds communs de
    créances

http://www.legifrance.gouv.fr/affichTexte.do?cidTexte=JORFTEXT000000445664
   art 18 116
Loi n° 67-5 du 3 janvier 1967 relative au statut des navires et autres bâtiments de mer
http://www.idit.asso.fr/legislation/documents/Loi%203%20janv%201967%20statut
%20navires.pdf
   art 43 24
   art 48 24

Germany

Civil Code (Bürgerliches Gesetzbuch) 84, 97, 165–66, 219
http://www.gesetze-im-internet.de/englisch_bgb/index.html
   s 398 ....83, 131
   s 403 ....82–83, 133
   s 407 133
   s 408 133
   s 409(1) 79
   s 410(1) 79, 83
   ss 1279–90 5
   s 1280 ....83, 85, 132
   s 1290 134
Criminal Code (Strafgesetzbuch)
http://www.gesetze-im-internet.de/englisch_stgb/index.html
   s 267 134
   s 278 134
Insolvency Statute (Insolvenzordnung)
http://www.gesetze-im-internet.de/englisch_inso/index.html
   s 131 169
Law of 5 April 2004 implementing Directive 2002/47/EC of the European Parliament
   and of the Council of 6 June 2002 on financial collateral arrangements (Gesetz
   vom 5/4/2004 zur Umsetzung der Richtlinie 2002/47/EG vom 6/6/2002 über
   Finanzsicherheiten und zur Änderung des Hypothekenbankgesetzes und anderer
   Gesetze) 146–50, 165–66
Law implementing the amended Banking Directive and the amended Capital Adequacy
   Directive (Gesetz zur Umsetzung der geänderten Bankenrichtlinie und der geänderten
   Kapitaladäquanzrichtlinie)...149

Japan

Civil Code (民法) 30, 32, 77, 79, 112, 114, 164–66, 199, 220
http://www.japaneselawtranslation.go.jp/law/detail/?id=1928&vm=04&re=02&new=1
   art 345 ....31, 36
   art 364 113
   art 365 29
   art 466(1) 113
   art 467(1) 29, 76
   art 467(2) 28–29, 75–76, 113, 198
   art 469 29
   art 473 29

Act Concerning Restrictions on Businesses in Specified Claims ('Specified Claims Act')
(特定債権等に係る事業の規制に関する法律)
http://law.e-gov.go.jp/haishi/H04HO077.html
    art 2(1) 29
Act on Special Provisions, etc of the Civil Code Concerning the Perfection
    Requirements for the Transfer of Movables and Claims
    ('Transfer Registration Act') 30, 32, 62–63, 66, 79, 82, 114, 161,
                                                                  189, 197–98, 214, 215, 217, 227
(動産及び債権の譲渡の対抗要件に関する民法の特例等に関する法律) 30–31
http://www.japaneselawtranslation.go.jp/law/detail/?id=1881&vm=04&re=02&new=1
    art 3 ....31, 36
    art 3(1) 31
    art 4(1) 31, 36, 113, 199
    art 4(2) 79
    art 5(2) 216
    art 7(2) 53
    art 7(2)(iii) 161
    art 8(2) 53, 224
    art 8(2)(iii) 54
    art 8(3) 54
    art 8(3)(i) 54
    art 8(3)(ii) 54
    art 11(1) 67
    art 11(2) 67
    art 13 67
    art 14 ....31, 36, 82, 112–13
Transfer of Movable Assets and Receivables Registration Order ('Transfer Registration
    Order') (動産・債権譲渡登記令)
    art 9 62
    art 12(1) 63
    art 12(2) 63
    art 15 67
Transfer of Movable Assets and Receivables Registration Rules ('Transfer Registration
    Rules') (動産・債権譲渡登記規則)
    art 8(1)(i) 189
    art 8(1)(ii) 190
Act on General Rules for Application of Laws (法の適用に関する通則法)
http://www.japaneselawtranslation.go.jp/law/detail/?id=1970&vm=04&re=02&new=1
    art 23 156

Korea

Civil Code (민법) 79, 97, 112, 165, 220
    art 188 34
    art 189 34
    art 332 31
    art 345 ....23, 31

art 346...111
art 349...111
art 350...29
art 351...29
art 450...34, 76–77, 111
art 450(1)..29, 35, 76, 109
art 450(2)...28–29, 75–76, 109–11, 198
art 508...29
art 523...29
Asset-Backed Securitisation Act ('ABS Act') (주택저당채권유동화회사법) 32, 34, 35, 73, 88, 97, 109, 111, 189
    art 2(2)...33
    art 3...33
    art 3(1)...161
    art 6(1)..110, 112
    art 7(1)..33, 79
    art 7(2)...33, 110, 112
    art 8(1)...110
Mortgage-Backed Securitisation Company Act ('MBS Company Act') (자산유동화에 관한 법률) 34–35, 97, 109, 111, 189
    art 4...33
    art 5(1)..110, 112
    art 6(1)..33, 79
    art 6(2)...33, 110, 112
    art 7...110
Act Regarding Security Rights in Movable Assets and Claims etc ('Security Registration Act') (동산·채권 등의 담보에 관한 법률) ....vi, 31, 33, 47, 57, 73, 87, 97, 112, 197, 223, 227
    art 2(1)...35
    art 2(3)...36
    art 2(5)...216
    art 3(1)...35
    art 3(2)...214
    art 3(2)(i)...36
    art 10...53
    art 12...53
    art 34(1)..35–36, 111
    art 34(2)..36, 214
    art 35(2)...79
    art 35(3)..111, 198
    art 39(1)...34
    art 39(2)...34
    art 41(1)..62, 224
    art 42(i)...62
    art 42(ii)..62
    art 43(1)...48
    art 47(2)..53, 161

art 47(2)(iv) 161, 216
Korean Security Registration Rules (동산·채권의 담보등기 등에 관한 규칙)
 art 34 161
 art 35(1)(ii) 53
Private International Act (국제사법)
 art 34(1) 156

The Netherlands

Civil Code
http://www.dutchcivillaw.com/legislation/dcctitle33044.htm
 art 3:84(3) 137
 art 3:94 136
 art 3:94(3) 137–38
Law of 22 December 2005 to implement Directive 2002/47/EC of the European
 Parliament and European Council of 6 June 2002 concerning financial collateral
 arrangements (Wet van 22 december 2005 tot uitvoering van Richtlijn nr. 2002/47/EG
 van het Europees Parlement en de Raad van de Europese Unie van
 6 juni 2002 betreffende financiëlezekerheidsovereenkomsten) 146–50, 165–66
Law of 21 April 2011 amending the Civil Code and the Bankruptcy Act to implement
 Directive 2009/44/EC of the European Parliament and the European Council of
 6 May 2009 amending Directive 98/26/EC on settlement finality in the settlement of
 payments and securities transactions in payment and securities settlement systems
 and Directive 2002/47/EC on financial collateral arrangements as regards linked
 systems and credit claims (Wet van 21 april 2011 tot wijziging van het Burgerlijk
 Wetboek en de Faillissementswet ter implementatie van Richtlijn 2009/44/EG van het
 Europees Parlement en de Europese Raad van 6 mei 2009 tot wijziging van Richtlijn
 98/26/EG betreffende het definitieve karakter van de afwikkeling van betalingen en
 effectentransacties in betalings- en afwikkelingssystemen en Richtlijn
 2002/47/EG betreffende financiëlezekerheidsovereenkomsten wat gekoppelde
 systemen en kredietvorderingen betreft) 146–50, 165–66

New Zealand

Personal Property Securities Acts 1999 ....20, 54–55, 93, 106, 192
http://legislation.govt.nz/act/public/1999/0126/latest/DLM45900.html
 s 16 107
 s 17(1)(b) 106
 s 30(a) 156
 s 31 178
 s 41(1) 106
 s 43 179
 s 44 179
 s 47 183
 s 53(1) 176–77, 180
 s 66 82
 s 66(a) 107
 s 66(b)(i) 107
 s 66(c) 107

xl Table of Statutes, Conventions and Model Laws

s 72 108
s 73 184
s 75A 185
s 103(1) 94, 107
s 103(1A) 107
s 135 59
s 142(1) 52, 269
s 146 107
s 148 58
s 162 59
s 163 59
s 165(1)(a) 59
s 167(1) 59

United Kingdom

Bills of Sale Act 1878 .... 16, 95, 101, 121, 139
http://www.legislation.gov.uk/ukpga/Vict/41-42/31/contents
Bills of Sale Act (1878) Amendment Act 1882
http://www.legislation.gov.uk/ukpga/Vict/45-46/43/contents
  s 8 16
Companies Act 1900 (63 & 64 Vict Cap 48)
  s 14 17
Companies Act 2006 .... 5, 17, 57, 70, 87, 89, 173, 175, 178, 214
http://www.legislation.gov.uk/ukpga/2006/46/contents
  s 1085(1) 65
Companies Act 2006 (Amendment of Part 25) Regulations 2013
http://www.legislation.gov.uk/uksi/2013/600/contents/made
  ss 859A–G 17, 173
  s 859A 62
  s 859A(4) 52, 95, 101, 121, 125
  s 859A(6) 17
  s 859D(1) 53
  s 859D(2) 53
  s 859D(2)(c) 186
  s 859F 95, 101, 121, 173
  s 859H 16, 95, 121, 173,
  s 859Q(2) 66
  s 859Q(3) 66
  s 859Q(8) 65
Insolvency Act 1986 .... 90, 101
http://www.legislation.gov.uk/ukpga/1986/45/contents
  s 123(1)(e) 3
  s 123(2) 3
  s 238 169
  s 344 95
  s 344(3)(a) 121
  s 344(3)(b)(i) 121

Law of Property Act 1925
http://www.legislation.gov.uk/ukpga/Geo5/15-16/20
  s 136(1) 76, 92, 101, 123–24
Merchant Shipping Act 1995
http://www.legislation.gov.uk/ukpga/1995/21/contents
  s 16 17
Schedule 1 17
Mortgaging of Aircraft Order 1972 17
http://www.legislation.gov.uk/uksi/1972/1268/contents/made
Patents Act 1977
http://www.legislation.gov.uk/ukpga/1977/37
  ss 30–33 17
Trade Marks Act 1994
http://www.legislation.gov.uk/ukpga/1994/26/contents
  s 25 17
Registered Designs Act 1949
http://www.legislation.gov.uk/ukpga/Geo6/12-13-14/88/enacted
  s 19 17
Financial Collateral Arrangements (No 2) Regulations 2003, SI 2003/3226
http://www.legislation.gov.uk/uksi/2003/3226/contents/made
reg 3 149
Financial Markets and Insolvency (Settlement Finality and Financial Collateral
  Arrangements) (Amendment) Regulations 2010, SI 2010/2993
http://www.legislation.gov.uk/uksi/2010/2993/contents/made
  reg 4(2)(b)(i) 149
  reg 4(2)(b)(ii) 149

The US

Uniform Commercial Code Article 9 .... 12, 18–19, 38–39, 49–50,
54–55, 58–59, 64, 66, 70, 78, 81, 87, 91, 94,
105, 157, 166, 172, 182, 186–87, 193, 197–99,
204, 214, 219, 228, 244, 247, 251, 262
http://www.law.cornell.edu/ucc/9/article9.htm
  s 9-102(a)(61) 82, 104
  s 9-109(a)(1) 82, 103
  s 9-109(a)(3) 82, 103
  s 9-204 179
  s 9-204(c) 104
  s 9-301(1) 156, 158, 161
  s 9-307(b) 158, 161
  s 9-307(c) 158, 161
  s 9-309(2) 70
  ss 9-310–9-314 39
  s 9-310(a) 82, 104
  s 9-315(a)(1) 173, 175
  s 9-315(d) 183
  s 9-316 176

s 9-320	176
s 9-320(a)	176–77, 180
s 9-322	175
s 9-322(a)	104
s 9-322(b)	104
s 9-322(c)	104
s 9-324	184
s 9-404(a)(2)	78
s 9-406(c)	78
s 9-502(a)	51
s 9-502(d)	104
s 9-507(a)	175
s 9-509(a)(1)	60
s 9-509(b)	60
s 9-510(a)	60
s 9-518(a)	61
s 9-518(c)	61

United Nations

United Nations Convention on the Transfer of Receivables in International Trade ('UN Receivables Convention') 3, 10, 187, 192, 202, 219, 254, 256, 259
http://www.uncitral.org/uncitral/en/uncitral_texts/payments/2001Convention_receivables.html

art 1(1)(a)	201
art 2	193, 263
art 3	201
art 8	41
art 9	41
art 24(2)	254
art 30(1)	163
art 45(1)	40
Annex	40
Section I	40
Section II	40

Convention on International Civil Aviation ('Chicago Convention') 190
http://www.icao.int/icaonet/dcs/7300.html
UNCITRAL Legislative Guide on Secured Transactions.........14, 19, 48, 50, 60, 62, 182, 197
http://www.uncitral.org/uncitral/en/uncitral_texts/payments/Guide_securedtrans.html

Terminology	264
Recommendation 33	49
Recommendation 84	264

UNCITRAL Model Law on Secured Transactions..........................12, 37, 51, 58–59, 61, 70, 192–93, 197, 214
http://www.uncitral.org/uncitral/en/uncitral_texts/security/2016Model_secured.html

art 2(o)	263
art 2(dd)	264

Table of Statutes, Conventions and Model Laws xliii

    art 2(kk) 194, 264
    art 6(1) 49
    art 18 39
    art 29(a) 50
Model Registry Provisions
    art 2(4) 61
    art 2(5) 61
    art 2(6) 61
    art 3 50
    art 4 50
    art 7(2) 52
    art 7(3) 52
    art 8 52

UNIDROIT

Convention on International Interests in Mobile Equipment (Cape Town, 2001)
('Cape Town Convention') 40–41, 58, 62–64, 68, 80, 188–92, 196, 202,
                                                219, 222–26, 232, 241, 259, 262
http://www.unidroit.org/english/conventions/mobile-equipment/main.htm
    art 1(c) 217
    art 1(p) 264
    art 2(3) 217
    art 3(1) 217–18
    art 3(2) 206
    art 16(1) 268
    art 17 268
    art 18(1)(a) 65
    art 20(1) 65
    art 29(5) 256
    arts 31–37 217
    art 31(1)(b) 239
    art 31(4) 193
    art 35 239
    art 36(1)(a) 218
    art 36(1)(b) 218
    art 39 252
    art 60 ....209, 265
Protocol to the Convention on International Interests in Mobile Equipment on
    Matters Specific to Aircraft Equipment (Cape Town, 2001)
    ('Aircraft Protocol') 41, 63–64, 68, 191, 196, 217, 223, 225, 241
http://www.unidroit.org/english/conventions/mobile-equipment/main.htm
    art I(2)(e) 202
    art I(2)(l) 202
    art VII 202
Regulations and Procedures for the International Registry 192
http://www.icao.int/publications/Documents/9864_4ed.pdf

Regulations
  s 2.1.7 263
  s 2.1.9 264
  s 4.1 225
  s 5.1 ....190, 202
Procedures
  s 12.1 269
  s 12.2 ....65, 270
  s 12.2(a) 65
  s 12.2(b) 65
  s 12.3 270
  s 12.6 270
  s 12.7 ....65, 270
Appendix, Fee Schedule
  s 1.8 68
Protocol to the Convention on International Interests in Mobile Equipment on Matters Specific to Space Assets (Berlin, 2012) ('Space Protocol') 41, 191, 217
http://www.unidroit.org/english/conventions/mobile-equipment/main.htm
  art X(3) 80, 193

Organization of American States (OAS)

Model Inter-American Law on Secured Transactions 37, 197
http://www.oas.org/dil/CIDIP-VI-securedtransactions_Eng.htm
  art 10 38

TABLE OF ONLINE REGISTERS

Canada

Ontario Personal Property Security Registration
https://www.ontario.ca/page/register-security-interest-or-search-lien-access-now

Saskatchewan Personal Property Registry
https://www.isc.ca/SPPR/Pages/default.aspx

Austria Personal Property Securities Register

http://www.ppsr.gov.au

Japanese Transfer Registration

http://www.touki-kyoutaku-online.moj.go.jp/index.html

New Zealand Personal Property Securities Register

http://www.ppsr.govt.nz/cms

United States

Utah UCC Filing
https://secure.utah.gov/uccsearch/uccs

Florida UCC Filing
http://www.floridaucc.com/UCCWEB/search.aspx

Tennessee UCC Filing
http://www.tn.gov/sos/bus_svc/iets3/ieuc/PgUCCSearch.jsp

Wisconsin UCC Filing
http://publicrecords.onlinesearches.com/Wisconsin-UCC-Filings.htm

Iowa UCC Filing
https://sos.iowa.gov/search/ucc/search.aspx?ucc

Washington UCC Filing
https://fortress.wa.gov/dol/ucc

New York UCC Filing
https://appext20.dos.ny.gov/pls/ucc_public/web_search.main_frame

UK Companies House

www.companieshouse.gov.uk

International Registry of Mobile Assets website under the Cape Town Convention

www.internationalregistry.aero

LIST OF TABLES

1.1	Receivables financing	7
2.1	Non-possessory security rights v possessory security rights	15
2.2	Mortgage v pledge	22
2.3	The effect of registration of mortgages in China	25
2.4	Creation requirements of pledges in China	26
2.5	Usages of the Japanese Transfer Registration	32
2.6	Comparison of Chinese, Korean and Japanese registration systems for movable assets and receivables	36
2.7	World Bank Group, enterprise surveys	45
2.8	Contents of registration (in the case where the grantor is a company)	54
2.9	Three types of registration certificates in Japan	67
3.1	Summary table of answers	74
3.2	Comparison of outright sale of and security rights in receivables (where the transferor is a company)	86
3.3	Perfection requirements (priority) for the transfer of receivables	88
3.4	Legal terms for insolvency administrators	90
3.5	Perfection of transfer and security right	95
3.6	Conclusion of agreement v notice to the debtor	97
3.7	Potential transferee's check points for prior transfers and security rights (answers to Question 6)	98
3.8	Classification of jurisdictions	99
3.9	Equivalent legislation and provisions in Group SR (England, Singapore and Hong Kong)	101
3.10	The Application of *Dearle v Hall*	123
3.11	Perfection methods of transfer and pledge in Dutch law	136
3.12	Implementation of the EU Directive on financial collateral arrangements	148
4.1	The governing law in the transfer of receivables	156
4.2	What should a transferee do in order to perfect a transfer against third parties in international receivables financing where the transferor is a company? (Groups R, RN, N, SR and C refer to the classification of jurisdictions in section 3-6)	160

4.3	What should a potential transferee check before concluding a contract for a transfer of a receivable or a security right in a receivable in order to secure his priority over any prior transfer of or security right in the receivable?	162
4.4	The double debtor problem	172
6.1	The double debtor problem	242

1

Introduction

1-1. Receivables

The transfer of receivables is critical in raising finance and there are various problems involved in international transfers. It is proposed that the best way to solve such problems is through an international register of transfers of receivables. An international registration system for the transfer of receivables could be an effective method to facilitate international capital movements. The purpose of this book is to propose a model international registration system for the transfer of receivables. This introduction will review the use of receivables in financing. It will make it clear that this proposal is focused on receivables other than tangible movable assets. Furthermore, it will give an overview of the structure of this book.

The term 'receivable' is a generic description of a right to payment of a monetary obligation. It includes rights to payment for goods sold or leased, facilities made available or services rendered.[1] Receivables form an integral part of the assets of every trading company, for example, insurance premiums, credit card debts, freights, and real and personal property rentals. They may be used to provide working capital by outright sale with discounting or as security for a loan. Therefore, they are generally considered an ideal basis for short-term finance.[2] Receivables financing also helps small and medium-sized companies that do not have sufficient real estate to mortgage for a loan. Receivables are potentially the single largest category of assets transferred in cross-border financing transactions.[3]

With respect to transfers of and security rights in receivables, a domestic registry and an international registry have different purposes. The main purpose of a domestic registry for the transfer of receivables is to help companies (especially small and medium-sized companies which do not have enough collateral) to finance using their receivables as collateral.

The main purpose of an international registry for the transfer of receivables, which would include both outright transfers and security transfers, is to facilitate

---

[1] Fidelis Oditah, *Legal Aspects of Receivables Financing* (London, Sweet & Maxwell, 1991) 19.
[2] ibid 2–3.
[3] Steven L Schwarcz, 'Towards a Centralized Perfection System for Cross-border Receivables Financing' (1999) 20 *University of Pennsylvania Journal of International Economic Law* 455, 455.

international receivables financing that could solve national financial crises. Where the effect of a financial crisis is within a national boundary, domestic receivables financing could not help to solve such a crisis because all companies in the nation are affected, but international receivables financing can help eliminate non-performing loans in the affected nation. Receivables financing could help the disposal of non-performing loans and mitigate liquidity risk. International receivables financing is particularly important when a financial crisis affects a country. During a financial crisis, an influx of foreign capital is necessary to combat the frozen cash-flow circulation.

For example, after the collapse of the bubble economy in Japan in 1991, Japan disposed of non-performing loans to foreign investors through securitisation. At that time, many American and European investment companies created branch offices or Special Purpose Companies (SPCs) in Japan for the sole purpose of perfecting the transfer of receivables under Japanese law. After the financial crisis in Korea in 1997, Korea disposed of non-performing loans to foreign investors through securitisation. Subsequently, a number of Korean financial institutions created SPCs both in Korea and Hong Kong to sell securitisations in the Hong Kong financial markets. For example, Japan has a domestic registration system for the transfer of receivables. Nevertheless, in international transfers of receivables between Japan and the US, legal practitioners would usually register the transfer of receivables both in Japan and in the US in order to ensure the perfection of the transfer.[4]

1-2. Transfers of Receivables

1-2-1. International Transfers of Receivables

International transfers of receivables are important in the disposal of non-performing loans, securitisation and factoring. With rapid globalisation, goods and services are traded across national borders, among which capital specifically moves across national borders. Capital mobility enables the total savings of the world to be distributed among countries that have the highest investment potential. Under these circumstances, one country's growth is not constrained by its own domestic savings.[5] International capital movements have been made mostly through stock and bond markets. However, this was one of the causes of financial

---

[4] Email from Takashi Asada (Head of Legal Engineering Group, Legal Department, Sumitomo Mitsui Banking Corporation) to the author (25 August 2008).

[5] C Rangarajan, 'Responding to Globalization: India's Answer', 4th Ramanbhai Patel Memorial Lecture on Excellence in Education (New Delhi, 25 February 2006) 3, https://www.scribd.com/document/27251741/Responding-to-Globalization-India-s-Answer.

crisis as stock markets are quite unstable. The volatility in stock markets and the ease with which funds can be withdrawn from countries and consequent liquidity risk have often created financial crises. Transfers of receivables can mitigate such liquidity risk, since by selling outstanding receivables, a company may receive an immediate cash influx.

Receivables are the objects of investment through factoring, block discounting, securitisation and other similar methods. Such receivables financing provides liquidity and prevents insolvency from temporary cash-flow shortage or liquidity risk.[6] However, there are various legal barriers involved in international transfers of receivables, details of which are discussed later in this book.

1-2-2. Securitisation

Securitisation is defined as creating tradable financial instruments from a number of non-tradable financial assets.[7] In a typical securitisation transaction, the originator sells rights to payment from income-producing financial assets, such as credit card receivables, loans or lease, to a special purpose vehicle (SPV). The SPV issues securities to capital market investors and uses the proceeds of the issuance to pay the originator for the receivables. The investors in the securities are repaid from the collection of the receivables. Thus, the investors buy the securities based on their assessment of the value of the receivables. The main function of securitisation is to transfer and spread risk from one party to another.

Financial markets promote the availability of capital and credit at optimal rates.[8] Currently, however, if companies in countries without established capital markets wish to raise funds from established capital markets such as New York, London, Hong Kong and other major financial centres,[9] these companies will have to structure deals that cross national borders through securitisation. For this reason, securitisation has an increasingly international focus.[10] Securitisations are often used for cross-border fundraising for the reason that the cross-border transfer of receivables confronts difficult legal issues due to the different legal systems of each jurisdiction.

---

[6] 'Cash flow insolvency' is described in s 123(1)(e) of the Insolvency Act 1986 as follows: 'A company is deemed unable to pay its debts— ... (e) if it is proved to the satisfaction of the court that the company is unable to pay its debts as they fall due.' The opposite concept of 'cash flow insolvency' is 'balance sheet insolvency', which is described in s 123(2) of the Insolvency Act 1986: 'A company is also deemed unable to pay its debts if it is proved to the satisfaction of the court that the value of the company's assets is less than the amount of its liabilities, taking into account its contingent and prospective liabilities.'

[7] Steven L Schwarcz, 'Securitisation Post-Enron' (2004) 25 *Cardozo Law Review* 1539, 1540.

[8] UNCITRAL 'Explanatory Note on the United Nations Convention on the Transfer of Receivables in International Trade' A/CN.9/557, 3.

[9] Steven L. Schwarcz, 'The Universal Language of International Securitization' (2002) 12 *Duke Journal of Comparative & International Law* 285, 288 n 10.

[10] ibid 288.

1-2-3. Factoring

A company may also enter into factoring on the strength of its receivables, where it has the receivables to be transferred. As a result, receivables are no longer simply claims and contractual obligations between two parties who made the original contract, but become reified objects that could be bought or sold as assets in the financial markets.

In factoring, a business sells its accounts receivable at a discounted price. Factoring[11] is classified according to whether a factor provides a debt collection service and whether a factor offers the acceptance of the risk of debtor's non-payment.[12]

Non-recourse factoring is the traditional method of factoring and puts the full risk of debtor's non-payment on the factor (transferee). If the debtor cannot pay the debt, it is the factor's responsibility and the factor cannot seek payment from the seller (transferor). The factor will only purchase solid creditworthy receivables and often turns away average credit quality customers. The price for the receivables transferred to the factor is typically lower with a non-recourse factoring since the factor assumes a greater risk.

On the other hand, a transferor who is not concerned about risk will sell on a *recourse basis*, giving a factor the right to resell debts that go into default to the transferor (original creditor). Here, the credit risk that the factor might not be able to collect the debt due to the debtor's non-payment or bankruptcy does not transfer to the factor. In this respect, recourse factoring is closer to the security transfer of receivables than the absolute transfer of receivables because in the absolute transfer, the risk is transferred to the transferee. The price for the receivables transferred to the factor is typically higher with a recourse factoring because the risk for the factor is lower.[13]

For such factoring, differing perfection requirements and priority criteria with respect to the transfer of receivables in each jurisdiction cause problems.[14] This book proposes that the best way to solve such problems is an internationally unified registration system for the transfer of receivables.

1-3. Security Rights in Receivables

Using receivables as security is advantageous in raising finance. Creating a security right in receivables could be safer for a debtor company than encumbering

---

[11] This terminology is used in English law. Internationally 'factoring' has a wider meaning.

[12] Roy Goode and Ewan McKendrick, *Goode on Commercial Law*, 4th edn (London, Penguin, 2010) 788–90.

[13] UNCITRAL, 'Receivables Financing: Analytical Commentary on the Draft Convention on Transfer of Receivables in International Trade' (A/CN.9/489, UNCITRAL 2001) [10].

[14] See section 4-6-1-2.

inventory, equipment, machines or real estates. This is because such movable assets and real estate are commonly essential for manufacturing products or providing services. If a secured creditor enforces the security right, the debtor company would lose encumbered movable assets and real estate, and consequently would not be able to operate the business. Receivables are different. Even after a debtor company grants security over its receivables, the debtor company can continue to operate the business. In addition, receivables provide extra collateral where lenders would want all assets encumbered. An international registration system for security rights in receivables would be able to assist international financiers with obtaining security rights in receivables internationally.

There is a noticeable difference in the terminology of security rights in receivables as used between English common law and French and German civil law. For a security right in receivables, English law uses the term 'charge' over receivables.[15] Article 9 of the US Uniform Commercial Code (UCC) and the Personal Property Security Acts (PPSAs) of Canada, New Zealand and Australia use the term 'security interest' in receivables.[16]

German law and French civil law use the term 'pledge' of receivables. The English translation of the German Civil Code provided by the Federal Ministry of Justice (*Bundesministerium der Justiz*) of Germany uses the term 'pledge' rather than 'charge' for a security right in receivables.[17] Likewise, the English translation of the French Civil Code provided by *Légifrance*, the official website of the French government for the publication of legislation, regulations and legal information, uses the term 'pledge' rather than 'charge' for a security right in receivables.[18] The pledge (*Pfandrecht*)[19] of a claim under the German Civil Code[20] and the pledge (*nantissement*)[21] of a debt under the French Civil Code[22] signify security rights generally over movable personal property, the creation of which is made public by physical transfer of the object. From the English law point of view, one cannot have a 'pledge' of receivables since one cannot have physical possession of receivables. This shows slightly different understanding of or approach towards security rights in receivables in English law and in German and French law.

---

[15] For example, 'charge on book debts of the company' in the Companies Act 2006. 'Charge' in the Companies Act 2006 includes 'mortgage'. Under English law, only tangible property may be pledged.

[16] Hugh Beale, Michael Bridge, Louise Gullifer and Eva Lomnicka, *The Law of Personal Property Security* (Oxford, Oxford University Press, 2007) 328 n 33. By comparison, a pledge under English law is called a 'security right perfected by possession' in art 9 UCC and in the PPSAs of Canada, New Zealand and Australia.

[17] www.gesetze-im-internet.de/englisch_bgb/englisch_bgb.html#Section%20405.

[18] http://195.83.177.9/code/liste.phtml?lang=uk&c=22&r=7815.

[19] www.gesetze-im-internet.de/bgb/BJNR001950896.html.

[20] German Civil Code, ss 1279–90.

[21] www.legifrance.gouv.fr/affichCode.do;jsessionid=10CE907B0C1018B38E574A6B23720541.tpdjo01v_3?idSectionTA=LEGISCTA000006150366&cidTexte=LEGITEXT000006070721&dateTexte=20090220.

[22] French Civil Code, ss 2356–66.

1-4. Security Transfer of Receivables

In addition to an outright transfer of receivables and a security right in receivables, there are hybrid security rights, ie, security transfers of receivables. In other words, it is a transfer of receivables for security purposes. The international registration system this book proposes should cover all these three categories of receivables transactions.

Security transfers of receivables are transfers of receivables for security purposes. The difference between a security transfer and an outright transfer is that in a security transfer, the transferor (grantor) may get back his right to the receivables after fulfilling the debt payment to the transferee (creditor), which the receivables secured. A security transfer of receivables functions to induce an economically similar result as an outright transfer of receivables with recourse. In a transfer of receivables with recourse, if debtors of receivables fail to pay the receivables to the transferee, the transferee can request the transferor to buy back the receivables.

For example, in an English mortgage (security transfer) on receivables, the receivable is transferred to the transferee (secured creditor). This means that the transferee (secured creditor) may collect the proceeds directly from the debtor of the receivable.

Let us suppose a case where V borrows money from B and provides its receivable (V-D)[23] to B as security. If V pays the debt to B before the due date, V has the right to request B to transfer the receivable (V-D) back to V. If V fails to pay the debt to B by the due date, B may give notice of the transfer of the receivable (V-D) to the debtor of the receivable (D) and collect the receivable directly from the debtor (D), returning the remainder to V after satisfying its debt.

A transfer *with recourse* operates in a similar way to a security transfer. In a transfer with recourse, V may transfer its receivable (V-D) to C with recourse and obtain the price of the receivable as consideration. C may give notice of the transfer of the receivable (V-D) to the debtor of the receivable (D) and collect the receivable directly from the debtor (D). If the debtor of the receivable (D) fails to pay the receivable to C, C may ask V to repurchase the receivable from C at the same price as sold. The difference between a security transfer and a transfer with recourse is that in a security transfer, the debtor of the receivable (D) would back up the transferor's credit risk, whereas in a transfer with recourse, the transferor would back up the credit risk of the debtor of the receivable (D). See Table 1.1.

In some jurisdictions, a security transfer of receivables is treated as an *outright transfer* of receivables because a security transfer is a transfer.[24] In other

---

[23] '(V-D)' indicates that the receivable is V's monetary claim against D and that V is the creditor and D is the debtor of the receivable.

[24] Germany. See section 3-7-12 Q 2-2.

jurisdictions, a security transfer of receivables is treated as a *security right* in receivables because both of them serve the same economic function.[25]

Table 1.1: Receivables financing

		Notice of the transfer to the account debtor (usually)	Debt collection	Account debtor default risk
Sale transfer	Factoring without recourse	At the outset	Transferee (factor)	
	Factoring with recourse	At the outset	Transferee	Transferor
	Block discounting without recourse	In/before transferor's insolvency	Transferor	Transferee
	Block discounting with recourse	In/before transferor's insolvency	Transferor	
Trust/sale	Securitisation	In/before transferor (originator)'s insolvency	Transferor (originator)	General investors
Security purpose	Security transfer (transfer for security purposes)	After transferor (debtor)'s default	Transferee (secured creditor)	Transferee (secured creditor) if transferor (debtor) defaults
	Security right	After grantor (debtor)'s default	Secured creditor	Secured creditor if grantor (debtor) defaults

1-5. Transfers Rather than Security Rights

An outright transfer of receivables and a security right in receivables appear differently on the balance sheet in the financial statement of a transferor or a grantor. A business balance sheet consists of two vertical columns. Assets are set out in one column, and liabilities and equity are set out in the other column. An outright

---

[25] France. See section 3-7-8 Q 2-1.

transfer of receivables eliminates the receivables on the asset column and instead a cash income for the consideration will appear on the asset column. By contrast, a security right in receivables does not eliminate the receivables on the asset column, but the debt that the receivables are encumbered for will appear on the liability column and a cash income from the debt will appear in the asset column.

For a bank to increase the capital adequacy ratio, an outright transfer of receivables is more advantageous than a security right in receivables. The capital adequacy ratio is measured by the percentage of a bank's core capital divided by its risk-weighted assets. Under the Basel III, the percentage of 'Common Equity Tier 1' (which comprises of a bank's core capital) divided by its risk-weighted assets should be no less than 4.5 per cent. Since in calculating risk weighted assets, cash is to be multiplied by zero, a cash income from selling receivables or borrowing has nothing to do with the capital adequacy ratios. However, decreasing bad receivables results in decreasing risk weighted assets, and thus may have an effect of increasing the capital adequacy ratio, although bad receivables are sold at a discounted price.

Considering potential reorganisation proceedings of the debtor (transferor or grantor), an outright transfer of receivables is more advantageous for the transferee (or secured creditor) than a security right in receivables. In the potential reorganisation proceedings of a debtor (a grantor or transferor), *secured creditors* with security rights might be pressured to sacrifice for the reorganisation of the debtor, whereas a transferee is not involved with the reorganisation proceedings of the transferor.[26] In this respect, creditors sometimes prefer a transfer of receivables.

1-6. Proposal of an International Receivables Registry

To facilitate the international transfer and collateralisation of receivables, this book proposes an international registration system for transfers of and security rights in receivables, which is referred to here as the 'International Receivables Registry'.

This book proposes that under the International Receivables Registry, foreign investors (transferees) would only have to register the transfer of receivables at the international registry in the case of cross-border transfers of receivables. A transferor could directly dispose of its receivables to foreign investors. A foreign investor could directly purchase the receivables without concerning itself with perfection requirements under domestic laws. If an investor (transferee) registers

---

[26] Under English law, a transfer by way of security could mean a mortgage, where the security taker is very much involved in a reorganisation. It is only when there is a transfer that the transferee can sue the account debtor without having to account to the grantor for the surplus, and so is completely outside the reorganisation. Beale et al (n 16) 326 [7.09]

the transfer of receivables in an international registry, the investor would be entitled to enforce his priority based on the registration in any country that has joined the international convention for it.

If transfers of receivables were regulated by a single international registration system, international financiers would not need to give notice to debtors of receivables or register their security rights in a domestic registry of a foreign country. All they would have to do is to register their transfers of or security rights in receivables with the International Receivables Registry for perfection against third parties. This would substantially reduce transaction costs in international financing.

Under the proposed International Receivables Registry, companies located in states with no established capital market would be able to raise funds from established capital markets across national borders through international receivables financing, including factoring and securitisation. Factoring, block discounting without recourse and securitisation are receivables financing structures using the outright transfers of receivables.

Furthermore, an International Receivables Registry would facilitate international bank loans using receivables as collateral. A company could easily obtain loans using its receivables as collateral from a foreign bank of a neighbouring country or international banks such as the International Monetary Fund (IMF). For example, a Spanish company could easily obtain loans using its receivables as collateral from a German bank, while a Korean company could easily obtain loans using its receivables as collateral from a Chinese bank.

The International Receivables Registry would remove the barriers against the cross-border transfer of receivables and could help receivables financing to cross national borders, thus enabling entrepreneurs to raise funds from a greater range of investors around the world *without* a need to heed foreign domestic laws or cope with foreign languages. It would ultimately result in a more efficient distribution of capital at a global level.

The International Receivables Registry would also facilitate international project financing. For example, in the case of a power station construction project in a country in Africa, the power station would provide a stable cash-flow of future receivables. A foreign investor could perfect transfers of or security rights in the future receivables of the power station by registering them in the International Receivables Registry without having to be concerned with the domestic laws of the country involved.

1-7. Research Methods

This book conducts a comparative analysis on perfection against third parties, priority and registration systems of multiple jurisdictions. Section 2-3 compares laws on security rights in common law jurisdictions. Section 2-4 compares laws on security rights in civil law jurisdictions. Section 2-7-4 compares the information required for registration in each jurisdiction. Section 2-8-2 compares what the registrant and the other counterparty to the transfer (or security right) agreement are required to do in the registration procedure in each jurisdiction. Section 2-9 compares the system of searching the registry in each jurisdiction. Sections 3-2 and 3-8 analyse and compare such laws in each jurisdiction by a way of giving answers to the same set of six questions about the effectiveness and perfection of transfers and security rights.

The purpose of employing this comparative analysis is to suggest a desirable model of the regulatory system on the transfer of receivables that best fits an international convention. The system should be functionally efficient as well as widely acceptable. There are two different factors for a successful international model: efficiency and universality. The first reason to conduct comparative analysis is to find the most efficient system among the legal systems of each jurisdiction. The second reason is to find the legal system that is most widely acceptable. However, the most efficient legal system is not always the most widely acceptable because states vary in terms of the degree of their legal sophistication. The lesson of the UN Receivables Convention shows that the most efficient model is not necessarily the best strategy for an international convention if it is not widely acceptable. Even though the UN Receivables Convention presents an ideal model for the transfer of receivables, the model has not been widely accepted.[27] For a successful international convention, therefore, wide acceptability is one of the most important considerations.

1-8. Overview of this Book

This book consists of seven chapters. Chapter 1 is the introduction. Chapter 2 explores current general security rights registries in the world and finds the need for an international registration system for security rights in receivables. Chapter 3 gives a general analysis on the current laws of priority and perfection with respect to transfers of and security rights in receivables. Chapter 4 explains conflicts of laws and private international law rules with respect to the transfer of receivables, and the so-called double-debtor problem and priority rules of floating charges and reservation of title. Chapters 5 and 6 show a model for the International Receivables Registry. Chapter 5 defines the limits of application scope of the International Receivables Registry and illustrates how to implement and operate the International Receivables Registry in practice. Chapter 6 sets out priority rules of the proposed International Receivables Registry Convention. Chapter 7 is the conclusion.

---

[27] It is because each state does not want to revise its domestic laws, especially basic laws such as civil codes in civil law jurisdictions. In order to adopt the UN Receivables Convention, many states need to revise their domestic civil codes.

2

Security Rights Registries

2-1. Introduction

The International Receivables Registry covers both the transfers of and security rights in receivables. In Chapter 1, it was shown that in order to determine priority among transfers of or security rights in a receivable, the International Receivables Registry should cover both transfers of and security rights in receivables.[1]

Chapter 2 analyses the merits of a registration system for security rights in receivables. It reviews existing registration systems under current laws in different jurisdictions. The UK, Singapore, Hong Kong, the US, Canada, New Zealand, Australia, Japan, Korea and China have registration systems. No registration system for security rights exists for transfers of and security rights in only receivables (without tangible movable assets) in any jurisdiction.

Sections 2-2 to 2-4 comparatively analyse national laws on security rights, registration systems for movable assets and receivables. Sections 2-3 and 2-4 compare the difference between common law jurisdictions and civil law jurisdictions with respect to registration, with a focus on why a registration system for security rights in movable assets and receivables has not been developed in European civil law jurisdictions. Section 2-4 also investigates how China, Korea and Japan compromised between the civil law jurisdictions and the common law jurisdictions. China, Korea and Japan have hybrid systems, where they adopted the registration systems influenced by the US and other countries in addition to their civil law legal systems.

Section 2-5 reviews global movements to harmonise laws on a general security rights registry facilitating security rights in movable assets and receivables as well as global movements to establish international registration systems for each specific type of assets, including receivables. Section 2-6 analyses the pros and cons of a general security rights registry and seeks to show the economic value of a general security rights registry.

Section 2-7 compares the notice-filing system and the document-filing system. Some jurisdictions have notice-filing systems and other jurisdictions have document-filing systems. Section 2-7-3 further deals with the so-called advance

---

[1] See section 1-6.

registration issue. It reviews the English legal system as the origin of a general security rights registry. Section 2-7-4 examines UCC Article 9 of the US as the originator of a notice-filing system, the UNCITRAL Model Law on Secured Transactions, which adopted a notice-filing system, and the Personal Property Security Acts of Canada, New Zealand and Australia, which follow the UCC Article 9 model. It reviews information that a registrant should submit to the registry for registration of a transfer of or security right in receivables in each jurisdiction.

Section 2-8 reviews whether the systems in each jurisdiction require the consent of a transferor or grantor upon the registration application of a transferee or secured creditor for verifying the authenticity of the contents of the registration. Section 2-9 shows how to search security rights registries in each jurisdiction. Section 2-10 provides a conclusion.

2-2. Publicity

Before investigating the general security rights registry of each jurisdiction, this section examines whether publicity is required for perfection of a security right against third parties in order to explain the function of a general security rights registry.

2-2-1. Methods of Publicity

Registration is one method of obtaining publicity. With respect to tangible movable assets, there are four methods of publicity. The steps that must be taken for the perfection of security rights in *tangible movable assets* fall into the following four categories: (1) registration or filing a notice in a public records system established for that purpose; (2) taking possession of collateral; (3) taking control of the collateral by means of the stakeholder's agreement to hold for the secured creditor; and (4) posting a notice on the property or where it will be seen by persons dealing with the property.[2]

With respect to transfers of and security rights in *receivables*: (1) registration or filing is required in some jurisdictions; and (2) notice of the transfer of the receivable to the debtor is required in other jurisdictions.

---

[2] Lynn M LoPucki and Elizabeth Warren, *Secured Credit: A Systems Approach*, 6th edn (Alphen aan den Rijn, Aspen Publishers, 2009) 280. In England, the US and France, because there are registries for security rights in movable assets, a third party can check the status of a movable asset by referring to the relevant registry. In Germany, there is no security rights registry where a third party can check the status of a movable asset. As such, a potential secured creditor could only ask the debtor or the grantor for that information.

2-2-2. The Function of Publicity

There are two main functions of publicity. First, it allows the public to be aware of the existence of a transfer of or a security right in a receivable. Second, it publicly certifies the existence and the date of a transfer of or a security right in a receivable.

2-2-2-1. Providing Information to the Public

By providing information to the public, publicity may prevent incorrect assumptions of the financial health of a company and may also prevent double transfers. With respect to transfers of and security rights in receivables, publicity gives information on the status of a certain receivable to third parties interested in purchasing or taking security rights in the receivable. Not only registration but also notification to the debtor is good publicity.

In the jurisdictions where registration is required for publicity, potential investors can refer to a registry. On the other hand, in the jurisdictions where notification of the transfer to the debtor is required for publicity, potential investors can enquire of the debtor whether there has been a prior transfer of the receivable. However, for future receivables for which debtors would not yet be specified, giving notice of the transfer is impossible. Furthermore, for bulk receivables for which there are numerous account debtors, giving notice of the transfer is impractical, time-consuming and costly.[3] For this reason, registration is a more desirable system of publicity than notification to the debtor for receivables financing.

In addition, a registration system for security rights in movable assets facilitates non-possessory security rights in movable assets. Under traditional civil law, the transfer of an *in rem* right should be publicised since it is effective *erga omnes* (enforceable against any person with respect to the object). Delivery of possession is required for the pledge of a tangible movable asset. With respect to non-possessory security rights, on the other hand, since a grantor is still in possession of the encumbered asset, third parties cannot easily find whether there is a security right in that asset. Traditionally in civil law, non-possessory security rights in tangible movable assets depend on exceptional legal conceptualisation because there is no physical delivery of possession. Because it is not publicised, a non-possessory security right creates uncertainty about its existence since there is no physical delivery for a third party to 'see'. A lender (bank) might be able to undertake an extensive search to minimise the uncertainty of any hidden prior security rights in a certain encumbered asset, but this is time-consuming, costly and increases the cost of credit. In this regard, a registration system can publicise non-possessory security rights in tangible movable assets and, as a result, can facilitate such non-possessory security rights.

---

[3] See section 4-6-1.

2-2-2-2. Evidence

A second purpose of publicity for some jurisdictions is to provide a mechanism for secured creditors to prove the existence and effective date of their security rights as an evidentiary matter.[4] Publicity is useful for a secured creditor to verify the effective date of a security right to preserve priority of the security right.

Publicity ensuring the veracity of the timing and the existence of a security right could eliminate the possibility that a debtor and a secured creditor could conspire to claim that a security right was created earlier than it actually was.[5] In the jurisdiction where priority is generally determined by the time order of registration, there is little risk that such collusion concerning the time of creation might affect the priority of other competing security rights.[6]

2-3. The Security Rights System in Common Law Jurisdictions

2-3-1. Security Rights Registries in English Law

2-3-1-1. English Courts of Equity Allowing Non-possessory Charges

Registration of charges over movable assets and receivables was first developed under English law. England has a relatively long history of non-possessory security rights, namely charges and mortgages. Although English law does not formally limit the permissible categories of security right, there are broadly four categories of consensual security known to English law: (1) pledge; (2) contractual lien; (3) mortgage; and (4) charge.[7] Whereas pledges require transfer of possession and mortgages require transfer of ownership, charges require neither transfer of possession nor transfer of ownership.[8]

---

[4] UNCITRAL Legislative Guide on Secured Transactions, 47 [70]. In some jurisdictions, publicity is a requirement for creation of a security right. But under UCC art 9, parties may file the financing statement even before a security agreement has been <u>concluded</u>. <u>Once</u> the security right is created by a security agreement, priority <u>is determined by the time order when the financing statement</u> covering the security right <u>has been filed, regardless of the time when the security agreement is concluded</u>: UCC, art 9-322(a).

[5] Charles W Mooney, Jr, 'The Mystery and Myth of Ostensible Ownership and Article 9 Filing: A Critique of Proposals to Extend Filing Requirements to Leases' (1988) 39 *Alabama Law Review* 683, 752.

[6] ibid 752, fn 264.

[7] Roy Goode and Louise Gullifer, *Goode on Legal Problems of Credit and Security*, 4th edn (London, Sweet & Maxwell, 2008) 30–31, fn 153 [1-42].

[8] *Carreras Rothmans Ltd v Freeman Mathews Treasure Ltd* [1985] Ch 207 (Ch).

All charges are equitable.[9] The scope of charges includes equitable mortgages and therefore all equitable mortgages are charges.[10] Thanks to equity in English law, non-possessory security rights could develop without the formality of *in rem* rights of the civil law,[11] and accordingly its registration system could develop under English law first. Common law jurisdictions could adopt registration systems for non-possessory security rights without changing their existing laws. A secured creditor with a non-possessory security right holds the right to request the debtor (grantor) to return the collateral if the debt is fully paid, while the debtor (grantor) possesses and uses the collateral. See Table 2.1.

Table 2.1: Non-possessory security rights v possessory security rights

	Non-possessory security right	Possessory security right (pledge)
Secured creditor	Right to request the debtor to return back the collateral	Possession
Debtor (grantor)	Possession	Ownership

2-3-1-2. The Publicity Problem of Non-possessory Charges

In England, the original reason for the development of a registration system for security rights was to prevent hidden non-possessory security rights. *Twyne's Case*[12] shows us the problem of a hidden non-possessory security right. In 1601, Pierce was indebted to Twyne and was also indebted to C. However, in secret, Pierce disposed by deed of all his goods, including the sheep, to Twyne in satisfaction of his debt. He continued in possession of the goods. He then sold some of the goods to third parties. Pierce then sheared the sheep and branded them with his own mark. C subsequently brought an action of debt against Pierce. C obtained a judgment against Pierce and had a *fieri facias* directed to the Sheriff of Southampton. When the Sheriff came to make execution of the goods by force of the writ, Twyne resisted the sheriff with force. Twyne claimed that he owned the goods by force of the gift, and it was a gift made on a good and lawful consideration. Twyne was criminally convicted of fraud according to the Fraudulent Conveyances Act 1571.[13]

---

[9] Goode and Gullifer (n 7) 5.
[10] *Shea v Moore* [1894] IR 158 (CA), 168, per Walker LC. Mortgages are divided into legal mortgages, which require transfer of ownership, and equitable mortgages.
[11] In contrast, in civil law jurisdictions, because security rights are *in rem* rights, the *numerus clausus* principle applies to security rights and therefore the parties may not freely create a new type of security right. This prevented the development of non-possessory security rights in civil law jurisdictions until the economic demand of non-possessory security rights increased unbearably.
[12] *Twyne's Case* [1558–1774] All ER Rep 303; 3 Co Rep 80 b; Moore KB 638; 76 ER 809 (Court of Star Chamber).
[13] 13 Eliz I Cap 5.

This case was a criminal action involving imputed fraud.[14] One way to understand fraudulent or hidden non-possessory security rights was as an affront to community norms.[15]

The problem with fraudulent or hidden non-possessory security rights appears to have had a significant influence on the development of a registration system, which functions as an information proxy for possession that could deter or correct the problems of hidden non-possessory security rights like those in *Twyne's Case*.[16]

2-3-1-3. Registration as an Ex Ante *Method*

A creditor may recover his loan insofar as the debtor can be brought under the jurisdiction of the court and recovery of the fraudulent transaction can be performed *ex post*. However, since the Victorian era, England had colonies around the world and English merchants travelled the world to places like Australia, New Zealand, Singapore, Hong Kong, Shanghai, India and Africa. Therefore, it would have been easy for an English merchant to effectively 'run away'. Because of this historical circumstance, there was a vital need to prevent fraudulent or hidden non-possessory security rights by an *ex ante* method.

Registration of company charges can function as an *ex ante* method. Under a transparent registration system, a debtor *cannot* hide non-possessory security rights. By checking the registry, a creditor can *ex ante* avoid those debtors who have created non-possessory security rights. Since a security right that is not registered would not be effective, a creditor may rely on the registry. An unregistered charge created by a company is not perfected against the insolvency administrator.[17] An unregistered security bill of sale is completely ineffective.[18]

2-3-1-4. The Origin of Security Rights Registries in English Law

The English courts of equity allowing non-possessory charges accelerated the creation of a registration system for company charges. In England, a general security rights registry was invented for non-possessory security rights in the late nineteenth century. The Bills of Sale Act 1878 provides for the registry of written chattel mortgages created by individuals. Registration of charges created by companies was introduced by the Companies Act 1862, but it required each company to maintain a registry of all mortgages and charges affecting the properties of

---

[14] Mooney, Jr (n 5) 727.
[15] Jonathan C Lipson, 'Secrets and Liens: The End of Notice in Commercial Finance Law' (2005) 21 *Emory Bankruptcy Developments Journal* 421, 438.
[16] ibid 437.
[17] Companies Act 2006 (Amendment of Part 25) Regulations 2013, s 859H. Still, an unregistered charge is valid against the company itself. Registration is required for perfection against other secured creditors and against unsecured creditors on insolvency.
[18] Bills of Sale Act (1878) Amendment Act 1882, s 8. This is because registration is a creation requirement for a security bill of sale.

the company.[19] A centralised registry that is searchable by any member of the public was introduced for company charges over certain types of assets stipulated in the Company Charges Act 1890.[20]

The scheme for registering company charges dates from the Companies Act 1900.[21] Originally, this registration system was for tangible personal property such as equipment, machines and inventory. Companies often create non-possessory security rights in factory machines or inventory. Companies also create charges over company receivables and create floating charges over future and present properties. To reflect companies' practices, the scope of the register of charges at Companies House has been expanded. Currently, the Companies Act 2006 and the Companies Act 2006 (Amendment of Part 25) Regulations 2013 provide for the register of charges created by companies.[22] The register of charges at Companies House is a general security rights registry which covers various types of assets unless the asset is exempted or regulated by other laws.[23] In addition, there are other kinds of registries for specific types of assets, such as mortgages or charges of registered ships,[24] registered aircraft[25] and intellectual property[26] that is able to be registered.

2-3-1-5. The Debtor-Based Indexed Registration System

A general security rights registry can hardly be systemised as an asset-indexed registry, because a general security rights registry covers various different types of assets. Thus, it needs to be designed as a debtor-indexed registry. In addition, a debtor-indexed registry is suitable for floating charges (universal charges) because a creditor with floating charges only knows his debtor (grantor) and would not necessarily know future assets that could be potentially encumbered.

In contrast, asset-indexed registries are exemplified by the land registry and special registries for particular movable assets such as cars, ships and planes. In most modern countries, each tract of land is given a unique address number on a map, and thus one can find the number of the land in question on the maps and search the index under the tract number in the land registry. Also, each car, each ship and each plane is given a registration number and can be searched accordingly.

In England and Wales, there are two existing parallel systems of providing title to land and investigating third-party rights in land. *Unregistered land* is governed

---

[19] Hugh Beale, Michael Bridge, Louise Gullifer and Eva Lomnicka, *The Law of Personal Property Security* (Oxford, Oxford University Press, 2007) 324 [7.03].
[20] ibid, following the report of the Davey Committee on Company Law Amendment (C 7779, 1895), paras 46–50.
[21] Companies Act 1900 (63 & 64 Vict Cap 48), s 14.
[22] Companies Act 2006 (Amendment of Part 25) Regulations 2013, ss 859A–G.
[23] ibid s 859A(6).
[24] Merchant Shipping Act 1995, s 16 and sched 1.
[25] Mortgaging of Aircraft Order 1972, SI 1972/1268.
[26] Patents Act 1977, ss 30–33; Trade Marks Act 1994, s 25; Registered Designs Act 1949, s 19. There is no registration of copyright in the UK.

by the older system of title deeds and the Land Charges Registry under the Land Charges Act 1925. Title deeds, where titles are recorded genealogically, show ownership of lands,[27] whereas the Land Charges Registry records all equitable interests in land.[28] The Land Charges Registry is indexed by the owner of the land (the debtor) at the time that the charge is created and therefore it is a debtor-indexed registry.

Registered land is governed by the newer system under the Land Registration Act 1925, which provides for the Land Registry.[29] The Land Registration Act 2002 has increased the number of interests which must be registered in order to make the Land Registry as self-contained and all-encompassing as possible and, accordingly, all creations, changes and discharges of ownership of and security rights in each piece of land need to be registered.[30] The Land Registry is indexed by the land and is therefore an asset-indexed registry.

2-3-2. Uniform Commercial Code Article 9 of the US

2-3-2-1. Historical Background

The US established the financial statement filing system under Article 9 of the US Uniform Commercial Code (UCC)[31] in 1952. The scope of the filing system has been expanded from charges over personal property including receivables to include outright transfers of receivables. This is because of historical reasons. Before the enactment of UCC Article 9, different rules had been developed by the various state courts. For example, in California and Pennsylvania, courts followed the English *Dearle v Hall* rule. On the other hand, in New York, the courts followed the German rule.

In 1943, in *Corn Exchange National Bank v Klauder*,[32] the US Supreme Court held that transferees who engaged in a transfer of receivables without giving notice to the debtors of the receivables in a state following the English rule[33] were not protected in the insolvency of the transferor in other states. As a result, in interstate transactions of receivables, the transferor or the transferee had to give notice

---

[27] Elizabeth Cooke, *The New Law of Land Registration* (Oxford, Hart Publishing, 2003) 5–9.
[28] Land Charges Act 1972, s 2.
[29] This is title registration and contains tabular data wherein the state of the title can be seen and thus a searcher need not look behind the final registration. See Cooke (n 27) 5–9.
[30] Cooke (n 25) 9–12.
[31] The UCC is a set of standardised business laws, created by the National Conference of Commissioners on Uniform State Laws (NCCUSL) and the American Law Institute (ALI), and first published in 1952. The UCC has been adopted by most states of the US with a few modifications. Its purpose is to harmonise, and further unify, the laws of business and commercial transactions throughout the US. The latest version of UCC art 9 was made in 2010.
[32] *Corn Exchange National Bank v Klauder* 63 S Ct 679, 318 US 434 (1943).
[33] *Dearle v Hall* (1828) 3 Russ 1.

of the transfer to the debtor in order for the transferee to be protected from the insolvency of the transferor. However, giving notice of the transfer to the debtor is costly and time-consuming.

After this decision, a codification of these various priority rules was accelerated.[34] In 1952, UCC Article 9 unified all these rules, and now the transferor or the transferee only has to file a financing statement for a transfer of a receivable to be perfected against the insolvency administrator of the transferor and for the receivable transferred to the transferee not to be included in the insolvency estate of the transferor. As a result, UCC Article 9 includes both security rights in receivables and outright transfers of receivables. All 50 states in the US have adopted UCC Article 9 with some amendments.

2-3-2-2. The Notice-Filing System

The US invented a notice-filing system that was significantly different from the commonly accepted concept of registration systems, where the state guarantees the contents.[35] In the US, land registries differ by county and the application criteria vary and can be lax at the county level. In such circumstances, a lax concept of registration, which is a notice-filing system under UCC Article 9, could be invented.[36] The goal of notice-filing under UCC Article 9 was to replace the cumbersome document-filing system with the registration of a simple notice containing only the basic details about the security right to which it related.[37] In a notice-filing system, 'a registrant need not submit the underlying security documentation or provide other evidence of the security right to which the registration relates in order to register a notice'.[38]

The main function of notice filing is to confirm that a debtor has made full disclosure and to provide warning of the need for further investigation.[39] In addition, a notice-filing registry could also provide support for due diligence and the discovery of potentially competing secured creditors.[40]

---

[34] Hein Kötz, 'Rights of Third Parties: Third Party Beneficiaries and Transfer' in Arthur von Mehren (ed), *International Encyclopedia of Comparative Law*, vol 7 (Tubingen, Möhr, 1992) 56.
[35] UNCITRAL Legislative Guide on Secured Transactions, 111.
[36] In the US, with respect to the financing statement filing under UCC Article 9, each of the 50 states has its own registration system for filing financing statements in the state level. But land registries exist at the county level. The contents of the land registration are more detailed than the contents of the financing statement filing under UCC Article 9. The registry officers do not examine the substance of a filing at the UCC Article 9 registries and a filing at land registries; they only examine and reject filings that are not in the proper form. For example, the omission of required data results in the rejection of an art 9 filing. The omission of a notarisation or tax stamps might result in the rejection of a real estate filing. With respect to land registries, deeds are recorded and deeds evidence the ownership of land.
[37] UNCITRAL Legislative Guide on Secured Transactions, 111 [32].
[38] ibid 174 [98].
[39] Harry C Sigman and Eva-Maria Kieninger (eds), *Cross-border Security over Tangibles* (Munich, Sellier, 2007) 43.
[40] ibid 42.

2-3-3. The Personal Property Security Acts (PPSAs)

In Canada, all provinces except Quebec follow the common law and have had registration requirements with respect to a general assignment of receivables since the 1920s, and each has its own registry. The current Canadian registry provisions are merged in the PPSAs of each province, but the basic principles remain the same.

New Zealand enacted the PPSA in 1999, which came into force on 1 May 2002 when the Personal Property Securities Register (hereinafter the PPS Register) became operational.[41] The New Zealand PPSA provides for the PPS Register, a registration system for security rights in personal property including the transfer of receivables. The registration system is operated online on the official website, where security rights over personal property may be registered and can be searched for.[42]

The Australian PPSA was passed in December 2009 and entered into force in May 2011. Since May 2011, there is one national personal property securities law and one national online PPS Register under the PPSA 2009.[43] The Australian PPS Register started operating on 30 January 2012 and is managed by the Insolvency and Trustee Service Australia (ITSA). The Australian government Attorney-General's Department has responsibility for personal property securities policy.

2-4. The Security Rights System in Civil Law Jurisdictions

2-4-1. The *Numerus Clausus* Principle

In civil law jurisdictions, there has been an obstacle to the development of registration system for security rights: the *numerus clausus* principle. The civil law countries explicitly restricted the available range of *in rem* rights and set up a closed list, known as the *numerus clausus* principle.[44]

Merrill and Smith argue that the *numerus clausus* principle strikes a balance between a proliferation of *in rem* rights in English common law jurisdictions and a 'one-size-fits-all' system of *in rem* rights in continental civil law jurisdictions.[45] On the one hand, a 'one-size-fits-all' system of *in rem* rights would frustrate those

---

[41] www.med.govt.nz/templates/StandardSummary____15299.aspx.
[42] The official website for the PPS Register of New Zealand is: www.ppsr.govt.nz/cms.
[43] The official website for the PPS Register of Australia is: www.ppsr.gov.au.
[44] Bernard Rudden, 'Economic Theory v Property Law: The Numerus Clausus Problem' in J Eekelaar and J Bell (eds), *Oxford Essays in Jurisprudence* (Oxford, Clarendon Press, 1987).
[45] Thomas Merrill and Henry Smith, 'Optimal Standardization in the Law of Property: The *Numerus Clausus* Principle' (2000) 110 *Yale Law Journal* 1, 69.

legitimate objectives that can be achieved only by using different *in rem* rights that fall short of full ownership. On the other hand, permitting free customisation of new forms of *in rem* rights would be problematic because third parties must ascertain and measure the legal dimensions of *in rem* rights in order to avoid violating the rights of others and to assess whether to acquire the rights, and it would also impose significant information costs or transaction costs. The *numerus clausus* principle pertains to the protection of all third parties from unexpected novel *in rem* rights.

In rem rights require publicity. In the past, the methods of publicity were costly and time-consuming. However, with the development of internet technology, publicity through online registration becomes very convenient and economical. As a result, today, the *numerus clausus* principle might be allowed to be relaxed. This is because third parties could easily and clearly check the contents of the contract arrangement of the parties through the online registration system. Thanks to the development of internet technology, people can use many online registration systems. People can search the online registry at home and in the office without visiting the registry office in person. This technical change could result in changes in the property law systems, including security rights. Traditionally, in civil law jurisdictions, the types of *in rem* rights are restricted because of the *numerus clausus* principle. However, nowadays, with the use of internet technology, the *numerus clausus* principle might not need to be strictly maintained.

There is a critical view towards the *numerus clausus* principle based on the historical background. Hansmann and Kraakman argue that the *numerus clausus* principle results from a 'unitary theory of property rights' of the civil law. They observe the historical background of the French Revolution in 1789 during which the *numerus clausus* doctrine was born. At that time, since divided property rights came to be associated with feudal social relations, it was argued that divided property rights must be closely regulated and restricted.[46] The liberal bourgeoisie were keen on protecting natural rights including property rights. Since then, the civil law countries of Europe have adhered to a 'unitary theory of property rights' under which all *in rem* rights in an asset must be concentrated in the hands of a single owner rather than divided into partial rights shared among two or more persons and the king under the feudal system, and only a relatively small, closed number ('numerus clausus') of specifically defined exceptions are permitted.[47]

In any case, Merrill and Smith, and Hansmann and Kraakman all agree that the *numerus clausus* principle is more strictly valued in civil law jurisdictions than in common law jurisdictions.[48]

---

[46] Henry Hansmann and Reinier Kraakman, 'Property, Contract, and Verification: The *Numerus Clausus* Problem and the Divisibility of Rights' (2002) 31 *Journal of Legal Studies* S417.

[47] ibid S375. Such exceptions include mortgages on real property and security rights in personal property.

[48] Merrill and Smith (n 45); Hansmann and Kraakman (n 46) 38.

There is a principle that *in rem* rights require publicity letting third parties know about the *in rem* rights since they are effective against everyone in the world, ie, *erga omnes*. Without publicity, an agreement to create a security right in an asset is not effective against third parties. As for real estates, registration is required to satisfy the publicity requirement.[49]

Under the German Pandekten system, security rights belong to *in rem* rights and are thus governed by the *numerus clausus* principle. First, mortgages must be perfected by registration.[50] Second, pledges must be perfected by delivery of possession. See Table 2.2. Third, a lien is not a contractual security right, but a statutory security right, which arises automatically once the requirements stipulated by law are fulfilled. These core concepts of three basic types of security rights are common in civil law jurisdictions. Due to the *numerus clausus* principle, the types of *in rem* rights are strictly limited in civil law jurisdictions and parties may not create a new type of *in rem* right.

Table 2.2: Mortgage v pledge

	Collateral	Publicity
Mortgage	Real estates, land, building, cars, ships, planes	Registration
Pledge	Movable assets, *in personam* rights	Possession

The pledge (*pignus* in Latin) is the oldest security right and was well known from Roman law.[51] In civil law jurisdictions, pledges are divided into two types: pledges

---

[49] In civil law jurisdictions, registration is required either for the creation of a title or at least for third-party effectiveness. In Germany and Korea, registration in a title registry is required for the creation or change of a title. This approach is called formalism (*Formalismus* in German) because it requires strict formality for the creation of a title that registration is a creation requirement (*Entstehungsvoraussetzung* in German). In France and Japan, registration in a title registry is required for the third-party effectiveness of a title. This approach is called legal will theory (*Rechtwillenstheorie* in German) because a title is created merely by the parties' will or intention, and registration is only a perfection requirement (*Einwendungsvoraussetzung* in German). Mortgages on real estate are registered in the real estate registry and mortgages in aircraft are registered in the aircraft registry.

[50] A mortgage is a non-possessory security right, which must be registered. A mortgage in Chinese, Korean and Japanese law is not exactly a mortgage in English law, in that the former is not involved with the transfer of ownership of the encumbered asset to the secured creditor. In Chinese, Korean and Japanese law, a mortgage is registered in the title registry of the relevant asset as a mortgage. For example, a mortgage in land is registered in the land registry and a mortgage in a plane is registered in the aircraft registry. An asset that cannot be registered cannot be an object of a mortgage. The title ownership of the encumbered asset is not influenced by a mortgage. The mortgagor (grantor) still has the title ownership of the encumbered asset.

[51] This Roman institution has spread over Europe and has been incorporated into all continental civil codes. See Ulrich Drobnig, 'Security Rights in Movables', 15 January 2010, 2. Available at SSRN: http://ssrn.com/abstract=1537137.

of movable assets and pledges of *in personam* rights to claim against obligors.[52] A pledge of a tangible movable asset is perfected by delivery of the possession. A pledge of an *in personam* right requires the transfer of that right. Thus, with respect to movable assets, a pledge is a possessory security right.[53] For this reason, a non-possessory security right in movable assets could not be incorporated into civil codes. In civil law jurisdictions, non-possessory security rights were almost non-existent in the nineteenth century and therefore did not appear in the civil codes of that century, only appearing in the last decade of the twentieth century.[54]

2-4-2. The Fiduciary Transfer of Title for Security Purposes

In Germany, due to the increasing economic demands for non-possessory security rights, the court acknowledges a non-possessory security right in practice, developing the fiduciary transfer of title for security purposes, which is called 'Sicherungsübereignung'. Title may be transferred without a change in actual possession, and no publicity is required. The fiduciary transfer of title for security purposes allows the parties to agree on their preferred enforcement mechanism outside of insolvency proceedings and gives the secured creditor a preferential right to liquidation proceeds in the insolvency of the debtor (grantor).[55] This principle also applies to receivables.[56]

Japan and Korea adopted the fiduciary transfer of title for security purposes from Germany, and the courts in Japan and Korea acknowledge non-possessory security rights as 'YangDoDamBo'[57] in practice.

In China, the legal regime has not introduced specific provisions on the transfer of title to the creditor as an alternative approach to security rights.[58] However, it is possible to arrange such contracts.[59] Under Chinese law, reservation-of-title arrangements and financial leases are allowed, but they are treated as contractual

---

[52] In Korea, any rights other than the right to use and take profits from immovables may be the subject of pledges: Korean Civil Code, art 345. In China, the Property Law and the Security Law stipulate types of rights that can be objects of pledges: Chinese Property Law, art 180; Chinese Security Law, art 34.

[53] In common law jurisdictions, secured transactions law have always recognised the possessory pledge, and this traditionally explained that the possession of the collateral by the pledgee provides publicity. See Sigman and Kieninger (n 39) 40.

[54] Drobnig (n 51).

[55] Sigman and Kieninger (n 39) 69.

[56] See section 3-7-12 Q 2-2.

[57] Fiduciary transfer of title for security purposes is '讓渡擔保' in Chinese characters. The pronunciation of '讓渡擔保' is YangDoDamBo in Korean and JyouToTanPo in Japanese. In this book, for convenience of reference, '讓渡擔保' is referred to as YangDoDamBo.

[58] John Hou, Cherry Chow and Zhen Zhao, 'International Secured Transactions (People's Republic of China Section)' in Dennis Campbell (ed), *International Secured Transactions, Binder 1* (Dobbs Ferry, NY, Oceana Publications, 2008) CHI-7.

[59] ibid.

arrangements and thus are not subject to the general rules on security rights, such as requirements of formality, publicity and effects.[60]

2-4-3. Special Registers

2-4-3-1. Germany

In Germany, in addition to the fiduciary transfer of title for security purposes, a few very specific statutes for registration were enacted in the twentieth century. There are registration systems for real estate and some movable assets that can be easily identified and specified. Germany has three special statutes of limited practical importance: the agricultural tenants' inventories of 1951; the agricultural fruits of 1949; and the overseas cables of 1925.[61] A security rights registry for general personal property including receivables does not exist in Germany.

2-4-3-2. France

France developed many special registers for each type of movable asset and enacted the *Dailly* Act[62] for transfers of receivables. In France, there are special registers for security rights in: ships,[63] planes,[64] motor vehicles,[65] motion picture,[66] patents,[67] trademarks[68] and rights in computer software.[69] Furthermore, there are special regulations for the security rights in: pledges of hotel equipment and furniture,[70] warrants for oil,[71] charges over tooling and equipment,[72] pledges of securities accounts[73] and financial leases.[74]

In addition, the French Commercial Code allows charges over businesses as a going concern,[75] where registration must take place within 15 days of the date of the memorandum and articles of association.[76] Priority among secured creditors shall be determined by the date of their registration.[77]

---

[60] ibid CHI-7–CHI-8.
[61] Drobnig (n 51) fn 27.
[62] The *Dailly* Act, enacted in 1981, provides that a transfer of receivables may be perfected against third parties by the simple delivery of a transfer deed (*bordereau*) signed by the transferor and dated by the transferee without notification to the debtor.
[63] Loi no 67-5 du 3 janvier 1967 relative au statut des navires et autres bâtiments de mer, arts 43 and 48.
[64] French Civil Aviation Code (Code de l'aviation civile), arts 121-2 and 122-7.
[65] French Civil Code, arts 2351, 2352 and 2353.
[66] French Industrial Cinema Code (Code de l'industrie cinématographique), art 33.
[67] French Intellectual Property Code (Code de la propriété intellectuelle), art L613-9.
[68] ibid art L714-7.
[69] ibid art L132-34.
[70] French Commercial Code, arts L523-1–L523-15.
[71] ibid arts L524-1–L524-21.
[72] ibid arts L525-1–L525-20.
[73] French Monetary and Financial Code, art L211-20.
[74] ibid arts L133-7–L133-11.
[75] French Commercial Code, arts L142-1–L143-23.
[76] ibid art L142-4.
[77] French Commercial Code, art L142-5.

2-4-3-3. China

2-4-3-3-1. Registries of Mortgages

The Chinese Property Right Law stipulates types of property that can be objects of mortgages, which include buildings, land use rights and certain types of movable assets.[78] Mortgages on buildings or land use rights etc are created upon the registration of the mortgage.[79] Mortgages on manufacturing facilities, raw materials, semi-manufactured products, finished products,[80] ships under construction, aircrafts under construction[81] or means of transportation[82] are created upon the mortgage agreement of the parties.[83] See Table 2.3.

Such mortgages are perfected against third parties by registration. If they are not registered, mortgages are not effective against bona fide third parties.[84] Registration of such mortgages should be conducted with the county-level administrative department for industry and commerce at the address where the mortgagor (grantor) resides.[85]

The Chinese Property Right Law introduces mortgages on future assets. Companies, individual industrial and commercial households and agricultural producers may mortgage manufacturing equipment, raw materials, semi-manufactured products or finished products, which they own at present or in the future.[86] Such mortgages shall be registered in the administrative department for industry and commerce at the address where the mortgagor (grantor) resides.[87]

Table 2.3: The effect of registration of mortgages in China

Objects of mortgages under the Chinese Property Right Law[88]	Registration
(1) Buildings and other things firmly fixed on the land	Creation requirement[89]
(2) Land use right for construction	
(3) Land management right for barren land etc contracted by the mortgagor by way of bidding, auction and public consultation etc	
(4) Buildings under construction	

(continued)

---

[78] Chinese Property Right Law, art 180; Chinese Security Law, art 34.
[79] Chinese Property Right Law, art 187.
[80] ibid art 180(1)(iv).
[81] ibid art 180(1)(v).
[82] ibid art 180(1)(vi).
[83] ibid art 188.
[84] ibid.
[85] Measures for Registration of the Mortgage on Movable Assets (Order No 30 of the State Administration for Industry and Commerce), art 2.
[86] Chinese Property Right Law, arts 181 and 189.
[87] ibid art 189.
[88] ibid art 180.
[89] ibid art 187.

Table 2.3: (*Continued*)

Objects of mortgages under the Chinese Property Right Law	Registration
(5) Manufacturing equipment, raw materials, semi-manufactured products or finished products (existing or future)[90]	Perfection requirement[91]
(6) Ships and aircrafts that are under construction	
(7) Means of transportation	
(8) Manufacturing facilities, raw materials, semi-manufactured goods and products[92]	

2-4-3-3-2. Registries of Pledges of Movable Assets

In China, the Property Right Law and the Security Law stipulate the types of rights that can be objects of pledges.[93] The Chinese Property Right Law provides creation requirements of pledges of several types of rights. Pledges of bills of exchange, cheques, promissory notes, bonds, certificates of deposit, warehouse receipts and bills of lading are created by the delivery of such negotiable instruments or documents.[94] If there is no title certificate, pledges are created by registration.[95] Pledges of shares are created by registration in the securities depository and clearing institution.[96] Pledges of intellectual property are also created by registration in the relevant department.[97] See Table 2.4.

Table 2.4: Creation requirements of pledges in China

Objects of pledges of rights under the Chinese Property Right Law[98]	Creation requirement
Bills of exchange, cheques, promissory notes	Delivery of possession or registration[99]
Bonds, certificates of deposit	
Warehouse receipts, bills of lading	
Shares of stocks or certificates of stocks which are transferable	Registration in the securities depository and clearing institution[100]

(*continued*)

[90] ibid arts 181 and 189.
[91] ibid art 188.
[92] ibid art 181.
[93] ibid art 180; Chinese Security Law, art 34.
[94] Chinese Property Right Law, art 224.
[95] ibid.
[96] ibid art 226.
[97] ibid art 227.
[98] ibid art 223.
[99] ibid art 224.
[100] ibid art 226.

Table 2.4: (*Continued*)

Objects of pledges of rights under the Chinese Property Right Law	Creation requirement
Exclusive trademark rights, patent rights, copyrights or other property rights in intellectual property which are transferable according to law	Registration in the relevant department[101]
Account receivables	Registration in the Credit Information Centre of the People's Bank of China[102]

2-4-3-3-3. The Registry of Pledge of Receivables

In 2007, the Chinese Property Right Law has greatly expanded the range of movable collateral available to borrowers and lenders in secured finance transactions to include receivables. Accordingly, account receivables can be used as pledges.[103]

Under the Chinese Property Right Law, the pledge of receivables must be registered in the Credit Centre of the People's Bank of China, which is China's central bank.[104] Registration is required for the creation of pledges of receivables. Without registration, the pledge is not effective even as between the parties to the pledge agreement.[105] Article 228 of the Chinese Property Right Law stipulates that, where receivables are pledged, the pledgor (debtor) and the pledgee (creditor) shall conclude a contract in writing and the pledge shall become effective upon registration with the Credit Information Centre. Such registration is compulsory.

In order to provide the registration system for pledge of receivables in accordance with Article 228 of the Chinese Property Right Law, the People's Bank of China made the Measures for Registration of the Pledge of Receivables (MRPR)[106] and established the Credit Information Centre. The MRPR addresses this issue by introducing a centralised registration system for pledges of account receivables. A pledge of account receivables is perfected by registering it in the Credit Information Centre. The Credit Information Centre establishes a system for publicising the registration of receivables pledge to handle the registration of receivables pledge and provide inquiry services for the general public to search registration.[107]

China has a registration system for the pledge of receivables under the MRPR. The MRPR provides a centralised scheme and system for registration of security rights over account receivables. This was welcomed especially by small and

---

[101] ibid art 227.
[102] ibid art 228.
[103] ibid art 223(6).
[104] ibid art 228.
[105] In comparison, under the Chinese Contract Law, if the creditor transfers its claim, it shall notify the debtor of the claim; such transfer is not binding upon the debtor of the claim if notice was not given; and a notice of the transfer of the claim given by the creditor may not be revoked, except with the consent of the transferee. Chinese Contract Law, art 80.
[106] Adopted in 2007, Order No 4 (2007) of the People's Bank of China, entered into force as of 1 October 2007.
[107] MRPR, s 2.

medium-sized companies and other enterprises engaged in manufacturing with high levels of account receivables and inventory.[108] The MRPR enables a lender to access the centralised system and obtain information about a borrower (debtor) and registered pledges of receivables with ease and efficiency.[109]

In China, the MRPR defines account receivables as the creditor's right to ask the debtor to make payments, which the creditor obtains from the debtor's offering goods, services or facilities, including existing and potential monetary claim and the proceeds thereof, but not including the right to claim a payment incurred from bills or other negotiable securities.[110] Still, there is currently the registration system for only *pledges* of receivables, but there is no registration system for *transfers* of receivables in China.

2-4-4. The General Security Rights Registry

2-4-4-1. France

Under the revised French Civil Code of 2006, a non-possessory pledge of movable assets may be perfected by registration. Since 2006, a pledge is perfected by publicity,[111] which is achieved by transfer of the encumbered asset to the creditor or a third party,[112] or by registration in a special registry.[113] Where the same asset has been the subject of several non-possessory pledges, priority is determined by the order of their respective registrations.[114]

2-4-4-2. Optional Registration

In Korea and Japan, as receivables financing developed, the problems with notice to debtors became unbearable. Under the Korean and Japanese Civil Codes, a transfer of receivables is perfected against third parties only if a transferor gives notice to a debtor by means of a certified document with a fixed-date stamp.[115] Notice to debtors in receivables financing is time-consuming and costly, and is simply impracticable. In order to circumvent this notification requirement, Japan and Korea have developed registration systems for the transfer of receivables in specified types of receivables financing.

In Korea and Japan, the pledge of an *in personam* right becomes effective by the method of the transfer of the right. Under the Korean and Japanese Civil Codes, the transfer of an ordinary *in personam* right[116] (other than *in personam*

---

[108] Joshua T Klein, 'Recent Legal Changes that Affect Secured Financing in the People's Republic of China' (2009) *American Bankruptcy Institute Journal* 38, 73.
[109] ibid 72.
[110] MRPR, s 4.
[111] French Civil Code, art 2337.
[112] ibid.
[113] ibid art 2338. The details of the special registry are regulated by a decree in the Conseil d'Etat.
[114] ibid art 2340.
[115] Korean Civil Code, art 450(2); Japanese Civil Code, art 467(2).
[116] This means the claim should be performed to the specific creditor who is a party to the agreement from which the claim arises, or a transferee of the claim, the transfer to whom the debtor is notified of or consents to.

rights embodied in negotiable instruments or negotiable documents) *may not* be effective against the debtor of the *in personam* right or other third parties, *unless* the transferor gives notice of the transfer of the *in personam* right to the debtor of the *in personam* right or the debtor of the *in personam* right consents to the transfer of the *in personam* right.[117] Such a notice to the debtor or the debtor's consent must be done by a certified document with a fixed-date stamp in order for the transfer of the *in personam* right to be effective against third parties other than the debtor of the *in personam* right.[118]

An *in personam* right embodied in a negotiable instrument or a negotiable document may be transferred by means of endorsement on and delivery of the instrument or document.[119] A pledge of an *in personam* right embodied in a negotiable instrument or a negotiable document is perfected by endorsement of the instrument or document and its delivery to the secured creditor.[120] A debt payable to the bearer may be transferred by means of delivery of the bearer instrument.[121] A pledge of a bearer instrument is effective upon delivery of the instrument to the secured creditor.[122]

Korea and Japan initially adopted registration systems with respect to the transfer of receivables to facilitate securitisation for the purpose of disposing non-performing loans. In Japan, it expanded to include pledges of receivables and the transfer of movable assets, abolishing the original law for securitisation.[123] In Korea, the registration of security rights in movable assets and receivables was adopted *without* abolishing the law on securitisation. When adopting registration systems, the legislators in Korea and Japan did not want to revise their respective Civil Codes because it would incur costs and confusion. For this reason, they adopted alternative optional registration systems that co-exist with the existing laws.

2-4-4-3. Japan

2-4-4-3-1. The Specified Claims Act

After the collapse of Japanese bubble economy in 1991,[124] Japan enacted the Act Concerning Restrictions on Businesses in Specified Claims[125] (hereinafter the Specified Claims Act) in 1992 with the aim of helping lease companies and credit card companies to raise funds through securitisations.[126] The Specified Claims Act

---

[117] Korean Civil Code, art 450(1); Japanese Civil Code, art 467(1).
[118] Korean Civil Code, art 450(2); Japanese Civil Code, art 467(2).
[119] Korean Civil Code, art 508; Japanese Civil Code, art 469.
[120] Korean Civil Code, art 350; Japanese Civil Code, art 365.
[121] Korean Civil Code, art 523; Japanese Civil Code, art 473.
[122] Korean Civil Code, art 351.
[123] See section 2-4-4-3-3.
[124] At that time, many real estate brokers in Japan became bankrupt and consequently many banks which lent money to those real estate brokers also went bankrupt.
[125] Act No 77 of 1992, enacted on 5 June 1992 and entered into force 1 June 1993. This Act is also translated as 'Business Asset Securitisation Act'.
[126] This Act covers auto loans and lease receivables, eg, industrial leases and computer leases: Japanese Specified Claims Act, art 2(1).

provided for the reporting system of securitisation plans to the Finance Committee and public notice of such a report in a daily newspaper. Such public notice in a daily newspaper could replace giving notice of the transfer to the debtor under the Japanese Civil Code. Thus, once such public notice was given to debtors through a daily newspaper, the transferor did not need to give notice of the transfer to debtors in accordance with the Japanese Civil Code. However, the Specified Claims Act was abolished as of 30 December 2004.[127]

2-4-4-3-2. The Special Act for the Transfer of Receivables

After the financial crisis in Asia in 1997 and the moratorium of Russia in 1998, worries about insolvency due to temporary cash-flow shortages prevailed and how to convert receivables to cash on a balance sheet became a critical issue. As a response, securitisation was widely encouraged. In June 1998, Japan enacted the Act Prescribing Exceptions to the Civil Code Requirements for Perfection of the Transfer of Receivables (hereinafter the Special Act for the Transfer of Receivables),[128] which provides that the transfer of receivables can also be perfected against third parties by registering it in the registration system administrated by the Ministry of Justice.[129] This is an alternative to notification of the transfer to the debtor under the Japanese Civil Code,[130] and only applies to the transfer of receivables where the transferor is a legal person.[131] Under the Special Act for the Transfer of Receivables, the scope of registration includes general receivables in addition to lease receivables and credit card receivables, which were covered by the Specified Claims Act enacted in 1992. It was seen as a way to promote securitisations,[132] which in turn would contribute to improving the financial strength of markets through a diversification of the methods by which companies could raise funds.[133]

2-4-4-3-3. The Japanese Transfer Registration Act

In 2005, Japan amended the Special Act for the Transfer of Receivables and renamed it the Act on the Exceptions to the Civil Code Requirements for Perfection of the Transfer of Movable Assets and Receivables (hereinafter the Japanese

---

[127] Although the Specified Claims Act was still valid until 2004, it was not often used after 1998 because transfers covered by the Specified Claims Act were also applicable to the Special Act for the Transfer of Receivables enacted in 1998, which provides for the registration system for general receivables. Finally, the Specified Claims Act was repealed on 30 December 2004.
[128] Act No 104 of 1998, enacted on 12 June 1998 and entered into force on 1 October 1998.
[129] Japan has been operating the electronic registration system since 1 October 1998.
[130] See section 3-7-7 Qs 1, 2, 3, 4-2.
[131] See section 6-3-1.
[132] Because there are a great number of account debtors in securitisation, it is impracticable to send notice of the transfer to all of the account debtors.
[133] Kazumoto Kitamura, 'Perfection Law Clears Way for Financing Opportunities', *The IFLR Guide to Japan 2006*, January 2006.

Transfer Registration Act).[134] The Japanese Transfer Registration Act expands the scope of registration to include transfers of movable assets, and provides a registration system for the transfer of movable assets and receivables.[135] Furthermore, the Japanese Transfer Registration Act provides for registration of the transfer of future receivables against unspecified debtors. Also, perfection of the transfer of a pool of receivables or movable assets could be achieved with one registration.

Under the Japanese Transfer Registration Act, the transfer of receivables, whose transferor is a legal person, may be registered. The Ministry of Justice is in charge of the management of the registration system for the transfer of movable assets and receivables under the Japanese Transfer Registration Act. A transferor and a transferee may request the registration of a transfer to the Transfer Registry Office, which is the Registration Department, Civil Administration Division of the Tokyo Legal Affairs Bureau. In Japan, there is only one centralised Transfer Registry Office in Tokyo.

Under the Japanese Transfer Registration Act, only transfers of movable assets[136] and receivables[137] and security rights in receivables[138] can be registered. A security right in movable assets cannot be registered under the Japanese Transfer Registration Act. It is said that this is because Article 345 of the Japanese Civil Code stipulates that a pledgee may not allow a pledgor to possess the movable asset pledged on behalf of the pledgee.[139]

In Japan, the Japanese Transfer Registration Act has been enacted mainly for fiduciary transfer of title for security purposes ('*JyouToTanPo*' in Japanese), and *JyouToTanPo* in Japan is regarded as an outright transfer.[140] Accordingly, other acquisition financing that is not regarded as an outright transfer such as reservation of title and financial lease cannot be registered under the Japanese Transfer Registration Act.

---

[134] Act No 104 of June 12, 1998, amended on 26 July 2005 and entered into force on 3 October 2005.
[135] This was intended to primarily cover the fiduciary transfer of title for security purposes (*JyouToTanPo* in Japanese), which is regarded as a transfer in Japan. According to art 178 of the Japanese Civil Code, the transfers of real rights concerning movables may not be perfected against third parties, unless the movables are delivered. For this delivery, art 3(1) of the Japanese Transfer Registration Act stipulates that when a registration of transfer is made in a movable assets registry with regard to the transfer of the movable assets, it shall be deemed that the movable assets have been delivered as set forth in art 178 of the Japanese Civil Code. Thus, if a non-possessory security right is registered, it is perfected against third parties.
[136] Japanese Transfer Registration Act, art 3.
[137] ibid art 4(1). Receivables are limited to nominative claims for monetary payment.
[138] ibid art 14. With respect to receivables, the Japanese Transfer Registration Act is mutatis mutandis applied to the pledge of receivables.
[139] Katsuhiro Uekaki (植垣勝裕) and Hideki Ogawa (小川秀樹), *Ichi Mon Ichi Tou Dousan Saiken Jouto Tokurei Hou* (『一問一答・動産・債権譲渡特例法』), 3rd edn (Tokyo, Shouji Houmu (商事法務) 2008) 15–16. In fact, the same provision exists in the Korean Civil Code as well. Article 332 of the Korean Civil Code stipulates that a pledgee cannot let the pledgor hold possession of the pledged article on his behalf. However, the Korean Security Registration Act enables security rights in movable assets to be registered and makes them non-possessory security rights in movable assets.
[140] ibid

Under the Japanese Transfer Registration Act, registration is a *creation* requirement for a transfer of *movable assets*, but is a *perfection* requirement for a transfer of and a security right in *receivables*. Such registration is optional in that if a transfer of movable assets or a transfer of or a security right in receivables is not registered, it would be regulated by the Japanese Civil Code.

In Japan, the Transfer Registration is used more for the transfer of receivables than for that of movable assets. With respect to movable assets, fiduciary transfer of title for security purposes (*JyouToTanPo*) is still used rather than the Transfer Registration. This is because fiduciary transfer of title for security purposes is not disclosed to third parties. See Table 2.5.

Table 2.5: Usages of the Japanese Transfer Registration (www.e-stat.go.jp)

Year	Registration of transfers of movable assets		Registration of transfers of receivables		Registration of pledges of receivables	
	Registrations	Items	Registrations	Items	Registrations	Items
2005	228	14,774	19,954	66,649,300	215	2,131,054
2006	860	30,780	19,733	51,899,814	181	3,048,887
2007	1,446	50,924	21,291	66,246,234	265	3,242,149
2008	2,306	36,443	25,336	76,274,375	318	3,609,800
2009	2,899	50,549	19,701	86,233,466	248	3,552,655
2010	3,566	133,648	18,295	89,892,483	324	4,259,340
2011	2,135	135,568	13,819	77,467,590	259	2,571,150
2012	1,554	66,112	12,611	92,693,590	148	2,362,348
2013	2,282	37,220	11,970	71,792,153	115	2,273,669
2014	3,905	20,931	13,228	59,204,946	147	3,610,817
2015	5,211	18,888	14,361	70,736,028	210	3,272,233
2016	5,207	85,793	14,891	51,278,012	157	2,079,800

2-4-4-4. Korea

2-4-4-4-1. The Asset-Backed Securitisation Act

After the financial crisis in Korea in late 1997, which resulted in the sudden halt of corporate bond circulation, the government swiftly codified the Asset-Backed Securitisation Act (hereinafter the ABS Act)[141] in September 1998. The purpose of the ABS Act was to facilitate the restructuring of financial institutions through the efficient resolution of non-performing loans (NPLs).

---

[141] Act No 5555, enacted on 16 September 1998 and entered into force on 16 September 1998.

The ABS Act provides a filing system for the transfer of receivables in asset-backed securitisations,[142] where an originator is a financial institution or public corporation stipulated in Article 2(2) of this Act. The ABS Act does not apply to securitisations where an ordinary private company is the originator. This is because the legislators thought that preferential exceptions to the Civil Code imposed by this Act might be misused.[143]

Facilitating such receivables financing is very important because it could prevent insolvencies caused by a temporary cash-flow shortage. The rapid enactment in 1998 of the ABS Act helped the Korean economy to recover from the crisis facing it quickly. Under the ABS Act, an SPV can perfect a transfer of receivables against third parties by filing the securitisation plan and the transfer of receivables at the Financial Services Commission.[144] For perfection against the debtor of the receivable, it is required to send notice of transfer of the receivable to the debtor. If such notice was returned back because of the failure to locate the debtor's address twice, public notice in two or more daily newspapers is required.[145]

2-4-4-4-2. The Mortgage-Backed Securitisation Company Act

Subsequently, in 1999, the Korean government codified the Mortgage-Backed Securitisation Company Act (hereinafter the MBS Company Act)[146] to facilitate mortgage-backed securitisations. The MBS Company Act has many provisions that parallel the ABS Act. It provides for the filing system for the transfer of receivables in mortgage-backed securitisations.[147] The transfers of receivables in a mortgage-backed securitisation can be perfected against third parties by filing the securitisation plan at the Financial Services Commission.[148] For perfection against the debtor of the receivable, it is required to send notice of transfer of the receivable to the debtor. If such notice was returned back because of the failure to locate the debtor's address twice, public notice in two or more daily newspapers is required.[149]

2-4-4-4-3. The Korean Security Registration Act

Since the financial crisis of 1998, many banks in Korea have been privatised and foreign investors have taken over the management of many Korean banks. As a result, it became more difficult to raise funds for small and medium-sized companies, especially those that did not have sufficient real estate to satisfy a bank's collateral requirements.[150]

---

[142] Korean ABS Act, art 3.
[143] Chae-Jin Lee, 'Study on Development and Evolving Process of Securitisation Laws in Korea', (2005) 18(2) *Commercial Case Study (Sang Sa Pan Rye Yeon Gu)* 208–09.
[144] Korean ABS Act, art 7(2). See section 3-7-6 Q 1, 3-2.
[145] Korean ABS Act, art 7(1).
[146] Act No 5692, enacted on 29 January 1999 and entered into force on 29 April 1999.
[147] Korean MBS Company Act, art 4.
[148] ibid art 6(2). See section 3-7-6 Qs 1, 3-3.
[149] Korean MBS Company Act, art 6(1).
[150] This is because foreign investors tend to avoid the risks posed by small and medium-sized companies and will not provide them with long-term policy loans.

In order to help these small and medium-sized companies with their financing, and pave the way for companies to use receivables and tangible movable assets as collateral, on 10 June 2010, Korea enacted the Act concerning Security Rights in Movable Assets and Receivables, etc (hereinafter the Korean Security Registration Act).[151] This Act provides for another convenient method to perfect security rights in movable assets or receivables against third parties. The Act provides for the registration system for security rights in movable assets and receivables.[152] The Act entered into force on 11 June 2012. The Supreme Court of Korea is in charge of the management of the registration system for the security rights in movable assets and receivables under the Korean Security Registration Act. There are many registration offices in Korea.[153] These registration offices are linked to each other online and thus information is searchable at any of the registration offices or even at home or in the office.

Under the Korean Security Registration Act, only security rights in movable assets and receivables[154] can be registered. The registration system under the Korean Security Registration Act does not cover an outright transfer of movable assets or receivables. The reason why the Act does not include the transfer of receivable is that the drafters did not want to change the Civil Code regime of the transfer of receivables. In addition, transfers of receivables in asset-backed securitisations and mortgage-backed securitisations are regulated by the Korean ABS Act and the Korean MBS Company Act respectively, under which the transfer of receivables is perfected by filing with the Financial Services Commission even after the enforcement of the Korean Security Registration Act, whereas Japan abolished the Specified Claims Act[155] after adopting the registration system for general receivables. See Table 2.6.

Outright transfers of movable assets and receivables are regulated by the Korean Civil Code.[156] For an outright transfer of a movable asset, delivery of possession is required. The Korean Civil Code stipulates that the transfer of a real right over a movable asset takes effect by delivery of the movable asset.[157] For an outright transfer of a receivable, notice of the transfer to, or consent of, the debtor

---

[151] *DongSan·ChaeKwon DeungEui DamBoE GwanHan BeobLyul* (동산・채권등의담보에관한법률) in Korean, enacted on 10 June 2010, entered into force on 11 June 2012.

[152] This provides for two kinds of registry: the movable assets registry and the receivables registry. Security rights in movables assets should be registered in the movable assets registry, and security rights in receivables should be registered in the receivables registry.

[153] Korean Security Registration Act, art 39(1) and (2).

[154] This covers, among claims, only nominative claims for payment of money: Korean Security Registration Act, art 34(1).

[155] '*Tokutei Saiken Tou Kakaru Jigyou no Kisei nikansuru Houritsu*' (特定債権等に係る事業の規制に関する法律) enacted on 5 June 1992, Act No 77 of 1992, entered into force on 1 June 1993.

[156] For movable assets, see Korean Civil Code, arts 188 and 189; for receivables, see Korean Civil Code, art 450.

[157] Korean Civil Code, art 188(1).

is required.[158] For securitisation, transfers of receivables in securitisation assets are regulated by the ABS Act or the MBS Company Act.

Acquisition financing including fiduciary transfer of title for security purposes, reservation of title and financial lease can be registered under the Korean Security Registration Act, insofar as such acquisition financing is an agreement to create security rights in movable assets or receivables.[159] No matter what the form of the security agreement is, regardless of whether it is *YangDoDamBo* (fiduciary transfer of title for security purposes) or not, any agreement to create security rights in movable assets, receivables or intellectual property in accordance with the Korean Security Registration Act is the 'security agreement' that applies to this Act.[160] A financial lease right can be registered by the lessor as a secured creditor and the lessee as a grantor.[161] A reservation-of-title right can be registered by the seller as a secured creditor and the buyer as a grantor.

If a legal person encumbers movable assets or receivables according to a security agreement (either pledge or fiduciary transfer), it can register its security right.[162] The parties may decide whether to register a financial lease right or a reservation-of-title right and be treated as a secured creditor under the Korean Security Registration Act, or not to register it and remain in an uncertain status as before.[163]

Once *YangDoDamBo* is registered, it should be regulated under the Korean Security Registration Act regardless of the content of the *YangDoDamBo* contract,[164] and it would cease to be a real *YangDoDamBo* anymore. *YangDoDamBo* does not have to be registered. If it is not registered, it would be regulated by uncertain case law as it used to be. Once a financial lease right or a reservation-of-title right is registered in the security rights registry under the Korean Security Registration Act, it is treated as a security right and is regulated by the Korean Security Registration Act.[165] Alternatively, a financial lease or a reservation-of-title transaction can be created and used by an agreement of parties without registration, in which case it is regulated by the Korean Civil Code and case laws.

Under the Korean Security Registration Act, registration is a *creation* requirement for a security right in *movable assets*, but is a *perfection* requirement for a security right in *receivables*. Such registration is optional in that if a security right

---

[158] ibid art 450(1). The Korean Civil Code, stipulates that the transfer of a receivable cannot be set up against the debtor of the receivable or third parties, unless the transferor has given notice thereof to the debtor of the receivable or the debtor of the receivable has consented thereto.
[159] Korean Security Registration Act, art 2(1).
[160] ibid.
[161] Kwang-Hyun Suk and Woo-Jung Jon, 'International Secured Transactions (South Korea Section)' in Dennis Campbell (ed), *International Secured Transactions, Binder 2* (Dobbs Ferry, NY, Oceana Publications, 2010).
[162] For a movable asset, see Korean Security Registration Act, art 3(1); and for a nominative claim for the purpose of monetary payment, see Korean Security Registration Act, art 34(1).
[163] ibid.
[164] Jae Hyung KIM, 'Organisation and Contents of the Draft of the Act Concerning Security Rights in Movable Assets, Receivables, etc.' (2009) 58(11) *Lawyers Association Journal* 5, 12.
[165] ibid.

36   Security Rights Registries

in movable assets or receivables is not registered, it would be regulated as a pledge of movable assets or receivables under the Korean Civil Code.

Table 2.6: Comparison of Chinese, Korean and Japanese registration systems for movable assets and receivables

	China	Korean Security Registration Act	Japanese Transfer Registration Act
Transfer of movable assets	Not registered	Not registered	Registrable (optional)[166]
Pledge (or mortgage) of movable assets	Manufacturing facilities, raw materials, semi-manufactured goods and products[167]	Registrable (optional)	Not registered[168]
Reservation of title	Not registered		
Financial lease	Not registered		
A pool of movable assets / Future movable assets	Registrable (compulsory)[169]	Registrable (optional)[170]	No provision
Outright transfer of receivables	Not registered	Not registered[171]	Registrable (optional)[172]
Pledge of receivables	Registrable (compulsory)[173]	Registrable (optional)[174]	Registrable (optional)[175]
Future receivables	Registrable (compulsory)[176]	Registrable (optional)[177]	No provision

[166] Japanese Transfer Registration Act, art 3.
[167] Chinese Property Right Law, art 180(1)(iv).
[168] Uekaki and Ogawa (n 139) 15–16. See Japanese Civil Code, art 345: 'A pledgee may not allow a pledgor to possess the movable asset pledged on behalf of the pledgee.'
[169] Chinese Property Right Law, arts 181 and 189.
[170] Korean Security Registration Act, art 3(2)(i). However, a group of movable assets and receivables cannot be registered together. Movable assets and receivables should be separated from each other. Security rights in movable assets cannot be registered in the receivables registry and security rights in receivables cannot be registered in the movable assets registry.
[171] Korean Security Registration Act, art 2(3).
[172] Japanese Transfer Registration Act, art 4(1).
[173] Chinese Property Right Law, art 223(vi).
[174] Korean Security Registration Act, art 34(1).
[175] Japanese Transfer Registration Act, art 14.
[176] Chinese Measures for the Registration of Pledge of Receivables, art 4.
[177] Korean Security Registration Act, art 34(2).

2-5. International Efforts of Harmonisation

A security rights registry was created for non-possessory security rights in England in the late nineteenth century. A notice-filing system was created in the US in 1952. Ever since, many countries have established a national domestic security rights registry. Establishing an international registry is much more difficult than establishing a national domestic registry, even though they share similar basic principles. A major barrier is language, including legal terminology, which results in accessibility difficulties for lay persons as well as problems with identification of registrants and specification of encumbered objects. As a result of international efforts at harmonisation, there have been soft laws and international conventions.

2-5-1. Soft Laws

There have been soft laws that recommend establishing a security rights registry at a national level. They include the UNCITRAL Model Law on Secured Transactions,[178] the European Bank for Reconstruction and Development (EBRD) Model Law on Secured Transactions[179] and the Organization of American States (OAS) Model Inter-American Law on Secured Transactions.[180] The Draft Common Frame of Reference (DCFR)[181] of the European Union also proposes the European registry for proprietary rights in movable assets.

2-5-1-1. The EBRD Model Law on Secured Transactions

The EBRD published the EBRD Model Law on Secured Transactions in early 1994. Many Central and Eastern European countries referred to the EBRD Model Law on Secured Transactions and established their national domestic registration systems for security rights in personal property.[182] The EBRD Model Law provides a model law regarding the registration system for security rights. Furthermore, the EBRD established the Guiding Principles for the Development of a Charges Registry in 2004.

---

[178] The UNCITRAL Model Law on Secured Transactions was adopted by the United Nations Commission on International Trade Law (UNCITRAL) at its session in New York on 1 July 2016. See www.uncitral.org/uncitral/en/uncitral_texts/security/2016Model_secured.html.

[179] The EBRD published the EBRD Model Law on Secured Transactions in early 1994.

[180] The OAS published the Model Inter-American Law on Secured Transactions.

[181] The Draft Common Frame of Reference is presented by the Study Group on a European Civil Code and the Research Group on Existing EC Private Law, commissioned by the European Commission in 2005. Part of the work is funded by the European Commission's Research Directorate-General. See *DCFR*, Outline edn (Munich, Sellier, 2009) 3–4.

[182] Jan-Hendrik Röver, *Secured Lending in Eastern Europe: Comparative Law of Secured Transactions and the EBRD Model Law* (Oxford, Oxford University Press, 2007).

The philosophy of the EBRD Model Law on Secured Transactions was to target first and foremost security transactions, and thus the EBRD Model Law does not apply to the transfer of receivables, even if it may serve the same function as security transactions.[183]

The EBRD Model Law on Secured Transactions produced a text that is compatible with the civil law concepts upon which many Central and Eastern European legal systems are based and, at the same time, that draws on common law systems, which have developed solutions to accommodate modern financing techniques.[184]

Under the EBRD Model Law on Secured Transactions, a charge may be only: (i) a registered charge; or (ii) an unpaid vendor's charge; or (iii) a possessory charge. A charge over a receivable can only fall into the first category,[185] and therefore a charge over receivables must be registered. Thus, the EBRD Model Law on Secured Transactions does not require notice to the account debtor for perfection against third parties.

2-5-1-2. The OAS Model Inter-American Law on Secured Transactions

The OAS drafted the Model Inter-American Law on Secured Transactions, and recently incorporated the registration for security rights regime. There are conflicts between the common law and the civil law among American states. Whereas North American states follow the common law, Central and South American states follow the civil law tradition. In addition, the state of Louisiana in the US and Québec province in Canada follow the civil law tradition. The OAS Model Inter-American Law shows the efforts to harmonise the common law and the civil law.

Nonetheless, the OAS Model Inter-American Law on Secured Transactions is much closer to the American UCC Article 9 in substance as well as terminology than the EBRD Model Law on Secured Transactions.[186] Perfection of a security right against third parties requires the security right to be publicised by registration or by delivery of possession or control of the encumbered asset to the secured creditor or to a third person on its behalf.[187]

The OAS Model Inter-American Law covers a transfer of receivables as well as a security right in receivables. Article 13 of the OAS Model Law stipulates that if the transfer is not for security, it must comply only with the publicity provisions of the OAS Model Law; if it fails to so comply, it will be subject to the priority rules of the OAS Model Law.

---

[183] Email from Frédérique Dahan (Lead Counsel and Head of Financial Law Unit, European Bank for Reconstruction and Development) to the author (24 February 2011).
[184] 'Introduction' in *EBRD Model Law on Secured Transactions* (London, EBRD, 1994).
[185] EBRD Model Law on Secured Transactions, art 6(1).
[186] Gerard McCormack, *Secured Credit and the Harmonisation of Law: The UNCITRAL Experience* (Cheltenham, Edward Elgar, 2011) 120.
[187] OAS Model Inter-American Law on Secured Transactions, art 10.

In practice, there are problems with respect to establishing the security rights registry in American states.[188] First, civil law jurisdictions are not familiar with the notice-filing system. In civil law jurisdictions, registry officers are supposed to examine and review the content of registration applications, and registrants should submit contract documents. Another problem is the description of encumbered assets. In civil law jurisdictions, a more detailed description is usually required. For these reasons, it is not common to have security rights registries in Central and South American states.

2-5-1-3. The UNCITRAL Model Law on Secured Transactions

The UNCITRAL Model Law on Secured Transactions contains model legislative provisions on all issues that need to be addressed in a modern law on security rights in all types of movable asset, whether tangible or intangible. It follows a modern approach to secured transactions that can be described as a functional, integrated and comprehensive approach, relying on a notice-based public registry for third-party and priority effects.[189] It also applies to outright transfers of receivables, although they are not secured transactions.[190] In broad terms, it follows the UCC Article 9 functional approach towards security. Under UCC Article 9, notice of all non-possessory security rights in tangible movable assets and all transfers of receivables must be filed in order to be perfected against third parties, including the insolvency administrator.[191] Likewise, the UNCITRAL Model Law on Secured Transactions recommends that all non-possessory security rights in tangible movable assets and all transfers of receivables must be registered to be perfected against third parties.[192] Such a functional, integrated and comprehensive approach to secured transactions is clear and simple.

2-5-1-4. The Draft Common Frame of Reference (DCFR)

The DCFR is an effort to accomplish a unified European Civil Code. The Study Group on a European Civil Code and the Research Group on Existing EC Private Law, commissioned by the European Commission in 2005, presented the DCFR in 2009.[193] Part of the work was funded by the European Commission's Research Directorate-General.

Because most European countries follow the civil law tradition, it is often claimed that the DCFR would involve marginalising the common law canon of

---

[188] Telephone Interview with John M Wilson, Senior Legal Advisor, Department of International Law, Organization of American States (UNCITRAL, Austria, Vienna, 22 September 2010).
[189] UNCITRAL Model Law on Secured Transactions, art 2(kk)(i).
[190] ibid art 2(kk)(ii).
[191] Under UCC art 9, one of three perfection methods is required: (1) filing of a financing statement; (2) possession; or (3) control. UCC, arts 9-310–9-314.
[192] UNCITRAL Model Law on Secured Transactions, art 18.
[193] *DCFR* (n 181) 3–4, http://ec.europa.eu/justice/contract/files/european-private-law_en.pdf.

experience in favour of the civil law.[194] Notwithstanding this claim, the DCFR adopts a registration system for priority of security rights. It sets up a rule under which priority among several security rights or between a security right and other limited proprietary rights in the same asset is determined according to the order of the time of registration, possession or control for security rights.[195] This rule applies to security rights in receivables. However, the rule does not apply to transfers of receivables. The DCFR states that where there are successive purported transfers by the same person of the same right to performance, the purported transferee whose transfer is first notified to the debtor has priority over any earlier transferee if, at the time of the later transfer, the transferee under that transfer neither knew nor could reasonably be expected to have known of the earlier transfer.[196]

2-5-2. International Conventions

There have been many international conventions addressing matters of public international law, such as human rights. But it appears to be more difficult to harmonise numerous and divergent legal systems and create a unified international convention in the areas of private law. Currently, there are only two international conventions relating to international registration systems: the UN Receivables Convention and the Cape Town Convention.

2-5-2-1. The UN Convention on the Transfer of Receivables in International Trade

The UN Convention on the Transfer of Receivables in International Trade (hereinafter the UN Receivables Convention)[197] was the first international effort to harmonise the laws on the transfer of receivables around the world. In order to facilitate international transfers of receivables, the UN Receivables Convention provides three options for Contracting States to adopt: first, it proposes the registration system as one option; second, it offers alternative priority rules based on registration;[198] and, third, it offers model provisions for an international registration system.[199]

---

[194] McCormack (n 186) 187.
[195] *DCFR* (n 181) 478, art IX-4:101(1) and (2).
[196] ibid art III-5:121.
[197] Adopted 31 January 2002, open for signature 31 December 2003. The Convention will enter into force upon ratification by five Member States (ibid art 45(1)). However, to date, the UN Convention has been signed by only three states and acceded to by only one: Luxembourg signed on 12 June 2002; Madagascar signed on 24 September 2003; the US signed on 30 December 2003; and Liberia acceded to the UN Convention on 16 September 2005. See www.uncitral.org/uncitral/en/uncitral_texts/payments/2001Convention_receivables_status.html.
[198] Annex to the Convention, s I.
[199] ibid s II.

In addition, the UN Receivables Convention removes statutory prohibitions from the transfer of future receivables and bulk transfers,[200] and prevents contractual prohibition on the transfer of trade receivables.[201]

However, the UN Receivables Convention adopted in January 2002 has not been successful in entering into force, despite presenting a desirable model for the transfer of receivables regime.

The proposed International Receivables Registry Convention differs from the UN Receivables Convention in that, under the proposed International Receivables Registry Convention, priority of transfers of and security rights in receivables is determined by the time order of registration in the International Receivables Registry uniformly.[202]

2-5-2-2. *The Convention on International Interests in Mobile Equipment*

The Convention on International Interests in Mobile Equipment (Cape Town, 2001) of UNIDROIT, called the 'Cape Town Convention',[203] established the first example of an international registration system for mobile equipment such as aircraft and railway rolling stock. The Cape Town Convention applies to all mobile equipment, but its Protocols have separate rules for each type of mobile equipment: aircraft equipment, railway rolling stock[204] and satellites.[205] This demonstrates that setting up an international registration system for transfers of and security rights in receivables is possible.[206]

---

[200] UN Receivables Convention, art 8.
[201] UN Receivables Convention, art 9.
[202] The transfer or security right registered first in the International Receivables Registry prevails over other transfers or security rights which are subsequently registered or not registered.
[203] The Convention on International Interests in Mobile Equipment (hereinafter the Cape Town Convention) and the Protocol to the Convention on International Interests in Mobile Equipment on Matters Specific to Aircraft Equipment (hereinafter the Aircraft Protocol) were adopted jointly in Cape Town on 16 November 2001. The Cape Town Convention entered into force on 1 March 2006. As of 11 May 2013, it has been ratified by 57 states and the Aircraft Protocol has been ratified by 51 states. In order for the Cape Town Convention to be enforced completely in an EU Member State, both the Member State and the EU must join the Cape Town Convention. Even though the EU has joined the Cape Town Convention, if a Member State does not, it does not give the Convention any effect whatsoever in the Member State. The Convention and the Protocol can only be ratified in its entirety, subject to permitted reservations or declarations. Adoption of the Cape Town Convention by the EU merely allows Member States to ratify the Convention. With respect to key insolvency provisions in the Aircraft Protocol, over which the EU has exclusive competence, the EU has made no declaration, which leaves it to Member States as to what declaration, if any, to make under art XI (Remedies on insolvency) of the Aircraft Protocol.
[204] Luxembourg Protocol to the Convention on International Interests in Mobile Equipment on Matters Specific to Railway Rolling Stock, adopted in Luxembourg on 23 February 2007, not yet entered into force.
[205] Protocol to the Convention on International Interests in Mobile Equipment on Matters Specific to Space Assets, adopted in Berlin on 9 March 2012, not yet entered into force.
[206] The International Registry of Mobile Assets under the Cape Town Convention and its Aircraft Protocol exemplifies the problems caused by the language barrier, including the specification of encumbered objects, the identification of registrants and interested parties, the incentive of registration, the enforcement regime, conflict-of-laws issues and the registration fee.

2-6. The Pros and Cons of a General Security Rights Registry

2-6-1. Pros

2-6-1-1. Using Movable Assets as Security

In order to gain finance, a company may borrow money from banks. Banks usually request security or collateral for loans. Historically, security rights in tangible movable assets are essentially possessory, ie, pledges. Security rights in real estate are non-possessory because they can be registered in the real estate registry. Because of the economic need for grantors' use of encumbered assets, non-possessory security rights in tangible movable assets have developed by registering the movable assets. Since non-possessory security rights are not visible to third parties, for non-possessory security rights in movable assets, a security rights registry is needed. Creating security rights in movable assets and receivables enables small and medium-sized companies that do not have sufficient real estate to pledge for a loan to finance, and thus provides entrepreneurs greater chances and opportunities to finance their business.

Lord Scott, in *Re Spectrum Plus Ltd*,[207] observed the preponderance of circulating capital of enterprises such as inventory and receivables, stating that:

> By the middle of the 19th century industrial and commercial expansion in this country had led to an increasing need by companies for more capital. Subscription for share capital could not meet this need and loan capital had to be raised. But the lenders required security for their loans. Traditional security, in the form of legal or equitable charges over the borrowers' fixed assets, whether land or goods, could not meet the need. The greater part of most entrepreneurial companies' assets would consist of raw materials, work in progress, stock-in-trade and trade debts. These were circulating assets, replaced in the normal course of business and constantly changing.

2-6-1-2. Civil Law Jurisdiction v Common Law Jurisdiction

In order to estimate and compare the rights of secured creditors in each jurisdiction, Rafael La Porta and others use four variables: (a) no automatic stay on assets; (b) secured creditors paid first; (c) creditor consent needed for a debtor to file for reorganisation; and (d) no debtor in possession (DIP) in reorganisation.[208] They take the perspective of senior secured creditors rather than unsecured creditors for concreteness and because much of the debt in the world has that character.[209]

---

[207] *Re Spectrum Plus Ltd* [2005] UKHL 41 (HL), [2005] 2 AC 680, para 95. See also Robert R Pennington, 'The Genesis of the Floating Charge' (1960) 23 *MLR* 630, 634–38.
[208] Rafael La Porta et al, 'Law and Finance' (1998) 106(6) *Journal of Political Economy* 1135.
[209] ibid 1134.

Their conclusion is that common law jurisdictions protect investors the most, French civil law jurisdictions protect them the least, and German civil law jurisdictions are in the middle, though closer to the civil law group.[210] Rafael La Porta and others argue that civil law countries which have weaker investor protections, measured by the character of legal rules and the quality of law enforcement, have less developed credit markets than common law countries.[211]

A general security rights registry makes it easy for a debtor to create a security right in movable assets and receivables by registering it and for a creditor to become a secured creditor. Thus, a general security rights registry would strengthen investor protections and ultimately develop credit markets.

2-6-1-3. The World Bank Report

Empirical studies by the Center for the Economic Analysis of Law with the World Bank show that the lack of a security rights registration system accounts for higher interest rates in Guatemala[212] than in the US, and that it results in limited access to credit in the agriculture sector of Nicaragua.[213] The Center for the Economic Analysis of Law also concluded that adopting a security rights registration system would increase the GDP of Argentina and Bolivia.[214] This is on the basis that businesses could obtain the cash necessary to purchase additional inventory and generate additional sales by using their portfolios of assets as collateral. Where such financing is possible, it allows a company to have an increased line of credit so that it can better respond to the needs of its business.[215]

For example, research by the World Bank shows that movable property accounts for approximately 60 per cent of company's capital stock in the US in 2004.[216] Among movable property, intellectual property was 30 per cent, accounts receivable 20 per cent, inventory 10 per cent, automobiles 1 per cent and other equipment 39 per cent.[217] To take one example, in Nigeria, due to the lack of a registration system, nearly 99 per cent of movable property that could serve as collateral for a loan

---

[210] ibid 1139.
[211] Rafael La Porta et al, 'Legal Determinants of External Finance' (1997) 52(3) *Journal of Finance* 1131.
[212] Steven L Schwarcz, 'Towards a Centralized Perfection System for Cross-border Receivables Financing' (1999) 20 *University of Pennsylvania Journal of International Economic Law* 455, 467–68, citing Heywood W Fleisig and Nuria de la Peña, 'Guatemala: How Problems in the Framework for Secured Transactions Limit Access to Credit', November 1998.
[213] Heywood W Fleisig and Nuria de la Peña, 'Nicaragua: How Problems in the Framework for Secured Transactions Limit Access to Credit', Center for the Economic Analysis of Law, February 1998, www.ceal.org/papers/Nicaversion26(cealp039)CovPage&ExecSum,v2.htm.
[214] Fleisig and de la Peña (n 212).
[215] Schwarcz (n 212) 466–68.
[216] Heywood Fleisig, Mehnaz Safavian and Nuria de la Peña, 'Reforming Collateral Laws to Expand Access to Finance', World Bank, August 2006, https://openknowledge.worldbank.org/bitstream/handle/10986/7100/370960Reformin101OFFICIAL0USE0ONLY1.pdf?sequence=1&isAllowed=y.
[217] ibid 8.

in the US would likely be unacceptable to a lender.[218] In some jurisdictions, there is a great disparity between the assets that firms possess or will need to possess, and the assets lenders will accept as collateral.[219] The data from surveys conducted by the World Bank Group in more than 60 low-income and middle-income countries from 2001 to 2005 shows this disparity (Figure 2.1).

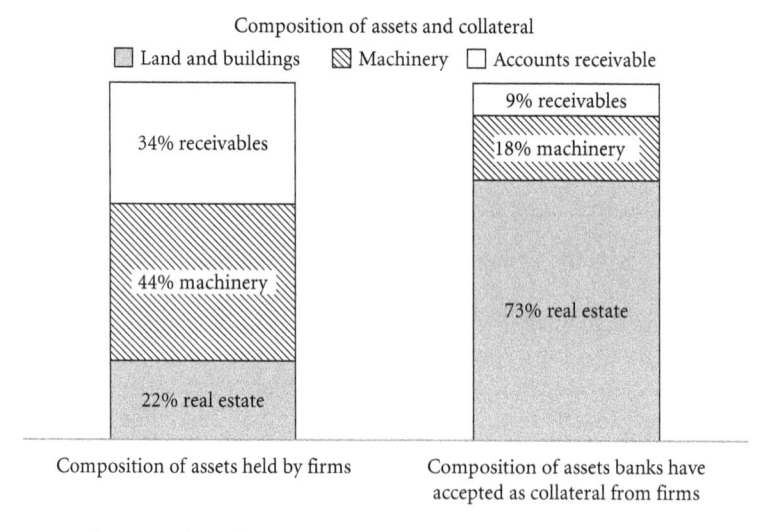

Composition of assets and collateral

☐ Land and buildings   ▨ Machinery   ☐ Accounts receivable

Composition of assets held by firms:
- 34% receivables
- 44% machinery
- 22% real estate

Composition of assets banks have accepted as collateral from firms:
- 9% receivables
- 18% machinery
- 73% real estate

Figure 2.1: The assets firms hold are a poor match for those banks accept as collateral[220]

There are several reasons why banks accept less machinery and account receivables as collateral from firms in the jurisdictions where a registration system is not developed. With respect to machinery, since companies need to use the machinery for production, a non-possessory security right must be used. However, if the grantor (debtor) still has possession of the machinery, it is quite difficult to perfect the security right in the machinery. With respect to account receivables, giving notice of the transfer to all account debtors is costly and time-consuming. Moreover, sometimes the grantor (transferor) does not wish to let account debtors know that their receivables are transferred.

The World Bank data below shows that many firms in low-income and middle-income countries cannot meet the collateral requirements for loans because of

---

[218] ibid 7.
[219] ibid 8.
[220] Mehnaz Safavian, Heywood Fleisig, and Jevgenijs Steinbuks, 'Unlocking Dead Capital: How Reforming Collateral Laws Improves Access to Finance', *Private Sector Development Viewpoint*, No 307 (World Bank, March 2006) 2. Data is from surveys conducted in more than 60 low- and middle-income countries in 2001–05. The source is World Bank Group, Enterprise Surveys database, http://rru.worldbank.org/documents/publicpolicyjournal/307Safavian_Fleisig_Steinbuks.pdf.

a lack of security right registries for movable assets and receivables. See Table 2.7. Thus, it is recommended that such countries set up security right registries.

Table 2.7: World Bank Group, enterprise surveys[221]

	Firms that are rejected because they have insufficient collateral (as a percentage of all firms that are rejected for credit)	Firms that do not apply for credit because the collateral requirements are too high (as a percentage of all firms that do not apply for credit)
Africa	51%	19%
East Asia	70%	20%
Eastern Europe and Central Asia	72%	13%
Latin America and the Caribbean	39%	23%
South Asia	72%	31%

2-6-2. Cons

2-6-2-1. Over-leverage

Most of the soft laws and international conventions recommend a registration system for security rights. However, there are also criticisms against these global movements in favour of such a system.

Secured credit law reform is generally promoted on the ground that it will foster market-based decision making on credit issues. It is often seen as part of an overall growth and development strategy.[222] One of the presumptions is that markets will intrinsically lead to efficient outcomes. However, the recent global financial crisis has highlighted the possibility of desirable government intervention that can guide economic growth and make everyone better off.[223]

When a debtor may use its movable assets and receivables as collateral, it might get excessive loans from creditors. Such over-leverage increases risks. With the excessive loans, the debtor would try expand the business. Such expansion of credit might introduce a source of error in the calculations of the entrepreneurs and thus cause them to misjudge business projects and to embark upon businesses

---

[221] Fleisig, Safavian and de la Peña (n 216) 9. Data is from surveys conducted in more than 60 countries in 2001–05, www.ifc.org/ifcext/sme.nsf/AttachmentsByTitle/BEE+Collateral+Access+to+Finance/$FILE/Reforming_Collateral.pdf.
[222] McCormack (n 186) 71.
[223] ibid 72.

which previously had been regarded as unprofitable.[224] If the business turns out to be successful, the debtor would be well off, but if the business fails, the debtor could lose more.

Expansion of credit increases a demand for land and accordingly raises the price of land. Price appreciation enlarges the amount that can be borrowed based on the collateral of land. This further expansion of credit may in turn raise land prices.[225] Overall, it could create economic bubbles in a society.

All of a sudden, people may discover that land is over-valued relative to the real economy sector cash flows, eg, businesses cannot pay escalating rents.[226] Then, land prices start to drop to the extent that land price becomes insufficient to cover the loans. As a result, debtors default on loans and dispose of land. Simultaneous sales of land would precipitate or accelerate a drop in the price of land.

2-6-2-2. Secured Creditor v Unsecured Creditor

Security runs counter to fairness in that it may involve secured creditors being paid, whereas unsecured creditors remain unpaid.[227] In case of a default, secured creditors may have a simple interest in getting possession of collateral regardless of what happens to the debtor company, whereas unsecured creditors may wish to preserve the debtor company as a going concern so that they can hope to get some of their money back if the company turns a profit.[228] In this sense, security might restrict vibrant economic activities of companies and cause adverse effects on the development of the economy. Bebchuk argues that giving full priority to secured creditors over unsecured creditors, and thus distorting the monitoring functions of companies, reduces the incentive of companies to take adequate precautions and therefore causes the excessive use of security rights.[229]

2-6-3. Analysis

Security rights registry enables a company to use its movable assets and receivables as collateral and raise more finance. It might cause vicious circles of expansion of credit and market bubble and collapse. However, collateralising receivables has different aspects from collateralising real estate. The latter could be more risky than the former since the price of real estate could fluctuate much more dramatically than the value of receivables. This is because the supply of land is limited, and

---

[224] Ludwig von Mises, *Interventionism: An Economic Analysis* (Indianapolis, Liberty Fund, 2011) ch 2. available at: http://oll.libertyfund.org/title/2394/226152.
[225] Jeffrey N Gordon and Christopher Muller, 'Confronting Financial Crisis: Dodd-Frank's Dangers and the Case for a Systemic Emergency Insurance Fund' (2011) 28 *Yale Journal on Regulation* 151, 169.
[226] ibid.
[227] McCormack (n 186) 70.
[228] La Porta et al (n 208) 1134.
[229] Lucian A Bebchuk and Jesse M Fried, 'The Uneasy Case for the Priority of Secured Claims in Bankruptcy' (1996) 105 *Yale Law Journal* 857, 895–904.

there is a gap between its use value and exchange value. Collateralising real estate carried with it the risk of market bubble and collapse, which are quite unpredictable. For example, mortgage-backed securitisation, which caused the subprime mortgage crisis in 2008, are based on mortgages on real estate which are susceptible to market bubble and collapse.

In contrast, receivables do not have any use value since one does not utilise receivables for other forms of production. Receivables only have exchange value. Therefore, they cannot be over-valued relative to their use value, and thus carry less risk of market bubble and collapse. With respect to receivables, the risk is debt default, which is calculated and reflected in discounting the value of receivables. For this reason, receivables could be safer to use as collateral than real estate.

The problem of secured creditors' tendency to liquidate the debtor company due to the full priority of secured creditors over unsecured creditors could be solved by national insolvency laws stipulating an automatic stay on assets in insolvency.

2-7. Filing Systems

2-7-1. Document-Filing System v Notice-Filing System

In a document-filing registration system, registrants must submit the document evidencing the transaction, such as a sales contract or a security contract, and the registry officials must scrutinise these documents before giving permission for their registration.[230] Only those that have satisfied the registration procedures may register in the registry. Therefore, registration can only be made after the contract, from which the security right arises, is concluded. Through such procedures, the registry tries to prevent void or false registration. A document-filing registration system provides searchers with actual or at least presumptive proof of the existence of the security right.

In some jurisdictions, original contract documents, which are manually made with great formality, are placed on the register. In the UK, only the registration form remains on the register once it had been checked against the charge document.[231] Under the Korean Security Registration Act, registrants must submit the

---

[230] For example, a land registry is a title registry, and the requirements and effect of the registration are strictly stipulated by law. The registration is the source of real rights. See Harry C Sigman, 'Security in Movables in the United States—Uniform Commercial Code Article 9: A Basis for Comparison' in Eva-Maria Kieninger (ed), *Security Rights in Movable Property in European Private Law* (Cambridge, Cambridge University Press, 2004) 78.

[231] There are proposals put forward by the Department for Business, Innovation and Skills (BIS), which would change this. Key elements of the revised scheme of August 2011 include the possibility of filing electronically. 'Registration of Charges Created by Companies and Limited Liability Partnerships—Proposals to Amend the Current Scheme and Relating to Specialist Registers' (BIS, 12 March 2010) 34, Proposal J(a), https://www.gov.uk/government/uploads/system/uploads/attachment_data/file/31493/10-697-registration-of-charges-created-by-companies-proposals.pdf.

document evidencing the cause of registration,[232] but such documents are reviewed only for verification of the registration application and are not searchable in the registry.

Jan-Hendrik Röver explains the function of a debtor-based indexed notice registration of security rights with comparison to a traditional title registry as follows:[233]

> Whereas traditional registers were understood as providing an accurate reflection of the facts registered, it is now being put forward that a security register for movables, at least, is not able to provide authenticity of the registered facts, i.e. good faith reliance on the registered information is not protected. A register for movables is seen as a tool of establishing priority between competing security holders and it provides a warning about existing security rights to potential creditors. Where registration is introduced it is also a creation requirement for the security right (hence, if a security is not registered it cannot exist or at least not perfected). However, the registration of a security right cannot be taken as showing that a security right legally exists. This would, however, limit the usefulness of the register in practice. The rationale that a register is a source of verified and guaranteed information is a misconception, since pledge registers should simply serve to publicize data as provided by the parties. The position of the pledge register is thus different from that of a land or companies register, which indeed has to establish a reliable record of the rights that exist in the land or the companies that have been created.

Because of the loophole in a debtor-based indexed notice registration of security rights, there is no point in having a document-filing registration system where parties must submit a document evidencing their contract and the documents themselves are registered. Such efforts might be wasted since a debtor-based indexed notice registration cannot ensure certainty or authenticity with respect to the legal validity or contents of registration.

2-7-2. The Effect of Notice-Filing

In a notice-filing system, 'registration only provides notice that the secured creditor may have a security right in the assets described in the notice'.[234] A notice-filing system 'does not provide even presumptive evidence of the existence of the security right'.[235] The UNCITRAL Legislative Guide on Secured Transactions[236] also explains that 'a notice-filing system is no guarantee of the actual existence of

---

[232] Korean Security Registration Act, art 43(1).
[233] Jan-Hendrik Röver, *Secured Lending in Eastern Europe: Comparative Law of Secured Transactions and the EBRD Model Law* (Oxford, Oxford University Press, 2007) 232 [16.83].
[234] UNCITRAL Legislative Guide on Secured Transactions, 111 [33].
[235] ibid 112 [37].
[236] The UNCITRAL Legislative Guide on Secured Transactions was prepared by the United Nations Commission on International Trade Law (UNCITRAL), and the General Assembly of the United Nations adopted the Guide on 11 December 2008. See: www.uncitral.org/uncitral/en/uncitral_texts/payments/Guide_securedtrans.html.

Filing Systems 49

a security right'[237] and recommends that 'the law should provide that registration of a notice does not create a security right and is not necessary for the creation of a security right'.[238] The UNCITRAL Model Law on Secured Transactions provides that: 'A security right is created by a security agreement, provided that the grantor has rights in the asset to be encumbered or the power to encumber it.'[239] LoPucki demonstrates the essence of the notice-filing system under UCC Article 9 as follows:

> The filing system is the principal means used to communicate the possible existence of a lien from a creditor who has one to a creditor who is thinking of acquiring one ... The difficulty in transmitting notice from the holder of a lien to the creditor who seeks to acquire one is that neither of these creditors has any way of knowing who the other is ... The solution to this problem is for each creditor who obtains a lien to leave a 'to whom it may concern' message. For an Article 9 security right, that message is in the form of a financing statement ... Each year, the creditors who take security rights leave millions of these messages in the filing system. And before they take their liens, many of these filers search the records to see whether prior secured creditors left message for them.[240]

Filing a financing statement is one method of perfecting security rights under UCC Article 9. It is simply a form of publicity for actual or potential rights.[241] Filing a financing statement does not evidence the existence of a security right.[242]

LoPucki explains that the filing system is a means for a secured creditor who takes a non-possessory security right in property of a debtor to communicate the existence of that security right to others who may later consider extending credit to that debtor.[243] Sigman[244] also emphasises that the filing of a financing statement under UCC Article 9 is just giving a warning about the need for further investigation. It is a form of advertisement, which indicates that a security right may then or thereafter exist in assets that fall within the description provided. In New Zealand, the PPS Register is often described as an electronic noticeboard.[245] It is like a public bulletin board where anybody may put a notice of their security rights in a debtor's assets.

A notice-filing system is like putting in a footnote. It is a reader's responsibility to refer to the original materials. The text does not have to contain all of the original text that it quotes; it only has to contain summarised contents and the exact citation by which readers can refer to the original materials. Notice-filing systems merely require the notice to contain summarised core information of the registered right and how to search for further information.

---

[237] ibid 112 [37].
[238] ibid Recommendation 33.
[239] UNCITRAL Model Law on Secured Transactions, art 6(1).
[240] LoPucki and Warren (n 2) 281.
[241] Sigman (n 230) 78.
[242] Sigman and Kieninger (n 39) 43.
[243] LoPucki and Warren (n 2) 404.
[244] Sigman and Kieninger (n 39) 43.
[245] Roger Fenton, *Garrow & Fenton's Law of Personal Property in New Zealand: Volume 2 Personal Property Securities*, 7th edn (London, LexisNexis, 2010) 36 [2.2.2].

2-7-3. Advance Registration of Notice-Filing

The notice filed under UCC Article 9 is independent of the security agreement.[246] Filing a financing statement may occur before or after the security right is created, before or after there is a security agreement, before or after the debtor has any rights in the collateral or even before any collateral comes into existence.[247] Priority between competing secured creditors is determined by the order of filing, regardless of the date of creation of the security rights.[248]

The UNCITRAL Model Law on Secured Transactions follows this first-to-register exception to the general principle of determining priority by reference to the date of perfection.[249] The UNCITRAL Model Law on Secured Transactions provides that: 'As between security rights that were made effective against third parties by registration of a notice in the Registry, priority is determined by the time order of registration, without regard to the order of creation of the security rights.'[250]

Under UCC Article 9, a single filed financing statement may support a number of transfers to the same party over an extended period of time.[251] This serves to reduce the cost of registration. Furthermore, the UNCITRAL Model Law on Secured Transactions provides that: 'The registration of a single notice may relate to security rights created by the grantor in favour of the secured creditor under one or more than one security agreement.'[252] A notice-filing system removes any practical necessity for the existence of a one-to-one relationship between the registration and the security agreement.[253]

The UNCITRAL Legislative Guide on Secured Transactions explains the primary reasons for, and advantages of, this flexible approach. First, registration in advance of the creation of a security right allows funds to be raised by using future assets. Advance registration accommodates efficient registration for security rights in future assets.[254] Advance registration also facilitates the extension of credit secured by future assets by providing a single date for establishing priority.[255]

Second, advance registration facilitates a grantor's access to credit. It avoids the risk of registration being ineffective in cases where the underlying security agreement is technically deficient at the point of registration but is later revised.[256] Therefore, it enables a secured creditor to establish its priority without having to worry about the timing of the execution of the security agreement.[257] It provides

---

[246] UNCITRAL Legislative Guide on Secured Transactions, 174 [98].
[247] Sigman and Kieninger (n 39) 43.
[248] Sigman (n 230) 73.
[249] UNCITRAL Model Law on Secured Transactions, Model Registry Provisions, art 4.
[250] UNCITRAL Model Law on Secured Transactions, art 29(a).
[251] Sigman and Kieninger (n 39) 48.
[252] UNCITRAL Model Law on Secured Transactions, Model Registry Provisions, art 3.
[253] UNCITRAL Legislative Guide on Secured Transactions, 174 [98].
[254] UNCITRAL Legislative Guide on Secured Transactions, 174 [100].
[255] ibid 195 [48].
[256] ibid 174 [99].
[257] ibid.

certainty by enabling secured creditors to determine the priority of their security rights before they extend credit.[258]

Third, advance registration encourages a secured creditor to register the notice as early as possible, which puts potential creditors on notice that a security right might have already encumbered the asset in question.[259]

The International Receivables Registry registrar would not have the resources to check or investigate the real time when a contract was actually concluded. Registration in the International Receivables Registry would be electronic registration, and the International Receivables Registry would only be able to record the time of registration when a transfer of or security right in receivables is registered. For this reason, it is inevitable that the International Receivables Registry will allow advance registration, which is in fact desirable. Since registration in the International Receivables Registry does not require submitting the contract document, it is possible for parties to register even future transfers in advance, as long as it is not expressly prohibited by the draft International Receivables Registry Convention. Thus, it would be possible for the parties to agree to register a transfer of or security right in a receivable before the agreement for the transfer or security right is concluded.

2-7-4. Information Required for Effective Registration

In a notice-filing system, only very basic information must be registered for the registered right to be identifiable. The information registered does not serve the function of verifying the right. This section considers what information should be included in registrations in the International Receivables Registry. In order to canvass the possibilities, this section compares the registration requirements of a number of jurisdictions. Since the International Receivables Registry only deals with receivables transferred by and to companies, this section limits the analysis of identification data to that pertaining to companies. As representative examples, it compares information to effect registration in the US, New Zealand and Australia under the UNCITRAL Model Law on Secured Transactions, and in the UK, Korea and Japan. See Table 2.8.

2-7-4-1. UCC Article 9

UCC Article 9 requires a financing statement to provide and indicate: (1) the name of the grantor; (2) the name of the secured party or a representative of the secured party; and (3) the collateral covered by the financing statement.[260] A financing statement is only sufficient if it contains all three elements.

---

[258] ibid 195 [48].
[259] ibid.
[260] UCC, art 9-502(a).

2-7-4-2. The New Zealand PPSA

The New Zealand PPSA stipulates that the following data must be contained in the financing statement to register it: (1) the name and address of the grantor and the name or job title, and contact details, of the person acting on behalf of the grantor; (2) the unique number transferred to the grantor on its incorporation; (3) the name and address of the secured creditor, and the name or job title, and contact details, of the person acting on behalf of the secured creditor; and (4) a description of the collateral.[261]

2-7-4-3. The Australian PPSA

The Australian PPSA 2009 stipulates that a financing statement consists of the following data: (1) the details of the secured creditor or a person nominated by the secured creditor who has authority to act on behalf of the secured creditor; (2) the grantor's details; (3) an address (including an email address or fax number) for the giving of notices to the secured creditor relating to the registration and details of any identifier provided for the giving of notices to the secured creditor; (4) a collateral description and a description of proceeds; and (5) an end time for registration.[262]

2-7-4-4. The UNCITRAL Model Law on Secured Transactions

According to the Model Registry Provisions of the UNCITRAL Model Law on Secured Transactions, the following information should be contained in the notice registration: (a) the identifier and address of the grantor; (b) the identifier and address of the secured creditor or its representative; (c) a description of the encumbered assets; (d) the period of effectiveness of the registration; and (e) a statement of the maximum amount for which the security right may be enforced.[263]

The Registry may not require verification of the information about a registrant's identity submitted[264] and may not scrutinise the form or content of a notice.[265]

2-7-4-5. UK Register of Company Charges

The Companies Act 2006 (Amendment of Part 25) Regulations 2013 stipulates that a company that creates charges must deliver the statement of particulars of the charge to the registrar for registration before the end of 21 days beginning with the day after the date of creation of the charge.[266] Where the charge is created or evidenced by an instrument, the registrar is required to register it only if a certified copy of the instrument is delivered to the registrar with the statement of

---

[261] New Zealand PPSA, s 142(1).
[262] Australian PPSA, s 153(1).
[263] UNCITRAL Model Law on Secured Transactions, Model Registry Provisions, art 8.
[264] ibid art 7(2).
[265] ibid art 7(3).
[266] Companies Act 2006 (Amendment of Part 25) Regulations 2013, s 859A(2) and (4).

particulars.[267] The registrar checks the application form against the certified copy of the instrument. This makes the registration consistent with the actual charge contract between the grantor and the secured creditor.

Where the charge is created or evidenced by an instrument, a statement of particulars must include the following information: the registered name and number of the company; the date of creation of the charge; the name of each of the chargees or of the security agents or trustees; whether it is a floating charge; whether there is a negative pledge clause etc.[268]

2-7-4-6. The Korean Security Registration Act

According to Article 47(2) of the Korean Security Registration Act, the following matters need to be recorded on the registration: (1) the head office or principal office and company registration number of the grantor; (2) the trade name or other name and head office or principal office of the debtor; (3) the trade name or other name, head office or principal office and company registration number of the secured creditor; (4) if the grantor, the debtor or the secured creditor is a foreign legal person, its business office or other office located in Korea; (5) the cause of registration regarding the registration of security and the date thereof; (6) matters necessary for identifying the encumbered movable assets and receivables, which are specified by Korean Security Registration Rules made by the Supreme Court;[269] (7) the amount of secured claim or the maximum amount of credit; (8) special agreements in accordance with Article 10 or Article 12;[270] (9) the duration of the security rights (duration of effectiveness of registration); (10) the receipt number of the application; and (11) the receipt date of the application.

2-7-4-7. The Japanese Transfer Registration Act

According to the Japanese Transfer Registration Act, the following matters need to be recorded on the registration of the transfer of movable assets or receivables:[271]

---

[267] ibid s 859A(3).
[268] ibid s 859D(1) and (2).
[269] In the case where the collateral is a receivable, the following must be recorded: (1) the type of the receivable; (2) the cause and the date of the accrual of the receivable, or the start date and the last date of the receivable; (3) the name and the address of the creditor of the receivable; and (4) the name and the address of the debtor of the receivable. Transfers of future receivables (if the debtor of the receivable is not specified) and bulk transfers of receivables may be exempted from recording the fourth item: Korean Security Registration Rules, art 35(1)(ii).
[270] Under art 10 of the Korean Security Registration Act, the effect of a security right in a movable asset will extend to all things that are attached to the encumbered movable asset, including its accessories, unless otherwise provided by law or a special agreement between the parties. If there is such a special agreement, it should be registered. In addition, according to art 12 of the Korean Security Registration Act, a security right in a movable asset will secure the principal, interest, penalty, expense for enforcement of the security right, expense for the preservation of the encumbered movable asset and damages arising from the non-fulfillment of the obligation or from latent defects in the encumbered movable asset, unless otherwise provided by a special agreement between the parties. If there is such a special agreement, it should be registered.
[271] Japanese Transfer Registration Act, arts 7(2) (for movable assets) and 8(2) (for receivables).

54   *Security Rights Registries*

(1) the trade name or other name of the transferor and its head office or principal office; (2) the name or other name and head office or principal office of the transferee; (3) the business office or other office located in Japan (if the head office or principal office of the transferor or the transferee is located in a foreign country); (4) the cause of registration regarding the registration of transfer of movable assets or receivables and the date thereof; (5) matters necessary for identifying the transferred movable assets or receivables, which are specified by the Japanese Transfer Registration Rule made by the Ministry of Justice;[272] (6) the duration of the registration of transfer of movable assets or receivables; (7) the registration number; (8) the date of registration; and (9) the total amount of the transferred receivables[273] (only for the transfer of receivables that have already been arisen—not for future receivables).

An agreement assigning a person's income for his whole lifetime is invalid. The valid term of registration for the transfer of existing receivables and the transfer of future receivables against a specified debtor may not exceed 50 years. It was taken into consideration that housing loans usually last for a long period.[274] With respect to future receivables against unspecified debtors, the valid term of registration must not be longer than 10 years.[275] The valid term of registration may be extended if there is a special reason to do so.[276]

Table 2.8: **Contents of registration (in the case where the grantor is a company)**

UCC Article 9	New Zealand PPSA	Australian PPSA	UNCITRAL Model Law
Notice-filing system	Notice-filing system	Notice-filing system	Notice-filing system
Name of the grantor	Name and address of the grantor and the job title, and contact details of the person acting on behalf of the grantor	Grantor's details	Name and address of the grantor

(*continued*)

---

[272] In the case where the collateral is a receivable, the following must be recorded: (1) if there is more than one receivable, the serial numbers of the receivables; (2) if the debtor of the receivable is specified, the name and the address of the debtor and the creditor of the receivable; (3) if the debtor of the receivable is not specified, the cause of the accrual of the receivable and the name and the address of the creditor of the receivable; (4) the type of the receivable; (5) the date of the accrual of the receivable; and (6) the amount of the receivable (only if the receivable has already accrued). See Japanese Transfer Registration Rule, art 9(1).
[273] ibid art 8(2)(iii).
[274] ibid art 8(3)(i).
[275] ibid art 8(3)(ii).
[276] ibid art 8(3).

Table 2.8: (*Continued*)

UCC Article 9	New Zealand PPSA	Australian PPSA	UNCITRAL Model Law
	Unique number transferred to the grantor on its incorporation		
Name of the secured party or a representative of the secured party	Name and address of the secured creditor and the name or job title, and contact details of the person acting on behalf of the secured creditor	Details of the secured creditor or a person nominated by the secured creditor who has authority to act on behalf of the secured creditor	Identifier and address of the secured creditor or its representative
		Address (including an email address or fax number) for the giving of notices to the secured creditor relating to the registration and details of any identifier provided for the giving of notices to the secured creditor	
Collateral covered by the financing statement	Description of the collateral	Collateral description and description of proceeds	Description of the encumbered assets
			Statement of the maximum amount for which the security right may be enforced (optional)
		End time for registration	Period of effectiveness of the registration (optional)

(*continued*)

Table 2.8: (*Continued*)

UK	Korean registration	Japanese registration
Notice-filing system	Combination of document-filing system and notice-filing system	Notice-filing system
Registered name and number of the company	Name, head office or principal office and company registration number of the grantor	Name and head office or principal office of the transferor
Name of each of the chargees or of the security agents or trustees	Name, head office or principal office and company registration number of the secured creditor	Name and head office or principal office of the transferee
Short description of the property	Type of the receivable Cause and date of the accrual of the receivable, or start date and last date of the receivable Name and address of the creditor of the receivable Name and address of the debtor of the receivable (may be exempted)	Serial numbers of the receivables (if there is more than one receivable) Name and address of the creditor of the receivable Name and address of the debtor of the receivable (and, if it is not specified, the cause of the accrual of the receivable) Type of the receivable Date of the accrual of the receivable
Date of creation of the charge	Cause of registration regarding the registration of security Date of the cause	Cause of registration regarding the registration of transfer of movables or receivables Date of the cause
Obligations secured by the charge	The amount of secured claim or the maximum secured amount	The total amount of the transferred receivables (only for the transfer of receivables that have already been arisen, not for future receivables)
	Duration of the security rights (no longer than five years, renewal possible)	Duration of the registration of transfer of movables or receivables (no longer than 10 years, renewal possible)
	Receipt number	Registration number
	Date of receipt	Date of registration

2-8. Parties' Reciprocal Confirmation Instead of Registrar's Review

2-8-1. Safeguards against Improper Registration under a Notice-Filing System

Section 2-7 concluded that an international registry should be a notice-filing system rather than a document-filing system. This is because, first of all, it would be impractical to store and manage documents from around the world. Second, reviewing documents in various languages for registration would be time-consuming and expensive.

However, a notice-filing system has an important shortcoming: the abuse of registration by secured creditors (or transferees). Because a notice-filing system does not require the contract document to be submitted, anyone could file a notice of intention to create a security right in relation to a person when there is actually no such proposal. They might do this maliciously to damage a person's credit record or they might be acting negligently. As such, on the one hand, a secured creditor (or transferee) would maximise the scope of registration of security rights (or transfers) to ensure the protection of his rights. On the other hand, a grantor (or a transferor) would wish to minimise the scope and amount of registration of security rights (or transfers). This is because if a security right is registered in the registry with respect to the grantor in question, it gives the impression that the grantor has such debts. A general security rights registry is a negative registry or a warning registry. Thus, if there are several assets registered as encumbered under the name of a grantor, this is not good for the grantor. It means that those registered assets are provided as collateral for debts. The assets registered in a security rights registry can no longer be used for security except where the value of the assets exceeds the amount secured.

Analysing these two aspects, a grantor's (or transferor's) cross-check on the registration contents submitted by a secured creditor (or transferee) would help to prevent a secured creditor's (or transferee's) abuse of registration.

Section 2-8 explores the legal systems of each jurisdiction with respect to the various possible remedies for this problem and the requirement of the parties' cooperation for registration. The issue considered is whether to require the parties' reciprocal confirmation in the International Receivables Registry. The conclusion is that an email request for consent from the transferor (or the grantor) is the best method.

In section 2-8, a 'secured creditor' includes a transferee, a 'grantor' includes a transferor, and a 'security right' in receivables includes a transfer of receivables except where it is used in the explanation regarding the Companies Act 2006 and the Korean Security Registration Act.

2-8-2. Comparative Research

Based on a comparative analysis, it appears that there are three general approaches to whether to require the grantor's consent or authorisation for registration. First, under the Canadian, New Zealand and Australian PPSAs, the law does not require the consent of the grantor for registration of a security right in a movable asset or a receivable owned by the grantor. Therefore, a secured creditor himself can apply for registration of a security right. In these jurisdictions, a secured creditor who registers his security right must give notice of its filing to the grantor (or transferor) within a certain period of time.

Second, under UCC Article 9 and the UNCITRAL Model Law on Secured Transactions and in English law, the authorisation of a grantor is required, but may be given either before or after registration. Furthermore, under UCC Article 9, the authorisation of a grantor is implied from the authentication of the security agreement. Thus, a secured creditor may file any financing statement unilaterally, but a grantor may at any time cancel an incorrect filing through a summary administrative or judicial procedure. The focus is how efficiently the grantor could cancel an incorrect filing affecting him after an incorrect filing has been registered.

Third, in Korea and Japan, and under the DCFR and the Cape Town Convention, the law requires the parties' reciprocal consent before the registration is actually registered. This may be achieved by requiring both a grantor and a secured creditor (or both a transferor and a transferee) to visit the registration office to apply for a registration. Alternatively, it can be achieved through an online registration system requiring the consent of a grantor (or a transferor) to be transmitted to the system in order for the registration application made by a secured creditor (or a transferee) to actually appear on the website.

2-8-2-1. Compulsory Notice to the Grantor

2-8-2-1-1. The Verification Statement

Under the PPSAs of Canada, New Zealand and Australia, a secured creditor may himself apply for the registration with respect to the security right. Then he must send a 'verification statement' of a registration, issued by the registrar, to a grantor, so that the grantor may have the opportunity to apply for a change to the registration if the registration is incorrect. If a secured creditor does not send a verification statement to a grantor within a certain period,[277] he will be fined. There are

---

[277] These are: 30 days under s 46(6) of the Ontario PPSA; 30 days under s 43(12) of the Saskatchewan PPSA; 15 working days under s 148 of the New Zealand PPSA; 'as soon as reasonably practicable after the time of the registration' in Australia under s 157(1)(b) of the Australian PPSA.

sanctions for failing to send a verification statement.[278] However, even though a secured creditor does not send a verification statement to a grantor, the registration is still effective until the grantor files a 'financing change statement'.

2-8-2-1-2. The Financing Change Statement

After a grantor (or a transferor) receives a verification statement of a registration, if the grantor believes that a certain financing statement is inaccurate or wrongfully filed, it may demand the secured creditor (or a transferee) to file a 'financing change statement' to amend or discharge the registration. 'Financing change statement' means a form that requires data authorised by the regulations to be entered into the register to renew, discharge or amend a financing statement.[279] Upon filing the financing change statement, the financing statement in question will disappear from the registry.

Under the PPSAs of Saskatchewan, Canada and New Zealand, the grantor may give the secured creditor a written demand[280] to register a financing change statement within 15 days after the demand is given.[281] If he does not, the grantor may register the financing change statement himself upon providing the registrar with satisfactory proof that the demand has been given to the secured creditor.[282] Upon application to the court by a secured creditor, the court may order that the registration be maintained, discharged or amended.[283]

Under the PPSAs of Ontario, Canada and Australia, a person registered as a grantor may make an amendment demand to the person registered as a secured creditor for a financing change statement to be registered to amend the registration.[284] In addition, the person registered as a grantor may also apply to the court for an order in relation to an amendment demand. Upon application, the court may consider the amendment demand and order the Registrar to register a financing change statement amending or removing the registration.[285]

2-8-2-2. Authorisation of the Grantor before or after Registration

Under UCC Article 9 and the UNCITRAL Model Law on Secured Transactions, the secured creditor is not obligated to send notice of the registration to the grantor as under the PPSAs of Canada, New Zealand and Australia.

---

[278] A total of $500 to the grantor (s 46(7) of the Ontario PPSA); punishment under the Australian Privacy Act 1988 (s 13) (s 157(4) of the Australian PPSA).
[279] Saskatchewan PPSA, s 2(1)(q); Ontario PPSA, s 49; New Zealand PPSA, s 135; Australian PPSA, s 150(2).
[280] Saskatchewan PPSA, s 50(3); New Zealand PPSA, s 162.
[281] Saskatchewan PPSA, s 50(4); New Zealand PPSA, s 163.
[282] Saskatchewan PPSA, s 50(5); New Zealand PPSA, s 165(1)(a).
[283] Saskatchewan PPSA, s 50(7); New Zealand PPSA, s 167(1).
[284] Ontario PPSA, s 56(2.1); Australian PPSA, s 178(1).
[285] Ontario PPSA, s 56(5)(b)(i); Australian PPSA, s 182(1), 182(4)(a).

2-8-2-2-1. UCC Article 9

Prior to its revision in 1998, UCC Article 9 required a financing statement to be signed by the debtor (grantor).[286] This was because the UCC filing offices were not up to the technological challenge.[287] Now, in order to facilitate the electronic filing of financing statements, the grantor's signature on a financing statement is no longer required.[288] Any person may file a financing statement if the grantor authorises the filing in an authenticated record.[289] Before filing a financing statement, the secured creditor must obtain authorisation from the grantor in an authenticated record. If the grantor has not authorised the filing, the financing statement is ineffective.[290] By authenticating a security agreement, a grantor (debtor) authorises the filing of financing statement covering the collateral described in the security agreement.[291] If a grantor consents to the security agreement in writing, he authorises the filing of the security agreement. As a result, a secured creditor only needs to get the grantor to authenticate a security agreement in order to obtain the right to file a financing statement.

However, a third party has no way of checking whether the grantor did not authorise the filing and therefore whether the filing is ineffective. If there is a dispute about the validity of a filing, it would be possible to challenge the validity by proving that the grantor did not authorise the filing.[292] If the filing is made in advance to concluding a security agreement, the filing is ineffective before the conclusion of the security agreement and becomes effective after the conclusion of the security agreement.[293]

UCC Article 9 does not require a secured creditor to send a notice of the registration of a security right to a grantor. If there is any prior registration of security right in the registry with respect to a grantor, a potential secured creditor would ask the grantor about the registration and thus let the grantor know about any such registrations. Furthermore, a potential secured creditor would use the fact that there is a prior registration, if any, as a point of negotiation.[294] Thus, in any case a grantor would get to know of any registration affecting him.

Under UCC Article 9, a grantor may file a correction statement with respect to a record indexed using the grantor's name if it is believed that the record is

---

[286] Even when the debtor's signature was required by law, the filing of unauthorised financing statements was a serious problem.
[287] LoPucki and Warren (n 2) 322.
[288] ibid.
[289] UCC, art 9-509(a)(1).
[290] ibid art 9-510(a).
[291] ibid art 9-509(b).
[292] LoPucki and Warren (n 2) 322.
[293] ibid.
[294] 'For example, a prospective buyer or secured creditor can refuse to go ahead with a financing transaction unless a pre-existing registration is cancelled or unless the secured creditor identified in the registered notice undertakes to subordinate its right to that of the prospective buyer or secured creditor.' UNCITRAL Legislative Guide on Secured Transactions, 153 [18].

inaccurate or was wrongfully filed.[295] Still, an initial financing statement or other filed record is not affected by the filing of a correction statement.[296] As a result, both the filing of the financing statement and the filing of the correction statement will be shown on the registry.[297]

2-8-2-2-2. UNCITRAL Model Law on Secured Transactions

Article 2 of the Model Registry Provisions in Chapter IV of the UNCITRAL Model Law on Secured Transactions provides as follows:

Article 2. Grantor's authorization for registration

1. Registration of an initial notice with respect to a security right in an asset of a grantor is ineffective unless authorized by that grantor in writing.

2. Registration of an amendment notice that adds encumbered assets [or increases the maximum amount for which the security right may be enforced] or extends the period of effectiveness of the registration of a notice is ineffective unless authorized by the grantor in writing.

3. [With the exception of an amendment notice to add a buyer of an encumbered asset as a grantor in accordance with Article 26 of these Provisions, registration] of an amendment notice that adds a grantor is ineffective unless authorized by the additional grantor in writing.

Furthermore, the UNCITRAL Model Law on Secured Transactions provides that: 'A written security agreement is sufficient to constitute authorization by the grantor for the registration of an initial or amendment notice covering an encumbered asset described in that security agreement.'[298] It also provides that: 'Authorization may be given before or after the registration of an initial or amendment notice.'[299] Thus, a registration in advance of a security agreement may be authorised afterwards. The UNCITRAL Model Law on Secured Transactions further provides that: 'The Registry may not require evidence of the existence of the grantor's authorization.'[300] Thus, the practical result is much the same as in the US, which does not explicitly require formal written authorisation from the grantor on the assumption that the security agreement constitutes consent. This is because if a registration is inaccurate or was wrongfully filed, 'modern regimes enable the grantor to request cancellation of the registration through summary judicial or

---

[295] UCC, art 9-518(a).
[296] UCC, art 9-518(c).
[297] LoPucki and Warren (n 2) 322.
[298] UNCITRAL Model Law on Secured Transactions, Model Registry Provisions, art 2(5).
[299] ibid art 2(4).
[300] ibid art 2(6).

administrative proceedings and other law may provide penalties for fraudulent registrations'.[301]

2-8-2-2-3. The UK

In the UK, under the Companies Act 2006 (Amendment of Part 25) Regulations 2013, the company or any person interested in the charge may deliver to the registrar a statement of particulars.[302] In practice, the grantor usually signs the security contract, a secured creditor usually registers his security right by himself, and the registrar checks the security contract on which the grantor signed (although in theory these need not be in a written agreement).

2-8-2-3. Consent of the Grantor Required before Registration

In Korea and Japan, and under the Cape Town Convention and the DCFR, the consent of the grantor (or transferor) is required before registration. In Korea and Japan, both a grantor and a secured creditor (or both a transferor and a transferee) must apply together for registration. Under the Cape Town Convention and the DCFR, both parties must consent to the registration before the registration is complete.

2-8-2-3-1. The Korean Security Registration Act

Under the Korean Security Registration Act, both the grantor and the secured creditor are required to apply for a registration of a security right.[303] This is to increase the authenticity of the contents of registration. The parties or their agents may apply for a registration of a security right either in person by visiting the Registry Office to submit the application form in writing,[304] or online in accordance with the Supreme Court Regulations.[305]

2-8-2-3-2. The Japanese Transfer Registration Act

Under the Japanese Transfer Registration Act, both a transferor and a transferee of a receivable (and, in the case of a pledge of a receivable, both a pledgor and a pledgee) are required to apply for a registration of a transfer (or a pledge). The parties or their agents may apply for a registration of a transfer (or a pledge) in person by visiting the Registry Office, by post[306] or online.

Since 2001, the Japanese Ministry of Justice has provided an online application system for registration of a transfer of movable assets and receivables. Thus, both a

---

[301] UNCITRAL Legislative Guide on Secured Transactions, 176 [8].
[302] Companies Act 2006 (Amendment of Part 25) Regulations 2013, s 859A.
[303] Korean Security Registration Act, art 41(1).
[304] ibid art 42(i)
[305] ibid art 42(ii)
[306] Japanese Transfer Registration Order, art 9.

transferor and a transferee may register their transfer of receivables on the official website administrated by the Ministry of Justice after downloading the program for online application at http://www.touki-kyoutaku-online.moj.go.jp/index.html. The registrants should register with their user ID and password and establish an electronic signature. An application that does not satisfy the legal requirements will be rejected. Once registered, even if a mistake is made in the online registration application, the parties cannot easily correct the mistake.

Online application has not been commonly used.[307] The reason is that the applicants cannot easily correct mistakes, but can only delete the previous registration and reapply for the registration after fixing the mistake unless the error or defect is due to a mistake on the part of the registry office.[308] Thus, applicants want to confirm with the registry officer in person that all items to be registered are correct on the application form, so that if there is a defect, they can revise the form or add necessary documents immediately.[309] For this reason, applicants prefer to physically appear in person at the registration office in Tokyo.[310]

A system that can allow corrections or modifications in its online application must be designed to build a successful registration in the International Receivables Registry system, since registrants from all over the world cannot come to the International Receivables Registry Office each time they register. This problem could be solved if parties could check and confirm a registration application or a registration amendment application submitted by the other party, as is the case with the operation of the International Registry of Mobile Assets under the Cape Town Convention and its Aircraft Protocol.

2-8-2-3-3. The DCFR

Under the DCFR, only a secured creditor may apply for registration unilaterally and a grantor must subsequently consent to the application for registration completed by the secured creditor.[311] The DCFR stipulates that 'an entry in the register can be made only if the grantor has consented to it by declaration to the register'.[312]

---

[307] For example, during December 2005, only 34 (0.9 per cent) out of 3,808 registration applications were submitted online. The rest were submitted either in person or by post. Toshiyuki Dote, 'Current Utilization and Future Trends of Registration of Transfers of Movable Assets and Receivables' (2006) 831 *New Business Law* 26.

[308] If the registry officer finds an error or defect in the registration of receivables transfer, and the error or defect is due to the registry officer's mistake, the registry officer must modify the error or defect with the permission of the Legal Affairs Bureau and notify the applicant of the registration of the fact (Japanese Transfer Registration Order, art 12(1)). In this case, the registry officer must also notify the Legal Affairs Bureau where the head office of the transferor is located (Japanese Transfer Registration Order, art 12(2)).

[309] Interview with Hiroto Dogauchi, Professor, Tokyo University, Faculty of Law, Japan, 30 May 2008.

[310] There is only one registration office for the transfer of movable assets and receivables under the Japanese Transfer Registration Act in Japan, which is located at Nakano in Tokyo.

[311] *DCFR* (n 181) 466, art IX-3:306(1)(d); 467, art IX-3:309.

[312] ibid 467, art IX-3:309(1).

The DCFR sees that the need for a requirement of the grantor's consent could be replaced as in UCC Article 9 'only if it is sufficiently certain that the grantor can reply on an efficient enforcement of its position before the court'.[313] However, the DCFR explains that it requires the consent of the grantor for the registration because court proceedings are not yet satisfactorily quick and cost-effective in all EU Member States.[314]

Since the consent of a grantor is separate from the registration, the grantor does not always consent to a specific registration that has already been registered. Therefore, a discrepancy could occur between the scope of the consent of the grantor and the scope of the registration that has actually been registered. If the grantor gives his consent before the registration is actually registered or separately from the application procedure for the registration, there could be a discrepancy between the grantor's consent and the registration in terms of scope.

There are two ways to give a consent that would exactly match an actual registration. Either the consent of the grantor is given in the registration application or the consent to a specific registration is made after it is registered. In the other ways, there could be discrepancy between the registration and the consent for the registration.

For this reason, the DCFR creates three possible types of consent declarations: (1) unlimited consent in favour of a specified secured creditor; (2) consent to an application with a specified content; and (3) partially limited consent.[315] Still, because an online system of registration cannot evaluate whether the content of the entry inputted by a secured creditor is the same as that provided by the grantor, the second type is not able to be used in an online system with automatic registration.[316]

2-8-2-3-4. The Cape Town Convention

In the International Registry of Mobile Assets under the Cape Town Convention and the Aircraft Protocol, there is no authority review or human intervention in the process of registration.[317] Thus, it requires the reciprocal consent of the parties without the registrar's review to increase the authenticity of the contents of registration. It requires consent from both the security provider and the secured creditor before the registration appears on the website of the International Registry of Mobile Assets.

---

[313] *Draft Common Frame of Reference Full Edition*, Vol 6, Book IX (Munich, Sellier, 2009) 5508, Comments to art IX-3:309.
[314] ibid.
[315] ibid 5509–10, Comments to art IX-3:309.
[316] ibid 5510, Comments to art IX-3:309.
[317] See Roy Goode, *Official Commentary on the Convention on International Interests in Mobile Equipment and the Protocol thereto on Matters Specific to Aircraft Equipment* (revised edn, 2008) 201 [4.132].

Under the Cape Town Convention, either a security provider or a secured creditor applies for registration and the other party gives consent to the application by email. Each named party, other than the registering party, is required to consent in order for a registration to become effective.[318] If a party to a security agreement registers the security interest on the official website of the International Registry of Mobile Assets (www.internationalregistry.aero), the other party to the security agreement must log on to the website, check the information and transmit his consent electronically.[319] Likewise, either a transferor or a transferee may apply for the registration and then the other party will have to give consent to the application.[320] Once a registering party has entered the information on the website and electronically signed it, each party identified in the registration will be notified by email automatically sent by the system and will be given 36 hours to give consent on the website.[321] Upon receipt of the final consent, the registration becomes searchable.[322] If the other party fails to give its consent within the 36-hour period, the registration application will be automatically cancelled.[323] Registrations, amendments or discharges that are initiated but not completed will not appear on any search results on the website.[324]

2-9. Search for Registration

This section explores the possibilities relating to search for registration in the UK, the US and Japan, and under the Cape Town Convention as meaningful examples of differing approaches.

2-9-1. Register of Charges in the UK at Companies House

Any person may inspect the register under the Companies Act 2006.[325] If the company and a person wishing to carry out an inspection agree, the inspection may be carried out by electronic means.[326] Extracts of each of the charges registered against a company are searchable online on the Companies House website (www.companieshouse.gov.uk).

---

[318] Cape Town Convention, art 20(1).
[319] ibid art 18(1)(a).
[320] Goode (n 317) 207 [4.146].
[321] Regulations and Procedures for the International Registry, Procedures, s 12.2(a) and (b).
[322] In practice, usually all relevant parties gather together in an office bringing laptop computers and immediately afterwards, one party registers online, the other parties immediately transmit their consent online. In this way, it can be a real-time registration.
[323] Regulations and Procedures for the International Registry, Procedures, s 12.2.
[324] ibid s 12.7.
[325] Companies Act 2006, s 1085(1).
[326] Companies Act 2006 (Amendment of Part 25) Regulations 2013, s 859Q(8).

A party searching the registry and obtaining details of a registered charge may further inspect a copy of the charge document at the company's registered office.[327] The documents and a company's register of charges must be made available for inspection at the company's registered office.[328]

2-9-2. UCC Article 9

On the official UCC Article 9 filing websites of some states in the US, a log-in is required to search the registry, but on the official websites of other states, a log-in is not required.

On the official UCC Article 9 filing websites of some states in the US, it is possible to conduct a free unofficial search;[329] in some states, searching the registry is free, while in others, it is not.

2-9-3. The Japanese Transfer Registration Act

In Japan, a potential transferee needs to apply for the issuance of a registration certificate of sorts and then wait a couple of days for it. A potential transferee can apply for the issuance of a registration certificate online, but cannot search the registry online directly.

In Japan, there are three types of certificate with regard to the registration of movable assets and receivables: (1) the Certificate of Registered Matters;[330] (2) the Certificate of Summary of Registered Matters;[331] and (3) the Certificate of Matters Recorded in Summary.[332] These differ in terms of what information is included on the certificate, who can apply for the issuance of the certificate and which office issues the certificate. See Table 2.9.

---

[327] The documents and register shall be open to the inspection of any creditor or member of the company without charge, and of any other person on payment of the fee. See ibid s 859Q(4).
[328] ibid s 859Q(2) and (3).
[329] For example, Utah: https://secure.utah.gov/uccsearch/uccs;
Florida: www.floridaucc.com/UCCWEB/search.aspx;
Tennessee: www.tn.gov/sos/bus_svc/iets3/ieuc/PgUCCSearch.jsp;
Wisconsin: http://publicrecords.onlinesearches.com/Wisconsin-UCC-Filings.htm;
Iowa: https://sos.iowa.gov/search/ucc/search.aspx?ucc;
Washington: https://fortress.wa.gov/dol/ucc;
New York: https://appext20.dos.ny.gov/pls/ucc_public/web_search.main_frame.
[330] 登記事項証明書.
[331] 登記事項概要証明書.
[332] 概要記録事項証明書.

Table 2.9: Three types of registration certificates in Japan

	Certificate of Registered Matters[333]	Certificate of Summary of Registered Matters[334]	Certificate of Matters Recorded in Summary[335]
Applicant	Anybody	Anybody	Anybody
Certified items	1. Transferor's name and address 2. Transferee's name and address 3. Debtor's name and address 4. Registration number 5. Registration date 6. Type of contract upon which the receivables accrue and the contract date 7. Total amount of receivables transferred at the time of the transfer 8. Valid term of registration 9. Purpose of registration 10. Reason of extension registration 11. Number of transferors and number of transferees	1. Transferor's name and address 2. Transferee's name and address 3. Registration number 4. Registration date 5. Type of contract upon which the receivables accrue and the contract date 6. Total amount of receivables transferred at the time of the transfer 7. Valid term of registration	1. Transferor's name and address 2. Transferee's name and address 3. Registration number 4. Registration date 5. Recorded date
Issuing Office	Registry Office for the Transfer of Movable Assets and Receivables (Receivables Registration Department, Civil Administration Division of the Tokyo Legal Affairs Bureau in Nakano ward, Tokyo)		District Registry Offices of Commercial Registry covering the transferor's domicile

[333] Japanese Transfer Registration Act, art 11(2); Japanese Transfer Registration Order, art 15.
[334] Japanese Transfer Registration Act, art 11(1).
[335] ibid art 13.

2-9-4. The Cape Town Convention

The general public is permitted to search the International Registry of Mobile Assets under the Cape Town Convention and its Aircraft Protocol to determine the priority of interest in particular assets on the official International Registry of Mobile Assets website (www.internationalregistry.aero). The search is not free.[336]

2-10. Conclusion

A registration system for security rights in movable assets and receivables was originally developed in common law jurisdictions. England invented the general security rights registry. The US invented a notice-filing registration. Owing to the strict principle of *numerus clausus*, civil law jurisdictions could not develop registration systems for security rights in movable assets and receivables until the increasing economic demands of non-possessory security rights became unbearable. Today, many civil law countries, such as Korea and Japan, established registration systems for security rights in movable assets and receivables. Korea and Japan invented optional registration.

Furthermore, there have been global movements to establish a general security rights registry to facilitate creating security rights in movable assets and receivables, and to try to establish international registries for each specific type of assets, including receivables.

---

[336] Regulations and Procedures for the International Registry, Appendix, Fee Schedule, s 1.8.

3

Transfers of and Security Rights in Receivables

3-1. Introduction

Chapter 3 comparatively analyses current laws on the priority and perfection of transfers of and security rights in receivables and private international law. These comparative analyses have three purposes: first, to demonstrate the need for an international registration system by showing how divergent the current systems are compared to one another; second, to demonstrate the complexity of investigations that have to be made by a potential transferee under the current laws; and, third, to consider and discuss possible models for an international convention and to suggest the most widely acceptable legal system.

This chapter examines the current laws in the following jurisdictions: the US, Canada, New Zealand, Australia, Korea, Japan, France, Belgium, England, Singapore, Hong Kong, China, Germany, Austria, the Netherlands, Singapore and Hong Kong. These jurisdictions have been selected partly because they represent different legal systems that are sufficiently divergent from one another for the purposes of this book and partly because it was impossible to study additional jurisdictions due to reasons of space.

Section 3-2 presents a case scenario and six questions with respect to perfection and priority of a transfer of and a security right in a receivable.

Section 3-3 compares the priority rules of each jurisdiction with respect to transfers of and security rights in a receivable. It analyses criteria to determine priority, ie, notice to the debtor, registration and time of creation doctrine. It further explores the methods of giving notice of the transfer to the debtor of the receivable.

Section 3-4 compares perfection methods for a transfer of and a security right in a receivable in each jurisdiction.

Section 3-5 explores the check points where a potential transferee of a receivable or a potential secured creditor who would be provided a receivable as collateral needs to check before the transaction.

Section 3-6 categorises these jurisdictions into five groups according to perfection methods and the potential transferee's check point.

Section 3-7 provides a direct comparison of the laws in each jurisdiction, answering the same six questions on priority vis-a-vis third parties and perfection against the insolvency administrator with respect to a transfer of and a security right in a receivable.

Section 3-8 introduces the EU Directive on Financial Collateral Arrangements.

3-2. Comparative Analysis on Priority and Perfection

3-2-1. The Definition of Perfection

Priority is determined by the order of perfection against third parties. Let us first analyse the term 'perfection'. 'Perfection' is the step required to make a transfer or a security right effective against third parties and, in the case of insolvency, of the transferor or the grantor.[1] It is different from the creation of a security. In some cases, an additional step beyond the creation of a security must be taken for perfection. For example, under the UK Companies Act 2006, an unregistered charge is not perfected against third parties or in the insolvency of the charger (debtor),[2] but it is valid against the company itself. This is because registration is a perfection requirement for a company charge. In other cases, the creation requirement is also the perfection requirement.[3] The UNCITRAL Model Law on Secured Transactions (2016) uses the term 'third-party effectiveness' instead of 'perfection'. A security right either achieves 'third-party effectiveness' or there is no priority contest at all.[4]

Perfection against third parties means third-party effectiveness, which preserves priority over another transferee.[5] Perfection of a transfer of receivables is regulated by the laws on transfers of receivables. Perfection of a *security right* in receivables

---

[1] Hugh Beale, Michael Bridge, Louise Gullifer and Eva Lomnicka, *The Law of Personal Property Security* (Oxford, Oxford University Press, 2007) 327 [7.13].

[2] See section 3-7-10 Q 2.

[3] For example, the situation referred to as 'automatic perfection' under UCC art 9. A transfer of accounts that does not transfer a significant part of the outstanding accounts of the transferor is automatically perfected upon attachment under UCC, s 9-309(2).

[4] UNCITRAL Model Law on Secured Transactions, art 29; Harry C Sigman and Eva-Maria Kieninger (eds), *Cross-border Security over Tangibles* (Munich, Sellier, 2007) 37.

[5] There are exceptions to this principle. The followings are examples of where perfection does not secure priority. Under English law, the exceptions are subordination of a floating charge to a fixed charge (see section 4-8-2-1) and a bona fide purchaser (see section 4-7-2-2). Under UCC Article 9, a secured creditor who has his security right perfected can be subordinated to a buyer in the ordinary course of business (see section 4-7-3-2).

is regulated by the laws on security rights in receivables. Thus, this book examines transfers and security rights separately.

Third parties include insolvency administrators. However, perfection against an insolvency administrator will be examined separately because it is regulated by the insolvency laws of each state. Perfection of a transfer of a receivable against an insolvency administrator of a transferor means that the transferred receivable is not included in the insolvency estate of the transferor, and thus the insolvency administrator of the transferor cannot claim against the debtor of the receivable, but the transferee can claim against the debtor of the receivable.

If a security right in a receivable is perfected against an insolvency administrator of the grantor, the creditor holding the security right is entitled to be treated as a *secured* creditor in the insolvency procedures (reorganisation proceedings or liquidation proceedings) of the grantor.

If a security right in a receivable has *not* been perfected against an insolvency administrator of the grantor, the creditor holding the security right is treated as an *unsecured* creditor in the insolvency procedures (reorganisation proceedings or liquidation proceedings) of the grantor.

Section 3-6 analyses the priority of *transfers* of receivables vis-a-vis third parties (section 3-6-1) and separately analyses the priority of *security rights* in receivables vis-a-vis third parties (section 3-6-2), because in many jurisdictions the priority of transfers and the priority of security rights are regulated differently. Section 4-7 analyses perfection of a transfer of receivables against the insolvency administrator (section 4-7-1) and perfection of a *security right* in receivables against the insolvency administrator (section 4-7-2). Section 4-8 explores priority between transfers of and security rights in the same receivable (section 4-8-1) and the check points when a third party would purchase a receivable or would be given a receivable as collateral (section 4-8-2).

3-2-2. Case Study

Section 3-7 analyses the laws with respect to transfers of and security rights in receivables in the following jurisdictions: the US, Canada, New Zealand, Australia, Korea, Japan, France, Belgium, England, China, Germany, Austria, the Netherlands, Singapore and Hong Kong. To provide a direct comparison of the laws in each jurisdiction, the same six questions are asked and answered. The six questions relate to priority vis-a-vis third parties and perfection against the insolvency administrator with respect to a transfer of a receivable and a security right in a receivable.

These questions are prepared and asked for the purpose of making an analysis from the following two perspectives. The first perspective is to determine for each jurisdiction what a transferee must do to achieve perfection against third parties and priority over other transferees or secured creditors in receivables financing.

There could be a security right in a receivable as well as a transfer of that same receivable.[6] In other words, a transferor may create a security right in his receivable for a creditor and later sell the same receivable to a third party, or vice versa. In such situations, in order to determine the priority, the court must compare both the perfection of a transfer of the receivable and the perfection of a security right in the receivable. This is examined in section 3-5-1.

The second perspective is to determine what a potential transferee should investigate before executing a transfer contract or security right contract in order to secure his priority over any prior transferee of or secured creditor in the receivable. It demonstrates the complexity of investigations that have to be made under the current laws by a potential transferee. This is examined in section 3-5-2.

The six questions are based on the following case study:

— C is a company. In this case study, C (who is a transferor and a grantor) is a legal person (company), not a natural person.
— C is a creditor of D. C has a receivable R owed by D. D is the debtor of the receivable R. C sells its receivable to E for receivables financing such as factoring, block discounting or securitisation. C transfers the receivable to E. E is a transferee of the receivable.
— Further, C arranges for a loan from S, using its receivables as security. S is a secured creditor with a security right in C's receivables, including the receivable R that is owed by D. C also transfers the receivable R to E2, making E2 another transferee of the receivable R. C arranges for another loan from S2, using its receivables R as security, thus making S2 another secured creditor with a security right in the receivable R.
— P is a potential transferee of the receivable R or a potential secured creditor with a security right in the receivable R.

3-2-3. Six Common Questions

Q1. What should the transferee E do to be perfected against the insolvency administrator of the transferor C in the event of C's insolvency? In other words, what should E do in order to make the receivable transferred to E not included in the insolvency estate of C?

Q2. What should the secured creditor S do to be perfected against the insolvency administrator of C in the case of C's insolvency? In other words, what should S do in order to be treated as a secured creditor in the insolvency procedures (reorganisation proceedings or liquidation proceedings) of C?

Q3. How is priority between E and E2 determined?

Q4. How is priority between S and S2 determined?

---

[6] See section 1-6.

Q5. How is priority between E and S determined?

Q6. What should a potential transferee P check before executing the transfer contract or the security right contract in order to secure priority over any prior transfer of or security right in the receivable R?

3-2-4. Table of Preliminary Answers

Table 3.1 below shows the answers to the six common questions asked for the 15 jurisdictions listed above. Details of the answers to the six common questions are elaborated upon in section 3-7, which provides answers to the same six questions regarding the requirements for perfection against different parties. This allows direct comparisons to be made among the different jurisdictions.

Table 3.1 simplifies the answers and uses abbreviations for the answers. In this table, 'notice' means notice to the debtor of the receivable. For example, in most jurisdictions, effectiveness against a debtor of a receivable is achieved by notification to the debtor of the receivable. In particular, in Korea, Japan and France, notice to the debtor requires specific formality stipulated by law. Such notice with specific formality under the law is indicated as 'formal notice'.

In Table 3.1, 'registration' means registration. In Korea especially, there are two methods of registration for transfers of receivables and security rights in receivables. The first registration at the Financial Services Commission of Korea under the ABS Act[7] and the MBA Company Act[8] is indicated as 'securitisation registration', and the second registration in the Korean Security Registration Act is indicated as 'registration'.

For the purposes of Table 3.1, 'agreement' means the conclusion of the transfer or security right agreement. 'Notarised contract' means the notarisation of the contract or registration of the contract at the Tax Registration Department (Belastingdienst/Registratie en successie) in the Netherlands. 'Transfer deed' means a transfer deed (*bordereau*) in France, and 'Company book' means a record in the company book of the transferor in Austria, which is a perfection method for a pledge of receivables.

In Table 3.1, 'debtor' means enquiring of the debtor of the receivable whether it received notice of a prior transfer or security right. In the jurisdictions where priority is determined by the order of notice to the debtor of the receivable, a potential transferee should ask the debtor of the receivable to check whether there is any prior transfer of or security right in a receivable. Even though in Germany, Austria and the Netherlands, it is not required to give notice to the debtor of the receivable for perfection and therefore enquiring of the debtor would not necessarily give a complete picture, a potential transferee is still advised to ask this of the debtor.

---

[7] See section 2-4-4-4-1.
[8] See section 2-4-4-4-2.

Table 3.1: Summary table of answers

	Group R			Group RN		Group N		Group SR		Group C		
	US	Canada	New Zealand	Australia	Korea	Japan	France	Belgium	England Singapore Hong Kong	China	Germany	Austria	The Netherlands
Q1	registration	registration	agreement	registration	securitisation registration, formal notice	registration, formal notice	formal notice, transfer deed	agreement	agreement	notice	agreement	agreement	notarised agreement, notice
Q2	registration	registration	agreement	registration	registration, formal notice	registration, formal notice	agreement, transfer deed	agreement	registration	registration	notice	company book, notice	notarised agreement, notice
Q3	registration	registration	registration	registration	securitisation registration, formal notice	registration, formal notice	formal notice, transfer deed	notice	notice, constructive notice	agreement	agreement	agreement	notarised agreement, notice
Q4	registration	registration	registration	registration	registration, formal notice	registration, formal notice	agreement, transfer deed	notice	notice, constructive notice	registration	notice	company book, notice	notarised agreement, notice
Q5	registration	registration	registration	registration	securitisation registration, registration, formal notice	registration, formal notice	formal notice, agreement, transfer deed	notice	notice	registration, notice	agreement, notice	agreement, company book, notice	notarised agreement, notice
Q6	registration	registration	registration	registration	securitisation registration, registration, debtor	registration, debtor	debtor	debtor	registration, debtor	registration, debtor	debtor	debtor	debtor

3-3. Priority

3-3-1. Priority of Transfers vis-a-vis Third Parties (Question 3)

For the convenience of explanation, section 3-3 explores the answers to Questions 3 and 4 first prior to the answers to Questions 1 and 2, which will be examined in section 4-7.

Section 3-3-1 analyses priority of absolute transfers only. The priority of security rights are addressed in section 3-3-2. In Korea, France, China, Germany and Austria, the perfection of a transfer of receivables against third parties is different from the perfection of a *security right* in receivables against third parties. In the other jurisdictions, they are the same.

If a transfer of a receivable is perfected against third parties, it has priority over third parties. Perfection against third parties preserves priority among competing transferees and secured creditors. In principle, the transferee that first achieves perfection against third parties has priority over the other transferees.

Perfection against third parties can be achieved by publicity such as: (i) notification of the transfer of the receivable to the debtor of the receivable; (ii) registration; and (iii) conclusion of the transfer agreement.

3-3-2. Notification

3-3-2-1. Notice of the Transfer to the Debtor

In many jurisdictions, priority between competing transferees is determined by the time order in which a debtor receives notice of the transfer. Accordingly, notification to the debtor is required for perfection of the transfer. In Korea, Japan, France, Belgium, England and China, priority between competing transferees is determined by the time order in which the account debtor receives notice of the transfer.

In Korea and Japan, a transferor must give notice of the transfer to the debtor to perfect the transfer against competing transferees, the insolvency administrator and an execution creditor of the transferor.[9] If the transferor becomes insolvent and no notice of the transfer has been given to the debtor, the insolvency administrator prevails over the transferee and therefore the transfer is void and ineffective against any third party, including the insolvency administrator.

The French Civil Code stipulates that a transfer is perfected against third parties only by the transferor's or the transferee's notification of the transfer with an

---

[9] Korean Civil Code, art 450(2); Japanese Civil Code, art 467(2).

official letter (*signification*) to the debtor.[10] It also stipulates that, alternatively, the transfer may be made effective against third parties by the debtor's acceptance of the transfer in a notarised deed (*acte authentique*).[11] Such notification is also required for effectiveness against the debtor. Until notification, the debtor may discharge the debt by paying the transferor (original creditor) regardless of any actual knowledge of the transfer on the part of the debtor.[12] Korea and Japan follow this approach of the French Civil Code, except that they generally omit such strict formality requirements.

In Korea and Japan, the transfer of a receivable is not effective against the debtor of a receivable unless the transferor gives notice of the transfer to the debtor or the debtor has consented to the transfer.[13] Furthermore, for perfection against third parties and priority, such notification requires formality of a certified document with a fixed date stamp.[14] However, in order to sue the debtor, notice of the transfer to the debtor does not require any formality.

English law takes the opposite position from the laws of Korea and Japan with respect to the formality of notification for priority and for suing the debtor. According to the holding of *Dearle v Hall*,[15] priority between competing transferees is determined by the time order that the debtor receives notice of the transfer. This is the 'first in time' rule. Therefore, notice of the transfer to the debtor is required for priority. Such notice does not require any formality. However, to sue the debtor, notification to the debtor must be in writing.[16]

However, under English law, notification is not required for perfection against the insolvency administrator. A transfer without notice to the debtor is still valid as an equitable assignment.[17] The concept of 'equitable assignment' under English law, which does not require notice to the debtor,[18] does not exist in many civil jurisdictions, including France, Korea and Japan.

In France,[19] Korea[20] and Japan,[21] the priority of competing transferees and perfection in the insolvency of the transferor is determined according to the time order in which the debtor of the receivable receives notice of the transfer. In these

---

[10] French Civil Code, art 1690. See section 3-7-8 Q 1-1.
[11] French Civil Code, art 1690.
[12] James Leavy, 'France' in Sigman and Kieninger (n 4) 129.
[13] Korean Civil Code, art 450(1); Japanese Civil Code, art 467(1).
[14] Korean Civil Code, art 450(2); Japanese Civil Code, art 467(2).
[15] *Dearle v Hall* (1828) 3 Russ 1. In fact, the decision of *Dearle v Hall* relates to interests held in trust. According to the decision, if the equitable owner of an asset purports to dispose of his equitable interest on two or more occasions, the claimant who first notifies the trustee or legal owner of the asset shall have priority.
[16] In English law, the benefit of a contract may be transferred to a third party by a process called 'statutory transfer' under s 136(1) of the Law of Property Act 1925.
[17] See section 3-7-10 Q 3-2.
[18] See section 3-7-10 Q 1-1.
[19] French Civil Code, art 1690.
[20] Korean Civil Code, art 450.
[21] Japanese Civil Code, art 467.

countries, if the debtor of the receivable has not received notice of the transfer, the transfer is not effective against any third party other than the transferor and cannot be protected in the insolvency of the transferor; thus, the transferred receivable would be included in the insolvency estate of the transferor. The English law principle that an equitable assignee may defeat a trustee in bankruptcy (insolvency administrator) has no equivalent counterpart in these civil law jurisdictions, France, Korea and Japan. This indicates how essential it is to give notice of the transfer to the debtor of the receivable in these jurisdictions. However, giving notice of the transfer to debtors of receivables is time-consuming and costly. Thus, it has been an obstacle to receivables financing, especially to transfers of future receivables and bulk transfers of receivables.[22]

Under *Dearle v Hall*, there is an exception to the first in time rule. If a subsequent transferee (E2) knew of the prior transfer at the time of his transfer, even if the subsequent transferee (E2) gave notice of the transfer to the debtor earlier than the prior transferee (E1) or while the prior transferee (E1) does not give notice to the debtor, the subsequent transferee (E2) cannot have priority over the prior transferee (E1).[23] Thus, under English law, priority is influenced by the subsequent transferee's knowledge of the prior transfer.

This is different from the approaches taken in France, Korea and Japan. In these jurisdictions, priority is determined by the time order of notice to the debtor, regardless of the subsequent transferee's knowledge of the prior transfer. Thus, even though a subsequent transferee (E2) knew of the prior transfer at the time of his transfer, he may still have priority over the prior transferee (E1) by earlier notification of his transfer to the debtor. This is because prior transfer without notification to the debtor is not perfected against the subsequent transferee (E2). Under the French, Korean, and Japanese Civil Codes, a transfer of receivables is not perfected against third parties unless the debtor is notified of the transfer.

3-3-2-2. *Transferees not Entitled to Give Notice to the Debtor of the Receivable*

In some jurisdictions, only the transferor is entitled to give notice of the transfer of the receivable to the debtor of the receivable. Under the Korean and the Japanese Civil Codes, in order to perfect a transfer of a receivable against third parties, a transferor is required to give notice of the transfer of the receivable to the debtor of the receivable, or the debtor of the receivable is required to consent to the transfer of the receivable.[24]

Only the transferor can give valid notice of the transfer of the receivable to the debtor by means of a certified document with a fixed date stamp in order to

---

[22] See section 4-6-1.
[23] *Dearle v Hall* (n 15); Beale et al (n 1) 437 [13.09]. See section 3-7-10 Q 3.
[24] Korean Civil Code, art 450; Japanese Civil Code, art 467.

perfect the transfer against third parties, including the insolvency administrator.[25] A transferee is not entitled to give such notice of the transfer of the receivable to the debtor of the receivable. Notice of a transfer of a receivable by a transferee is not effective to the debtor of the receivable. This is because a transferee is unfamiliar or unknown to the debtor of the receivable. Thus, a transferee needs the cooperation of a transferor to give notice of the transfer of the receivable to the debtor of the receivable.

However, in receivables financing, transferors do not want to give notice of the transfer of receivables to the debtors of the receivables because this might damage the transferor's financial health or credit reputation. Therefore, in practice, the transferor and the transferee do not usually give notice of the transfer of receivables to the debtors of the receivables, and the transferor reserves the right to collect debts from the debtors of the receivables even after the transfer of the receivables to the transferee.

If the transferor enters into insolvency proceedings before the transferor gives notice of the transfer to the debtors, the transferee himself cannot give notice of the transfer to the debtors. As a result, the transferee cannot claim the debt directly against the debtors and can only participate in the distribution process of the insolvency estate of the transferor as an unsecured creditor. This is a serious problem for the transferee. For this reason, in Korea and Japan, a transferee needs to ensure that the transferor gives notice of the transfer to the debtors before the transferor enters into insolvency proceedings. In receivables financing where too many debtors of receivables are involved, it is very expensive to give notice of the transfer to all of the debtors of receivables.

3-3-2-3. *Transferees Entitled to Give Notice to the Debtor of the Receivable*

In many jurisdictions, both a transferor and a transferee may give notice of the transfer of the receivable to the debtor of the receivable. In these jurisdictions, when a transferee gives notice of the transfer of the receivable to the debtor of the receivable, the transferee needs evidence to prove the fact that he is a lawful transferee to the debtor of the receivable.

Under UCC Article 9 of the US, both a transferor and a transferee may give notice of the transfer of the receivable to the debtor of the receivable.[26] Where a transferee gives notice of the transfer of the receivable to the debtor of the receivable, the transferee 'shall seasonably furnish reasonable proof that the transfer has been made' if requested by the debtor.[27]

---

[25] By contrast, the debtor of the receivable may send consent to the transfer of the receivable to either the transferor or the transferee.
[26] UCC, s 9-404(a)(2). This stipulates that the rights of a transferee are subject to any defence or claim of the account debtor against the transferor, which accrue before the account debtor receives a notification of the assignment authenticated *by the transferor or the transferee*.
[27] ibid s 9-406(c).

In the US, France and Germany, both a transferor and a transferee may give notice of the transfer of the receivable to the debtor of the receivable. Under the French Civil Code, both a transferor and a transferee may give notice of the transfer of the receivable to the debtor of the receivable.[28] However, such notification to the debtor must be done by an official letter (*signification*) delivered by a court bailiff (*huissier*).[29]

Under German law, notice of the transfer of the receivable to the debtor of the receivable is not required for the transfer of the receivable to be effective.[30] Still, a transferee needs to give notice of the transfer of the receivable to the debtor of the receivable in order to sue the debtor of the receivable.[31] Where a transferee gives notice of the transfer to the debtor of a receivable, the transferee should deliver the document relating to the transfer of the receivable issued by the transferor to the debtor of the receivable. If a transferor has issued a document that relates to the transfer of the receivable to a transferee named in the document, the transferee's presentation of the document to the debtor of the receivable is equivalent to giving notice of the transfer of the receivable.[32] The debtor's obligation to the transferee is to perform only in exchange for the delivery of the document relating to the transfer of the receivable issued by the transferor.[33]

Under the Korean and the Japanese Civil Codes, a transferee cannot give notice of the transfer to the debtor. However, there are exceptions under special acts. According to the Korean Security Registration Act,[34] the Korean ABS Act, the Korean MBS Company Act[35] and the Japanese Transfer Registration Act,[36] a transferor and a transferee (or a grantor and a secured creditor) are both entitled to give notice of the transfer of or the security right in a receivable to the debtor of the receivable by delivering a certificate of registration.[37] This is because a certificate of registration can evidence the transfer of or the security right in the receivable.[38]

---

[28] French Civil Code, art 1691. This stipulates that a debtor of a receivable may be discharged of the debt by paying the transferor before the debtor has been given notice *by the transferor or the transferee*.
[29] ibid art 1690.
[30] See section 3-7-12 Q 1-1.
[31] Even though notice of the assignment to the debtor is not required by law, it is typical to notify the debtor that the receivable is transferred to the transferee before filing a lawsuit against the debt. No one would file such a lawsuit without first asking the debtor to pay the debt.
[32] German Civil Code, s 409(1).
[33] ibid s 410(1).
[34] Act No 10366, enacted on 10 June 2010, entered into force on 11 June 2012.
[35] Korean ABS Act, art 7(1); Korean MBS Company Act, art 6(1). Both a transferee and a transferor are entitled to give effective notice of the assignment to the debtor of the receivable if the securitisation plan, according to which the receivables are transferred, is filed at the Financial Services Commission of Korea.
[36] Act No 87 of 2005, amended on 26 July 2005 and entered into force on 3 October 2005.
[37] Korean Security Registration Act, art 35(2); Japanese Transfer Registration Act, art 4(2).
[38] Under the Korean Security Registration Act, both a security provider and a secured creditor are required to apply for a registration of a security interest. Under the Japanese Transfer Registration Act, both a transferor and a transferee are required to apply for a registration of an assignment. As a result, once a security interest or an assignment is registered, it means that a security provider or a transferor has agreed on the registration unless its consent is fraudulent in some way. See section 2-8-2-3.

3-3-2-4. Perfection against the Debtor of the Receivable

Notice of the transfer of the receivable to the debtor of the receivable entitles the transferee to sue the debtor of the receivable. If the debtor of the receivable has received notice of the transfer, the transferee can sue and collect the receivable from the debtor. Thus, the debtor needs to be notified of the transfer.[39] In both a transfer of and a security right in a receivable, notice of the transfer or the security right to the debtor of the receivable is required for the transferee or the secured creditor to directly sue the debtor of the receivable. Where a transferee who is unfamiliar or unknown to the debtor of the receivable gives notice of the transfer to the debtor, the transferee must present the debtor with evidence of the transfer.

3-3-2-5. Set-off

In the transfer of a claim, the debtor of the claim may preserve his rights of set-off even after the transfer of the claim. This is because the rights of the transferee against the debtor of the claim could be no more than the rights enjoyed by the transferor.[40]

A debtor may rely on the cross-claims, which the debtor could enforce against the transferor until notified of the transfer, against a transferee. A debtor may set off against a transferee the cross-claims that the debtor has against the transferor only to the extent that such cross-claims are accrued until notified of the transfer.[41] Notice of the transfer to the debtor of the receivable prevents the debtor from setting off any cross-claims that the debtor has against the transferor that arise after notice to the debtor. Once the debtor receives notice of the transfer, the debtor cannot reduce his liability to the transferee by the set-off arising after the debtor receives notice of the transfer. The law should not protect the debtor's right of set-off where the debtor has voluntarily obtained his cross-claims against the transferor with knowledge that the transferor already transferred the claim to the transferee.[42] Such set-off is related to the notice of the transfer of the claim.

For such set-off, the debtor's cross-claim does not have to be closely connected to the transferor's claim.[43] At the time when the debtor receives notice of the

---

[39] Naturally, a creditor would first ask the debtor to pay the debt before bringing the case to the court. If a transferee sues a debtor without giving notice of the assignment, a court would deny the transferee's claim on the fact that the transferee does not have a proper cause of action.

[40] *Mangles v Dixon* (1852) 3 HLC 702, 10 ER 278, PC; James LJ in *Phillips v Lovegrove* (1873) LR 16 Eq 80, 88.

[41] It is not a mandatory rule, and thus a debtor may voluntarily waive any defences or rights of set-off before or even after being notified of the transfer. Article 31(40 of the Cape Town Convention and art X(3) of its Space Protocol stipulate the obligor's waiver of defences and rights of set-off by agreement in writing.

[42] Roy Goode and Louise Gullifer, *Goode on Legal Problems of Credit and Security*, 4th edn (London, Sweet & Maxwell, 2008) 320 [7-67].

[43] ibid 298–99 [7-36].

transfer of the claim, the cross-claim does not have to fall due for payment or be payable,[44] but the debtor's cross-claim against the transferor must have arisen and accrued before the debtor receives notice of the transfer. Set-off is excluded in some receivables which are likely to be transferred, such as certain bank loans.

Such set-off is statutory set-off in many jurisdictions because there are provisions regulating such set-off. Under English law, such set-off is referred to as independent set-off, as opposed to equitable or transaction set-off. Under English law, independent set-off can arise in relation to receivables subject to a floating charge, until both the floating charge has crystallised and the debtor of the receivable receives notice of the crystallisation.

There is another type of non-contractual set-off under English law besides the independent set-off explained above. This is the equitable or transaction set-off, which does not exist in civil law jurisdictions. For equitable set-off, the debtor's cross-claim must be closely or inseparably connected to the transferor's claim.[45] An equitable set-off will arise when a claim and a cross-claim are so closely connected that it would be inequitable for the transferred claim to proceed without giving credit for the debtor's cross-claim[46] and that it would be unconscionable for a transferee to deny the debtor's cross-claim.[47] Close connection will exist only when the debtor's cross-claim impeaches the title of the transferor's claim.[48] The transferee takes the claim subject to equitable set-off, because the equitable set-off results in an impeachment of the title taken by the transferee.[49] Thus, equitable set-off will be permitted, even if the debtor's cross-claim accrues after the debtor receives notice of the transfer.[50]

3-3-3. Registration

The meaning of a registration system for the transfer of receivables is related to the different cultures of transfer in common law jurisdictions and civil law jurisdictions. In the US, Canada, New Zealand and Australia, priority is determined by the time order of registration. Under registration systems such as UCC Article 9 and the PPSAs of Canada, New Zealand and Australia, the transfer of receivables is perfected against third parties by registration, and priority between competing transferees is determined by the time order of registration. In these jurisdictions and in Japan, the registration system covers both transfers of receivables and security rights in receivables. In contrast, in the UK, Korea and China, the

---

[44] *Roxburghe v Cox* (1881) 17 Ch D 520, CA; *In Re Pinto Leite and Nephews* [1929] 1 Ch 221.
[45] *Bim Kemi AB v Blackburn Chemicals Ltd (No 1)* [2001] EWCA Civ 457; [2001] 2 Lloyd's Rep 93.
[46] R Derham, 'Recent Issues in Relation to Set-Off' (1994) 68 *Australian Law Journal* 331, 332.
[47] Gregory Tolhurst, *The Transfer of Contractual Rights* (Oxford, Hart Publishing, 2006) [8.64]–[8.65] 435–37.
[48] ibid [8.64] 436.
[49] ibid [8.65] 437.
[50] *Banco Central SA v Lingos & Falce Ltd (The Raven)* [1980] 2 Lloyd's Rep 266.

registration system covers only security rights in receivables, but does not cover transfers of receivables.

In the US, the filing system includes both security rights in and transfers of receivables.[51] In 1952, UCC Article 9 was drafted with the intent of unifying the rules regarding the perfection of transfers of receivables that varied among the states. UCC Article 9 includes not only security rights in receivables but also transfers of receivables.[52] Thus, the transferee only has to file a financing statement at the UCC filing office generally with the Secretary of State of the state where the transferor is located for the transferred receivable not to be included in the insolvency estate of the transferor in the insolvency of the transferor. Most of the laws on the transfer of receivables are stipulated not in general contract law, but in UCC Article 9. As a result, the laws on the transfer of receivables appear to be treated as a subsection of the broader laws regarding transfers of personal property security under UCC Article 9.[53] The creditor holding a security right in a receivable only has to file a financing statement at the UCC filing office of the state where the grantor is located for the creditor to be treated as a secured creditor in the insolvency procedures of the transferor.

The PPSAs of Canada, New Zealand and Australia also include both security rights in receivables and transfers of receivables. Under the PPSAs, registration of a transfer of a receivable is required for perfection of the transfer against third parties.[54] Priority between competing transferees is determined by the time order of filing or registration of the transfer.

In Japan, there is a registration system for the transfer of movable assets and receivables under the Japanese Transfer Registration Act. This also covers pledges of receivables.[55]

3-3-4. The Time of Creation Doctrine

3-3-4-1. Neither Notice nor Registration

In Germany,[56] Austria and the Netherlands, priority between competing transferees is determined according to the order of conclusion of the transfer contract,

---

[51] UCC, s 9-109(a)(3).

[52] ibid s 9-310(a). UCC art 9 applies to the transfers of accounts, chattel paper, payment intangibles and promissory notes (s 9-109(a)(3)), as well as all security rights in personal property (s 9-109(a)(1)). 'Payment intangible' refers to general intangibles where the debtor's primary obligation is monetary (UCC, s 9-102(a)(61)).

[53] Hein Kötz, 'Rights of Third Parties: Third Party Beneficiaries and Transfer' in Arthur von Mehren (ed), *International Encyclopedia of Comparative Law*, vol 7, ch 13 (Tubingen, Möhr, 1992) 56.

[54] Saskatchewan PPSA, s 35(2); Ontario PPSA, s 30(1)1; New Zealand PPSA, s 66; Australian PPSA, ss 267, 267A.

[55] Japanese Transfer Registration Act, art 14.

[56] In Germany, if the transferee demands, the transferor must issue the transferee with a publicly certified document on the transfer, and the transferee must bear and advance the costs; German Civil Code, s 403. This is to verify the time of conclusion of the transfer contract. See section 3-7-12 Q 1-1.

regardless of notification to the debtor of the receivable. In Germany,[57] Austria and the Netherlands, notice to the debtor is not required for a transfer (*Zession*) of a receivable to be perfected in the insolvency of the transferor and for the transferred receivable to be excluded from the insolvency estate of the transferor. Therefore, a transfer without notice is absolutely valid. The distinction between the statutory assignment and the equitable assignment under English law does not exist in these jurisdictions. The prior transferee in terms of the time of the transfer agreement has priority, regardless of notification.

Until the debtor receives notice of the transfer, the debtor of the receivable may discharge the debt by paying the transferor (the original creditor). In the case of double transfers, in which the transferor makes a transfer to a transferee (the first transferee) and subsequently makes another transfer to another transferee (the second transferee), the debtor who did not receive notice of the first transfer from the transferor may also discharge the debt by paying the second transferee if the second transferee presents the document evidencing the transfer issued by the transferor.[58] In Germany, Austria and the Netherlands, however, the second transferee must surrender the money to the first transferee once the second transferee has collected the debt from the debtor, because the first transferee has priority over the second transferee. This is the case even though the second transferee gave proper consideration to the transferor and knew nothing of the first transfer.[59] The second transferee may cancel the transfer contract with the transferor and make a claim for damages from the transferor. In Germany, the date of the transfer is verified by a publicly certified document evidencing the transfer (if it is issued), which a transferor must issue upon a transferee's demand.[60]

In a jurisdiction following the German approach where notice to debtors is not required for the transfer, priority between transferees, the insolvency administrator and an execution creditor is determined according to the time order of (a) conclusion of the transfer agreement, (b) bankruptcy adjudication or (c) attachment notice.

The German concept of the transfer of receivables is peculiar in that it has an *in rem* (*dingliche* in German) nature. Once a receivable is transferred to a transferee (E1), the transferor no longer has a right in the receivable and a later transfer by the transferor gives the subsequent transferee (E2) no right in the receivable.[61] A transfer is effective towards everyone (*erga omnes*) even if particular formality

---

[57] German Civil Code, s 398. In contrast, for a pledge of a receivable to be effective against third parties, the debtor of the receivable must be notified of the pledge; German Civil Code, s 1280. However, because of the inconvenience of notification, pledges of receivables are seldom used in practice in Germany.

[58] German Civil Code, s 410(1).

[59] See section 3-7-12 Q 3.

[60] Section 403 of the German Civil Code stipulates that the transferor must, upon demand, issue the transferee with a publicly certified document on the transfer. The transferee must bear and advance the costs.

[61] Julia Klauer Rakob, 'Germany' in Sigman and Kieninger (n 4) 112.

is not required.[62] The German Civil Code does not require any publicity for the transfer of receivables. For this reason, there is no strong need to develop a registration system for the transfer of receivables. In Germany, a transferor functions as the information centre since the law requires that a potential transferee should consult with the transferor regarding the status of a receivable. This is sensible because the transferor is in the best position to report on the status of his own receivable.

How then could the law prevent a transferor from attempting double transfers of receivables? The German view on double transfers or fraudulent non-possessory security rights is that such conduct is a tort or breach of contract, so that the transferor who sells a receivable twice, or sells a receivable that has been pledged as security, will be liable for the damages incurred by third parties and be punished criminally.

3-3-4-2. The Delivery of the Transfer Deed (Bordereau)

Under the French Monetary and Financial Code, a transfer of receivables may be perfected against third parties by simple delivery of a transfer deed (*bordereau*).[63] A transferor must sign a transfer deed (*bordereau*) and the transferee must date it. The date of a '*Dailly* transfer'[64] is indicated on a transfer deed (*bordereau*). A transfer deed (*bordereau*) is made between a transferor and a transferee without any involvement or verification of a third party or even the debtor of the receivable. Delivering a transfer deed (*bordereau*) is not the same as publishing it. It is neither a notice to a debtor nor a registration. A transfer deed (*bordereau*) is simply a written document, the provisions of which are stipulated by law, evidencing the date of the conclusion of the relevant contract.

The priority rule under the French Monetary and Financial Code is, from a functional point of view, close to the German law, where no notification is required for third-party effectiveness. To the extent that the French Monetary and Financial Code applies and a transfer deed (*bordereau*) could perfect a transfer of receivables,[65] the French regime for the transfer of receivables has almost the same effect as the German system.

First, in both the situation where *no* competing creditor gives notice to a debtor of the receivable and the situation where *all* competing creditors give notice to a debtor, the priority rule is the same in France and Germany. Priority is determined by the time order of conclusion of the relevant contract.

---

[62] Lina Aleknaitė, 'Why the Fruits of Capital Markets are Less Accessible in Civil Law Jurisdictions or How France and Germany Try to Benefit from Asset Securitisation' (2007) 5 *DePaul Business & Commercial Law Journal* 191, 219.

[63] French Monetary and Financial Code, arts L313-23–L313-34.

[64] '*Dailly* transfer' means a transfer of receivables in accordance with the *Dailly* Act, which was enacted in 1981 and incorporated into the Monetary and Financial Code as arts L313-23–L313-34 in 2000.

[65] See section 3-7-8 Q 1-2.

By comparison, under Korean and Japanese law, if *no* competing creditor gives notice of the transfer of a receivable, the debtor of the receivable may pay the transferor (the original creditor) and competing creditors could only claim against the transferor.

In the situation where *one* competing transferee gives notice to the debtor of the receivable and the others do not, in France, the transferee who gave notice to the debtor has priority over any other transferees who have not given notice to the debtor. This is different from the priority rules under the German Civil Code.

Let us suppose a case where C is a transferor, E1 and E2 are transferees and the transfer to E1 is prior to the transfer to E2. In Germany, if E2 gives notice of the transfer of the receivable to the debtor of the receivable and requests the debtor to pay the debt to him (E2) by showing the transfer contract between C and E2, the debtor without knowledge of the prior transfer to E1 may discharge its debt by paying E2. Still, E1 has priority over E2 between E1 and E2, and thus E1 can claim against E2 for unjust enrichment. E2 can then claim against C for breach of the transfer contract.

In France, if E1 has not given notice of the transfer to the debtor of the receivable, E2 may request the debtor of the receivable to pay the debt to him (E2), and the debtor may discharge its debt by paying E2. In this regard, France is the same as Germany. However, in France, E2, who gave notice of the transfer of the receivable to the debtor of the receivable while E1 does not give notice to the debtor, has priority over E1, who has not given notice to the debtor. Thus, unlike in Germany, E1 has no right to claim against E2 for unjust enrichment.[66]

In comparison, under Korean and Japanese law, if only E2 gives notice of the transfer to the debtor of the receivable while E1 does not give notice to the debtor, E2 has priority over E1 because only the transfer to E2 is effective against the debtor of the receivable as well as third parties.[67]

The primary difference between French law and German law lies in the scope of this priority regime focused on the time of creation and supplemented by notice. In France, this time-of-creation regime only applies to transfers and pledges under the French Monetary and Financial Code and pledges of receivables under the revised French Civil Code. By contrast, in Germany, the time-of-creation regime generally applies to the transfer of receivables, but not to pledges of receivables under the German Civil Code. In Germany, because of difficulties involving notification, a pledge of receivables is rarely used, whereas a security transfer is often used. Notification is not required for a security transfer in Germany,[68] since a security transfer is not a pledge, and therefore section 1280 of the German Civil Code does not apply to a security transfer of receivables.[69]

---

[66] If in theory, Y1 could be allowed to give notice to the debtor, even after the debtor of the receivable paid, Y1 might be able to have priority over Y2 and then accordingly sue Y2 for unjust enrichment.
[67] See section 3-7-6 Qs 1, 3-1 and section 3-3-7 Qs 1, 2, 3, 4-1.
[68] Klauer Rakob (n 61) 96–97.
[69] See section 3-7-12 Q 2-2.

Table 3.2: Comparison of outright sale of and security rights in receivables (where the transferor is a company)

		Requirement for perfection against third parties	
		Transfer of receivables	**Security rights in receivables**
R	US, Canada, New Zealand, Australia	Registration	
RN	Korea	Notice or filing at the Financial Services Commission	Notice or registration
	Japan	Notice or registration	
N	France	Notice	No publicity
	Belgium	No publicity	
SR	England Hong Kong Singapore	No publicity for equitable assignment	Registration at Companies House
		Notice for statutory assignment	
	China	Notice	Registration in the Credit Reference Centre
C	Germany	No publicity	Notice
	Austria	No publicity	Notice or recording in the company book of the transferor
	The Netherlands	Notice, notarisation of the deed or registration with the TRD[70]	

3-3-5. The Priority of Security Rights vis-a-vis Third Parties (Question 4)

This section analyses the perfection of *security rights* in receivables, comparing the difference between a security right in receivables and a transfer.

In the US, Canada, New Zealand, Australia, Japan, Belgium and the Netherlands, the requirement for perfection of a transfer of a receivable is *the same* as the requirement for perfection of a security right in a receivable.

In contrast, in France, England, Singapore, Hong Kong, China, Germany and Austria, the requirement for perfection of a security right in a receivable is *different* from the requirement for perfection of a transfer of a receivable. This difference

---

[70] Tax Registration Department (Belastingdienst/Registratie en successie).

means that a potential transferee should check both the perfection of a transfer and the perfection of a security right.

Under UCC Article 9 and the PPSAs of Canada, New Zealand and Australia, and in England and China, registration is required for the perfection of a security right in a receivable. Most existing registration systems are for security rights in movables assets and receivables. Under UCC Article 9 of the US and the PPSAs of Canada, New Zealand and Australia, as well as in Japan, the registration system covers security rights in movable assets and receivables, and transfers of receivables. In the US, Canada, New Zealand and Australia, the scope of the registration system has been expanded from charges over personal property including receivables to include outright transfers of receivables. Japan has the registration system for transfers of movable assets and receivables, and security rights (pledges) in receivables.

In contrast, in England, Korea and China, the registration system covers only security rights in movable assets and receivables, and includes only security rights in (and not transfers of) receivables.

In England, the Companies Act 2006 provides for registration of company charges. Under the Companies Act 2006 (Amendment of Chapter 25) Regulations 2013, all charges (including charges over receivables) created by a company can be registered in the register of charges at Companies House. Under English law, registration of charges created by a company does not guarantee priority.[71] The priority of competing charges is determined by the usual priority rules established at common law for the particular type of asset in question.[72] According to *Dearle v Hall*,[73] priority is determined by the time order in which the debtor receives notice of the charge. If fixed charge F1 is registered, fixed charge F2 will take the security right subject to F1 because of constructive notice.[74] *Dearle v Hall* does not apply to floating charges.

Korea has a registration system for security rights in movable assets and receivables. The Korean Security Registration Act provides for such a registration system. This Act only applies to security rights in receivables and does not apply to outright transfers of receivables.

China adopted registration systems for security rights in specified types of movable assets and receivables separately. Under the Chinese Property Law, a pledge of an account receivable becomes effective upon its registration in the Credit Reference Centre.[75] It must be registered to be perfected against third parties. Notification to the debtor is not required for the creation of a pledge.[76]

---

[71] Roy Goode and Ewan McKendrick, *Goode on Commercial Law*, 4th edn (London, Penguin, 2010) 705.
[72] ibid.
[73] *Dearle v Hall* (n 15).
[74] The second limb of *Dearle v Hall* (ibid).
[75] Chinese Property Law, arts 228 and 223(6).
[76] William Johnston (ed), *Security over Receivables: An International Handbook* (Oxford, Oxford University Press, 2008) 644.

The registration system is only for pledges of receivables and not for transfers of receivables. A transfer of a receivable does not have to be registered.

In Germany, notice to the debtor is required for a pledge of receivables and not for the transfer of receivables. For this reason, transfer of title for security purposes (*Sicherungsabtretung*) is used more frequently for security rights in receivables than the pledge of receivables to circumvent the notification requirement.[77]

In France, notice to the debtor is not required for a pledge of receivables since 2006.[78] As such, the German and French Civil Codes have contrasting approaches with respect to requirements for transfers and pledges. Nevertheless, in both German law and French law, notice to the debtor is not required for security transfers of receivables.

3-4. Perfection

Table 3.3: Perfection requirements (priority) for the transfer of receivables

Perfection against			Competing transferee	Execution creditor[79]	Insolvency administrator
US			Filing of the financing statement		
Canada			Registration		
New Zealand			Registration	Registration[80]	Agreement of the transfer
Australia			Registration		
Korea	a		Notice		
		sec[81]	Filing at the Financial Services Commission		
	Security		Notice or registration		
Japan			Notice or registration		
France	a		Notice		
		d[82]	Delivery of a transfer deed (*bordereau*)		
	Security		Conclusion of pledge contract		

(continued)

---

[77] See section 3-7-12 Q 2-2.
[78] See section 3-7-8 Q 2-1.
[79] An execution creditor is the creditor who has recovered a judgment against the debtor for his debt or claim and has caused an execution such as seizure or a garnish order to be issued thereon.
[80] New Zealand PPSA, s 103.
[81] Korean ABS Act; Korean MBS Act.
[82] *Dailly* Act; French Monetary and Financial Code.

Table 3.3: *(Continued)*

Perfection against		Competing transferee	Execution creditor	Insolvency administrator
Belgium		Notice	Agreement of the transfer	
England Singapore Hong Kong	cc[83]	Notice Registration	Equitable assignment	
China	transfer	Notice	Not certain	
	security	Registration in the Credit Reference Centre		
Germany	transfer	Conclusion of the transfer contract		
	security	Notice		
Austria	transfer	Conclusion of the transfer contract		
	security	Notice or recording on the company book of the transferor		
The Netherlands		Notice or notarisation of the deed or registration with the TRD[84]		

Note: a: transfer, d: transfer under the *Dailly* Act, security: security right, sec: securitisation, cc: charges over company book debts

3-4-1. Perfection of Transfers against the Insolvency Administrator (Question 1)

The most critical perfection is that against the insolvency administrator of the transferor.[85] The concept of 'insolvency administrator' in this book includes an insolvency representative, a receiver, a trustee in bankruptcy, a bankruptcy administrator in reorganisation procedures and a liquidator in liquidation procedures.

If the transfer of a receivable is perfected, the receivable that has effectively been transferred to the transferee is excluded from the insolvency estate of the transferor. This depends on the insolvency law of the jurisdiction. With respect to outright transfers of receivables, in England, Singapore, Hong Kong, New Zealand, Belgium, China, Germany and Austria, a transfer of receivables is perfected against an insolvency administrator of the transferor upon the conclusion of the transfer contract. In the US, Canada and Australia, for a transfer of a receivable, filing or registration is required for perfection against the insolvency administrator of the transferor and for the receivable to be excluded from the insolvency estate of the transferor.

---

[83] Charges over company book debts under the Companies Act 2006.
[84] Tax Registration Department (Belastingdienst/Registratie en successie).
[85] See section 4-8-4.

Table 3.4: Legal terms for insolvency administrators

	Insolvency administrator	
	Reorganisation	Liquidation
England	Administrator, receiver, trustee in bankruptcy[86]	Liquidator[87]
Singapore	Official Assignee, trustee in bankruptcy[88]	Liquidator[89]
Hong Kong	Receiver, trustee[90]	Liquidator[91]
Canada	Receiver, trustee[92]	Liquidator[93]
New Zealand	Assignee, receiver[94]	Liquidator[95]
Australia	Administrator[96]	Liquidator[97]
US	US trustee[98] (bankruptcy administrator)	US trustee[99] (bankruptcy administrator)

In England, Singapore and Hong Kong, an equitable assignment under English law is perfected against the insolvency administrator, and thus the receivable assigned to the assignee by an equitable assignment without notification to the debtor of the receivable is not included in the insolvency estate of the assignor.[100] In New Zealand, an unregistered transfer of a receivable is perfected against the insolvency administrator of the transferor. In the other jurisdictions, the method of perfection against the insolvency administrator is the same as the method of perfection against third parties.

3-4-2. The Insolvency Administrator as a Transferee

In order for a transfer of a receivable to be perfected against an insolvency administrator of the transferor, the transfer must be perfected against third parties prior

---

[86] Insolvency Act 1986.
[87] ibid.
[88] Bankruptcy Act (Cap 20).
[89] Companies Act (Cap 50).
[90] Bankruptcy Ordinance (Cap 6).
[91] Companies Ordinance (Cap 622).
[92] Bankruptcy and Insolvency Act.
[93] Winding-up and Restructuring Act.
[94] Insolvency Act 2006.
[95] Companies Act 1993 Liquidation Regulations 1994.
[96] Corporations Act 2001.
[97] ibid.
[98] 11 US Code Section 11.
[99] 11 US Code Section 7.
[100] See section 3-4-1-3.

to the insolvency adjudication of the court or bankruptcy petition[101] in most jurisdictions other than England, Singapore, Hong Kong and New Zealand. If a transfer is perfected against third parties prior to the insolvency adjudication and an attachment, it is deemed to be perfected against the insolvency administrator and an execution creditor.

In France, Korea and Japan, upon the insolvency adjudication of the transferor, every right and every obligation of the transferor is considered to be transferred to the insolvency administrator of the transferor. Therefore, an insolvency administrator of the transferor is regarded as similar to a kind of transferee, in that an insolvency administrator of the transferor becomes in competition with other transferees. This is a critical difference between civil law jurisdictions and common law jurisdictions.[102] As a result, priority between a transferee and an insolvency administrator is determined according to the order in which the debtor receives notice of the transfer or the insolvency adjudication of the transferor is made.

Let us imagine a case where C transferred its receivable (C-D)[103] to E, and C subsequently filed for bankruptcy. T was appointed as the insolvency administrator. The perfection rule determines priority between E and T. The transfer of the receivables must be perfected against third parties before the insolvency adjudication or bankruptcy petition[104] in order for E to win against T.

Under UCC Article 9, a financing statement must be filed in order for the transfer to be perfected against third parties, including the insolvency administrator.[105] Likewise, under the PPSAs of Canada and Australia, the transfer of receivables must be registered in order to be perfected against the insolvency administrator in the insolvency procedures of the transferor.[106] If parties have not filed a financing statement of the transfer of the receivable, the transferred receivable might be included in the bankruptcy estates of the transferor upon the transferor's insolvency and the transferee might lose his rights. This is a policy decision to punish a transferee for not having registered or filed a transfer of a receivable.

In the jurisdictions where publicity is not required, such as Germany and Belgium, a transferee can assert a transfer of a receivable against the insolvency administrator of the transferor if the transfer contract is concluded before the insolvency adjudication is made.[107]

---

[101] In the US: 11 US Code, s 362(a).
[102] Upon attachment, the attached receivable is considered to be transferred to a judgment creditor. So, a judgment creditor is also regarded as a kind of transferee. As a result, priority between a transferee and a judgment creditor is determined according to the order in which the debtor receives a notice of the transfer or an attachment notice.
[103] '(C-D)' indicates that the receivable is C's monetary claim against D and that C is the creditor and D is the debtor of the receivable.
[104] In the US: 11 US Code, s 362(a).
[105] See 3-7-2 Qs 1, 2.
[106] See 3-7-3 Qs 1, 2 and 3-3-5 Qs 1, 2.
[107] See 3-7-12 Q 1-1 and 3-3-9 Q 1.

3-4-3. The Insolvency Administrator as a Trustee

3-4-3-1. Equitable Assignment under English Law

In English law, the original common law rule was that a chose in action was not transferable, with only a few permitted exceptions.[108] However, equity took the view that a chose in action is property which ought to be transferable in the interests of commercial convenience, eg, to provide security for a loan.[109] Even when equity gave effect to a transfer of a legal right, equity did not enforce the transferee's claim, which was enforced in the common law courts and in the transferor's name.[110] An equitable assignee must join the assignor in any proceedings against the debtor of the receivable to enforce the thing in action,[111] as either a co-claimant or a co-defendant.[112]

Section 25(6) of the Judicature Act 1873 introduced a form of statutory assignment effect at law, which is a variant of the equitable system. Under section 136(1) of the Law of Property Act 1925, the benefit of a contract may be transferred to a third party by a process called 'statutory assignment'. Only if the requirements of section 136(1) of the Law of Property Act have been met may the transferee claim directly against the debtor of the receivable without joining the transferor.

As a result, there are two kinds of assignment under English law: a statutory assignment and an equitable assignment. A statutory assignment is an assignment that satisfies the requirements stipulated in section 136(1) of the Law of Property Act 1925.[113] Section 136(1) of the Law of Property Act 1925 stipulates three requirements: (1) that the assignment must be expressed in writing; (2) that notice of the assignment must be given to the obligor in writing; and (3) that the assignment must be of the whole of the obligation, ie, not merely part of the choses or an assignment of future or contingent rights.

An equitable assignment is the assignment which does not fulfil the requirements of a statutory assignment stipulated in section 136(1) of the Law of Property Act 1925. For example, an assignment without a written notification to the debtor is an equitable assignment. The chief difference between the two types

---

[108] There were two main reasons for non-assignability. The first reason was that the personal relationship between the debtor and the creditor forbids the substitution of any other party for the original creditor. The second reason was that the transfer of a chose in action would multiply contentions and suits and bring about great oppression of the people including terre-tenants (eg, *Lampet's* Case (1612) 10 Co Rep 46b). See Oshley Roy Marshall, *Transfer of Choses in Action* (London, Pitman, 1950) 35–36.

[109] Guenter Treitel, *The Law of Contract* (London, Sweet & Maxwell, 2003) 674.

[110] Tolhurst (n 47) [8.83] 452-53.

[111] *Three Rivers District Council v Governor and Company of the Bank of England* [1996] QB 292, 298, 308–09, CA.

[112] *Holt v Heatherfield Trust Ltd* [1942] 2 KB 1.

[113] Section 9 of the Law Amendment and Reform (Consolidation) Ordinance (Cap 23) of Hong Kong and s 4(8) of the Civil Law Act of Singapore are equivalent to s 136(1) of the Law of Property Act 1925.

of assignment is that a statutory assignee can sue the debtor in his own name, whereas an equitable assignee cannot sue the debtor himself in his own name, but must join the assignor as a party in any such proceedings to sue a debtor.

Not only statutory assignments but also equitable assignments are perfected against the insolvency administrator and execution creditors of the transferor.[114] Thus, notice of the transfer to the debtor of the receivable is not required for perfection against the insolvency administrator and execution creditors of the transferor. As such, under English law, perfection against the insolvency administrator and execution creditors of the transferor differs from priority against competing third parties.

Unless it is a security transfer that must be registered, a transferee can assert an equitable assignment against the insolvency administrator of the transferor even without giving notice of the equitable assignment of the receivable to the debtor of the receivable. The transfer contract is valid between the transferor and the transferee regardless of whether notice of the transfer is given to the debtor of the receivable.

Under English law, an insolvency administrator functions like a trustee of the insolvent transferor. An insolvency administrator must fulfil every obligation that the insolvent transferor should have fulfilled. Before notification of the transfer of the receivable to the debtor of the receivable, the transferee cannot collect the money from the debtor of the receivable. Thus, the transferor is obliged to collect the money from the debtor and give the money to the transferee. Likewise, an insolvency administrator is also obliged to collect the money from the debtor for the transferee. The transferor or the insolvency administrator of the transferor should hold the money on trust for the transferee.

An equitable assignment is still perfected against the insolvency administrator without giving notice of the transfer to the debtor of the receivable. Thus, regardless of whether notice of the transfer is given to the debtor of the receivable, the receivable transferred to the transferee is separated from the insolvency estate of the transferor under English law.

The transferor generally wishes to maintain its relationship with its customers (account debtors of receivables) and to continue to collect the receivables. For this reason, notice of the transfer is initially not normally given to the debtor of the receivable in common law jurisdictions. In the case of the transferor's insolvency or reneging on the debt, the transferee himself can give notice of the transfer to the debtors under English law. A transferee may give notice of the transfer to the debtor if and when necessary.

3-4-3-2. New Zealand

New Zealand has a registration system under the New Zealand PPSA, which covers both security rights in and transfers of receivables. The interest of an assignee

---

[114] *Holt* (n 112).

should be registered in the PPS Registry in order to be perfected against third parties and execution creditors.[115] An assignment of a receivable is perfected against third parties, including execution creditors, upon registration in the PPS Registry, with the exception for the insolvency administrator.

Perfection against the insolvency administrator is different from perfection against other third parties in New Zealand, where there is no provision that declares unregistered interests to be void against the insolvency administrator or a company liquidator.[116] As a result, an unregistered security interest in a receivable is perfected against the insolvency administrator of the grantor.[117] An unregistered transfer of a receivable is also perfected against the insolvency administrator of the transferor. This is different from the PPSAs of Canada and Australia.[118] In addition, the Property Law Act 2007 of New Zealand abolished the notification requirement for a statutory assignment.[119]

3-4-4. Perfection of Security Rights in the Insolvency Procedures of the Grantor (Question 2)

In order for a security right in a receivable to be perfected in the insolvency procedures of the grantor, it must be perfected against third parties by registration or notice to the debtor or by creation of the security right according to the applicable national domestic laws prior to the insolvency adjudication or bankruptcy petition.[120] If a security right in a receivable is perfected against the insolvency administrator of the grantor, the creditor having the security right will be treated as a secured creditor in the insolvency procedures (reorganisation proceedings or liquidation proceedings) of the grantor.

In the US, Canada and Australia, filing or registration is required for perfection of a security right in a receivable against the insolvency administrator of the grantor. Under registration systems such as UCC Article 9 and the PPSAs of Canada and Australia, the perfection method of a security right in a receivable is the same as the perfection method of a transfer of a receivable; both of them are registration.

In England, charges created by a company are required to be registered in the register of charges at Companies House for perfection against the insolvency

---

[115] New Zealand PPSA, s 103(1).
[116] Roger Fenton, *Garrow & Fenton's Law of Personal Property in New Zealand: Volume 2 Personal Property Securities*, 7th edn (Auckland, LexisNexis, 2010) 49 [2.2.18].
[117] ibid; New Zealand Law Commission, Report No 8, *A Personal Property Securities Act for New Zealand* (NZLC R8) (1989).
[118] Australian Attorney-General's Department, *Personal Property Securities Discussion Paper 2: Extinguishment, Priorities, Conflict of Laws, Enforcement, Insolvency* (March 2007) 85 [342].
[119] New Zealand Property Law Act 2007, s 50.
[120] In the US: 11 US Code, s 362(a).

administrator of the chargor.[121] All charges (including charges over receivables) created by a company can be registered in the register of charges at Companies House. If a charge created by a company is not registered within a period of 21 days (or such later time as is permitted by the court) beginning from the day after the date of creation of the charge,[122] it is not perfected against a liquidator, administrator and creditor of the company.[123]

In New Zealand, a security right in a receivable is perfected against third parties upon registration in the PPS Register. Nevertheless, an unregistered security interest in a receivable is perfected against the insolvency administrator in the insolvency procedures of the grantor.[124]

Table 3.5: Perfection of transfer and security right

		Perfection	
		Transfer	Security right
		What should the transferee do to be perfected against the insolvency administrator of the transferor?	What should the secured creditor do to be perfected against the insolvency administrator of the grantor?
		What should the transferee do in order to separate the transferred receivable from the insolvency estate of the transferor?	What should the secured creditor do in order to be treated as a secured creditor in the insolvency procedures (reorganisation proceedings or liquidation proceedings) of the grantor?
R	US Canada Australia	Registration	Registration
	New Zealand	Agreement of the transfer	Agreement of the security right
RN	Korea, Japan	Registration or notice	Registration or notice
N	France (*bordereau*)	Notice to the debtor	Agreement of the security right
	Belgium		Notice to the debtor

(continued)

---

[121] See section 3-7-10 Q 2. In addition, a general transfer of book debts by a person must be registered under the Bills of Sale Act 1878 in order to be perfected in the insolvency of the transferor: Insolvency Act 1986, s 344.
[122] Companies Act 2006 (Amendment of Chapter 25) Regulations 2013, s 859A(4).
[123] ibid ss 859H and 859F.
[124] Fenton (n 116) 49 [2.2.18]; New Zealand Law Commission (n 117).

Table 3.5: *(Continued)*

		Perfection	
		Transfer	**Security right**
SR	England Hong Kong Singapore China	Agreement of the transfer	Registration
C	Germany	Agreement of the transfer	Notice to the debtor
	Austria (recording in the book of the transferor company)	Agreement of the transfer	Recording in the book of the pledgor company
	The Netherlands	Registration with the TRD	Registration with the TRD

3-5. Check Points

3-5-1. Priority between Transfers and Security Rights (Question 5)

In the US, Canada, New Zealand, Australia, Japan, Belgium and the Netherlands, the same requirements apply to both determining priority of transfers of receivables and determining the priority of security rights in receivables.

In the US, Canada, New Zealand, and Australia, the priority of both transfers and security rights is determined by the time order of filing or registration.

In Japan, the priority of both transfers and security rights is determined by the time order of notice to the debtor or registration.[125]

In England, Singapore and Hong Kong, under English law, priority of both transfers and security rights is determined by the *Dearle v Hall* rule. Thus, priority is determined by the time order of notice to the debtor of the receivable. In addition, registration of charges over company book debts in the register of charges at Companies House may constitute constructive notice of the first transfer to the second transferee. So, if the first transfer is registered, the second transferee does not have priority, even though the second transferee gave notice of the second transfer to the debtor first.[126]

---

[125] See section 3-7-7 Qs 1, 2, 3, 4.
[126] ibid.

Check Points 97

In Belgium, with respect to both transfers and security rights, even though the notification requirement for perfection against third parties has been abolished after the revision of its Civil Code, priority is still determined by the time order in which the debtor of the receivable receives notice of the transfer of the receivable or the security right in the receivable.[127]

In the Netherlands, with respect to both transfers and security rights, priority is determined by the time order of notarisation of the contract, registration in the Tax Registration Department (*Belastingdienst/Registratie en successie*) or notice to the debtor of the receivable.[128]

In the other jurisdictions, priority of transfers is different from priority of security rights. For example, under the French Civil Code, notification is required for an outright transfer of a receivable, but notification is not required for a pledge of a receivable. The opposite is the case under the German Civil Code, where notification is not required for an outright transfer of a receivable, whereas notification is required for a pledge of a receivable. In these jurisdictions, in order to determine priority between transfers of and security rights in a receivable, both perfection of transfers and perfection of security rights must be compared.

In Korea, priority of transfers is determined by the time order of notice to the debtor of the receivable under the Korean Civil Code or registration under the Korean ABS Act or the MBS Company Act,[129] and priority of security rights is determined by the time order of notice to the debtor of the receivable under the Korean Civil Code or registration under the Korean Security Registration Act.[130]

Table 3.6: Conclusion of agreement v notice to the debtor

	France	Germany	Belgium	New Zealand
Perfection of transfer of receivable	notice	agreement	agreement	agreement
Perfection of security right in receivable	agreement	notice	agreement	agreement
Priority of transfers of receivable	notice	agreement	notice	registration
Priority of security rights in receivable	agreement	notice	notice	registration

---

[127] See section 3-7-9 Qs 3, 4, 5.
[128] See section 3-7-14 Qs 3, 4, 5.
[129] See section 3-7-6 Qs 1, 3.
[130] See section 3-7-6 Qs 2, 4.

3-5-2. The Potential Transferee's Check Points (Question 6)

When a potential transferee purchases a receivable from a transferor, there must be an investigation to determine whether the transferor is a legitimate right holder of the receivable, whether there was any prior transfer of the receivable and whether there was any prior security right in the receivable. Question 6 asks what a potential transferee should investigate and check before concluding the transfer or security contract in order to secure priority over any prior transfer of or security right in the receivable.

Table 3.7 below provides the answers to this question. It combines the information centre for perfection of an outright transfer of receivables and the information centre for perfection of a security right in receivables. In most cases, publicity is required for perfection, but there are exceptions where it is not required that perfection be publicised.[131] Unpublicised perfection produces hidden priority, which causes uncertainty in transactions with receivables. It is best for a potential transferee, buyer or investor to check all of the publicised perfection methods.

Table 3.7: Potential transferee's check points for prior transfers and security rights (answers to Question 6)

	Country	Potential transferee's check points	Unpublicised perfection
R	US	UCC Registry	
	Canada	PPS Register	
	New Zealand	PPS Register	
	Australia	PPS Register	
RN	Korea	Security Registry Financial Services Commission Debtor of the receivable	
	Japan	Transfer Registry Debtor of the receivable	
N	France	Debtor of the receivable	Delivery of a transfer deed (*bordereau*) Conclusion of pledge contract
	Belgium	Debtor of the receivable[132]	Agreement between the parties

(continued)

---

[131] For example, registration in the Tax Registration Department (Belastingdienst/Registratie en successie) in the Netherlands, conclusion of a contract in Germany and delivery of a transfer deed (*bordereau*) in France.

[132] A transfer or pledge of a receivable is perfected by conclusion of the transfer or pledge agreement, but priority is determined by the time order of notice of the transfer or pledge to the debtor of the receivable.

Table 3.7: *(Continued)*

	Country		Potential transferee's check points	Unpublicised perfection
SR	England Singapore Hong Kong	cc[133]	Debtor of the receivable	
			Register of charges at Companies House	
			Debtor of the receivable	
	China		Credit Reference Centre	
C	Germany		Debtor of the receivable	Agreement between the parties
	Austria		Debtor of the receivable	Agreement between the parties
	The Netherlands		Debtor of the receivable	Notarisation of a deed
				Registration with the TRD[134]

3-6. Classification of Jurisdictions

3-6-1. Classification

Table 3.8: Classification of jurisdictions

Group		The transferor or grantor is a company (legal person).		
		Priority		**Check point**
		What should a transferee (or secured creditor) do to achieve third-party effectiveness and priority over any other transferees or secured creditors?		What should a potential transferee check before concluding the transfer contract (or the security contract) in order to secure his priority over any prior transferee of or secured creditor in the receivable?
		Transfer	**Security right**	
R	US Canada New Zealand Australia	Registration	Registration	Registry
RN	Korea Japan	Registration or notice	Registration or notice	Registry and debtor of the receivable

(continued)

---

[133] Charges over a company's book debts.
[134] Tax Registration Department (Belastingdienst/Registratie en successie).

Table 3.8: *(Continued)*

N	France (*bordereau*)	Notice to the debtor	Agreement of the security right	Debtor of the receivable
	Belgium		Notice to the debtor	
SR	England Singapore Hong Kong China	Notice to the debtor	Registration	Registry and debtor of the receivable
C	Germany	Agreement of the transfer	Notice to the debtor	Debtor of the receivable
	Austria (recording in the book of the transferor company)	Agreement of the transfer	Recording in the book of the pledgor company	
	The Netherlands	Registration with the TRD	Registration with the TRD	

This book categorises jurisdictions into five groups according to: (i) the perfection method of transfers of and security rights in receivables where the transferor is a legal person; and (ii) the points that a potential transferee should check before concluding the transfer contract in order to ensure that there are no prior transferees or secured creditors of the receivable.

In the jurisdictions of Groups R and RN, a financier may perfect a transfer of receivables by registering them. The difference between Group R and Group RN is that in the jurisdictions of Group R, registration is the only method to perfect the transfer of receivables. In contrast, in the jurisdictions of Group RN, both registration and notice of the transfer to the debtor of the receivable are available methods to perfect the transfer of receivables. Therefore, in order to be certain that there is no prior transfer of or security right in the receivable, a potential transferee should both check the registry and ask the debtor of the receivable whether it received notice of a prior transfer of or security right in the receivable.

In the jurisdictions of Groups N and SR, a financier may perfect a transfer of receivables by notification of the transfer to the debtors of the receivables. The difference between Group N and Group SR is that in the jurisdictions of Group N, there is no registration system for transfers or security rights of movable assets or receivables. In contrast, in the jurisdiction of Group SR, there is a security rights registration system and security rights in the receivable are registered with the registry. Therefore, to ensure that there is no prior transfer of or security right in the receivable, a potential transferee should both check the registry and ask the

Classification of Jurisdictions 101

debtor of the receivable whether it received notice of a prior transfer of or security right in the receivable.

The jurisdictions of Group SR (England, Singapore and Hong Kong) have equivalent legislation and provisions.

Table 3.9: Equivalent legislation and provisions in Group SR (England, Singapore and Hong Kong)

England	Singapore	Hong Kong
Law of Property Act 1925, s 136(1)	Civil Law Act, s 4(8)	Law Amendment and Reform (Consolidation) Ordinance (Cap 23), s 9
Bills of Sale Act 1878	Bills of Sale Act (Cap 24)	Bills of Sale Ordinance (Cap 20)
Insolvency Act 1986	Bankruptcy Act (Cap 20)	Bankruptcy Ordinance (Cap 6)
s 344(2)	s 104(2)	s 48(1)
s 344(3)	s 104(3)	s 48(2)
Companies Act 2006 (Amendment of Chapter 25) Regulations 2013	Companies Act (Cap 50), Chapter IV, Division 8	Companies Ordinance (Cap 622), Chapter 8, Division 2
s 859A(1)	s 131(3)(f)	s 334(1)(d)
s 859A(2)	s 131(1)	s 335(1)
s 859A(4)—'21 days'	s 131(1)—'30 days'	s 335(5)(a)—'one month'
s 859F	s 137	s 346(1)(a)
s 859H(3)	s 131(1)	s 337(4)
Companies House	Accounting and Corporate Regulatory Authority	Companies Registry

In the jurisdictions of Group C, a financier may perfect a transfer of receivables by the conclusion of the transfer contract. However, due to German law regarding pledges of receivables, notice of the pledge to the debtor of the receivable is required. A potential transferee should ask the debtor of the receivable whether the debtor received notice of a prior pledge of the receivable to ensure that there is no other prior pledge of the receivable.

Austrian law with respect to the transfer of receivable is the same as German law. In addition, Austria has the recording system of pledges in the book of the pledgor company.

Under Dutch law, there are disclosed and undisclosed transfers of receivables and pledges of receivables. For a disclosed transfer or pledge of a receivable, notice of the transfer or pledge to the debtor of the receivable is required. Therefore, a potential transferee should ask the debtor of the receivable whether it received notice of a prior transfer or pledge of the receivable to ensure that there is no prior disclosed transfer or pledge of the receivable.

3-6-2. The Information Centre

One question to think about is which party should be the information centre where third parties may obtain information about a particular receivable. In jurisdictions where publicity is required, a potential transferee may seek the status of a receivable through a neutral third party (the registry, an account debtor etc) other than the direct counterparty to the contract. Publicity evidences the existence of the transfer of or security right in receivables through a neutral third party's confirmation.

A *registry* can be a neutral third party to confirm the transfer of or security right in receivables.[135] A neutral third party serves as an information centre for the public. In the jurisdictions of Groups R and RN, where the transfer of receivables needs to be registered or filed to be perfected against third parties, the law designates the registry as an information centre for security rights. For example, in the US, filing is required for perfection of the transfer of receivables, and therefore a third party can check the status of a receivable by referring to the filing registry.

A *debtor* of a receivable can also be a neutral third party to confirm the transfer or security right. The parties to a contract for the transfer of receivables are the transferor and the transferee. Thus, a debtor of receivables is not a direct party to a transfer contract. In the jurisdictions of Groups RN, N and SR, where notice of the transfer to a debtor is required for the perfection of a transfer of receivables against third parties, the law intends for a debtor of receivables to be an information centre so that anyone may seek the status of a receivable from the debtor. A potential transferee may inquire as to the status of a receivable by asking the debtor of the receivable, who must have been notified if there was any prior transfer of the receivable. In these jurisdictions, priority is determined by the time order in which a debtor receives notice of the transfer.

In the jurisdictions of Group C, where publicity is not required (for example, in Germany), a transfer of receivables does not have to be confirmed by a third party outside the parties to the contract. Priority among claimants is determined by the order of the conclusion of the transfer contracts rather than depending on publicity. Therefore, a potential transferee is not able to check the status of a receivable

---

[135] 'Registry' refers to the institution that fulfils the registration function. 'Register' refers to the physical file or database that contains all the information that has been registered, and 'registrar' refers to the person responsible for operating the registry (including the agent or the representative of the registrar with whom a user has contact). See EBRD, *Publicity of Security Rights: Guiding Principles for the Development of a Charges Registry* (2004) 4, fn 10, www.oas.org/dil/ebrd-publicity.pdf.

other than by asking the transferor. In these jurisdictions, investors have to trust and rely on the transferor, who is the direct counterparty to the contract. Thus, a transferor can function as an information centre.

3-7. Answers to the Six Common Questions

3-7-1. The Six Common Questions

Q1. What should the transferee E do to be perfected against the insolvency administrator of the transferor C in the event of C's insolvency? In other words, what should E do in order to make the receivable transferred to E not included in the insolvency estate of C?

Q2. What should the secured creditor S do to be perfected against the insolvency administrator of C in the event of C's insolvency? In other words, what should S do in order to be treated as a secured creditor in the insolvency procedures (reorganisation proceedings or liquidation proceedings) of C?

Q3. How is priority between E and E2 determined?

Q4. How is priority between S and S2 determined?

Q5. How is priority between E and S determined?

Q6. What should a potential transferee P check before executing the transfer contract or the security right contract in order to secure priority over any prior transfer of or security right in the receivable R?

	Transfer	Security right
Perfection	Question 1	Question 2
Priority	Question 3	Question 4
	Question 5	

3-7-2. The US

Qs 1, 2. Perfection

UCC Article 9 applies both to a transaction that creates a security interest in personal property[136] and a sale of accounts. Thus, the priority and perfection

---

[136] UCC, s 9-109(a)(1) and (3).

rules under UCC Article 9 apply to both a security interest in receivables and a transfer of receivables.[137] A 'security interest' includes any interest of a buyer of receivables.[138]

UCC Article 9 stipulates that a security interest is subordinate to the rights of a person that becomes a trustee in bankruptcy upon the filing of the bankruptcy petition before the security interest is perfected.[139] From the time when a bankruptcy petition is filed, it operates as a stay of any act to perfect any security interest against the property of the debtor.[140] Security interests in and transfers of receivables must be filed at the UCC filing office in the Secretary of State before a bankruptcy petition of the transferor is filed to the court in order to be perfected against the trustee in bankruptcy. A financing statement must be filed to perfect all security interests (including the transfer of a payment intangible).[141] 'Payment intangible' refers to only those general intangibles under which the debtor's main obligation is a monetary obligation.[142]

Qs 3, 4, 5. Priority

In the US, the priority of transfers of and security interests in receivables is determined by the order of filing the financing statement under UCC Article 9. A perfected security interest has priority over a conflicting unperfected security interest.[143] A filed transfer or security interest has priority over a conflicting transfer or security interest that is not filed.[144] Conflicting filed transfers or security interests are ranked according to priority in terms of time of filing.[145]

A financing statement may be filed before a security agreement is concluded or a security interest otherwise attaches, ie, advance filing.[146] Priority dates from the time of filing.[147] A security agreement may provide that collateral secures future advances, regardless of whether the advances are made.[148] If they are made, the priority established by the original filing applies to all future advances so long as the perfection is continuous.

---

[137] In the US, there is no need for a security transfer of receivables, because both an outright transfer of receivables and a charge over receivables should be filed under UCC art 9. For a security transfer of receivables, see section 1-4.

[138] UCC, s 1-201(b)(35) (providing that: "'Security interest' includes any interest of ... a buyer of accounts, chattel paper, a payment intangible, or a promissory note in a transaction that is subject to Article 9').

[139] ibid s 9-317(a)(2) and s 9-102(a)(52)(c).

[140] 11 US Code, s 362(a).

[141] ibid s 9-310(a).

[142] ibid s 9-102(a)(61).

[143] ibid s 9-322(a)(2).

[144] ibid s 9-322(b) The first transfer or security right to become effective has priority if conflicting transfers or security rights are not filed: ibid s 9-322(c).

[145] ibid s 9-322(a).

[146] ibid s 9-502(d).

[147] ibid s 9-322(a).

[148] ibid s 9-204(c).

Q6. The Potential Transferee's Check Points

A potential transferee only has to check the UCC Article 9 filing registry to confirm whether there is any prior transfer of or security interest in the receivable in question.

3-7-3. Canada

The Canadian provinces are governed by their respective provincial laws, which are similar in many respects but not identical. For the present purposes, the laws of Ontario and Saskatchewan will be examined.

Qs 1, 2. Perfection

In Canada, the registration system covers charges over personal property, including receivables and the outright sales of receivables. Under the Ontario PPSA, 'security interest' includes 'the interest of a transferee of an account', regardless of whether the interest secures the payment or performance of an obligation.[149] Under the Saskatchewan PPSA, 'security interest' includes 'the interest of a transferee pursuant to a transfer of an account' that does not secure payment or performance of an obligation.[150] Thus, the priority and perfection rules under the Saskatchewan and Ontario PPSAs apply to both a security interest in and a transfer of receivables.

Until perfected, a security interest in collateral is subordinate to the interest of a person who causes the collateral to be seized through execution, attachment, garnishment, charging order, equitable execution or other legal process.[151]

In order to be perfected against the insolvency administrator, a transfer of or a security interest in a receivable has to be registered before the insolvency of a transferor. A security interest in collateral is not perfected against a trustee in bankruptcy if a financing statement of the security interest is not registered at the date of bankruptcy.[152] A security interest in collateral is not perfected against a liquidator if a financing statement of the security interest is not registered on the day that the winding-up order is made.[153]

Registration is filed electronically at the PPS Register established under their respective PPSAs and does not require a signed authorisation from the debtor (grantor).[154]

---

[149] Ontario PPSA, s 1(1).
[150] Saskatchewan PPSA, s 2(1)(qq)(ii)(A).
[151] Ontario PPSA, s 20(1)(a).
[152] ibid s 20(1)(b); Saskatchewan PPSA, s 20(2).
[153] Ontario PPSA, s 20(1)(b); Saskatchewan PPSA, s 20(2).
[154] Simon Finch, 'Canada' in Johnston (n 76) 81 [6.13].

Qs 3, 4, 5. Priority

Under the Ontario and Saskatchewan PPSAs, in relation to transfers of and security interests in receivables, priority is determined by the time order of registration of financing statements.[155] If a transfer or a security interest is perfected by registration of a financing statement and another transfer or security interest is not, the registered transfer or security interest has priority over the unregistered transfer or security interest. If no transfers or security interests are registered, priority is determined by the time order of attachment.[156] Under the Ontario and Saskatchewan PPSAs, the financing statement may be registered before or after the security agreement is concluded by the debtor (grantor) and the secured creditor.[157] In fact, it is industry practice in Ontario to pre-register against a debtor (grantor), so that searches confirming no prior registrations may be obtained prior to funding.[158]

Q6. The Potential Transferee's Check Points

A potential transferee only has to check the PPS Register of the transferor's province[159] to confirm whether there is any prior transfer of or security interest in the receivable in question.

3-7-4. New Zealand

Qs 1, 2. Perfection

Under the New Zealand PPSA, a security interest includes 'an interest created or provided for by a transfer of an account receivable', whether or not the transfer secures payment or performance of an obligation.[160] The priority and perfection rules under the New Zealand PPSA apply to both a security interest in and a transfer of receivables with a few exceptions. Section 23 of the New Zealand PPSA lists the types of receivables to which it does not apply.[161] The Property Law Act 2007 of New Zealand abolished the notification requirement for a statutory assignment.[162]

A security interest is perfected if the security interest has attached and a financing statement has been registered in respect of the security interest.[163] Registration

---

[155] Ontario PPSA, s 30(1)1; Saskatchewan PPSA, s 35(2).
[156] Ontario PPSA, s 30(1)4.
[157] ibid s 45(3); Saskatchewan PPSA, s 43(4).
[158] Finch (n 154) 81 [6.13].
[159] In Canada, each province has an independent PPS Register as in the US.
[160] New Zealand PPSA, s 17(1)(b). The New Zealand PPSA is designed as a code for all transactions giving rise to security over personal property.
[161] Rights of such exceptions will be determined in accordance with existing common law and equitable principles. In order to achieve priority of these types of transfers, a transferee must give notice to the debtor in accordance with the rule in *Dearle v Hall*.
[162] New Zealand Property Law Act 2007, s 50.
[163] New Zealand PPSA, s 41(1).

of a financing statement needs to be done in the PPS Register at the Companies Office of New Zealand.

New Zealand does not have provisions that declare unregistered interests to be void against the insolvency administrator or a company liquidator.[164] As such, an unperfected security interest is still effective against the grantor and its insolvency administrator as an equitable security interest.[165] However, given that competing secured creditors may easily perfect their security interests, an unperfected security interest might be of little commercial value.[166]

An execution creditor has priority over unperfected security interests. A transfer of or security interest in a receivable is not perfected against an execution creditor if the transfer or security interest is not registered at the time of execution of a judgment.[167]

Qs 3, 4, 5. Priority

The rule in *Dearle v Hall*[168] continues to apply to interests that do not fall within the PPSA priority system. However, where the PPSA applies,[169] a transferee should ensure that the transfer is perfected by registration so as to preserve priority.[170]

A registered transfer of or security interest in receivables has priority over an unregistered transfer or security interest.[171] Priority between registered transfers of, between registered security interests in or between registered transfers of and registered security interests in the same receivables is determined according to the time order of registration of financing statements.[172] The transferee or secured creditor that was first to register a financing statement in respect of the transfer or security interest has priority, regardless of whether attachment occurred at the time of registration.

A financing statement may be registered before or after a security agreement is made, or a security interest has attached.[173] For this reason, it is common for a party that intends to take a security interest in a particular receivable to register a

---

[164] New Zealand Law Commission (n 117); Fenton (n 116) 49 [2.2.18].
[165] Australian Attorney-General's Department, *Discussion Paper 2 (Extinguishment, Priorities, Conflict of Laws, Enforcement, Insolvency), Review of the Law on Personal Property Securities* (March 2007) 85 [342].
[166] Matt Yarnell and Richard May, 'New Zealand' in Johnston (n 76) 403.
[167] New Zealand PPSA, s 103(1). 'Time of execution' means: (a) if the collateral is seized by an execution creditor or on an execution creditor's behalf, the time of seizure; or (b) in any other case, the time when a charging order or a garnishee order is made. See New Zealand PPSA, s 103(1A).
[168] *Dearle v Hall* (n 15).
[169] The New Zealand PPSA applies to account receivables. Under the New Zealand PPSA, 'account receivables' means a monetary obligation that is not evidenced by chattel paper, an investment security, or by a negotiable instrument, whether or not that obligation has been earned by performance (s 16).
[170] Fenton (n 116) 390 [9.14].
[171] New Zealand PPSA, s 66(a). Priority between unregistered transfers or security rights in the same receivables is determined by the order of attachment of the transfer or security right (s 66(c)).
[172] ibid s 66(b)(i).
[173] ibid s 146.

financing statement relating to that security interest in advance of the transaction being consummated.[174] If the security agreement extends to future advances, the priority established by the original registration applies to all future advances so long as the perfection is continuous.[175]

Q6. The Intending Transferee's Check Points

A potential transferee only has to check the PPS Register to confirm whether there is any prior transfer of or security interest in the receivable in question.

3-7-5. Australia

Qs 1, 2. Perfection

With respect to perfection and priority, the Australian PPSA unified the laws of each state. The Australian PPSA was passed in December 2009 and entered into force in May 2011. Under the Australian PPSA, a security interest includes 'the interest of a transferee under a transfer of an account', regardless of whether transaction concerned, in substance, secures payment or performance of an obligation.[176] A security interest in receivables includes a transfer of receivables. Therefore, the priority and perfection rules under the Australian PPSA apply to both a security interest in and a transfer of receivables.

Perfection is done by registration of a financing statement in the PPS Register at the Securities and Investments Commission of Australia. In order for a security interest to be perfected, the security: (i) must have attached to the collateral; (ii) must be enforceable against third parties; and (iii) must have its financing statement registered in the PPS Register.[177] The financing statement should contain detailed information of the security interest, for example, the parties involved and the collateral in concern. If not registered prior to a winding-up or bankruptcy, a transfer of or a security interest in receivables is not perfected upon such winding-up or bankruptcy of the transferor or grantor.[178]

An execution creditor has priority over unperfected security interests. The interest of an execution creditor in collateral has priority over any security interest in the same collateral that is not perfected at the time covered by the time of seizure or the time when an order is made by a court in respect of a judgment in relation to the execution creditor or when a garnishee order is made in relation to the execution creditor.[179]

---

[174] Yarnell and May (n 166) 394 [27.14].
[175] New Zealand PPSA, s 72.
[176] Australian PPSA, s 12(3)(a).
[177] ibid s 21(1).
[178] ibid ss 267 and 267A.
[179] ibid s 74(1) and (4).

Qs 3, 4, 5. Priority

A registered transfer of or security interest in certain receivables has priority over an unregistered transfer of or security interest in the same receivables.[180] Priority between registered transfers of, between registered security interests in or between registered transfers of and registered security interests in the same receivables is to be determined according to the time order in which a financing statement with respect to the transfer or security interest is registered.[181] A financing statement with respect to a transfer or security interest may be registered before or after it is made or attached.[182]

Q6. The Potential Transferee's Check Points

A potential transferee only has to check the PPS Register to confirm whether there is any prior transfer of or security interest in the receivable in question.

3-7-6. Korea

Qs 1, 3. Transfers

In Korea, an insolvency administrator of a transferor is treated as a third party, and therefore perfection against third parties includes perfection against the insolvency administrator. Thus, perfection against the insolvency administrator is the same as the perfection against third parties by which priority is determined. So, the answers to Questions 1 and 3 are the same. Perfection and priority are made and determined by notification of transfers under the Korean Civil Code or filing of securitisations under the ABS Act or the MBS Company Act.

Qs 1, 3-1. Transfer under the Korean Civil Code

Under the Korean Civil Code, the transfer of a receivable is not perfected against third parties, including the insolvency administrator, unless the transferor gives notice of the transfer to the debtor of the receivable or the debtor consents to the transfer.[183] Such notice or consent must be made by means of a certified document with a fixed date stamp in order for the transfer of the receivable to be perfected against third parties.[184] This regime intends to designate a debtor as an information centre, so that a potentially interested party may inquire of the debtor of the receivable regarding notice of a transfer. Priority among competing trans-

---

[180] ibid s 55(3). Priority between unregistered transfers of or security rights in the same receivables is to be determined by the order of attachment of the transfer or security rights (s 55(2)).
[181] ibid s 55(4) and 55(5)(a).
[182] ibid s 161.
[183] Korean Civil Code, art 450(1).
[184] ibid art 450(2).

ferees is determined by the time order in which the debtor receives notice of the transfer.[185] There are exceptions to the Civil Code: the ABS Act and the MBS Company Act.

Qs 1, 3-2. The ABS Act

Under the ABS Act, an SPV can perfect a transfer of receivables against third parties by filing a securitisation plan and a transfer of receivables in accordance with the plan at the Financial Services Commission.[186] Upon filing the transfer of receivables in accordance with the securitisation plan at the Financial Services Commission, the perfection requirement under Article 450(2) of the Korean Civil Code will be deemed satisfied. Thus, the transfer of the securitised receivables is perfected against third parties, even if no notice is given to the debtor. Upon filing, the receivables transferred to the SPV will no longer belong to the insolvency estate of the transferor, and creditors of the transferor may not attach the receivable thus transferred to the SPV.[187]

Qs 1, 3-3. The MBS Company Act

If the mortgage-backed securitisation plan and the transfer of receivables in accordance with the plan are filed at the Financial Services Commission, the perfection requirement under Article 450(2) of the Korean Civil Code will be deemed satisfied. Thus, the transfer of receivables is perfected against third parties on the date of filing.[188] If the receivables transferred in accordance with a mortgage-backed securitisation plan are secured by a pledge or a mortgage, the transferee of the receivables (the SPV) will acquire the pledge or the mortgage upon filing the transfer of receivables in accordance with the mortgage-backed securitisation plan at the Financial Services Commission.[189]

Qs 2, 4. Security Rights

As discussed above, in Korea, perfection against the insolvency administrator is the same as the perfection against third parties by which priority is determined. Thus, the answer to Question 2 is the same as the answer to Question 4.

---

[185] Korean Supreme Court Decision 2011Da83110 Decided on 28 June 2013; Supreme Court Decision 93Da24223 Decided on 26 April 1994; Supreme Court Decision 71Da2697 Decided on 31 January 1972.
[186] Korean ABS Act, art 7(2).
[187] Mee-Hyon Lee, 'Securitisation in Korea' (2002) 2(1) *Journal of Korean Law* 116.
[188] Korean MBS Company Act, arts 6(2) and 5(1). *cf* Korean ABS Act, arts 7(2) and 6(1).
[189] Korean MBS Company Act, art 7. *cf* Korean ABS Act, art 8(1).

Qs 2, 4-1. Pledges under the Korean Civil Code

Under the Korean Civil Code, the method of creating a pledge of a receivable is to transfer the receivable.[190] A pledge of a receivable becomes effective by the method of a transfer of a receivable. In order to perfect a pledge of a receivable against third parties, a pledgor is required to give notice of the pledge of the receivable to the debtor of the receivable, or the debtor of the receivable is required to consent to the pledge of the receivable.[191] The notice must be made by means of a certified document with a fixed date stamp.[192]

Qs 2, 4-2. The Korean Security Registration Act

Korea enacted the Korean Security Registration Act in order to provide a registration system for security rights in movable assets and receivables. This Act entered into force on 11 June 2012. It covers security rights in and security transfers of receivables,[193] but does not cover outright transfers of receivables.

The Korean Security Registration Act creates a new form of security right guaranteed by registration in addition to the pledge under the Korean Civil Code. It does not replace the notification requirement for a pledge of receivables under the Korean Civil Code. Pledges co-exist with security rights under the Korean Security Registration Act. Priority is determined by the order of notification of pledges under the Korean Civil Code or registration of security rights under the Korean Security Registration Act.[194]

As a result, parties may choose to use either a pledge of receivables under the Korean Civil Code or a security right in receivables under the Korean Security Registration Act. If parties choose to use a pledge of a receivable under the Civil Code, notice of the pledge to the debtor by means of a certified document with a fixed date stamp is required for perfecting the pledge against third parties. If parties choose to use a security right under the Korean Security Registration Act, they may perfect the security right against third parties by simply registering it.

Q5. *Priority between Transfers and Security Rights*

With respect to receivables, there could be transfers or pledges under the Korean Civil Code, security rights under the Korean Security Registration Act, or securitisations under the ABS Act or the MBS Company Act. The person who completes any one of these perfection methods first will have priority.

Priority between competing transfers of, pledges of or security rights in receivables is determined by the order of notice of the transfers or pledges to

---

[190] Korean Civil Code, art 346.
[191] ibid arts 349 and 450.
[192] ibid arts 349 and 450(2).
[193] Korean Security Registration Act, arts 34(1) and 2(1).
[194] ibid art 35(3).

(or consent of) the debtor of the receivable under the Korean Civil Code or registration of the security rights under the Korean Security Registration Act.[195] In addition, if the transfer of receivables is made in accordance with a securitisation plan, upon filing the transfer of receivables at the Financial Services Commission of Korea, the perfection requirement under the Korean Civil Code will be satisfied.[196]

As a result, priority is determined by the order of notice to the debtor, filing at the Financial Services Commission or registration under the Korean Security Registration Act.

Q6. The Potential Transferee's Check Points

In Korean law, to ensure there is no prior transferee or prior secured creditor of the receivable, a potential transferee of a receivable should: (1) ask the debtor of the receivables whether it has received notice of any prior transfer of or security right in the receivable in question; (2) check the securitisation filing registry at the Financial Services Commission of Korea; and (3) check the security registry for receivables under the Korean Security Registration Act.

3-7-7. Japan

Qs 1, 2, 3, 4. Perfection and Priority

In Japan, the perfection against the insolvency administrator is the same as the perfection against third parties by which priority is determined. Furthermore, the notification requirement for the transfer of receivables under the Japanese Civil Code also applies to pledges of receivables. The registration system under the Japanese Transfer Registration Act applies to both transfers of and pledges of receivables.[197] As a result, the answers to Questions 1, 2, 3 and 4 are all the same.

Qs 1, 2, 3, 4-1. The Japanese Civil Code

Under the Japanese Civil Code, both perfection and priority of transfers as well as pledges of receivables are all determined by notification to the debtor of the receivable.

A transfer of a receivable is perfected against third parties, including the insolvency administrator, if the transferor gives notice of the transfer to the debtor of the receivable by means of a certified document with a fixed date stamp or the debtor has consented to the transfer by means of a certified document with a

---

[195] ibid.
[196] Korean ABS Act, arts 7(2) and 6(1); Korean MBS Company Act, arts 6(2) and 5(1).
[197] Japanese Transfer Registration Act, art 14.

fixed date stamp.[198] Therefore, priority between or among competing transferees is determined by the time order in which the debtor receives notice of the transfer (or the pledge) of the receivable.

Under the Japanese Civil Code, the method of creating a pledge of a right is to transfer the right.[199] The pledge of a right becomes effective by a transfer of the right. To perfect a pledge of a receivable against the debtor of the receivable and third parties, the pledgor is required to give notice of the pledge to, or receive consent from, the debtor of the receivable regarding the creation of the pledge.[200]

Qs 1, 2, 3, 4-2. The Japanese Transfer Registration Act

Under the Japanese Transfer Registration Act, both perfection and priority of transfers as well as pledges of receivables are all determined by registration. The provisions of the Japanese Transfer Registration Act may apply mutatis mutandis to pledges of receivables.[201]

Japan has adopted registration systems without revising the Japanese Civil Code. Registration is optional and co-exists with notification of the transfer to the debtor under the Japanese Civil Code. The Japanese Transfer Registration Act does not replace the notification requirement for the transfer of receivables under the Japanese Civil Code,[202] but provides registration as an alternative to perfecting a transfer of receivables against third parties.

Where a legal person has transferred a receivable and when a transfer of a receivable has been registered, notice shall be deemed given to third parties by means of a certified document with a fixed date stamp under Article 467 of the Japanese Civil Code.[203] Here, the date of the registration is dealt as the fixed date of the notice under the Civil Code. Thus, registration is a method of perfection. If a transfer of receivables is registered, it is perfected against third parties, including the insolvency administrator.

Priority between or among competing transferees is determined by the time order of registration. Therefore, the debtor of a receivable needs to know the exact time of the registration to determine the proper payee. For this reason, notice should be given to the debtor with the certificate of registration. For a transferor to give notice of the transfer to the debtor in accordance with the Japanese Civil Code, he should provide it by means of a certified document with a fixed date stamp.[204]

---

[198] Japanese Civil Code, art 467(2). Notice or consent of the transfer of receivables must be done by a certified document with a fixed date stamp.
[199] ibid art 364.
[200] Japanese Civil Code, art 466(1).
[201] Japanese Transfer Registration Act, art 14.
[202] Japanese Civil Code, art 467.
[203] Japanese Transfer Registration Act, art 4(1).
[204] Japanese Civil Code, art 467(2).

If a transferor fraudulently transfers the same receivable to two transferees, both transfer contracts are valid,[205] but the second transferee may rescind the second transfer contract by the reason of the transferor's fraud.

Q5. Priority between Transfers and Security Rights

Under the Japanese Transfer Registration Act, if a transfer is registered, it is perfected against third parties without giving notice of the transfer to the debtor. In addition, even if a transfer is not registered, the transferor may perfect it against third parties by notification to the debtor according to the Japanese Civil Code. The same rule applies to a pledge of receivables.

Transfers or pledges of the same receivable may be perfected by either notice to (or consent of) the debtor of the receivable under the Japanese Civil Code or registration under the Japanese Transfer Registration Act. If both perfection methods exist with respect to a receivable, the transfer or pledge that is perfected first will prevail.[206] Priority is thus determined by the time order of registration or notice to the debtor. The transferee who first gives notice to the debtor will have priority over the other transferee that registers the transfer at a later time, and vice versa.

Q6. Potential Transferee's Check Points

A potential transferee should both check the registry under the Japanese Transfer Registration Act and enquire of the debtor of the receivable whether it has received notice of any prior transfer of or security right in the receivable in question.

3-7-8. France

Q1. Perfection of Transfers

Q1-1. Transfer of Receivables (*Cession de créances*)

The basis of the French legal system is laid out in the Napoleonic Civil Code, which was originally drawn up in 1804 and has been updated many times to take account of changes in society. Under the French Civil Code, notification to or consent of a debtor of a receivable is required for the transfer of a receivable to be perfected against third parties, including the insolvency administrator.[207] Notification to a debtor requires formality. Notification to a debtor must be done by an official

---

[205] The transfer contract between a transferor and a transferee is always valid in law between the transferor and the transferee. Thus, the transferor bears an obligation to the transferee. The question of priority is different from that of validity.
[206] Takashi UCHIDA, *Civil Code III Credit General and Security Right*, 3rd edn (Tokyo, University of Tokyo Press 2006) 223.
[207] French Civil Code, art 1690.

letter (*signification*)[208] delivered by a court bailiff (*huissier*).[209] Alternatively, a debtor may give consent of the transfer in a notarised deed (*acte authentique*).[210] Because of this strict formality, an outright transfer of receivables is rarely used as a financing device in France. If a transfer of receivables is used for security purposes, it would be characterised as a pledge of receivables.[211]

Q1-2. Transfer under the French Monetary and Financial Code

In 1981, France enacted the *Dailly* Act (Loi Dailly)[212] in order to circumvent the notification requirement under the French Civil Code. In 2000, the *Dailly* Act was incorporated into the Monetary and Financial Code (Le Code Monétaire et Financier)[213] as Articles L313-23–L313-34. The Monetary and Financial Code groups the legislative and regulatory provisions concerning the activities of banking, finance and insurance professionals.

The French Monetary and Financial Code applies to both transfers and pledges of receivables in which: (1) the transferee is a credit institution (établissement de crédit);[214] (2) the transferor is a private law or public law corporation or a natural person; (3) the transferor transfers a bulk of claims (present or future) that he has over one or more debtors, where the transfer is related to his business activities;[215] and (4) the debtor of the receivable is a third party private law or public law corporation, or natural person. This Code largely applies to receivables financing transaction.

Under the French Monetary and Financial Code, a transfer of receivables may be perfected against third parties by simple delivery of a transfer deed (*bordereau*) signed by the transferor and dated by the transferee, where the transferee is a credit institution (*établissement de crédit*) and the transferor is a corporation or a natural person conducting business activity.[216] The transfer deed (*bordereau*) must include the signature of a transferor[217] and must be dated by a transferee to be perfected against third parties.[218]

---

[208] 'Signification' is the official letter that the transferee needs to give to the debtor to be perfected against third parties.
[209] French Civil Code, art 1690. See Eva-Maria Kieninger (ed), *Security Rights in Movable Property in European Private Law* (Cambridge, Cambridge University Press, 2004) 538; Philip Wood, *Principles of International Insolvency* (London, Sweet & Maxwell, 2007) 297. If a notification is served by a bailiff (*huissier*), it costs approximately €250 per debtor. See Olivier Hubert, 'France' in Johnston (n 76) 179.
[210] 'Acte authentique' is the notarised deed which the debtor needs to consent to the transfer. This notarised deed must exist for the transfer to be effective against third parties; French Civil Code, art 1690.
[211] Leavy (n 12) 136. See also Hubert (n 209) 179.
[212] Loi no 81-2 du 2 janvier 1981. *Dailly* is the surname of the senator who initiated this Act.
[213] Loi no 2006-64 du 23 janvier 2006.
[214] French Monetary and Financial Code, art L313-26.
[215] ibid art L313-23.
[216] ibid art L313-23–L313-34.
[217] The signature is affixed either by hand or by any non-manual process.
[218] French Monetary and Financial Code, art L313-25. See Arthur F Salomons, 'Deformalisation of Transfer Law and the Position of the Debtor in European Property Law' (2007) 15 *European Review of Private Law* 639, 644.

Where the transferor becomes bankrupt and even if no notice is given to the debtor of the receivable, the transferee credit institution with the transfer deed (*bordereau*) can declare his claim to the insolvency administrator of the transferor and can claim payment directly from the debtor of the receivable.[219] However, if the debtor of the receivable has already paid the transferor by cash or by bank transfer[220] before receiving notice of the transfer, the transferee only has the option of joining in the insolvency proceedings,[221] since the cash payment would have been commingled with other cash in the transferor's account.

Q1-3. Securitisation under the French Monetary and Financial Code

In securitisation, a transfer of receivables is perfected against third parties simply upon delivery of a transfer deed (*bordereau*) to the transferee from the date indicated on the transfer deed (*bordereau*) by the transferee when it is handed over to the transferee.[222] The terms of a transfer deed (*bordereau*) are determined by decree.[223] A transfer deed (*bordereau*) must be named an act of transfer of receivables. It must indicate that it is subject to the provisions of the Monetary and Financial Code addressing asset securitisation. The name of the transferee must be included. The transferred receivables must also be indicated and identified.[224]

A transfer of future receivables is possible. A transfer of future receivables that come into existence after the date of the transfer contract is not affected by the commencement of insolvency proceedings against the transferor.[225] According to a decision of the Commercial Chamber of the Cour de Cassation in December 2004, a transfer of future receivables can be perfected against third parties and, once perfected, future cash-flows arising from the collection of the transferred receivables are not affected by the insolvency of the transferor.[226] This decision applies to *Dailly* transfers as well as securitisations under the French Monetary and Financial Code.

---

[219] Kieninger (n 209) 541.
[220] Cass Com 4 July 1995, Bull civ IV, No 203; D 1996, Som, 208, obs Piedelièvre; JCP 1995, II, 22553, note Legeais; RTDC 1996, 192, obs Gauthier.
[221] Kieninger (n 209) 541–42.
[222] French Monetary and Financial Code, art L214-43.
[223] ibid.
[224] Décret no 2004-1255 du 24 novembre 2004 pris en application des articles L. 214-5 et L. 214-43 à L. 214-49 du code monétaire et financier et relatif aux fonds communs de créances, art 18.
[225] Fabrice Grillo and Hervé Touraine, 'France' in *The International Comparative Legal Guide to: Securitisation 2007* (London, Global Legal Group, 2007) 139 [4.10].
[226] Sharon Lewis and Philip Boys, 'France' in *The International Comparative Legal Guide to: Securitisation 2005* (London, Global Legal Group, 2005) 95 [4.2].

Q2. Perfection of Security Rights

Q2-1. The Pledge under the Revised French Civil Code of 2006

Under the revised French Civil Code of 2006,[227] for a pledge of a receivable (*Nantissement de créance*), an executed pledge contract document (*l'acte*) is sufficient for the pledge to be perfected against third parties.[228] Neither notification to the account debtor nor registration is required for a pledge of a receivable to be perfected against third parties. This is an exception to the new general rule that pledges of tangible movable assets must be registered under Article 2337 of the French Civil Code. The pledge of a receivable (*créance*), including a future receivable, is perfected against third parties as of the date of concluding the pledge contract document (*l'acte*).[229] In France, a security transfer of receivables is treated as a security right in receivables, and therefore notice to the debtor is not required.

Q2-2. The Pledge under the French Monetary and Financial Code

A pledge as well as a transfer is perfected against third parties from the date indicated on the transfer deed (*bordereau*) when it is handed over, regardless of the origination date, maturity date or due date of the receivables.[230] It provides a simple method to pledge or transfer commercial receivables to a bank as security for financing.[231]

Q3. Priority of Transfers

Under the French Civil Code, priority of transfers of receivables (*cession de créances*) is determined by the time order in which the debtor receives notice of the transfers. The transferee who first gives notice to the debtor has priority.[232]

Under the French Monetary and Financial Code, if all *Dailly* transferees[233] give notice to the debtor of the receivable, priority is determined by the date indicated on the transfer deed (*bordereau*) by the transferee when it is handed over to the transferee.[234] If no *Dailly* transferee gives notice to the debtor of the receivable, priority is determined by the date indicated on the transfer deed (*bordereau*) by the transferee.[235]

---

[227] Loi no 2006-399 du 4 avril 2006 renforçant la prévention et la répression des violences au sein du couple ou commises contre les mineurs (1).
[228] French Civil Code, art 2361.
[229] French Civil Code, art 2361.
[230] French Monetary and Financial Code, art L313-27.
[231] Leavy (n 12) 123.
[232] *Draft Common Frame of Reference*, Full Edition, vol 2, Book III (Munich, Sellier 2009) 1051.
[233] In this book, a *Dailly* transferee means a transferee who has transferred a receivable by a transfer deed (*bordereau*) under the French Monetary and Financial Code.
[234] Cass Com 12 January 1999, D Aff 1999, 336; RTD com 1999, 479, obs *Cabrillac*.
[235] Cass Com 5 July 1994, RTD com 1995, 172, obs *Cabrillac*.

If one *Dailly* transferee gives notice to the debtor of the receivable and the others did not, the *Dailly* transferee who gives notice has priority over any other *Dailly* transferee or a transferee under the French Civil Code, regardless of the date of the transfer.[236]

For this reason, even though a prior *Dailly* transferee does not have to give notice to the debtor of the receivable immediately, in order to secure priority, he must give notice to the debtor of the receivable before payment would be made to any other competing transferee. The French priority regime encourages a *Dailly* transferee to give notice of the transfer to the debtor of the receivable.

Q4. Priority of Security Rights

Under the revised French Civil Code of 2006, priority of pledges or security transfers of receivables (*nantissement de créances*) is determined by the order of the date of concluding the pledge contract or the security transfer contract. All pledges or security transfers of receivables must be evidenced in writing.[237] Such writing is sufficient to perfect a pledge or a security transfer against third parties.[238]

Q5. Priority between Transfers and Security Rights

With respect to transfers under the French Civil Code, priority is determined by the time order in which the debtor receives notice of the transfer with formality. With respect to *Dailly* transfers and pledges, priority is determined by the order of the date of concluding the pledge contract or the date on the transfer deeds (*bordereau*), if neither a *Dailly* transferee nor a pledgee gives notice to the debtor of the receivable.[239] However, notification to the debtor of the receivable may trump the date of concluding the pledge agreement or the date on the transfer deeds (*bordereau*). If one transferee under the French Civil Code, *Dailly* transferee or pledgee gives notice to the debtor of the receivable while the others do not, the transferee or pledgee who gives notice to the debtor of the receivable has priority over the others.

Q6. The Potential Transferee's Check Points

If a potential transferee is a financial institution, it may use a *Dailly* transfer under the French Monetary and Financial Code. In France, it is possible that there might be a prior transfer or pledge under the French Civil Code or a prior *Dailly* transfer. A potential transferee should first enquire of the debtor of the receivable whether

---

[236] Leavy (n 12) 134.
[237] France Civil Code, arts 1326 and 1341.
[238] Leavy (n 12) 134.
[239] Cass Com 13 February 1996, Banque 1996, No 569, 91, obs *Guillot*.

it has received notice of any prior transfer, pledge or *Dailly* transfer. A potential transferee should also give notice to the debtor of the receivable as soon as possible.

However, this still does not guarantee the transferee's priority. If another pledgee or *Dailly* transferee subsequently gives notice to the debtor of the receivable, and the date of concluding the pledge agreement or the date on the transfer deed (*bordereau*) is prior to the transfer date of a potential transferee, the pledgee or *Dailly* transferee will have priority over a potential transferee.

3-7-9. Belgium

Q1. Perfection of Transfers

Under Article 1690 of the Belgian Civil Code, as altered by the Law of 6 July 1994, a transfer of a receivable is effective between a transferor and a transferee and is perfected against third parties, including the insolvency administrator, upon the conclusion of a transfer agreement. Belgium has abolished the notification requirement for a transfer of receivables. Compared with the French *Dailly* Act 1981, which abolished the notification requirement for the limited scope of transfers of credit institutions, the Belgian reform has uniformly abolished the notification requirement for a transfer of receivables and a pledge of receivables. The primary aim of this abolition is to facilitate securitisation.[240]

Q2. Perfection of Security Rights

A pledge of a receivable is perfected against third parties from the moment a valid pledge agreement is entered into. The Belgian Civil Code follows the principle that the transfer of possession of the pledged collateral is publicity for a pledge. The Belgian Civil Code stipulates that a pledge is effective as long as the pledgee (or a third party who the pledgor and the pledgee agree) holds possession of the pledged collateral,[241] and the pledgee is regarded as taking possession of a receivable upon the conclusion of an agreement for the pledge of the receivable.[242] Thus, a pledge of a receivable is effective upon the conclusion of the pledge agreement. Still, for enforcement of a pledge of a receivable against the debtor of the pledged receivable, giving notice of the pledge to the debtor of the pledged receivable or the consent of the debtor to the pledge is required.[243]

---

[240] Jan Peeters and Wouter Ghijsels, 'Increasing Activity in the Belgian Market', 2005, www.global-restructuring.com/05Europe/271_274.htm.
[241] Belgian Civil Code, art 2076.
[242] ibid art 2075.
[243] ibid.

Qs 3, 4, 5. Priority

Even though Belgium abolished the notification requirement for perfection against third parties including the insolvency administrator, priority among competing transferees or pledgees is still determined by the time order in which the debtor of the receivable receives notice of the transfer or the pledge.[244]

Q6. The Potential Transferee's Check Points

In order to secure priority, a potential transferee has to enquire of the debtor of the receivable whether it has received notice of any prior transfer of or security right in the receivable in question.

3-7-10. England

Q1. Perfection of Transfers

Q1-1. Transfer of Receivables

Under English law, a transfer without notice to the debtor is still valid as an equitable assignment.[245] Moreover, the receivables equitably transferred are separated from the insolvency estate of the transferor. As a result, an equitable assignee, like a statutory assignee, prevails against the trustee in bankruptcy or the liquidator of the transferor.[246] An equitable assignment is also perfected against an execution creditor.[247]

Equitable assignments in English law are close to transfers in German law in that they do not require notice of the transfer to the debtor for an equitable assignment which is perfected against the insolvency administrator and execution creditors.[248]

---

[244] ibid art 1690(1). See also Marc Vermylen, 'Belgium' Johnston (n 76) 54 [4.32].
[245] *Gorringe v Irwell India Rubber and Gutta Percha Works* (1886) LR 34 Ch D 128 (CA).
[246] For this reason, in England, at first notice will not normally be given to the debtors because an equitable assignment is effective even without notice to a debtor and the transferor generally wishes to maintain its relationship with its customers (debtors of receivables) and continue to collect on the debt. Since a transferee may give notice of the transfer to the debtor at any time, once the other requirements of a statutory transfer are satisfied, an equitable assignee is always able to change an equitable assignment into a statutory transfer without a transferor's cooperation. Thus, a transferee factor will usually send notice to debtors only if and when it needs to collect the debt itself, unless the arrangement is notification financing. For example, in the case of a transferor's insolvency or refusal to pay the debt, the transferee will give notice to the debtor.
[247] *Holt* (n 112).
[248] See section 3-4-3-1.

Q1-2. An Individual Person's General Transfer of Book Debts

If a natural person makes a general transfer of existing or future book debts, the transfer must be registered under the Bills of Sale Act 1878 in order to be perfected against the trustee of the bankrupt's estate.[249] A 'general assignment' does not include a transfer of book debts due at the date of the transfer from specified debtors or a transfer of debts becoming due under specified contracts.[250] In this context, an 'assignment' includes both a security transfer of and a charge over book debts.[251]

Q2. Perfection of Security Rights

Under the Companies Act 2006 (Amendment of Chapter 25) Regulations 2013, all charges (including charges over receivables) created by a company can be registered in the register of charges at Companies House.[252] If a charge created by a company (chargor) is not registered within a period of 21 days (or such later time as is permitted by the court)[253] beginning with the day after the date of creation of the charge,[254] it is not perfected against any other creditor, the liquidator, the insolvency administrator and execution creditors of the company.[255]

Q3. Priority of Transfers

Under English law, priority is not related to perfection. In *Dearle v Hall*, priority between competing transferees is determined by the time order in which the debtor receives notice of the transfer, unless the subsequent transferee E2 knew of the prior transfer at the time of his transfer.[256] However, there could be situational exceptions due to the concept of equity that exists in English law. The concept of 'equitable assignment', which does not exist in many civil law jurisdictions, is differentiated from a 'statutory assignment' of receivables. Thus, in the case described above, the transfers made to E and E2 are either equitable or statutory, producing three possible cases where first, both transfers are equitable, second, both are statutory and, third, one is equitable while the other is statutory.

---

[249] Insolvency Act 1986, s 344(2).
[250] ibid s 344(3)(b)(i).
[251] ibid s 344(3)(a).
[252] Companies Act 2006 (Amendment of Chapter 25) Regulations 2013, s 859A(1) and (2).
[253] ibid s 859F. See Goode and Gullifer (n 42) 187 [5-23].
[254] Companies Act 2006 (Amendment of Chapter 25) Regulations 2013, s 859A(4).
[255] ibid s 859H(3).
[256] *Dearle v Hall* (n 15). See section 3-3-2.

Q3-1. Priority of Equitable Assignments

Q3-1-1. The First View of Transferring Receivables

English law: *Dearle v Hall*	E	E2
Conclusion of the transfer agreement	1st	2nd
Debtor of the receivable receives notice of the transfer	4th	3rd
		E2 has priority over E

There are two views on how the doctrine of *Dearle v Hall* was framed and how it operates. According to the first view, the prior equitable assignment to E is valid between the transferor and the transferee even though no notice is given to the debtor, and consequently the transferred receivable no longer belongs to the insolvency estate of the transferor. Under the *nemo dat quod non habet* ('No one gives what he doesn't have') rule, a transferor cannot transfer what he does not have. Therefore, it might seem odd that the transferor can make a similar transfer to E2 which can have priority over the transfer to E.[257] See Table 3.10.

Nevertheless, E2 could be a bona fide purchaser if E2 purchased the receivable without notice of the prior equitable assignment made to E, even though E2 gave notice of his transfer to the debtor of the receivable. In order for E2 to be a bona fide purchaser, E2 should have enquired of the debtor of the receivable. During the process of the enquiry, while E2 enquires of the debtor of the receivable as to whether he has received notice of any prior transfer of the receivable, it is likely that E2 would naturally give notice of his transfer to the debtor of the receivable. In this view, the *Dearle v Hall* rule is framed in terms of the bona fide purchaser rule. This view explains why E2 prevails over E.

However, the shortcoming of this view is that it does not explain why E2 must give notice to the debtor. E2 would have to give notice of his transfer of the receivable to the debtor of the receivable to protect his position against a potential third party, since a potential third party cannot be a bona fide purchaser without notice once E2 has given notice of the transfer of the receivable. Still, it does not really explain why notice is necessary for E2 to have priority over E.

Q3-1-2. The Second View of Creating Equivalent Equitable Interests Engrafted upon Legal Interests

According to the second view, the *Dearle v Hall* rule is explained as resolving a particular case of conflict between mere equitable interests. Because each transfer

---

[257] Michael Bridge, Louise Gullifer, Gerard McMeel and Sarah Worthington, *The Law of Personal Property* (London, Sweet & Maxwell, 2013) [36-012].

in equity only creates a new claim against the transferor, the transferor can create multiple claims. An equitable assignment merely creates and vests in the transferee an equitable interest. Equitable interests are 'engrafted' or 'impressed' upon legal interests rather than 'carved out of' them.[258] Equitable interests are not drawn out of legal interests.[259] The underlying equitable nature of transfer is an engraftment of an equitable personal chose in action with a power of control onto the personal debt claim. Thus, an equitable assignment does not involve a disposition.[260] It is possible for the same transferor to create equally valid claims against himself by multiple intentional transfers of the same debt.[261] Priority between them is determined by the *Dearle v Hall* rule. See Table 3.10.

If there are two equitable assignments and neither transferee gives notice to the debtor, priority is determined by the order of conclusion of the transfer agreement.[262]

Table 3.10: The Application of *Dearle v Hall*

		Prior transfer to E1	Subsequent transfer to E2	
Equitable assignment	First view: transferring receivables	Valid	Void *nemo dat quod non habet*	Exception: bona fide purchaser for value without notice (or *Dearle v Hall*)
Statutory assignment	Substantive view			
Equitable assignment	Second view: creating equivalent equitable interests engrafted upon legal interests	Valid	Valid	*Dearle v Hall*
Statutory assignment	Procedural view			

Q3-2. Priority of Statutory Assignments

Q3-2-1. The Substantive View of Statutory Assignments

The two views of equitable assignments could similarly apply to statutory assignments under section 136(1) of the Law of Property Act 1925. The substantive view

---

[258] Tolhurst (n 47) [3.11] 40.
[259] ibid [3.12] 43.
[260] ibid [3.11] 40.
[261] David Fox, 'Relativity of Title at Law and in Equity' (2006) 65 *CLJ* 330, 354.
[262] Beale et al (n 1) 438 [13.09].

of statutory assignments follows the logic of the first view of equitable assignments. The primary argument for the substantive view flows from the words of section 136(1) of the Law of Property Act 1925, which stipulates that: 'Any absolute transfer ... is effectual in law ... to pass and transfer ... the legal right to such debt or thing in action'.[263] The substantive view is that the transfer actually takes effect as a transfer at law for all purposes. See Table 3.10.

Q3-2-2. The Procedural View of Statutory Assignments

On the other hand, the procedural view of statutory assignments follows the logic of the second view of equitable assignments. The procedural view is that it only enables the transferee to sue in its own name as a matter of procedure, but otherwise it does not change the position at all, so that the interest of the transferee is equitable for other purposes, such as priority. As a result, the *Dearle v Hall* rule still applies.[264] See Table 3.10.

However, since notice to the debtor is a requirement for a statutory assignment, there will rarely be a situation where the application of the substantive view will lead to a different result from that which would follow from the application of the procedural view. If there are two transfers that comply with the statutory requirements, priority is determined by the time order in which the debtor receives notice of the transfer in writing.

Q3-3. Priority of Equitable Assignment and Statutory Assignment

Let us suppose a case where there are a statutory assignment and an equitable assignment of the same receivable, and an equitable assignment is made first and where the debtor receives notice of the equitable assignment earlier than the notice of the statutory assignment.

If the substantive view of statutory assignments is taken, the statutory assignee is to take the claim subject to the equitable assignment.[265] Thus, the statutory assignment is subject to the prior equitable assignment. If the procedural view of statutory assignments is taken, the *Dearle v Hall* rule applies.

Let us suppose a case where a statutory assignment is made first and then an equitable assignment is made later. If the substantive view of statutory assignments is taken, *ex hypothesi* (according to the hypothesis itself) the statutory assignee is the first to give notice to the debtor and therefore the statutory assignee has priority over the equitable assignee. If the procedural view of statutory assignments is taken, the *Dearle v Hall* rule applies.

---

[263] Tolhurst (n 47) [5.06] 107.
[264] Bridge et al (n 257) [27-006].
[265] Section 136(1) of the Law of Property Act 1925 stipulates that a statutory transfer is 'subject to equities having priority over the right of the transferee'. See *E Pfeiffer Weinkellerei-Weineinkauf GmbH & Co v Arbuthnot Factors Ltd* [1987] BCLC 522 (QB), 533, [1988] 1 WLR 150, 162; *Compaq Computer Ltd v Abercorn Group Ltd* [1993] BCLC 602 (Ch), 621–22.

Q4. Priority of Security Rights

English law: *Dearle v Hall* and constructive notice	S	S2
Registration of charge over the receivable	1st	2nd
Debtor of the receivable receives notice of the transfer	4th	3rd
		S has priority over S2

Let us suppose a case where a chargor provides the same receivable as collateral twice to two different chargees by creating two charges over the receivable.

Priority of competing charges over a receivable is governed by the *Dearle v Hall* rule,[266] once the charges are registered within a period of 21 days (or such later time as is permitted by the court) beginning with the day after the date of creation of the charge.[267] A chargee who has a charge over a receivable must give notice of the charge over the receivable to the debtor of the receivable in order to perfect the charge over the receivable. The chargee who gives notice of the charge to the debtor before any other secured creditor will have priority.

However, if one chargee S2 is aware of a registered charge made by the other chargee S, S2 cannot have priority over S despite giving notice of its charge to the debtor of the receivable before S. Registration of a charge (including a charge over receivables) in the register of charges at Companies House constitutes a constructive notice of the charge to third parties if it would be reasonable for the subsequent claimant to have made a search of the register of charges.[268] Thus, a subsequent chargee cannot later give notice of the charge to the debtor of the receivable and obtain priority over the prior charge that has already been registered before.[269] The chargee who registered its charge first has priority over any subsequent chargee.

If neither of the chargees gives notice of their charges to the debtor of the receivable, priority is determined by the time order of creation of the charge according to the first in time rule. According to the *nemo dat quod non habet* rule, a transferee cannot obtain more rights than the transferor had. Therefore, a subsequent charge should be subject to a prior charge. If a subsequent chargee is a bona fide

---

[266] *Dearle v Hall* (n 15).
[267] Companies Act 2006 (Amendment of Part 25) Regulations 2013, s 859A(4).
[268] To whom registration of a charge over company book debts in the register of charges at Companies House constitutes a constructive notice is not firmly settled. However, many scholars agree that registration is constructive notice to subsequent chargees of the registered company book debt. Some scholars argue that a bank taking commercial security would be expected to search. They also argue that in practice, most transferees will search the registry because it is safer to scour the registry than to remain uncertain. See Beale et al (n 1) 441–42 [13.13]; Philip Wood, *Law and Practice of International Finance* (London, Sweet & Maxwell, 2008) 278 [17-27].
[269] The second limb of *Dearle v Hall* (n 15); *Ellerman Lines Ltd v Lancaster Maritime Co Ltd* [1980] 2 Lloyd's Rep 497 (QB), 503. Until it has been registered, the subsequent chargee will not be on constructive notice of the earlier charge.

purchaser for value without notice, it will take free of a prior charge. However, registration of a charge constitutes a constructive notice of the charge to third parties if it would be reasonable for the subsequent claimant to have made a search of the register of charges. Therefore, registration could prevent subsequent chargees from being a bona fide purchaser for value without notice.

Q5. Priority between Transfers and Security Rights

Q5-1. Prior Charge: Subsequent Transfer

If a charge over a receivable is perfected and the same receivable is later transferred to a third party, priority is determined by the time order in which the debtor of the receivable receives notice of the charge or the transfer.[270] For a charge over receivables that is to be registered in the register of charges at Companies House, if such registration constitutes a constructive notice, the subsequent transferee cannot have priority over the prior chargee by notification of the transfer to the debtor of the receivable. Most financiers of receivables would check the register in the ordinary course of business. Thus, registration might constitute a constructive notice.

Q5-2. Prior Transfer: Subsequent Charge

If a receivable is transferred to a transferee and a charge is subsequently created over the same receivable, the subsequent chargee would have no way to have actual or constructive notice of the prior transfer since a transfer is not registered.[271] Priority is determined by the time order in which the debtor of the receivable receives notice of the charge or the transfer.[272] Therefore, a subsequent chargee may give notice of his charge to the debtor of the receivable first (while the debtor of the receivable is not notified of the prior transfer) and obtain priority over the prior transfer.

Q6. The Potential Transferee's Check Points

Under English law, a potential transferee should both check the register of charges at Companies House and enquire of the debtor of the receivable whether it has received notice of any prior transfer of or security right in the receivable in question.

---

[270] *Dearle v Hall* (n 15).
[271] Beale et al (n 1) 442 [13.14]. However, in practice, many receivable financiers also take a charge over all the assets of a financial company.
[272] *Dearle v Hall* (n 15).

3-7-11. China

Q1. Perfection of Transfers

Q1-1. Transfer of Receivables under the Contract Law

Owing to Article 80 of the Chinese Contract Law, it is not clear whether a transfer is perfected against the insolvency administrator of the transferor if a debtor has not been notified of the transfer. This is because the Chinese Contract Law does not stipulate perfection of a transfer of a receivable against third parties.

Some scholars argue that notice of the transfer to the debtor is required for priority.[273] On the other hand, other scholars argue that even though a debtor has not been notified, a transfer can be perfected against the insolvency administrator of the transferor once the transferee has paid proper consideration to the transferor for the receivable.[274] They cite Article 31(2) of the Chinese Insolvency Law in support of this.[275] However, an avoidance provision that can set aside unfair preferences such as Article 31(2) of the Chinese Insolvency Law exists in many jurisdictions, regardless of which approach is taken for perfection against the insolvency administrator.[276]

It is controversial whether a transfer of a receivable is perfected against the insolvency administrator upon the conclusion of the transfer contract even without notice of the transfer to the debtor, unless the transfer of the receivable is set aside as an unfair preference according to the avoidance provision of the Chinese Insolvency Law.[277]

If a transfer of a receivable is perfected against the insolvency administrator without notice of the transfer to the debtor, the practice of transfers of receivables in China would be similar to that under the English equitable assignment, although China does not have the concept of equity.

---

[273] Xuezhong Zhang, 'Notification: Effectiveness Requirement of the Transfer of Rights' (2005) 7 *Legal Science Monthly* 97; Jianping Shen, *Research on the Transfer of Rights Focused on Transfer Notice* (Beijing, Law Press China, 2008) 167–71.

[274] See Jianyuan Cui, *Contract Law*, 3rd edn (Beijing, Law Press China, 2004) 178; Shiyuan Han, *Contract Law General Principles* (Beijing, Law Press China, 2004) 568–70.

[275] Article 31(2) of the Chinese Insolvency Law stipulates that, within one year before the court accepts an application for bankruptcy, the insolvency administrator has the right to plead to the court to revoke the following transactions of the debtor's assets: (1) transferring the assets free of charge; (2) transaction at an *obviously unreasonable price*; (3) providing asset guarantees to those debts without any asset guarantee; (4) paying off the undue debts in advance; or (5) giving up the creditor's right. Nonetheless, this method has a time limitation and sometimes it might be difficult to prove whether that consideration is obviously unreasonable.

[276] The avoidance of the insolvency administrator is for the protection of creditors of the insolvent transferor. For the purpose of preventing the unfair fraudulent trade of company assets, the insolvency laws of many jurisdictions provide that an insolvency administrator may avoid the transfer if the consideration for the transfer of receivables was an unreasonable price and the transfer was made within a certain period of time before the insolvency date.

[277] Chinese Insolvency Law, art 31(2).

Q1-2. Disposal of Non-performing Loans

In April 2001, the Supreme People's Court of China issued 'The Supreme People's Court Provisions Regarding Several Issues on Examining Applicable Laws Concerning Financial Asset Management Company's Acquisition, Management and Disposal of Non-Performing Loan Asset of State-Owned Bank Cases' (hereinafter 'SPC Provisions on Disposal of NPLs').[278] The SPC Provisions on Disposal of NPLs stipulate that if, after a state-owned bank transfers its receivables to an asset management company,[279] the state-owned bank publishes a notice about the transfer of receivables in an influential newspaper distributed nationally or provincially, then the court may acknowledge that the state-owned bank has completed its duty of notice under Article 80 of the Chinese Contract Law.[280] Such a transfer is perfected by publication in an influential newspaper distributed nationwide or province-wide. This provision exempts the difficulties of notification to debtors from the transfer of receivables by a state-owned bank to an asset management company in China.

Q1-3. Securitisation

For securitisation, China adopted the method of public notice in newspapers for the perfection of the transfer against the insolvency administrator of the transferor that is the originator. It was adopted by Article 6 of the SPC Provisions on Disposal of NPLs and Article 12 of the Administrative Measures for the Securitisation of Credit Assets (AMSCA).[281] The AMSCA regulates the pilot work of credit

---

[278] Supreme People's Court Judicial Interpretation [2001] No 12.

[279] In China, there are the 'big four' state-owned commercial banks: the Bank of China, the China Construction Bank, the Industrial and Commercial Bank of China (ICBC) and the Agricultural Bank of China. These banks have historically formed the bulk of the lending to state-owned companies or state-controlled companies and each is focused on particular industries and sectors. Years of government-directed lending resulted in the big four state-owned banks being left with many non-performing loans (NPLs). According to a People's Bank of China report, NPLs accounted for 21.4–26.1 per cent of the total lending of China's four big banks in 2002. Furthermore, it was said that the real ratio of bad loans was much higher. In 2003, the Chinese government estimated the amount of such NPLs at around $240 billion and independent estimates ranged from $410 to $815 billion. In 1999, the Chinese government established four asset management companies (资产管理公司) to deal with NPLs. They are the Orient (东方), Cinda (信达), Huarong (华融) and Great Wall (长城) asset management companies. About RMB 1,400 billion NPLs were transferred from the big four state-owned banks to the four asset management companies. Each of the four asset management companies mirrors one of the big four state-owned banks. See Baozhong Gao, *Institutional Analysis of Asset Securitisation in China* (Beijing, Social Science Academic Press, 2005) 155; Weitseng Chen, 'Legal Implications of a Rising China: WTO: Time's up for Chinese Banks—China's Banking Reform and Non-performing Loan Disposal' (2006) 7 *Chinese Journal of International Law* 239, 240–43; Yanrong Hong, *Studies of Legal Issues Concerning Asset-Backed Securitisation* (Beijing, Peking University Press, 2004) 223; Johnny P Chen, *Non-performing Loan Securitisation in the People's Republic of China* (Stanford, Stanford University Department of Economics, May 2004) 22.

[280] SPC Provisions on Disposal of NPLs, art 6.

[281] Announcement of the People's Bank of China and China Banking Regulatory Commission No 7 (2005), enacted on 20 April 2005.

asset securitisation.[282] After the success of these securitisations, there have been several securitisation practices in China.[283]

Perfection against the insolvency administrator is achieved by establishing a special purpose trustee (SPT) and public notice in accordance with the AMSCA. The AMSCA stipulates that an originator must publish a notice about the originator's establishing a SPT and that the credit assets are transferred to the SPT on a nationwide medium.[284] It also provides that a transfer of credit assets may be perfected by making a public announcement rather than giving individual notice to each debtor. The AMSCA also stipulates that in the event of originator's insolvency, the trust property is not included in the insolvency asset.[285] It provides that the assets transferred from the originator to the SPT is separated from the originator and will not be affected by the bankruptcy of the originator.

Q2. *Perfection of Security Rights*

The Chinese Property Law, which was enacted in 2007, stipulates that account receivables (*YingShouZhangKuan*) may be used as pledges.[286] A pledge of a receivable becomes effective upon its registration in the Credit Reference Centre.[287] Registration is required for a pledge of a receivable to be perfected against third parties, but notice of the pledge to the debtor of the receivable is not required for the creation of the pledge.[288]

In 2008, in order to provide a registration system for pledges of receivables under the Chinese Property Law, the People's Bank of China[289] formulated the

---

[282] AMSCA, art 1. The AMSCA was designed to parallel the pilot asset-backed securitisation scheme of the China Development Bank (国家开发银行) and the pilot residential mortgage-backed securitisation (RMBS) scheme of the China Construction Bank (建设银行). The China Development Bank issued asset-backed securitisations, and the China Construction Bank issued residential mortgage-backed securitisations on the same day (15 December 2005).

[283] For example, the China Development Bank (国家开发银行) issued the first asset-backed securitisation amounting to RMB 4.178 billion on 15 December 2005, the second asset-backed securitisation on 25 April 2006, and the third asset-backed securitisation amounting to RMB 7.8 billion on 22 June 2007. The Shanghai Pudong Development Bank (浦东发展银行) issued asset-backed securitisations amounting to RMB 4.383 billion on 14 September 2007. The Industrial and Commercial Bank of China (中国工商银行) issued the first asset-backed securitisation amounting to RMB 4 billion on 10 October 2007 and the second asset-backed securitisation amounting to RMB 8 billion on 27 March 2008. The Industrial Bank (兴业银行) issued asset-backed securitisations amounting to RMB 5.3 billion in 2007. As for mortgage-backed securitisations, the China Construction Bank (建设银行) issued the first RMBS amounting to RMB 3 billion, backed by mortgage receivables, whose average value is RMB 245,430 and whose average repayment period is 32 months, on 15 December 2005, and the second RMBS amounting to RMB 4 billion on 14 December 2007.

[284] AMSCA, art 12.
[285] ibid art 6.
[286] Chinese Property Law, art 223(6).
[287] ibid art 228.
[288] Johnston (n 76) 644.
[289] The People's Bank of China is China's central bank. It generally formulates and implements monetary policy and performs the functions of regulating the inter-bank lending market and the inter-bank bond market, maintaining the normal operation of the payment and settlement system etc.

Measures for the Registration of Pledge of Receivables (MRPR)[290] and established a registration system for pledges of receivables in the Credit Reference Centre.[291] However, the registration system is only for pledges of receivables and not for outright transfer of receivables. Therefore, outright transfers do not have to be registered. In this respect, it is similar to English law, where only charges over company receivables must be registered and an outright transfer of a receivable cannot be registered.

Q3. Priority of Transfers

Under Chinese law, it is not clear whether notice of transfer to the debtor is required for priority. This is because the Chinese Contract Law[292] only stipulates that notice of the transfer to the debtor is required for effectiveness against the debtor of the receivable, while it does not stipulate priority.

Although it is debatable whether notice of transfer to the debtor is required for priority, it seems that at least priority among competing transferees is determined by the time order in which the debtor receives notice of the transfer. For example, suppose there are two transferees, E1 and E2. Even though the date of conclusion of the transfer contract with E1 is prior to the transfer contract with E2, if the debtor received notice of the transfer made to E2 but has not received notice of the transfer made to E1, E2 has priority over E1 under Chinese law. Thus, it could be said that notice to the debtor is required for priority.

Q4. Priority of Security Rights

Priority of pledges of receivables is determined by the time order of registration of the pledge in the Credit Reference Centre.

Q5. Priority between Transfers and Security Rights

Priority between transfers or security rights is determined by the order of notification of the transfer to the debtor or registration of the pledge in the Credit Reference Centre.

---

[290] Adopted at the 21st governor's meeting on 26 September, 2007, promulgated by Order No 4 (2007) of the People's Bank of China, entered into force as of 1 October 2007.

[291] Article 2 of the MRPR provides for a centralised registration system for security rights in account receivables: the Credit Reference Centre of the People's Bank of China. This is especially welcomed by small and medium-sized enterprises and other enterprises engaged in manufacturing with high levels of account receivables and inventory. Now, lenders or other parties will be able to access a single centralised system in order to obtain information about a borrower or other registered security rights. See Joshua T Klein, 'Recent Legal Changes that Affect Secured Financing in the People's Republic of China' (2009) 27 *American Bankruptcy Institute Journal 38*, 72–73. The official website of the Chinese Credit Reference Centre is www.pbccrc.org.cn/chanpinfuwu_305.html.

[292] Chinese Contract Law, art 80. The title of this article is 'Duty to Notify When Assigning Rights; Revocation of Transfer Subject to Assignee's Consent'.

Q6. *Potential Transferee's Check Points*

A potential transferee should both check the registry for the pledges of receivables in the Credit Reference Centre and enquire of the debtor of the receivable whether it has received notice of any prior transfer of or security right in the receivable in question.

3-7-12. Germany

Q1. *Perfection of Transfers*

Q1-1. Transfer of Receivables

In German law, with respect to a transfer of receivables, there is no difference between the perfection of a transfer and the creation of a transfer. A transfer of receivables is perfected against third parties (including the insolvency administrator of the transferor) upon the conclusion of the transfer agreement of the parties.

For the creation of a transfer of receivables, only an agreement between a transferor and a transferee is required, and the participation of a debtor of a receivable is not required. A failure to give notice of the transfer to the debtor of the receivable does not void the transfer.

In German law, any third-party involvement or confirmation is not required for the transfer of receivables to be perfected against third parties. The transfer of a receivable does not have to be publicised, whereas the ownership transfer of land must be publicised by registration and the ownership transfer of tangible movable assets must be publicised by delivery of possession. The German Civil Code does not require publicity for the transfer of receivables. Instead, a transferor functions as the information centre. Thus, a potential transferee needs to enquire of the transferor about the status of a receivable. This is sensible because a transferor who is an original creditor of a receivable is the person in the best position to know the status of a receivable that belongs to him.

The German Civil Code stipulates that when the transfer contract is entered into, 'the new creditor (transferee) steps into the shoes of the previous creditor (transferor)'.[293] Therefore, a transferee acquires all the same rights over the receivables that the transferor possessed. A transferee is entitled to receive payments and may take any required actions independently without joining the transferor. If a debtor is not notified of the transfer, he is free to pay the transferor (the original creditor). Still, a transferee is entitled to claim and receive such payments from the transferor.[294]

---

[293] German Civil Code, s 398.
[294] Aleknaitė (n 62) 219, fn 187.

Q1-2. Global Transfer (*Globalzession*)

German provisions on the transfer of receivables permit a global transfer (*Globalzession*).[295] Global transfer is a contract pursuant to which a transferor transfers all its present and future receivables originating from certain legal acts or from certain designated debtors. However, in order for the global transfer agreement to be effective, it must be possible to identify the future receivables.[296]

Q1-3. Securitisation

Such liberal regulation like the German regime on the transfer of receivables allows more flexibility in structuring asset securitisation transactions that best suit the interests of a particular company. The transfer of receivables under the German Civil Code could be the best method of transferring receivables for asset securitisation. Jurisdictions following German law, such as Austria and Switzerland, are thus in a good position to facilitate receivables financing. Yet, statistics show that there have not been as many securitisation practices in these states as in the US.[297] This could be because their banks might not prefer securitisation.

Q2. Perfection of Security Rights

Q2-1. The Pledge of Receivables (*Forderungsverpfändung*)

The creation of a pledge (*Pfand*) of a receivable requires notice of the pledge to the debtor of the receivable.[298] Notice of the pledge must be given by the pledgor. Alternatively, if notice is given by the pledgee (secured creditor), it must be authorised by the pledgor (grantor).[299] Notification need not be in writing.[300]

Q2-2. Security Transfer of Receivables (*Sicherungsabtretung*)

Compared to a pledge of receivables, a security transfer of receivables does not require notice to the debtor of the receivable. The security transfer of receivables is only valid if the transferor (grantor) and the transferee (secured creditor) agree on the transfer for security purposes.[301] The transferee may collect the receivable

---

[295] ibid 221.
[296] Hendrik Haag and Oliver Peglow, 'Germany' in Johnston (n 76) 196.
[297] Interestingly, the statistics show that securitisation is issued and used incomparably more in the US than in Germany. See ESF (European Securitisation Forum) Securitisation Data Report Q2:2009 (SIFMA (Securities Industry and Financial Markets Association), 2009) 3, www.afme.eu/document.aspx?id=2788.
[298] Section 1280 of the German Civil Code stipulates that the pledging of a receivable, for whose transfer a contract of transfer suffices, is effective only if the creditor gives notice thereof to the debtor ('Die Verpfändung einer Forderung, zu deren Übertragung der Abtretungsvertrag genügt, ist nur wirksam, wenn die Gläubiger sie dem Schuldner anzeigt').
[299] Klauer Rakob (n 61) 118.
[300] ibid.
[301] Hansjörg Weber, *Kreditsicherungsrecht*, 8th edn (Munich, CH Beck, 2006) 302.

without joining the transferor, as if the transferee were the original creditor of the receivable.[302] Because of the burden that a pledge of a receivable requires giving notice to the debtors of the receivable, in Germany, security transfers have replaced pledges under the German Civil Code as the common form of security rights in receivables.[303]

Q3. Priority of Transfers

Under the German Civil Code, notice to a debtor is not required for the transfer of a receivable. The transferee prior in time of the transfer agreement has priority regardless of notification. Under German law, priority among a transferee, the insolvency administrator and an execution creditor is determined according to the order of conclusion of the transfer agreement,[304] bankruptcy adjudication and attachment (seizure) notice.

If a transferee asks a transferor for a publicly certified copy of the transfer contract, the transferor must provide it, but the transferee should pay the cost.[305] The date of conclusion of the transfer contract is verified by a publicly certified document evidencing the transfer (if it is issued). However, in practice, it is not often issued because it is time-consuming and costly.[306]

German Civil Code	E	E2
Conclusion of the transfer agreement	1st	2nd
Debtor of the receivable receives notice of the transfer	4th	3rd
	E has priority over E2	

The debtor who had no notice of the first transfer may discharge the debt by paying the second transferee E2.[307] However, if the second transferee E2 has collected the debt from the debtor, he must surrender the money to the first transferee E, even though he gave value and knew nothing of the first transfer.[308] If a second transferee E2 gives notice to a debtor first, a debtor may discharge the debt by paying the second transferee E2 until such time as the first transferee E gives notice to the debtor. The second transferee E2 must surrender any payment he received from the debtor to the first transferee E. If a debtor of a receivable is

---

[302] Haag and Peglow (n 296) 200 [14.16].
[303] Klauer Rakob (n 61) 93.
[304] German Civil Code, s 403.
[305] ibid.
[306] Interview with Professor Ulrich Drobnig, Max Planck Institute for Comparative and International Private Law (Hamburg, Germany, 20 October 2010).
[307] German Civil Code, ss 408 and 407.
[308] See section 3-3-4-1.

truly uncertain as to who has priority, the debtor may deposit the payment with the court, which will ultimately determine which transferee has priority.

If a transferor fraudulently or mistakenly transfers the same receivable to different transferees, the transferor will have to compensate the transferees for damages and be criminally charged with fraud. Usually, the transferor signs a document confirming that there is no prior transfer of or security right in the receivable before concluding the transfer agreement. If what is confirmed in the signed document is found to be untrue, the transferor will be punished for fraud against the transferee.[309] Such conduct by the transferor can also give rise to civil liability.

Q4. Priority of Security Rights

The priority of pledges of a receivable is determined by the time order in which the debtor of the receivable receives notice of the pledge of the receivable. In a case involving two pledges of one receivable, the pledge of which the debtor received notice earlier takes priority over the later one.[310] The right to enforce the pledge rests with the holder of the pledge having priority.[311]

Q5. Priority between Transfers and Security Rights

The priority of transfers or pledges of a receivable is determined by the order of conclusion of the transfer agreement or notification of the pledge to the debtor of the receivable.

Q6. The Potential Transferee's Check Points

A potential transferee should enquire of the debtor of the receivable whether it has received notice of any prior security right in the receivable in question. However, it does not guarantee the transferee's priority. If there is another transfer with a contractual effective date that is prior to that of the potential transferee, then the potential transferee would not have priority. A potential transferee may, of course, also ask the transferor whether there was any prior transfer of the receivable in question.

---

[309] With respect to forgery, even though the transferor signed a document that confirms there is no prior transfer of or security right in the receivable, and before or after signing such a document, the transferor transferred or transfers the receivable to another transferee, it does not constitute a forgery (*Urkundenfälschung*) under s 267 of the German Criminal Code. The transferor is a rightful composer of the document assuming that he did not use another person's name or title. This only creates an erroneous private document, which is not subject to criminal punishment, except in the case of health certificates under s 278 of the German Criminal Code.

[310] Haag and Peglow (n 296) 196 [14.07].
[311] German Civil Code, s 1290.

3-7-13. Austria

Qs 1, 3. Transfers

An outright transfer of receivables does not require notification to a debtor. The transfer of receivables is done simply by the agreement of the parties.[312] Notice to the debtor of the receivable is not required for a transfer of a receivable to be perfected against third parties, including the insolvency administrator of the transferor.[313] This is the same under German law. Priority is determined by the time order of conclusion of the transfer agreement.

Let us suppose a case where the second transferee E2 gives notice of the transfer to the debtor of the receivable, while the first transferee E does not give notice to the debtor of the receivable, and the debtor of the receivable pays the second transferee E2.

In this case, the first transferee E can claim against the second transferee E2 for unjust enrichment (*Bereicherungsanspruch*). Furthermore, if the second transferee E2 knew of, or was negligent of the first transfer to E, the first transferee E may also claim against the second transferee E2 under tort law (*Schadenersatzanspruch*), as in German law.

Qs 2, 4. Security Rights

The pledge of receivables requires an explicit act (*Zeichen*), which allows its existence to be ascertained by third parties.[314] Notification to a debtor qualifies as an explicit act (*Zeichen*). In addition, a pledgor company may have records in its book (*Buchvermerk*), which evidence each receivable, the pledge, its date and the transferee, in order for the explicit act (*Zeichen*) requirement to be satisfied.[315]

Thus, for the pledge of a receivable, either notice of the pledge to the debtor of the receivable or a written record in the book of the pledgor company is required in order to perfect a pledge of a receivable against third parties, including the insolvency administrator of the transferor. These records are not available for members of the public to check; they are solely intended to prevent any possibility of backdating by requiring the pledgor company to immediately record an exact date.

A potential transferee or pledgee may enquire of the debtor of the receivable whether it has received notice of any prior pledge. However, this is not definitive because there is the possibility of future transfers or hidden pledges made without full disclosure to the debtor of the receivable.

---

[312] Austrian Civil Code, s 1392.
[313] ibid s 1394. See Rudolf Welser, *Koziol-Welser Bürgerliches Recht Band II* (Vienna, Manz, 2007) 120.
[314] Austrian Civil Code, ss 452 and 427.
[315] Welser (n 313) 120.

136 *Transfers of and Security Rights in Receivables*

Priority is determined by the order of notification of the pledge to the debtor of the receivable or the recording of the pledge in the book (*Buchvermerk*) of the transferor, comparing the date of the notice of the pledge to the debtor and the date of the recording of the pledge in the book (*Buchvermerk*) of the transferor.

Q5. Priority between Transfers and Security Rights

Priority is determined by the order: (i) of conclusion of the transfer contract; (ii) in which the debtor of the receivable receives notice of the pledge; or (iii) of the recording of the pledge in the book (*Buchvermerk*) of the transferor company. The first in time has priority.

Q6. The Potential Transferee's Check Points

A potential transferee should enquire of the debtor of the receivable whether it has received notice of any prior security right in the receivable in question. The book (*Buchvermerk*) of a transferor company is not available for a potential transferee to check.

3-7-14. The Netherlands

Table 3.11: Perfection methods of transfer and pledge in Dutch law

Transfer	Pledge	
	Disclosed pledge (*openbaar pand*)	**Undisclosed pledge** (*stil pand*)
Notice to the debtor of the receivable	Notice to the debtor of the receivable	n/a
Notarisation of a transfer deed	n/a	Notarisation of a transfer deed
Registration of a transfer deed with the TRD	n/a	Registration of a transfer deed with the TRD

Q1. Perfection of Transfers

Q1-1. Outright Transfer

The Netherlands abolished the notification requirement for the outright transfer of receivables in 2004.[316] The Dutch Civil Code allows the following three

---

[316] Dutch Civil Code, art 3:94. Originally, Dutch law had not required notice of the transfer to the debtor, but in 1994 it was decided that the notification requirement was necessary, and finally on 1 October 2004, the notification obligation was revoked. See Wood (n 209) 297.

methods of perfection against the insolvency administrator: (1) notice of the transfer to the debtor of the receivable; (2) notarisation of a transfer deed (*akte*); and (3) registration of a transfer deed with the Tax Registration Department (Belastingdienst/Registratie en successie) (TRD).[317] See Table 3.11. Parties may choose one of these three perfection methods.

Methods (2) and (3) mean that a transfer of receivables can be perfected by the mere execution of a written transfer deed,[318] which must be signed by both a transferor and a transferee. They are available only for receivables that already exist at the time of the transfer and future receivables that arise directly from a legal relationship that already exists at the time.[319] However, neither notarisation of a transfer deed nor registration with the TRD constitutes publicity, since they are not available to members of the public; instead, they are only to certify the transfer of receivables. Registration is a substitute for notarisation that is costly.

Q1-2. Security Transfer

Under the Dutch Civil Code, transfer of title to a receivable for security purposes is, in principle, not permitted.[320] In the Netherlands, a security transfer of receivables was disallowed by a Dutch Supreme Court decision[321] referring to Article 3:84(3) of the Dutch Civil Code, which stipulates that a judicial act intended to transfer property for security purposes or which does not have the purpose of vesting title in the transferee after the transfer does not constitute a valid title transfer of that property.[322]

Q2. Perfection of Security Rights

Under Dutch law, there are two ways to use receivables as collateral: a pledge with notification (disclosed pledge, *openbaar pand*) and a pledge without notification (undisclosed pledge, *stil pand*). See Table 3.11.

A disclosed pledge (*openbaar pand*) is created through perfection method (1). Notification is not subject to any specific form requirement. Notification may be oral or in writing.[323]

An undisclosed pledge (*stil pand*) may be created by perfection methods (2) and (3). In a case of an undisclosed pledge, the pledgee is authorised to give

---

[317] Dutch Civil Code, art 3:94(3).
[318] Angelique Thiele, 'Dutch Securitisations: A Step Forward', *The In-House Lawyer* (February 2005) 30, www.legal500.com/assets/images/devs/nether/fi/nlfi_014.pdf.
[319] Dutch Civil Code, art 3:94(3). See Sander Timmerman and Michael Veder, 'The Netherlands' in Sigman and Kieninger (n 4) 183.
[320] Dutch Civil Code, art 3:84(3).
[321] *Sogelease* case, HR 19 May 1995, NJ 1996, 119.
[322] Timmerman and Veder (n 319) 185.
[323] Notification is not subject to any specific form requirement and may be oral or in writing (ibid 212).

138   *Transfers of and Security Rights in Receivables*

notice of the pledge to the debtor of the receivable if the pledgor is in default or if the pledgee has good reason to believe that such a default will occur.[324]

Qs 3, 4, 5. Priority

Priority is determined by the order of perfection of a transfer or a pledge. As discussed above, perfection of the transfer or the pledge can be made by one of the following three methods: (1) notice of the transfer to the debtor of the receivable; (2) notarisation of a transfer deed; and (3) registration of a transfer deed with the TRD.[325] Once one of these three methods has been achieved, the transfer or the pledge of receivables is perfected against third parties. The transferee or pledgee completing any one of three perfection methods first has priority over any subsequent transferee or pledgor. The rule for priority is that the earlier pledge prevails, ie, first in time, first in right. Therefore, any subsequently disclosed right of pledge will not have priority over earlier undisclosed rights of pledge, even if the second pledgee acted in good faith.[326]

Q6. The Potential Transferee's Check Points

A potential transferee should enquire of the debtor of the receivable whether it has received notice of any prior transfer of or security right in the receivable in question. The best approach for a potential transferee would be to register the transfer of a receivable with the TRD as soon as possible. However, even so, such registration does not guarantee a potential transferee's priority. If it is later found that another transferee (or another pledgee) has notarised a transfer (or a pledge) prior to a potential transferee's registration with the TRD, a potential transferee would lose priority over the transferee (or the pledgee) with earlier notarisation.

3-7-15. Singapore

Q1. Perfection of Transfers

Q1-1. Transfer of Receivables

A transfer without notice to the debtor is still valid as an equitable assignment under English law.[327] Moreover, the receivables equitably transferred are separated from the insolvency estate of the transferor. As a result, an equitable assignee, like a statutory assignee, prevails against the trustee in bankruptcy or the liquidator of

---

[324] ibid.
[325] Dutch Civil Code, art 3:94(3).
[326] William Rank, 'The Netherlands' in Johnston (n 76) 360 [25.29].
[327] *Gorringe* (n 245).

the transferor.[328] An equitable assignment is also perfected against an execution creditor.[329]

Equitable assignments in English law are close to the transfer in German law in that they do not require notice of the transfer to the debtor for an equitable assignment which is perfected against the insolvency administrator and execution creditors.[330]

Q1-2. An Individual Person's General Transfer of Book Debts

If a natural person makes a general transfer of existing or future book debts, the transfer must be registered under the Bills of Sale Act 1878 in order to be perfected against the Official Assignee of the transferor.[331] A 'general assignment' does not include a transfer of book debts due at the date of the transfer from specified debtors or a transfer of debts becoming due under specified contracts.[332] In this context, an 'assignment' includes both a security transfer of and a charge over book debts.[333]

Q2. Perfection of Security Rights

Under the Companies Act (Cap 50), Chapter IV, Division 8, a charge on the book debts of a company can be registered in the register of charges of the Accounting and Corporate Regulatory Authority.[334] If a charge is created by a company (chargor), the company shall lodge a statement containing the particulars of the charge with the Registrar within 30 days (or such later time as is permitted by the court)[335] after the creation of the charge.[336] If it is not registered within 30 days, the charge is not perfected against the liquidator and any creditor (including execution creditor) of the company.[337]

Q3. Priority of Transfers

Priority is not related to perfection under English law. In *Dearle v Hall*, priority between competing transferees is determined by the time order in which the debtor receives notice of the transfer unless the subsequent transferee E2 knew of the prior transfer at the time of his transfer.[338]

---

[328] See section 3-7-10 Q 1-1.
[329] *Holt* (n 112).
[330] See section 3-4-3-1.
[331] Bankruptcy Act (Cap 20), s 104(2).
[332] Bankruptcy Act (Cap 20), s 104(3).
[333] Bankruptcy Act (Cap 20), s 104(3).
[334] Companies Act (Cap 50), s 131(3)(f).
[335] Companies Act (Cap 50), s 137.
[336] Companies Act (Cap 50), s 131(1).
[337] ibid.
[338] *Dearle v Hall* (n 15). See section 3-3-2.

English law: *Dearle v Hall*	E	E2
Conclusion of the transfer agreement	1st	2nd
Debtor of the receivable receives notice of the transfer	4th	3rd
		E2 has priority over E

The prior transfer to E is valid between the transferor and the transferee, even though no notice is given to the debtor, and consequently the transferred receivable no longer belongs to the insolvency estate of the transferor. Under the *nemo dat quod non habet* rule, a transferor cannot transfer what he does not have. Therefore, it might seem odd that the transferor can make a similar transfer to E2 which can have priority over the transfer to E.[339]

Nevertheless, E2 could be a bona fide purchaser if E2 purchased the receivable without notice of the prior equitable assignment made to E even though E2 gave notice of his transfer to the debtor of the receivable. In order for E2 to be a bona fide purchaser, E2 should have enquired of the debtor of the receivable. During the process of the enquiry, while E2 enquires of the debtor of the receivable as to whether it has received notice of any prior transfer of the receivable, it is likely that E2 would naturally give notice of his transfer to the debtor of the receivable. In this view, the *Dearle v Hall* rule is framed in terms of the bona fide purchaser rule.

If there are two transfers that comply with the statutory requirements, priority is determined by the time order in which the debtor receives notice of the transfer in writing.

If there are two equitable assignments and neither transferee gives notice to the debtor, priority is determined by the order of conclusion of the transfer agreement.[340]

Q4. Priority of Security Rights

English law: *Dearle v Hall* and constructive notice	S	S2
Registration of charge over the receivable	1st	2nd
Debtor of the receivable receives notice of the transfer	4th	3rd
		S has priority over S2

Let us suppose a case where a chargor provides the same receivable as collateral twice to two different chargees by creating two charges over the receivable.

---

[339] Michael Bridge et al (n 257) [36-012].
[340] Beale et al (n 1) 438 [13.09].

Priority of competing charges over a receivable is governed by the *Dearle v Hall* rule,[341] once statements of particulars of the charges are lodged with the Registrar within 30 days after the creation of the charge.[342] A chargee who has a charge over a receivable must give notice of the charge over the receivable to the debtor of the receivable in order to perfect the charge over the receivable. The chargee who gives notice of the charge to the debtor before any other secured creditor will have priority.

However, if one chargee S2 is aware of a registered charge made by the other chargee S, S2 cannot have priority over S despite giving notice of its charge to the debtor of the receivable before S. Registration of a charge (including a charge on the book debts of a company) with the Registrar of the Accounting and Corporate Regulatory Authority constitutes a constructive notice of the charge to third parties if it would be reasonable for the subsequent claimant to have made a search of the register of charges.[343] Thus, a subsequent chargee cannot later give notice of the charge to the debtor of the receivable and obtain priority over the prior charge that has already been registered before.[344] The chargee who registered its charge first has priority over any subsequent chargee.

If neither of the chargees gives notice of their charges to the debtor of the receivable, priority is determined by the time order of creation of the charge according to the first in time rule. According to the *nemo dat quod non habet* rule, a transferee cannot obtain more rights than the transferor had. Therefore, a subsequent charge should be subject to a prior charge. If a subsequent chargee is a bona fide purchaser for value without notice, it will take free of a prior charge. However, registration of a charge constitutes a constructive notice of the charge to third parties if it would be reasonable for the subsequent claimant to have made a search of the register of charges. Therefore, registration could prevent subsequent chargees from being a bona fide purchaser for value without notice.

Q5. Priority between Transfers and Security Rights

Q5-1. Prior Charge: Subsequent Transfer

If a charge over a receivable is perfected and the same receivable is later transferred to a third party, priority is determined by the time order in which the debtor of the receivable receives notice of the charge or the transfer.[345] For a charge on book debts of a company that is to be registered with the Registrar of the Accounting

---

[341] *Dearle v Hall* (n 15).
[342] Companies Act (Cap 50), ss 131(1) and 137.
[343] See section 3-7-10 Q 4.
[344] The second limb of *Dearle v Hall* (n 15). *Ellerman Lines Ltd v Lancaster Maritime Co Ltd* [1980] 2 Lloyd's Rep 497 (QB), 503. Until it has been registered, the subsequent chargee will not be on constructive notice of the earlier charge.
[345] *Dearle v Hall* (n 15).

and Corporate Regulatory Authority, if such registration constitutes a constructive notice, the subsequent transferee cannot have priority over the prior chargee by notification of the transfer to the debtor of the receivable. Most financiers of receivables would check the register in the ordinary course of business. Thus, registration might constitute a constructive notice.

Q5-2. Prior Transfer: Subsequent Charge

If a receivable is transferred to a transferee and a charge is subsequently created over the same receivable, the subsequent chargee would have no way to have actual or constructive notice of the prior transfer since a transfer is not registered.[346] Priority is determined by the time order in which the debtor of the receivable receives notice of the charge or the transfer.[347] Therefore, a subsequent chargee may give notice of his charge to the debtor of the receivable first (while the debtor of the receivable is not notified of the prior transfer) and obtain priority over the prior transfer.

Q6. The Potential Transferee's Check Points

In Singapore, a potential transferee should both check the register of charges kept by the Registrar of the Accounting and Corporate Regulatory Authority and enquire of the debtor of the receivable whether it has received notice of any prior transfer of or security right in the receivable in question.

3-7-16. Hong Kong

Q1. Perfection of Transfers

Q1-1. Transfer of Receivables

A transfer without notice to the debtor is still valid as an equitable assignment under English law.[348] Moreover, the receivables equitably transferred are separated from the insolvency estate of the transferor. As a result, an equitable assignee, like a statutory assignee, prevails against the trustee in bankruptcy or the liquidator of the transferor.[349] An equitable assignment is also perfected against an execution creditor.[350]

Equitable assignments in English law are close to the transfer in German law in that they do not require notice of the transfer to the debtor for an equitable

---

[346] Beale et al (n 1) 442 [13.14]. However, in practice, many receivable financiers also take a charge over all the assets of a financial company.
[347] *Dearle v Hall* (n 15).
[348] *Gorringe* (n 245).
[349] See section 3-7-10 Q 1-1.
[350] *Holt* (n 112).

assignment which is perfected against the insolvency administrator and execution creditors.[351]

Q1-2. An Individual Person's General Transfer of Book Debts

If a natural person makes a general transfer of existing or future book debts or any class thereof, the transfer must be registered in the register of charges at the Companies Registry to be perfected against the trustee in bankruptcy of the transferor.[352] A 'general assignment' does not include a transfer of book debts due at the date of the transfer from specified debtors or a transfer of debts becoming due under specified contracts.[353] In this context, an 'assignment' includes both a security transfer of and a charge over book debts.[354]

Q2. Perfection of Security Rights

Under the Companies Ordinance (Cap 622), Chapter 8, Division 2, a charge on book debts of a company can be registered in the register of charges at the Companies Registry.[355] A company must deliver a statement of the particulars of every specified charge created by the company to the Registrar for registration,[356] within one month (or such later time as is permitted by the court)[357] after the date on which the specified charge is created.[358] If it is not registered within 30 days, the charge is not perfected against any liquidator and creditor (including execution creditor) of the company or registered non-Hong Kong company.[359]

Q3. Priority of Transfers

Priority is not related to perfection under English law. In *Dearle v Hall*, priority between competing transferees is determined by the time order in which the debtor receives notice of the transfer unless the subsequent transferee E2 knew of the prior transfer at the time of his transfer.[360]

English law: *Dearle v Hall*	E	E2
Conclusion of the transfer agreement	1st	2nd
Debtor of the receivable receives notice of the transfer	4th	3rd
	\multicolumn{2}{c}{E2 has priority over E}

---

[351] See section 3-4-3-1.
[352] Bankruptcy Ordinance (Cap 6), s 48(1).
[353] ibid.
[354] ibid s 48(2).
[355] Companies Ordinance (Cap 622), s 334(1)(d).
[356] ibid s 335(1).
[357] ibid s 346(1)(a).
[358] ibid s 335(5)(a).
[359] ibid s 337(4).
[360] *Dearle v Hall* (n 15). See section 3-3-2.

The prior transfer to E is valid between the transferor and the transferee, even though no notice is given to the debtor, and consequently the transferred receivable no longer belongs to the insolvency estate of the transferor. Under the *nemo dat quod non habet* rule, a transferor cannot transfer what he does not have. Therefore, it might seem odd that the transferor can make a similar transfer to E2 which can have priority over the transfer to E.[361]

Nevertheless, E2 could be a bona fide purchaser if E2 purchased the receivable without notice of the prior equitable assignment made to E, even though E2 gave notice of his transfer to the debtor of the receivable. In order for E2 to be a bona fide purchaser, E2 should have enquired of the debtor of the receivable. During the process of the enquiry, while E2 enquires of the debtor of the receivable as to whether it has received notice of any prior transfer of the receivable, it is likely that E2 would naturally give notice of his transfer to the debtor of the receivable. In this view, the *Dearle v Hall* rule is framed in terms of the bona fide purchaser rule.

If there are two transfers that comply with the statutory requirements, priority is determined by the time order in which the debtor receives notice of the transfer in writing.

If there are two equitable assignments and neither transferee gives notice to the debtor, priority is determined by the order of conclusion of the transfer agreement.[362]

Q4. Priority of Security Rights

English law: *Dearle v Hall* and constructive notice	S	S2
Registration of charge over the receivable	1st	2nd
Debtor of the receivable receives notice of the transfer	4th	3rd
	S has priority over S2	

Let us suppose a case where a chargor provides the same receivable as collateral twice to two different chargees by creating two charges over the receivable.

Priority of competing charges over a receivable is governed by the *Dearle v Hall* rule,[363] once statements of particulars of the charges are delivered to the Registrar within one month after the date of creation.[364] A chargee who has a charge over a receivable must give notice of the charge over the receivable to the debtor of the receivable in order to perfect the charge over the receivable. The chargee who gives notice of the charge to the debtor before any other secured creditor will have priority.

---

[361] Bridge et al (n 257) [36-012].
[362] Beale et al (n 1) 438 [13.09].
[363] *Dearle v Hall* (n 15).
[364] Companies Ordinance (Cap 622), ss 335(5)(a) and 346(1)(a).

However, if one chargee S2 is aware of a registered charge made by the other chargee S, S2 cannot have priority over S, despite giving notice of its charge to the debtor of the receivable before S. Registration of a charge (including a charge on the book debts of a company) in the register of charges at the Companies Registry constitutes a constructive notice of the charge to third parties if it would be reasonable for the subsequent claimant to have made a search of the register of charges.[365] Thus, a subsequent chargee cannot later give notice of the charge to the debtor of the receivable and obtain priority over the prior charge that has already been registered before.[366] The chargee who registered its charge first has priority over any subsequent chargee.

If neither of the chargees gives notice of their charges to the debtor of the receivable, priority is determined by the time order of creation of the charge according to the first in time rule. According to the *nemo dat quod non habet* rule, a transferee cannot obtain more rights than the transferor had. Therefore, a subsequent charge should be subject to a prior charge. If a subsequent chargee is a bona fide purchaser for value without notice, it will take free of a prior charge. However, registration of a charge constitutes a constructive notice of the charge to third parties if it would be reasonable for the subsequent claimant to have made a search of the register of charges. Therefore, registration could prevent subsequent chargees from being a bona fide purchaser for value without notice.

Q5. Priority between Transfers and Security Rights

Q5-1. Prior Charge: Subsequent Transfer

If a charge over a receivable is perfected and the same receivable is later transferred to a third party, priority is determined by the time order in which the debtor of the receivable receives notice of the charge or the transfer.[367] For a charge on the book debts of a company that is to be registered in the register of charges at the Companies Registry, if such registration constitutes a constructive notice, the subsequent transferee cannot have priority over the prior chargee by notification of the transfer to the debtor of the receivable. Most financiers of receivables would check the register in the ordinary course of business. Thus, registration might constitute a constructive notice.

Q5-2. Prior Transfer: Subsequent Charge

If a receivable is transferred to a transferee and a charge is subsequently created over the same receivable, the subsequent chargee would have no way to have actual

---

[365] See section 3-7-10 Q 4.
[366] The second limb of *Dearle v Hall* (n 15). See *Ellerman Lines Ltd v Lancaster Maritime Co Ltd* [1980] 2 Lloyd's Rep 497 (QB), 503. Until it has been registered, the subsequent chargee will not be on constructive notice of the earlier charge.
[367] *Dearle v Hall* (n 15).

or constructive notice of the prior transfer since a transfer is not registered.[368] Priority is determined by the time order in which the debtor of the receivable receives notice of the charge or the transfer.[369] Therefore, a subsequent chargee may give notice of his charge to the debtor of the receivable first (while the debtor of the receivable is not notified of the prior transfer) and obtain priority over the prior transfer.

Q6. The Potential Transferee's Check Points

In Singapore, a potential transferee should both check the register of charges at the Companies Registry and enquire of the debtor of the receivable whether it has received notice of any prior transfer of or security right in the receivable in question.

3-8. The EU Directive on Financial Collateral Arrangements

3-8-1. The Parties: Financial Institutions

Directive 2002/47/EC on financial collateral arrangements as amended by Directive 2009/44/EC is referred to as 'EU FCD' in this section. The EU FCD generally does not cover receivables, except those owed to financial institutions.

Directive 2002/47/EC on financial collateral arrangements[370] limits its scope of application to cases where none of the parties (the grantor or the secured creditor) is a natural person,[371] and at least one or both of the parties belong to one of the following categories: (a) a public authority;[372] (b) a central bank, the European Central Bank, the Bank for International Settlements, a multilateral development bank, the International Monetary Fund or the European Investment Bank;[373] (c) a financial institution subject to prudential supervision;[374] or (d) a central

---

[368] Beale et al (n 1) 442 [13.14]. However, in practice, many receivable financiers also take a charge over all the assets of a financial company.

[369] *Dearle v Hall* (n 15).

[370] Directive 2002/47/EC of the European Parliament and of the Council of 6 June 2002 on financial collateral arrangements [2002] OJ L168/43 For information on the national implementation of Directive 2002/47/EC on financial collateral arrangements, see EUR-Lex, Bibliographic notice 72002L0047, http://eur-lex.europa.eu/legal-content/EN/TXT/?uri=uriserv:OJ.L_.2002.168.01.0043.01.ENG&toc=OJ:L:2002:168:TOC.

[371] EU FCD, art 1(2)(e).

[372] ibid art 1(2)(a).

[373] Directive 2002/47/EC on financial collateral arrangements, art 1(2)(b), as amended by Directive 2009/44/EC, art 2(4)(a).

[374] Directive 2002/47/EC on financial collateral arrangements, art 1(2)(c), as amended by Directive 2009/44/EC, art 2(4)(b).

counterparty, settlement agent or clearing house.[375] If one party belongs to one of these four categories, the counterparty on the other side may be any legal person, including unincorporated firms and partnerships outside of the banking industry.[376] The EU FCD extends the scope of application beyond collateral arrangements between central banks and financial institutions.

3-8-2. Financial Collateral

3-8-2-1. Cash and Financial Instruments

Directive 2002/47/EC on financial collateral arrangements has removed any publicity requirements such as registration or notification[377] for the arrangement of financial collateral consisting of cash or financial instruments.[378]

Directive 2002/47/EC on financial collateral arrangements also recognises the transfer of credit claims for security purposes.[379]

3-8-2-2. Credit Claims

In 2007, the European Central Bank introduced credit claims as an eligible type of collateral for Eurosystem credit operations.[380] In line with the change, Directive 2009/44/EC[381] amended Directive 2002/47/EC on financial collateral arrangements and has expanded the scope of the Directive to include the financial collateral consisting of 'credit claims',[382] ie, receivables arising out of an agreement whereby a credit institution grants credit in the form of a loan.[383] Such credit claims are basically bank loans used as collateral for advances from the European Central Bank and other central banks.[384] Directive 2009/44/EC facilitates a transfer or pledge of bank loans to the central banks for security purposes.

---

[375] EU FCD, art 1(2)(d).
[376] ibid art 1(2)(e). However, states may opt out of this provision: ibid art 1(3).
[377] ibid recital 10 and art 3(1).
[378] ibid art 1(4)(a).
[379] ibid arts 2(1)(b) and 6.
[380] European Central Bank (ECB) press release of 15 September 2006, www.ecb.eu/press/pr/date/2006/html/pr060915_1.en.html.
[381] Directive 2002/47/EC of the European Parliament and of the Council of 6 June 2002 on financial collateral arrangements [2002] OJ L168/43 For information on the national implementation of Directive 2002/47/EC on financial collateral arrangements, see EUR-Lex, Bibliographic notice 72002L0047 http://eur-lex.europa.eu/legal-content/EN/TXT/?uri=uriserv:OJ.L_.2002.168.01.0043.01.ENG&toc=OJ:L:2002:168:TOC.
[382] Directive 2009/44/EC, art 2(4)(c).
[383] ibid art 2(5)(a)(ii).
[384] Louise Gullifer, 'What Should We Do about Financial Collateral?' (2012) 65 *Current Legal Problems* 377, 404.

3-8-3. Perfection

A financial collateral arrangement may not be declared invalid or void if the financial collateral arrangement has come into existence or the financial collateral has been provided prior to the order or decree making the commencement of insolvency proceedings or reorganisation measures.[385] It does not require any publicity for perfection against the insolvency administrator. As a result, credit claims can be pledged or transferred for security purposes in the same way as financial instruments or cash. In the insolvency of the grantor, the secured creditor can realise the credit claim as financial collateral even though the secured creditor did not give notice to the debtor of the credit claim prior to the insolvency adjudication. If an EU jurisdiction requires the registration of security rights in or security transfers of such credit claims under its national law for perfection against insolvency administrators,[386] it must repeal the legislation to the extent that it applies to interests over financial collateral. The EU FCD contributes to harmonising legal standards with respect to credit claims used among credit institutions in EU Member States.

3-8-4. Priority

Where credit claims are provided as financial collateral, priority is determined by the order of execution of financial collateral agreements. However, Member States are permitted to require publicity such as registration or notification for priority vis-a-vis third parties.[387]

3-8-5. Implementation

Table 3.12: Implementation of the EU Directive on financial collateral arrangements

	Directive 2002/47/EC on financial collateral arrangements	Directive 2009/44/EC amending Directive 2002/47/EC
France	Articles L211-36 to L211-40 of the French Monetary and Financial Code[388]	

(continued)

---

[385] EU FCD, art 8(1)(a).
[386] ibid art 8(1) and (2).
[387] Directive 2009/44/EC, art 2(6)(a).
[388] Inserted by Order No 2009-15 of 8 January 2009, art 1 Official Journal of 9 January 2009.

Table 3.12: *(Continued)*

	Directive 2002/47/EC on financial collateral arrangements	Directive 2009/44/EC amending Directive 2002/47/EC
Belgium	Financial Collateral Act of 15 December 2004	Act of 26 September 2011
UK	Financial Collateral Arrangements (No 2) Regulations 2003[389]	Financial Collateral Arrangements (No 2) Regulations 2003 (Amendment) Regulations 2009[390] Financial Markets and Insolvency (Settlement Finality and Financial Collateral Arrangements) (Amendment) Regulations 2010[391]
Germany	Law of 5 April 2004 implementing the Directive 2002/47/EC of the European Parliament and of the Council of 6 June 2002 on financial collateral arrangements[392]	Law implementing the amended Banking Directive and the amended Capital Adequacy Directive[393]

(continued)

---

[389] SI 2003/3226. Its scope of application with respect to parties is wider than that of the EU FCD, in that the UK 2003 Regulations apply to financial collateral arrangements where the collateral provider and the collateral taker are both non-natural persons: Financial Collateral Arrangements (No 2) Regulations 2003, reg 3. It does not require one of the parties to be a financial institution. There was an argument that it is ultra vires s 2(2) of the European Communities Act 1972, but such an argument is unlikely to succeed: *R (on the Application of Cukurova Finance International Limited) v Her Majesty's Treasury* [2008] EWHC 2567 (Admin).

[390] SI 2009/2462.

[391] SI 2010/2993. The amended Regulations cover receivables on loans made by credit institutions. Regulation 3 of the Financial Collateral Arrangements (No 2) Regulations 2003 was amended by regs 4(2)(b)(i) and (ii) of the Financial Markets and Insolvency (Settlement Finality and Financial Collateral Arrangements) (Amendment) Regulations 2010. Accordingly, for financial collateral arrangements with respect to receivables on loans made by credit institutions, no publicity (either registration or notice to the debtor) is required.

[392] Gesetz vom 5/4/2004 zur Umsetzung der Richtlinie 2002/47/EG vom 6/6/2002 über Finanzsicherheiten und zur Änderung des Hypothekenbankgesetzes und anderer Gesetze, Bundesgesetzblatt, (2004) part I, No 15, 502 http://ec.europa.eu/internal_market/finances/actionplan/transposition/germany/f_d7_de_en.htm.

[393] Gesetz zur Umsetzung der geänderten Bankenrichtlinie und der geänderten Kapitaladäquanzrichtlinie, Bundesgesetzblatt (2010) part I, No 58, 1592–613.

Table 3.12: *(Continued)*

	Directive 2002/47/EC on financial collateral arrangements	Directive 2009/44/EC amending Directive 2002/47/EC
Austria	Federal Law implementing the Federal Law governing safety on financial markets (Financial Markets Safety Act—FinSG) and modifying the Private International Law Act[394]	Financial Collateral Act (Finanzsicherheiten-Gesetz)[395]
The Netherlands	Law of 22 December 2005 to implement Directive 2002/47/EC of the European Parliament and European Council of 6 June 2002 concerning financial collateral arrangements[396]	Law of 21 April 2011 amending the Civil Code and the Bankruptcy Act to implement Directive 2009/44/EC amending Directive 98/26/EC on settlement finality in the settlement of payments and securities transactions in payment and securities settlement systems and Directive 2002/47/EC on financial collateral arrangements as regards linked systems and credit claims[397]

3-9. Conclusion

This chapter has shown us that there is considerable variation in terms of how legal systems around the world deal with transfers of and security rights in receivables. This legal variety makes it difficult for financiers to conduct international receivables financing business.

---

[394] Bundesgesetz, mit den ein Bundesgesetz über Sichereiten auf den Finanzmärkten (FINSG) erlassen wird und das Bundesgsetz über das internatoinale Privatrecht geändert wird, Bundesgesetzblatt für die Republik Österreich (BGBl) no 117 vom 16/12/2003, 1645, http://ec.europa.eu/internal_market/finances/actionplan/transposition/austria/f_d7_at_en.htm.

[395] Bundesgesetzblatt für die Republik Österreich (BGBl), I No 90/2010.

[396] Wet van 22 december 2005 tot uitvoering van Richtlijn nr 2002/47/EG van het Europees Parlement en de Raad van de Europese Unie van 6 juni 2002 betreffende financiëlezekerheidsovereenkomsten, Staatsblad 2006, 15, http://ec.europa.eu/internal_market/finances/actionplan/transposition/netherlands/f_d7_nl_en.htm.

[397] Wet van 21 april 2011 tot wijziging van het Burgerlijk Wetboek en de Faillissementswet ter implementatie van Richtlijn 2009/44/EG van het Europees Parlement en de Europese Raad van 6 mei 2009 tot wijziging van Richtlijn 98/26/EG betreffende het definitieve karakter van de afwikkeling van betalingen en effectentransacties in betalings- en afwikkelingssystemen en Richtlijn 2002/47/EG betreffende financiëlezekerheidsovereenkomsten wat gekoppelde systemen en kredietvorderingen betreft (PbEU L 146/37) Staatsblad 2011, 210.

Giving notice to the debtor of the receivable is still required in many cross-border transfers of receivables, which is a major obstacle to cross-border receivables financing. In receivable financing, it is impractical for financiers to enquire of the account debtors whether they have received notice of any prior transfer of or security right in the receivables they owe before each transaction. Also, it is impractical for financiers to give notice to the account debtors after the transaction.

In this world, where different laws on transfers of and security rights in receivables in each jurisdiction are commingled, an international registration system for transfers of and security rights in receivables is the best solution to facilitate cross-border receivables financing.

4

Conflicts of Laws and Technical Issues of the Debtor-Indexed Registration System

4-1. Introduction

In this chapter, sections 4-2–4-5 examine the private international laws of each jurisdiction in order to simulate which national law would be applied in international receivables financing. The simulation shows that deciding the governing law according to private international laws is not crystal-clear and such uncertainty in relation to private international law rules hinders international receivables financing. This suggests that unifying choice-of-law rules cannot solve the current situation and instead a unified substantive rule is needed to facilitate international receivables financing. Section 4-6 summarises the problems of conflicts of laws in international transfer of receivables and proposes that establishing an international registration system is the best solution to facilitate international receivables financing.

However, a general security rights registry has a systemic weakness due to the debtor-indexed registration system, ie, the so-called double debtor problem, and there are technical issues with respect to priority rules for floating charges in English law, reservation of title, purchase-money security interests and proceeds. These issues need to be dealt with sophisticatedly when designing an international receivables registry system. Section 4-7 explains the so-called double debtor problem, which is a systemic weakness of debtor-indexed registration system. Sections 4-8 and 4-9 analyse priority rules with respect to floating charges in English law, reservation of title, purchase-money security interests and proceeds.

4-2. The Governing Law

The transfer of receivables is a triangular relationship: between the transferor and the transferee; between the transferor and the debtor; and between the transferee and the debtor. In the transfer of receivables, each relationship between different parties is governed by different choice-of-law rules.

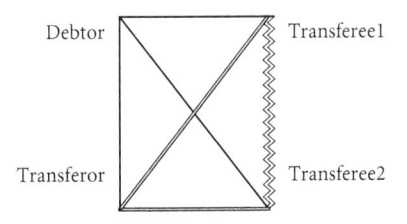

4-2-1. Transferor and Transferee

The relationship between the transferor and the transferee is governed by the governing law of the *transfer contract*. For example, formality of the contract, rights and obligations of the parties, and the effect of a transfer of future receivables are governed by the governing law of the transfer contract. Article 14(1) of the Rome I Regulation[1] stipulates the same rule.

If the receivable has been collected by the transferor, the transferor has the obligation to transfer the proceeds to the transferee. The transferee's right on the proceeds is governed by the governing law of the transfer contract.[2] If the transferee claims for the proceeds on the basis of unjust enrichment, Article 10 of the Rome II Regulation[3] will apply. In any case, the result is the same, in that it is governed by the governing law of the transfer contract.[4]

4-2-2. Transferor and Debtor, Transferee and Debtor

The relationship between the transferor and the debtor is governed by the governing law of the *contract generating the receivable* between the transferor and the debtor. The relationship between the transferee and the debtor is also governed by the governing law of the contract generating the receivable.[5] For example, the assignability of the receivable, the validity of the transferred obligation, the effect

---

[1] Regulation (EC) No 593/2008 of the European Parliament and of the Council of 17 June 2008 on the law applicable to contractual obligations (Rome I) [2008] OJ L 177/6.
[2] ibid art 14(1). The Rome I Regulation applies to contractual obligations. However, Recital 38 of the Rome I Regulation stipulates that art 14(1) also applies to the property aspects of a transfer as between the transferor and the transferee.
[3] Regulation (EC) No 864/2007 of the European Parliament and of the Council of 11 July 2007 on the law applicable to non-contractual obligations (Rome II) [2007] OJ L 199/40. The Rome II Regulation applies to non-contractual obligations.
[4] ibid art 10(1).
[5] Rome I Registration, art 14(2).

of an anti-assignment clause vis-a-vis the debtor[6] and discharge of the receivable are governed by the law regulating the obligation of the debtor as stipulated in the contract generating the receivable.

4-2-3. Insolvency Administrator and Transferee

In cases involving the insolvency of the transferor, the relationship between the insolvency administrator and the transferee is governed by the law of the state where the insolvent transferor is located.[7] This is because the insolvency proceedings are opened in the state where the transferor is located.

4-2-4. Attachment Creditor and Transferee

The relationship between the transferee and an attachment creditor of the transferor is not stipulated in the Rome Regulation.

In *Raiffeisen Zentralbank Osterreich AG v Five Star General Trading LLC*,[8] where an insurance policy is transferred to a transferee under English law and later the insurance policy is attached by a creditor of the transferor in a court in France, the English Court of Appeal decided that since the insurance policy had been validly transferred to the transferee under English law before the attachment, the transferor was no longer the owner of the insurance policy and therefore the creditor of the transferor cannot attach the insurance policy.

It is thought that if the insurance policy were first attached and then transferred to the transferor, it might be an issue of priority and thus French law might be the governing law. Under both French and English private international law, priority between competing transferees is governed by the law of the state in which the debtor is located.

4-2-5. Transferee 1 and Transferee 2

The relationship between competing transferees is not stipulated in the Rome Regulation. There are four choice-of-law rules: the law of the state in which the *debtor* is located ('Rule D'); the governing law of the transfer *contract* between the transferor and the transferee ('Rule C'); the governing law of the contract

---

[6] However, where the transfer is invalid due to an anti-assignment clause, the remedy of the transferee to the transferor is governed by the governing law of the transfer contract.
[7] Council Regulation (EC) No 1346/2000 of 29 May 2000 on insolvency proceedings [2000] OJ L 160/1, arts 4(1) and 4(2)(m).
[8] *Raiffeisen Zentralbank Osterreich AG v Five Star General Trading LLC* [2000] EWCA Civ 68, [2001] QB 825 (CA).

generating the *receivable* between the transferor and the debtor ('Rule R'); and the law of the state where the *transferor* is located ('Rule A').

Rule C has a serious disadvantage in the event that there are different transferees competing against each other, because different transfer contracts may be governed by different governing laws. Each of these would have to be examined.

Rule D has a serious disadvantage in receivables financing, which contains various receivables, since there could be various account debtors of receivables and different receivable contracts governed by different governing laws. Each of these would have to be investigated.

Rule A and Rule R[9] are desirable because there is only one single transferor in the case of competing transferees and in receivables financing. In addition, if the proceeds are already collected by the transferor, it is a matter of unjust enrichment between the transferor and the transferees. According to the Rome II Regulation, the governing law may be the law of the state where the unjust enrichment took place,[10] which is the law of the state in which the transferor is located.

4-3. The Governing Law for Priority

4-3-1. The Rome I Regulation

Under Article 14(1) of the Rome I Regulation, which governs the choice of law in the EU, the relationship between a transferor and a transferee is governed by the law that applies to the contract between the transferor and transferee. Furthermore, Article 14(2) of the Rome I Regulation only stipulates that the law governing the transferred receivable between the transferor (the original creditor) and the debtor determines the relationship between the transferee and the debtor, and thus is the governing law for the legal obligation between the transferee and the debtor.

The EC Commission's proposal for the Rome I Regulation[11] suggested that the law of the transferor's state should be the governing law for the priority among competing transferees or claimants of the transferred receivable.[12] However,

---

[9] According to international private law principles, in sales contracts, the governing law of the receivable is determined by the law of the country where the seller of goods is located. The seller of goods is the creditor of monetary claims and furthermore would be the transferor of monetary claims. Thus, in many cases, the law of the transferor's country would be the governing law according to Rule R.

[10] Rome II Regulation, art 10(3).

[11] Proposal for a Regulation of the European Parliament and the Council on the law applicable to contractual obligations (Rome I) (COM/2005/0650 final—COD 2005/0261), art 13(3).

[12] The benefit of this approach is that there would be only one governing law for all transfers. A transferee would only have to look at the laws of one jurisdiction for bulk transfers. In bulk international transfers of receivables for international receivables financing, though there might be multiple debtors, there will only be one transferor. See Harry C Sigman and Eva-Maria Kieninger (eds), *Cross-border Security over Receivables* (Munich, Sellier, 2009) 60–62. However, the law of the state of a transferor

unfortunately the EU Member States did not reach an agreement on this issue and this proposal has not been accepted. As a result, there is no clear regulation on the governing law for third-party effectiveness and priority in the Rome I Regulation at the moment.

4-3-2. Private International Law

At present, private international laws regarding priority vary from state to state. In international transfers of receivables, it is not always clear which state's law is the governing law for priority. The governing law of priority can be considered according to the applicable private international laws of the jurisdiction, but there is still uncertainty depending on the court involved.

Table 4.1 below displays the governing law of the relationship of each of the parties in the transfer of receivables according to the private international law of each jurisdiction. The governing law of priority is related to the information centre where a potential transferee can check whether there is any prior transfer or security right.

Table 4.1: The governing law in the transfer of receivables

		Transferee v Transferor	Transferor v Debtor, Transferee v Debtor	Insolvency administrator v Transferee	Priority between competing transferees
R	US	Rule C	Rule R	Rule A	Rule A[13]
	Canada				Rule A[14]
	New Zealand				Rule A[15]
	Australia				Rule A[16]
RN	Korea	Rule C	Rule R	Rule A	Rule R[17]
	Japan				Rule R[18]

(continued)

might not be enforceable in the state of the debtor. If a debtor does not pay the debt, the transferee must use the domestic court in the debtor's state to enforce payment. The court would decide priority and make judgments according to that state's law. Even if the governing law of the transfer contract is the law of the transferor's state, it is not clear whether the applicable court in the debtor's state would apply the foreign law of the transferor's state.

[13] US UCC, s 9-301(1).
[14] Ontario PPSA, s 7(1)(a)(i); Saskatchewan PPSA, s 7(2)(a)(i).
[15] New Zealand PPSA, s 30(a).
[16] Australian PPSA, ss 239(2) and 77(2).
[17] Korean Private International Act, art 34(1).
[18] Japanese Act on General Rules for Application of Laws (法の適用に関する通則法), art 23.

Table 4.1: *(Continued)*

		Transferee v Transferor	Transferor v Debtor, Transferee v Debtor	Insolvency administrator v Transferee	Priority between competing transferees
N	France	Rule C	Rule R	Rule A	Rule D[19]
	Belgium				Rule A[20]
SR	England	Rule C	Rule R	Rule A	Rule D[21]
	China				Unknown[22]
C	Germany	Rule C	Rule R	Rule A	Rule R[23]
	Austria				Rule R
	The Netherlands				Rule C[24]

In the Group R jurisdictions, where priority is determined by the time order of registration, the *registry* is an information centre. Registration of the transfer of receivables must be done in the registry of the transferor's state, because the registry is indexed by the transferor (or grantor). The transferor's state is where registrants register their transfers or security rights and searchers seek to discover them.[25] Thus, in these jurisdictions, the law of the transferor's state is the governing law for perfection and priority, although subject to the exceptions discussed in the next paragraph.

Under UCC Article 9, if a transferor is located in a foreign country, and the country has a central filing system that meets the UCC's requirements, the law of the transferor's country is the governing law with respect to perfection and

---

[19] CA Paris, 26 March 1986, D 1986, 374 2°, note *Vasseur*.
[20] Belgian Private International Law, art 87(3).
[21] *Re Queensland Mercantile and Agency Co* [1892] 1 Ch 219 (CA); Roy Goode and Ewan McKendrick, *Goode on Commercial Law*, 4th edn (London, Penguin Books, 2010) 1242, citing James Fawcett, Janeen Carruthers and Peter North, *Private International Law*, 14th edn (Oxford, Oxford University Press, 2008) 1234–35.
[22] The governing law of priority of competing transferees is not stipulated in the Law of the Application of Law for Foreign-Related Civil Relations (涉外民事关系法律适用法).
[23] BGH 20 June 1990, BGHZ 111, 376, at 379; BGH 26 November 1990, NJW 1991, 1414. In Germany, art 12(2) of the Convention on the law applicable to contractual obligations opened for signature in Rome on 19 June 1980 [1980] OJ L 266/1 ('Rome Convention') was applied.
[24] Property Law (Conflict of Laws) Act (*Wet Conflictenrecht Goederenrecht*) of 25 February 2008; HR 16 May 1997 Brandsma qq/Hansa Chemie, NJ 1998, 585; JOR 1997,77. In the Netherlands, art 12(1) of the Rome Convention was applied.
[25] Lynn M LoPucki, 'The Systems Approach to Law' (1996–97) 82 *Cornell Law Review* 479, 512; Maria Kieninger, 'General Principles on the Law Applicable to the Transfer of Receivables in Europe' in Jürgen Basedow, Harald Baum and Yuko Nishitani (eds), *Japanese and European Private International Law in Comparative Perspective* (Tubingen, Mohr Siebeck, 2008) 162.

priority of security rights.[26] If a transferor is located in a foreign country, but that country does not have a central filing system that meets the UCC's requirements, the transferor is considered for the purposes of the UCC to be located in Washington DC for filing purposes.[27] If a transferor is incorporated in a foreign country but has a place of business or a chief executive office in the US, the filing should be made in the US at its place of business or chief executive office as applicable.[28]

Under the Australian PPSA as interpreted by the Australian courts, if the law of the jurisdiction that governs the priority does not provide for public registration,[29] the transfer of receivables, perfected by registration under Australian PPSA before the other interest attaches to the receivables, has priority over the other transfer in proceedings.[30]

In the jurisdictions of Groups N and SR (except Belgium), where priority is determined by the time order in which the debtor of the receivable receives notice of the transfer, the law of the account debtor's state is generally the governing law for priority. This is because the *debtor* of the receivable is an information centre. A potential transferee would be expected to ask the debtor regarding a prior transfer or security right.[31] Moreover, the state where the debtor of the receivable is located is the place where the courts have control over the debtor and thus recovery of the debt.[32] Thus, potential transferees will naturally turn to the rules of the jurisdiction where the debtor is located.

Exceptionally, under the French Monetary and Financial Act, notice of transfer to the debtor is not required.[33] A transfer or pledge of receivables is perfected against third parties from the date indicated on the transfer deed (*bordereau*) when it is handed over, regardless of the law applicable to the receivables and the law of the debtor's country of residence.[34] The same principle applies to transfers to the *Fonds Communs de Créances* (FCC)[35] in securitisation.[36] Priority is also determined by the order of the date indicated on the transfer deed (*bordereau*) when it is handed over.

---

[26] UCC, ss 9-307(b) and (c), 9-301(1).
[27] ibid s 9-307(c).
[28] ibid s 9-307(b)(2) and (3). See also Elizabeth A Roff, 'New York' in William Johnston (ed), *Security over Receivables: An International Handbook* (Oxford, Oxford University Press, 2008) 372.
[29] Australian PPSA, s 77(1).
[30] ibid s 77(2).
[31] Goode and McKendrick (n 21) 1242, citing Fawcett, Carruthers and North (n 21) 1234–35.
[32] ibid.
[33] See section 3-7-8 Q 1-2.
[34] French Monetary and Financial Code, art L313–27.
[35] The French Monetary and Financial Code provides for the use of FCC, which can be either an incorporated entity (*société de titrisation*) or an unincorporated co-ownership between the holders of the participation interests in it (*fonds commun de titrisation*). The latter form does not have legal personality. See James Leavy, 'France' in Sigman and Kieninger (n 12) 142.
[36] See section 3-7-8 Q 1-3.

In the Group RN jurisdictions, where priority is determined by the time order of registration or notice of the transfer to the debtor, both the *debtor* of the receivable and the *registry* are information centres that a potential transferee should check. In these jurisdictions, the governing law for perfection and priority is the law governing the receivable, which is determined according to the characteristics of the contract generating the receivable.

For example, if the receivables transferred are trade receivables, the law of the seller's state is the law governing the receivable because it is the most closely related state. The seller of the goods is the transferor (the original creditor) of the receivables. As a result, the law of the transferor's state would be the governing law for priority of the transfer of trade receivables. This is suitable because in trade receivables, the parties would opt to register the transfer rather than give notice to each and every account debtor. For trade receivables, there are usually a number of small account debtors and it would be very costly and time-consuming to give notice of the transfer of receivables to each and every account debtor.

In the Group C jurisdictions, where neither notice nor registration is required for perfection, the *transferor* is an information centre. In these jurisdictions, eg, if the receivables transferred are trade receivables, the governing law for perfection and priority is the law of the transferor's state because it is the law governing the receivable.

In the Netherlands, parties may choose the governing law for priority.[37] If not chosen by the parties, priority is determined by the governing law of the transfer contract.[38]

4-4. Perfection Methods and Check Points

4-4-1. What to Do for Perfection in International Transfers

The governing law for priority in international transfers of receivables would be determined mostly by Rule R, Rule A or Rule D. Although the law governing the receivable (Rule R) varies according to the characteristics of the receivable, it is either the law of the transferor's state or the law of the account debtor's state. As a result, the governing law would be either the law of the state of the transferor (Rule A) or the law of the account debtor's state (Rule D). Thus, it is both the best and common practice to perfect the transfer of receivables under the law of the transferor's state and under the law of the account debtor's state. Table 4.2 below

---

[37] Rome Convention, art 3(1).
[38] Property Law (Conflict of Laws) Act (Wet Conflictenrecht Goederenrecht) of 25 February 2008; HR 16 May 1997 Brandsma qq/Hansa Chemie, NJ 1998, 585; JOR 1997,77. In the Netherlands, art 12(1) of the Rome Convention was applied.

shows what a transferee should do in order to perfect a transfer of a receivable against third parties in international receivables financing where the transferor is a company under the current laws.

Table 4.2: What should a transferee do in order to perfect a transfer against third parties in international receivables financing where the transferor is a company? (Groups R, RN, N, SR and C refer to the classification of jurisdictions in section 3-6)

Debtor Transferor	Group R	Group RN	Group N	Group SR	Group C
Group R	Registration in R	Registration in R Registration in RN	Registration in R Notice to the debtor in N	Registration in R Notice to the debtor in N	Registration in R
Group RN	Registration in RN	Registration in RN or Notice to the debtor in RN	Registration in RN Notice to the debtor in N	Registration in RN Notice to the debtor in SR	Registration in RN
Group N	Registration in R Notice to the debtor in R	Notice to the debtor in RN	Notice to the debtor in N	Notice to the debtor in SR	Notice to the debtor in C
Group SR	Registration in R Notice to the debtor in R	Notice to the debtor in RN	Notice to the debtor in N	Notice to the debtor in SR	Notice to the debtor in C
Group C	Registration in R	Registration in RN or Notice to the debtor in RN	Notice to the debtor in N	Notice to the debtor in SR	Agreement between the parties

The grey boxes in Table 4.2 above indicate international transfers of receivables where the transferor has to give notice of the transfer to the debtor of the receivable. If notice of the transfer to the debtor is required under either the law of the transferor's state or the law of the account debtor's state, the parties would give notice of the transfer to the debtor in order to be certain of priority. Currently, in many international transfers of receivables, notice of the transfer to the debtor is required. In block transfers of receivables and transfers of future receivables, giving notice to account debtors is too costly, time-consuming and impractical. This could be a barrier to the free international transfer of receivables.

For example, if the transferor is an American company (Group R) and the debtor is a French company (Group N), it is safest to file the transfer in the US in accordance with US law and give notice of the transfer to the French company in accordance with French law. By doing so, the transferee will have priority regardless of whether US law or French law governs priority.

If the transferor is a French company (Group N) and the debtor is an American company (Group R), it would be safest to give notice of the transfer to the American company under French law and file the transfer under US law. However, it is impossible to file the transfer in France because there is no filing or registration system for the transfer of receivables in France.

If the priority issue is considered by a US court, since the law of the transferor's state is the governing law for priority under UCC Article 9,[39] French law would be the applicable governing law for priority. As a result, priority will be determined by the time order in which the American company receives notice of the transfer.

By contrast, if the priority issue is considered by a French court, since under French private international law, which stipulates that the law of the debtor's state is the governing law for priority,[40] US law would be the applicable governing law for priority. As a result, priority will be determined by the order of filing. Since France does not have a registration system for the transfer of receivables, the transfer would have to be registered in Washington DC.[41] In conclusion, the parties might wish to both give notice of the transfer to the American company under French law and file the transfer of receivables in Washington DC under US law.

If the transferor is a German company (Group C) and the debtor is a Japanese company (Group RN), it is safest to register the transfer or give notice of the transfer to the Japanese company in accordance with Japanese law. In Japanese law, there are two perfection methods: registration and notice of the transfer to the debtor. A foreign legal person can also register the transfer of receivables as a transferor under the Japanese Transfer Registration Act.[42] Thus, it is safest to register the transfer in Japan.

Under the Korean ABS Act, a foreign legal person may file a securitisation plan and the transfer of receivables according to the plan with the Financial Services Commission as an originator (transferor), even if the foreign legal person does not have an office in Korea.[43] Thus, if the transferor is a German company, the debtor is a Korean company and the transaction is securitisation, it is safest to file the transfer and the securitisation plan in Korea in accordance with the Korean ABS Act. Furthermore, under the Korean Security Registration Act, a foreign legal person can also register security rights in receivables as a grantor or a secured creditor.[44]

As seen above, currently in many international transfers of receivables, notice of the transfer to debtors of the receivables is required, which hampers international

---

[39] UCC, ss 9-307(b) and (c), 9-301(1).
[40] CA Paris, 26 March 1986, D 1986, 374 2°, note *Vasseur*.
[41] UCC, s 9-307(c). See section 4-2-2.
[42] Japanese Transfer Registration Act, art 7(2)(iii).
[43] Korean ABS Act, art 3(1).
[44] Korean Security Registration Act, art 47(2)(iv); Korean Security Registration Rules, art 34.

transfers of receivables. Hence, the International Receivables Registry that liberates financiers from the notification requirement could facilitate international transfers of receivables.

4-4-2. The Potential Transferee's Check Point

In order for a potential transferee to secure priority over other transfers of or security rights in a receivable, the potential transferee must ensure that there is no prior transfer of or security right in the receivable. Table 4.3 below indicates information centres that a potential transferee should check before concluding a transfer contract under the current law, ie, without implementation of the proposed International Receivables Registry Convention. The shaded boxes indicate the cases where notice should be given to the debtors of the receivables.

Table 4.3: What should a potential transferee check before concluding a contract for a transfer of a receivable or a security right in a receivable in order to secure his priority over any prior transfer of or security right in the receivable?

Debtor \ Transferor	Group R	Group RN	Group N	Group SR	Group C
Group R	Registry in R	Registry in R / Debtors in RN	Registry in R / Debtors in N	Registry in R / Debtors in SR	Registry in R / Debtors in C
Group RN	Registry in RN	Registry in RN / Debtors in RN	Registry in RN / Debtors in N	Registry in RN / Debtors in SR	Registry in RN / Debtors in C
Group N	Debtors in R	Debtors in RN	Debtors in N	Debtors in SR	Debtors in C
Group SR	Registry in SR / Debtors in R	Registry in SR / Debtors in RN	Registry in SR / Debtors in N	Registry in SR / Debtors in SR	Registry in SR / Debtors in C
Group C	Debtors in R	Debtors in RN	Debtors in N	Debtors in SR	Debtors in C

In most cases, the parties have to search both the registry of the transferor's state and ask the debtor whether it received notice of any prior transfer of or security right in the receivable. In block transfers of receivables and transfers of future receivables, enquiring of account debtors is too costly, time-consuming and impractical. Under the current laws, priority issues in international transfers of receivables are very complicated, unsettled and often involve notification of the transfer to the debtor, which is often difficult or undesirable.

4-5. The Experience of the UN Receivables Convention

The UN Receivables Convention proposes that the law of a transferor's state should be applied to international transfers of receivables.[45] However, the UN Receivables Convention, adopted in January 2002, has not yet entered into force as of June 2017.[46] It is said that European countries hesitated to join the UN Receivables Convention because of the current uncertain situation whether the rule under the UN Receivables Convention might or might not be identical to, or at least compatible with, future European regulations.[47]

One of the reasons for the UN Receivables Convention's lack of success might be that priority issues are not adequately resolved by the choice-of-law rule. The UN Receivables Convention attempts to resolve priority issues with the choice-of-law rule that the law of the transferor's state determines priority disputes for international transfers.[48]

As analysed in section 4-2-2 above, the choice-of-law rule for priority issues is affected by what the information centre is under the substantive law on determining priority between competing transferees, and the substantive laws on priority differ by jurisdictions.[49] Thus, states which have different substantive laws, according to which priority is determined, could not easily agree on a unified choice-of-law rule that chooses the state, according to whose law priority is determined. Even within Europe, it is challenging to unify domestic choice-of-law rules that choose the state according to whose law priority is determined. It would be even more difficult to unify these rules worldwide. Thus, a unified substantive rule (rather than choice-of-law rule) is needed to facilitate international receivables financing.

4-6. Registration is the Solution

4-6-1. Problems of the Notification Requirement

In the jurisdictions of Groups RN, N and SR, where notice of the transfer to the debtor is required for the transfer of receivables, notification has always hampered

---

[45] UN Receivables Convention, art 30(1).
[46] See section 2-5-2-1.
[47] Sigman and Kieninger (n 12) 55.
[48] UN Receivables Convention, art 30(1).
[49] See section 4-7-2-2.

receivables financing.[50] As receivables financing developed, the problem of notification requirement became unbearable in these jurisdictions. Even though a transferee in a receivables financing does not usually intend to immediately collect the debt from the debtor, the transferor or the transferee nonetheless has to give notice of the transfer to the debtor for perfection against third parties, including the insolvency administrator or an execution creditor of the transferor.

However, as explained in the following two subsections, giving notice of the transfer to all debtors of bulk receivables in receivables financing is impractical, costly and time-consuming. Moreover, it is impossible to give notice of the transfer to the debtors of future receivables. To address these difficulties, many jurisdictions have adopted registration systems. One registration can replace innumerable notifications.

4-6-1-1. Facilitating Transfers of Future Receivables

To assist companies (especially small and mid-sized companies with insufficient collateral) in using their receivables as collateral, the ability to assign future receivables is important. Long-term receivables and future receivables are recommended for receivables financing. As it takes a long time to liquidate long-term receivables and future receivables, using long-term receivables and future receivables for receivables financing would be helpful to companies.

A registration system for the transfer of receivables facilitates the transfer of future receivables. Under traditional civil law, notification of the transfer of receivables to the debtor is required for the transfer of receivables. However, with respect to future receivables, the debtor of the receivable is not yet ascertainable, and therefore giving notice of the transfer to a debtor of a future receivable is impossible. A registration system would enable the transfer of future receivables as well as floating charges, which include future receivables. The registration system is also useful in project financing where the debtor's future cash flow is important collateral.[51]

4-6-1-2. Facilitating Bulk Transfers of Receivables

A registration system for the transfer of receivables facilitates bulk transfers of receivables. Many receivables financing transactions such as securitisation, factoring and block discounting consist of bulk transfers of receivables, which contain a large number of debtors of receivables and inevitably encounter notification problems. A registration system could solve these notification problems. On the one hand, if there is a highly valued receivable, a potential transferee would not

---

[50] Despite this, the transferee in a receivables financing does not usually intend to immediately collect the debt from the debtor, but has to give notice of the transfer to the debtor for perfection against the insolvency administrator or a judgment creditor of the transferor.
[51] See section 1-1.

just check the registry but would also directly contact the debtor of the receivable to enquire whether there is any prior security right in or transfer of the receivable. For example, where company D owes bank X £10,000,000 and bank Y purchases the receivable from bank X, bank Y would give notice to company D to ensure the transfer of the receivable.

In the case where a bulk transfer of receivables consists of a number of small consumer receivables, a potential transferee of the receivables could not enquire after each debtor. Also, transferors usually would not want to give notice to the debtors of the receivables because transferors would not want to let the debtors know of the transfer. A registration system for the transfer of receivables allows a bulk transfer of receivables to be perfected without giving notice of the transfer to each of the consumer debtors.

4-6-2. Registration or No Publicity

In the jurisdictions of Groups RN, N and SR, there have been developments to resolve the problems of notification requirement towards two movements: either no publicity or registration. Some states revised their civil codes or relevant laws to abolish the notification requirement, while some states enacted special laws for receivables financing adopting other methods to replace notice of the transfer to debtors. These legislative efforts provide us with references for establishing a unified international system in order to facilitate cross-border receivables financing.

For example, Belgium and the Netherlands revised their civil laws and abolished the notification requirement for the transfer of receivables and security rights in receivables. Belgium abolished the notification requirement in 1994[52] and the Netherlands abolished it in 2004. Furthermore, the EU Financial Collateral Arrangement Directive[53] does not apply any publicity requirement such as registration or notification for financial collateral arrangements of financial institutions.[54]

In comparison, France, Korea, Japan and China, where notice of the transfer to the debtor is required for priority, have enacted special laws for receivables financing and securitisations. Although the style of code and classification of rights were influenced by the German Civil Code (BGB), the Japanese Civil Code adopted the notification requirement from the French Civil Code for the transfer of receivables.[55] The Korean Civil Code follows the Japanese Civil Code. If the

---

[52] Still, in Belgium, priority is determined by the order of notification. See section 3-7-9 Qs 3, 4 and 5.

[53] EU Directive 2002/47/EC on financial collateral arrangements (amended by Directive 2009/44/EC).

[54] See section 3-8-3.

[55] According to art 1690 of the French Civil Code, either notification by an official letter (*signification* in French) delivered by a bailiff (*huissier*) or consent of the debtor by a notarised deed (*acte authentique*) with a certain fixed date is required for a transfer to be effective against third parties.

Japanese Civil Code had adopted the no-publicity approach for the transfer of receivables and followed the German time-of-creation doctrine,[56] the registration system would not have been needed in Japan.

There are three special methods that replace notice of the transfer to the debtor: (1) delivery of a transfer deed; (2) public notice in newspapers; and (3) filing or registration. France adopted the method of delivering a transfer deed (*bordereau*). By delivering a transfer deed (*bordereau*), a transfer of a receivable is perfected against third parties as well as the debtor of the receivable.[57] This solution under the French Monetary and Financial Code is in effect a no-publicity approach.[58]

Special legislative reformation tends to be influenced by the legal systems of neighbouring states. These influences are either towards the time-of-creation doctrine of Germany[59] or the registration system of the US. Japan is close to the US and thus adopted a UCC Article 9-style registration system. In Japan, special legislative actions were initially taken to facilitate securitisation for the purpose of disposing of non-performing loans[60] and then later extended the scope of registration from securitisation assets to other receivables.[61] Korea established a registration system referring to UCC Article 9 and the Japanese system.[62] China adopted the method of public notice in newspapers.[63] Public notice in newspapers is a kind of publicity. However, this publicity method is inconvenient for potential transferees to search.

This book argues that for a worldwide unified system, registration is more appropriate than no publicity. A no-publicity approach might be workable only for transactions by and between tightly interconnected financial institutions such as under the EU Financial Collateral Arrangement Directive.[64] However, for a global financial market, a registration system could provide certainty of transactions. In addition, it would be difficult in practice for jurisdictions familiar with publicity such as notification or registration under their current laws to adopt the concept of no publicity.

See section 3-7-8 Q 1-1. However, under the Japanese Civil Code, only a certified document with a fixed date stamp is required for notice of the transfer to a debtor or consent of a debtor. See section 3-7-7 Qs 1, 2, 3, 4-1.

[56] Under the German Civil Code, the transferee who concluded the transfer contract first has priority regardless of notification, and notice of the transfer to the debtor is not required for priority of the transfer of receivables. See section 3-7-12 Q 1-1.

[57] See section 3-7-8 Q 1-2.

[58] See section 3-3-4-2.

[59] The method of a transfer deed in France is rather similar to the time-of-creation doctrine.

[60] Non-performing loans are loans on which debtors have failed to make contractual payments for a pre-determined time. Usually, loans become non-performing after being in default for three months, but this can depend on the contract terms. See Chae-Jin Lee, 'Study on Development and Evolving Process of Securitisation Laws in Korea' (2005–06) 18(2) *Commercial Case Study (Sang Sa Pan Rye YeonGu)* 208–09.

[61] See section 2-4-4-3-2.

[62] See section 2-4-4-4.

[63] See section 3-7-4 Q 1-2.

[64] EU Directive 2002/47/EC on financial collateral arrangements (amended by Directive 2009/44/EC).

4-6-3. Problems with No Publicity of Transfers

In the jurisdictions of Group C, there is no *ex ante* measure for a potential transferee to investigate whether a specific receivable belongs to a transferor except by asking the transferor. This begs the question as to the acceptability of a system in which there is no publicity requirement for the transfer of receivables.

Nonetheless, the transfer system works very well in Germany without a notification requirement.[65] The system seems fine in a limited, interconnected and stable society like Germany where financier communities develop methods of communication that reliably distribute financial information of its members, so that fraudulent non-possessory security rights are difficult to hide.

Although neither notice to the debtor nor registration is required for the outright transfer of receivables, there is no public debate about clandestine transfers of receivables and no apparent lobbying or push for a change in this regard in Germany.[66] A German professor, Julia Klauer Rakob, found that the German banking and factoring industry appears satisfied with the current situation and does not perceive the risks of fraudulent transfers or of mistaken double transfers as serious.[67] Companies do not want the transfer information revealed to debtors or the public at large.

However, it seems that there could be problems for two reasons. First, there is no way for a potential transferee to check whether there is a prior transfer of or security right in the receivable that might be purchased or taken as collateral. A potential transferee's only option is to trust the transferor. There may be warranties or conditions in the transfer contract. Still, if there were a prior transfer, the subsequent transferee would have no rights in the receivable, but for merely a claim for damages, which is unsecure and impracticable if the transferor becomes insolvent. Furthermore, if a subsequent transferee gives notice of the transfer to the debtor of the receivable and the debtor pays the subsequent transferee, the prior transferee can theoretically claim against the subsequent transferee for unjust enrichment. However, it is a personal claim and therefore unsecured if the subsequent transferee became insolvent or otherwise unavailable.

Second, without any third-party involvement, it is easy for the transferor and the transferee to falsify the date of the transfer contract and to hide such conspiracy. Where X transferred his receivable to Y1 and then Y2 (X is a transferor, Y1 and Y2 are transferees, and the transfer to Y1 is prior in time to the transfer to Y2), X might have an incentive to backdate the execution of the transfer contract with Y2 prior to the transfer contract with Y1 if X favours Y2 over Y1. If X actually does so, X will be charged with *fraud* in case X signed the documents confirming there is no prior transfer when X transferred his receivable to Y1 and to Y2.

---

[65] Interview with Ulrich Drobnig, Professor, Max Planck Institute for Comparative and International Private Law (Hamburg, Germany, 20 October 2010).
[66] Julia Klauer Rakob, 'Germany' in Sigman and Kieninger (n 12) 112–13.
[67] ibid 113.

If X backdates the transfer contract with Y2 to a time prior to the date of the transfer contract with Y1 and, as there is no third-party involvement, the backdating is not revealed, it would appear that X transferred the receivable to Y2 before X signs the document confirming that there was no prior transfer and gives the document to Y1, and therefore Y2 would appear to have priority over Y1. This would constitute fraud against Y1.

If the backdating is revealed so that it turns out that Y1 has priority over Y2, such backdating committed by X would still constitute a fraud against Y2 because Y2 will lose his right to the receivable. In either case, the transferor X would be guilty of fraud.

4-6-4. Is Registration Necessary?

Registration informs the public of transfers of and security rights in receivables, and may be used as evidence in resolving disputes such as priority disputes. However, some legal practitioners argue that registration is not necessary for receivables financing. They argue that receivables transactions do not have to be publicised and that additional evidence of receivables transactions besides the relevant contract is not needed.

Priority between competing transferees is only relevant if a transferor sells the same receivable twice, grants competing security rights in a receivable or sells a receivable that has already been pledged as security. In this regard, an execution creditor of a transferor may be treated in the same way as a transferee. If a transferee has not completed the registration requirement before an attachment is perfected, the transfer is not perfected against the execution creditor.

Practitioners argue that such concerns with regard to priority issues between competing transferees are out-of-date because accidental double transfers are not prevalent in highly sophisticated financial markets where trading is managed with computer accounting systems. If a financial institution erroneously sold the same receivable twice or sold the receivable that had been pledged as security, it would be quickly discovered and noticed as such, and few would do business with such a suspicious financial institution in the future. Once a financial institution loses its goodwill, it cannot continue doing business. Accordingly, if a financial institution commits a wrong, it will be sufficiently punished and burdened with severe repercussions.

On the other hand, there is a counter-argument claiming that registration is necessary because a company running into insolvency might sell the same receivable twice or secretly sell the receivable that has been provided as security, or might grant a security right in the receivable that has already been transferred, before filing for insolvency. A person or a company on the brink of insolvency who has nothing to lose except possible criminal punishment might conduct such fraudulent behaviour intentionally. Small trading companies might well make a mistake or engage in fraudulent behaviour when they assign their receivables to a bank or receivables financier, and subsequently become bankrupt. As long as the transferor is solvent, the second transferee who does not have priority can recover the full amount of the receivable plus damages from the transferor, although the second transferee cannot claim directly against the debtor. But if the transferor becomes insolvent, the second transferee cannot obtain proper restitution.

Still, legal practitioners argue that those who know the financial situation of a potential transferor would not buy receivables from that company if it were on the verge of insolvency. As such, so the argument goes, the law does not have to require registration for the transfer of receivables, nor does it have to provide notification or registration for priority purposes. In such situations, ie, where registration is not required, an intending transferee or secured creditor should properly investigate the transferor's or grantor's financial situation to prevent double transfers. If there was no registration requirement, financiers would thus have to pay greater attention to the financial condition and creditability of the transferor or the grantor.

Such a duty of caution is already present in the insolvency laws of many jurisdictions. For the purpose of preventing fraudulent transactions relating to company assets, the insolvency laws of many jurisdictions provide that the insolvency administrator may ask the court to revoke the insolvent transferor's transactions made within a certain period, which is called the suspect period. The suspect period is calculated retrospectively from the date of the transferor's insolvency[68] or from the date of application for the insolvency proceedings.[69]

Accordingly, the insolvency administrator may avoid the transfer of receivables made within the suspect period if the consideration received for the receivables transferred is unreasonable. If a transferee purchased some receivables with an unreasonably low price, the transfer might be revoked. There is a high probability that the second transfer with an unreasonably low consideration could be avoided by the insolvency administrator if it is made within the suspect period. Such avoidance provisions would serve to protect creditors, or potential creditors, of the company that has transferred its receivables. For this reason, a potential transferee should have to pay greater attention to the probability for the transferor to become bankrupt. However, the difficulty and costs of enforcement by the insolvency administrator may mean that in fact the possibility of avoidance is not a great disincentive to fraudulent transactions.[70] Thus, registration is necessary to prevent fraudulent transfers.

Finally, since fraudulent double transfers rarely occur in sophisticated financial systems, the most important purpose of registration in practice is perfec-

---

[68] For example, UK Insolvency Act 1986, s 238; Chinese Insolvency Law, art 31(2).

[69] For example, German Insolvency Statute (*Insolvenzordnung*), s 131. Under the German Insolvency Statute, the suspect period is three months, but with some exceptions.

[70] Rebecca Parry et al, *Transaction Avoidance in Insolvencies*, 2nd edn (Oxford, Oxford University Press, 2011). Parry shows that the avoidance provision should not deter people from dealing with struggling companies and rescue efforts which would otherwise be viable.

tion against the insolvency administrator or an execution creditor of a transferor. It is necessary to establish a system verifying the date of the transfer that will be compared with the date of bankruptcy adjudication or attachment notice. Without such a system, where there is a transfer, the parties might be tempted to backdate another transfer contract to have priority over other transfer actually made earlier.

4-7. The Double Debtor Problem

4-7-1. The Systemic Weakness of the Debtor-Indexed Registration System

Previous sections suggested that establishing an international registration system is the best solution to facilitate international receivables financing. However, a debtor (grantor)-based indexed registration system has a systemic weakness, ie, the so-called double debtor problem, and there are technical issues with respect to priority rules for floating charges, reservation of title, purchase-money security interests and proceeds. These issues need to be dealt with sophisticatedly when designing an international receivables registry system:

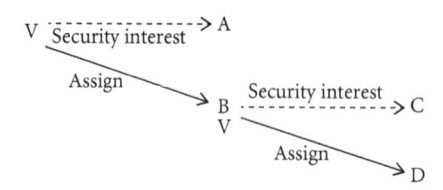

```
V ----Security interest----> A
  \
   Assign
        \
         > B    ----Security interest----> C
           V
            \
             Assign
                   \
                    > D
```

Let us suppose a case where a company (V) provides a security right in its receivable (V-R)[71] to A and registers the security right under the name of V in the general security rights registry indexed by debtors. Subsequently thereafter, V transfers the receivable (V-R) to B and registers the transfer of the receivable (V-R) under the name of V in the general security rights registry. A's security right in the receivable (V-R) has priority over B's right to the receivable (V-R), since A's security right was registered in the general security rights registry before the transfer of the receivable (V-R) to B. B should have checked the general security rights registry under the name of V before concluding the transfer of the receivable (V-R), and therefore

---

[71] '(V-R)' indicates that the receivable is V's monetary claim against R, and that V is the creditor and R is the debtor of the receivable.

B knew or should have known that A's security right was attached to the receivable (V-R). Thus, B's right to the receivable (V-R) is subject to A's security right.

If the security right in the receivable (V-R) continues to be perfected even after the receivable (V-R) is transferred to a third party B, the transferee B of the receivable (V-R) might take the receivable (V-R) subject to the security right of another creditor A previously registered under the name of V in the general security rights registry:

V
Security right for A
Security right for C

B
Security right for C
transferred to D

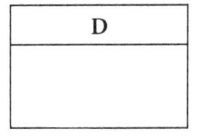

D

A problem arises where B transfers the receivable (B-R)[72] to D. According to the *nemo dat quod non habet* rule that a transferee cannot obtain more rights than the transferor had, D would obtain the receivable subject to A's security right just as B did. The question then becomes how can D know that the receivable (B-R) is subject to A's security right registered under the name of V? Such a problem is referred to as 'double debtor problem' since there are two debtors—an old debtor (V) and a new debtor (B)—creating security rights in the same receivable. Whether D or A should be protected is a problem.[73]

These problems have their origin in the transferor (or grantor)-based registration system. A general security rights registry is indexed by debtors, grantors or transferors. Because a general security rights registry includes various different types of collateral that can hardly be identified, a general security rights registry can hardly be indexed by each of the collateral objects.

If a security right in a receivable registered in the general security rights registry might become unperfected after the receivable is transferred to a third party, the validity of a security right registration would be invalidated and terminated by any subsequent registration of transfer of the receivable. Then, the security right in the receivable could not be protected. The question is how far the security right in a receivable registered in the general security rights registry should continue to be perfected after the receivable is transferred again and again to third parties away from the original creditor of the receivable.

---

[72] '(B-R)' indicates that the receivable is B's monetary claim against R, and that B is the creditor and R is the debtor of the receivable. Since the receivable (V-R) has been transferred to B, B becomes a new creditor of the receivable.

[73] This is the double debtor problem, about which there is considerable literature in the US and in the PPSA jurisdictions. See Jonathan C Lipson (ed), *Forms under Revised Article 9* (Chicago, American Bar Association, 2002) 37–39; Gerard McCormack, *Secured Credit under English and American Law* (Cambridge, Cambridge University Press 2004) 159–61.

Table 4.4: The double debtor problem

	A's security right	C's security right	D
Solution I	free of	free of	authority given by A and C
Solution II	free of	subject to	bona fide purchaser / change of jurisdiction
Solution III	subject to	subject to	*nemo dat quod non habet* rule
Solution IV	subject to	free of	buyer in the ordinary course of seller's business

There are four options to solve the double debtor problem: the first option is that B and subsequently D take the receivable free of A's security right (Solution I). The second option is that B takes the receivable subject to A's security right, but subsequently D takes the receivable free of A's security right (Solution II). This requires a potential transferee to check the registry with respect to his transferor. The third option is that B and subsequently D take the receivable subject to A's security right (Solution III). The fourth option is that B takes the receivable free of A's security right, but subsequently D takes the receivable subject to A's security right (Solution IV). Solution III and Solution IV require a potential transferee to check the registry with respect to his transferor and the former transferor if his transferor purchased the receivable from the former transferor. See Table 4.4.

Section 4-7 analyses how English law, UCC Article 9 and the PPSAs, under which the registries are indexed by person and thus debtor (grantor)-based, solve this problem where a receivable in which a security right is made is transferred to a third party.

There are two exceptions for the validity of a security right after the transfer of the receivable: (1) an authorised disposition; and (2) a bona fide purchase for value without notice in English law or a buyer in the ordinary course of business under UCC Article 9 and the PPSAs.[74] First, if the transferor has either actual or apparent authorisation from the secured creditor having the security right, the transferor may assign the receivable to the transferee free of the security right. The second exception is examined in sections 4-7-2-2 and 4-7-3-2.

If a secured creditor authorises disposition free of the security right, the security right is no longer attached to the receivable transferred to a transferee. In English law, apparent authorisation also counts. In the case of a floating charge, the chargor is held to be authorised to dispose of its assets.[75] Under UCC Article 9,

---

[74] This is similar but not identical to a bona fide purchaser because a buyer in the ordinary course of business takes goods free of a security right even if the buyer knows of the existence of the security right.

[75] Roy Goode and Louise Gullifer, *Goode on Legal Problems of Credit and Security*, 4th edn (London, Sweet & Maxwell, 2008) 176 [5-05].

if a secured creditor authorises the disposition, a buyer obtains the collateral free of the security right.[76] However, the secured creditor's receipt of the proceeds from the disposition does not in and of itself constitute an authorisation of disposition, and whether there is an authorisation will be decided by the courts.[77] This approach leads to the same result as Solution I mentioned above.

4-7-2. English Law

4-7-2-1. *The* Nemo Dat Quod Non Habet *Rule*

Let us suppose a case where a company X creates a fixed charge over its receivable for its creditor A and registers the A's fixed charge in the register of charges at Companies House, and subsequently X transfers the receivable to a third party transferee B. Does B obtain the receivable with A's fixed charge attached? According to the *nemo dat quod non habet* rule, B should obtain the receivable subject to A's fixed charge just as X did.

In the UK, under the Companies Act 2006, inter alia, a charge over a receivable of a company must be registered in the register of charges at Companies House in order to secure validity against other secured creditors and against a liquidator or administrator.[78] However, in English law, priority between a transfer and a fixed charge is not determined by the time order of registration in the register of charges.[79] An outright transfer of a receivable cannot be registered in the register of charges at Companies House.

Instead, priority is determined by *Dearle v Hall*,[80] according to which a transferee who is first to give notice of transfer to the debtor obtains priority over an earlier transferee or chargee that had not given notice of the earlier transfer or charge.[81] Thus, between A and B, whoever first gives notice of the charge or transfer to the debtor of the receivable has priority. If a prior fixed charge (of A) over a receivable is not registered in the register of charges, priority between an unregistered fixed charge (of A) and a transfer (of B) of the receivable is determined by the time order in which the debtor of the receivable received notice of the fixed charge or the transfer.

---

[76] UCC, s 9-315(a)(1).
[77] ibid s 9-315, Official Comment [2].
[78] Companies Act 2006 (Amendment of Part 25) Regulations 2013, sched 1, ss 859A–G.
[79] Registration of a fixed charge created by a company is meaningful for perfection against the insolvency administrator of the company. If a fixed charge of a company is not registered in the Company Charges Register within 21 days (or such later time as is permitted by the court), it is not perfected against the insolvency administrator of the company: ibid ss 859H and 859F. See section 3-7-10 Q 2.
[80] *Dearle v Hall* (1828) 3 Russ 1.
[81] Goode and Gullifer (n 75) 177 [5-08].

However, if a prior fixed charge (of A) over a receivable is registered in the register of charges at Companies House, the second limb of *Dearle v Hall* applies. According to the second limb of *Dearle v Hall*, if B knew of the prior fixed charge of A at the time of the transfer to B by any method, B has no priority over A even if B gave notice of the transfer to the debtor of the receivable earlier than A gave notice of its charge to the debtor. Registration of a fixed charge over a receivable in the register of charges at Companies House constitutes constructive notice to those who could reasonably be expected to search the registry, except a buyer in the ordinary course of business.[82] Therefore, the registration of fixed charges over receivables reduces the application of the *Dearle v Hall* rule in receivables financing because the second transferee (B) will usually have actual or constructive notice of a prior fixed charge (of A) by virtue of the registration.[83] A potential transferee wishing to purchase a receivable from a company would search the register of charges at Companies House against the company. Hence, B could reasonably have been expected to search the register of charges at Companies House against company X before B purchases the receivable from X. Thus, B takes the receivable subject to A's fixed charge.

4-7-2-2. Bona Fide Purchaser for Value without Notice

Under English law, once a person, who does not have actual or constructive notice of a prior equitable interest, provides value and acquires a legal interest, he takes priority over the holder of the prior equitable interest.[84] This doctrine is often called the 'bona fide purchaser for value without notice' rule.[85]

If B transfers the receivable to D, according to the *nemo dat quod non habet* rule, D should take the receivable subject to A's fixed charge just as B did. However, a chargee has no priority over a subsequent bona fide transferee who acquires the receivable in good faith without notice of the prior fixed charge.[86] If a transferee of a receivable is a bona fide purchaser for value without notice, the transferee takes the receivable free of any charge.

Registration in a public register may constitute constructive notice of matters recorded in the register, where the purchaser could reasonably have been expected to search the register.[87] In England, only companies can register their charges.

---

[82] ibid 92 [2-29].

[83] ibid 177 [5-08].

[84] *Pilcher v Rawlins* (1872) LR 7 Ch App 259, 268–89; *Heath v Crealock* (1874) LR 10 Ch App 22, 29–30; *Joseph v Lyons* (1884) 15 QBD 280 (CA); *Hallas v Robinson* (1885) 15 QBD 288 (CA), 292–93; *Taylor v London and County Banking Company* [1901] 2 Ch 231 (CA), 256; *Re Diplock* [1948] Ch 465 (CA).

[85] Hugh Beale, Michael Bridge, Louise Gullifer and Eva Lomnicka, *The Law of Personal Property Security* (Oxford, Oxford University Press, 2007) 434 [13.01].

[86] Goode and Gullifer (n 75) 193 [5-35].

[87] ibid 186 [5-22]. For example, a summons posted on a court house bulletin board or legally advertised in an approved newspaper may be regarded as constructive notice. Persons dealing with a company may be deemed to have constructive notice of the company's articles of association and memorandum of association. This is because a company must register its articles of association

Thus, in a transaction, if the grantor is a company, the secured creditor would have known that the grantor should have registered its charges if there are any, and the secured creditor could reasonably have been expected to search the registration of the grantor.

When B purchases the receivable from X, B has the obligation to check the register of charges at Companies House before purchasing the asset. If B fails to check the register of charges, B would be regarded as negligent, meaning B cannot be a bona fide purchaser for value without notice.[88]

Furthermore, if B transfers the receivable to another transferee D, D would be expected to search the Register of Company Charges with respect to B, but not against X. D could not find the record of A's fixed charge by searching B's registration record, since A's fixed charge is registered against X. Therefore, A's fixed charge which is registered under X does not constitute constructive notice to D. Thus, D takes the receivable free of A's fixed charge if D gave notice of the transfer to the debtor of the receivable before A gave notice of its charge to the debtor. Then, A would lose its fixed charge and registration of A's fixed charge under X would become of no use. This approach leads to the same result as Solution II mentioned above.

4-7-3. UCC Article 9 and the PPSAs

4-7-3-1. Taking Subject to the Perfected Security Right

Under UCC Article 9, both security rights in receivables and transfers of receivables must be filed in the UCC Article 9 filing system in order to preserve priority. The priority of competing transferees and secured creditors is determined by the order of filing under UCC Article 9.[89] If collateral in which a secured creditor has a security right perfected by filing under the law of the jurisdiction of the location of the debtor is transferred to a third party, the filing remains effective within the same jurisdiction and the security right continues in the collateral.[90] A security right continues in collateral notwithstanding sale or other disposition thereof.[91]

Let us suppose a case where a company (V) creates a security right in its receivable (R) for its creditor (A) and registers A's security right, and subsequently V transfers the receivable R to a third-party transferee (B). B creates a security right in the receivable R for its creditor (C) and registers C's security right, and subsequently B transfers the receivable R to another transferee (D).

---

according to s 18(2) of the Companies Act 2006. However, an internal resolution of the board of directors does not constitute a constructive notice; *Royal British Bank v Turquand* (1856) 6 E&B 327.

[88] Nevertheless, if Y is a purchaser in the ordinary course of business, Y does not have the duty to check the registry.
[89] UCC, s 9-322.
[90] ibid s 9-507(a); Lipson (n 73) 37.
[91] UCC, s 9-315(a)(1).

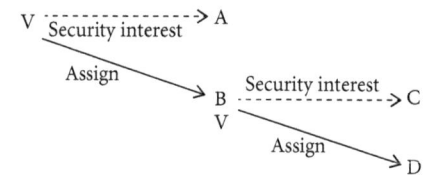

```
V  ----Security interest---->  A
  \Assign
        \→  B  ----Security interest---->  C
            V
              \Assign
                    \→ D
```

Under UCC Article 9, if V sells an asset to B not in the ordinary course of business, B acquires the asset subject to A's security right, and C's security right is subordinate to A's security right. This is because C could have investigated the source of the asset and could have searched the registry against V as well as B, and thus discovered A's security interest registered under the name of V before making an advance against the asset,[92] whereas A could not search for filing against B, since B's existence and identity at that stage were purely hypothetical.[93] Likewise, D takes the receivables subject to A's security right. This approach leads to the same result as Solution III mentioned above.

In Canada, New Zealand and Australia, according to the *nemo dat quod non habet* rule, D takes the receivable subject to A's security right. A security right continues in the collateral, unless the secured party expressly or impliedly authorised a disposal of the collateral, or expressly or impliedly agreed that a disposal would extinguish the security right.[94] This approach leads to the same result as Solution III mentioned above.

However, under UCC Article 9 and the PPSAs, there are two exceptions: (1) buyers in the ordinary course of business;[95] and (2) interstate transactions changing the jurisdiction.[96] The first exception is examined in section 4-7-3-2 and the second exception is examined in section 4-7-4.

4-7-3-2. Buyer in the Ordinary Course of Business

Under UCC Article 9 and the PPSAs, where the selling is in the ordinary course of the seller's business, a buyer in the ordinary course of business takes goods free of a security right created by the seller, even if the security right is perfected and the buyer knows of its existence.[97] 'Buyer in ordinary course of business' means a person who buys goods in the ordinary course of business from a person in the business of selling goods of that kind.[98] Only the buyer's knowledge of the

---

[92] Stephen L Sepinuck (ed), *Practice under Article 9 of the Uniform Commercial Code*, 2nd edn (Chicago, ABA UCC Committee, 2008) 438.
[93] McCormack (n 73) 160.
[94] Ontario PPSA, s 25(1)(a); Saskatchewan PPSA, s 28(1)(a); New Zealand PPSA, ss 45(1)(a) and 88; Australian PPSA, s 32(1)(a).
[95] UCC, s 9-320.
[96] ibid s 9-316.
[97] ibid s 9-320(a); Ontario PPSA, s 28(1); Saskatchewan PPSA, s 30(2); New Zealand PPSA, s 53(1); Australian PPSA, s 46(1).
[98] UCC, s 1-201(b)(9).

fact that the sale constitutes a breach of the security agreement under which the security right was created stops the purchaser from taking the goods free of a security right.[99] Thus, a secured creditor who has his security right perfected could be subordinated to a buyer in the ordinary course of business who buys goods from a seller in the business of selling goods of that kind.[100] When a buyer buys goods in the ordinary course of business from a seller in the business of selling goods of that kind, the buyer does not even need to check the security registry of the seller.

If B is a buyer in the ordinary course of V's business, B takes the receivable free of A's security right. Furthermore, if D is a buyer in the ordinary course of B's business, D takes the receivable free of C's security right. However, the ordinary course of business rule only applies to the security right created by the seller. Thus, D takes the receivable free of C's security right, but cannot take the receivable free of A's security right. As a result, D takes the receivable subject to A's security right. For this reason, if it is known that the receivable under sale had been transferred by another entity (V) to the seller (B), searches should be made by potential transferee (D) to see whether the entity (V) has created a security right in the receivable.[101] This approach leads to the same result as Solution IV mentioned above.

However, there is a possibility that the ordinary course of business rule does not apply to the sale of receivables, since UCC Article 9 and the PPSAs only stipulates that the rule applies to the sale of goods.[102]

4-7-4. Change of Jurisdiction

Under UCC Article 9 and the PPSAs, if a receivable is transferred to a different jurisdiction, the security right in the receivable registered in the original jurisdiction becomes unperfected unless it is re-registered in the new jurisdiction. Thus, if the collateral or the debtor is moved to a different jurisdiction from the jurisdiction where the security right was filed, the security right becomes unperfected after a grace period. This approach leads to the same result as Solution II mentioned above in the case of change of jurisdiction.

In addition, UCC Article 9 and the PPSAs provide grace periods, during which a secured creditor may file its security right in the new jurisdiction and obtain priority. If the secured creditor in the original jurisdiction re-perfects its security right in the new jurisdiction within the grace period, the security right trumps any

---

[99] ibid s 1-201(b)(9); Ontario PPSA, s 28(1); Saskatchewan PPSA, s 30(2); New Zealand PPSA, s 53(1); Australian PPSA, s 46(2)(b).
[100] Sigman and Kieninger (n 12) 38.
[101] Roger Fenton, *Garrow & Fenton's Law of Personal Property in New Zealand: Volume 2 Personal Property Securities*, 7th edn (Auckland, LexisNexis, 2010) 534 [13.3].
[102] UCC, s 9-320(a); Ontario PPSA, s 28(1); Saskatchewan PPSA, s 30(2); New Zealand PPSA, s 53(1); Australian PPSA, s 46(1).

security right in the new jurisdiction. Hence, there remains uncertainty during the grace period as to whether an unexpected security right might trump a security right registered in the new jurisdiction. After the lapse of the grace period, the security right registered in the old jurisdiction loses its effectiveness unless it is re-perfected in the new jurisdiction.

Under UCC Article 9, the grace period is one year for the interstate transfer of the collateral.[103] The 50 states that make up the US each have their own jurisdiction. The UCC Article 9 filing systems operate independently in each of the 50 states and are not connected to one another. A potential transferee is not expected to search the UCC Article 9 filing system of another state. So, in the case of an interstate transfer of a receivable, where the transferee is located in a jurisdiction different from that of the transferor, the secured creditor has a period of one year to perfect the security right under the law of the transferee's jurisdiction.[104]

Under the PPSAs, perfection continues temporarily after the transfer of the collateral to a foreign jurisdiction. In Saskatchewan in Canada and New Zealand, the period during which perfection continues temporarily is the earlier of: (i) 60 days after the day on which the debtor transfers an interest in the collateral to a person located in the other jurisdiction; or (ii) 15 days after the day on which the secured creditor has such knowledge of the transfer.[105] In Australia, the period during which perfection continues temporarily is the earlier of: (i) 56 days after the day of the relocation; or (ii) five business days after the day the secured creditor has actual knowledge of the relocation.[106] Once the temporary perfection period expires, the security right becomes unperfected in a foreign jurisdiction.

4-8. Floating Charges

4-8-1. English Floating Charges

Under English law, once a charge has been perfected by registration, the charge has priority over subsequent charges. This applies to a fixed charge created by a company registered under the Companies Act 2006. However, a registered floating charge may still lose to a subsequent fixed charge in the race for priority.[107] A floating charge, by definition, allows the chargor to dispose of his assets in the course of business until some act or event occurs on the part of the chargor or the chargee causes the floating charge to crystallise into a fixed charge.[108] A company

---

[103] UCC s 9-316(a)(3) and (b).
[104] Lipson (n 73) 37.
[105] Saskatchewan PPSA, s 7(3); New Zealand PPSA, s 31.
[106] Australian PPSA, s 40(3)(b).
[107] Beale et al (n 85) 330 [7.20].
[108] *Evans v Rival Granite Quarries Ltd* [1910] 2 KB 979 (CA), 999, per Buckley LJ.

may continue business as usual, and the assets covered by a floating charge would change from time to time.[109] The scope of collateral subject to a floating charge fluctuates, sometimes increases and sometimes decreases until the point of crystallisation. A fixed charge has priority over a prior floating charge.[110] The reason why a subsequent fixed charge has priority over a prior floating charge is because the chargor has permission to create it. This applies to charges over receivables.

Since a chargor has the power to dispose of the receivables subject to a floating charge without a specific consent of the floating chargee each time,[111] a floating charge is subordinated to a subsequent transfer of a specific receivable. The second limb of *Dearle v Hall*[112] does not apply to a floating charge. Even if a subsequent transferee had notice of the prior floating charge, the subsequent transfer trumps the prior floating charge and the subsequent transferee achieves priority over the prior floating chargee by notification of the subsequent transfer to the debtor of the receivable.[113]

4-8-2. Security Rights in After-Acquired Property under the UCC and the PPSAs

The US, Canada, New Zealand and Australia have no floating charge, and they only recognise security rights in after-acquired property which is subject to a bona fide purchaser in the ordinary course of business. Under UCC Article 9 of the US and the PPSAs of Canada, New Zealand and Australia, a security agreement may create or provide for a security right in all the grantor's present and after-acquired property (optionally excepting specified items or types of personal property).[114] A security right in after-acquired property makes it possible for the security right to float on encumbered assets, the components of which are subject to change, but which as a whole remains stable in terms of identity and value.[115] Security rights in after-acquired property are most frequently used with regard to inventory and account receivables <u>of the grantor</u>. A debtor continually sells some items and acquires others over time. A security right in after-acquired property enables the parties to a long-term financing relationship to think of the collateral as the

---

[109] *Re Yorkshire Woolcombers Association Ltd* [1903] 2 Ch 284 (CA), 295, per Romer LJ.
[110] ibid, per Romer LJ at 295; *Evans v Rival Granite Quarries Ltd* (n 108) per Buckley LJ at 999.
[111] *Agnew v Commissioner of Inland Revenue* [2001] UKPC 28, [2001] AC 710 [32]; *Re Spectrum Plus* [2005] UKHL 41, [2005] 2 AC 680 [107].
[112] *Dearle v Hall* (n 80).
[113] *In re Hamilton's Windsor Ironworks ex parte Pitman & Edwards* (1879) 12 Ch D 707; Beale et al (n 85) [14.11] fns 53, 54.
[114] UCC, s 9-204; Ontario PPSA, s 12; Saskatchewan PPSA, s 13; New Zealand PPSA, ss 43 and 44; Australian PPSA, ss 18(2) and (3), 20(2)(b) and 76(2)(b).
[115] *Stoumbos v Kilimnik*, 988 F 2d 949 (9th Cir 1993).

category rather than as the individual assets. A security right in after-acquired property is also referred to as a floating lien in the US.[116]

A security right in after-acquired property is defeated by a purchaser for value in the ordinary course of the seller's business. The concept of the ordinary course of seller's business was adopted to allow exceptions for a security right in after-acquired property. If selling of certain goods is in the ordinary course of the seller's business, the purchaser takes the goods free of a security right created by the seller.[117]

4-8-3. Floating Charges with Negative Pledge

In English law, a floating charge is subordinated to a subsequent fixed charge. In contrast, under UCC Article 9 and the PPSAs of Canada, New Zealand and Australia, a security right in after-acquired property is not subordinated to a subsequently registered security right.

Thus, in English jurisdictions, a floating chargee (creditor) often wants a negative pledge clause, which prohibits the floating chargor (debtor) from creating any subsequent security right in its property subject to the floating charge, while the floating chargee is happy for the proceeds to be disposed of. In practice, a floating charge under English law usually comes equipped with a negative pledge clause or an automatic crystallisation clause[118] and functions similarly as a security right in after-acquired property under UCC Article 9 and the PPSAs.[119]

4-9. Reservation of Title

4-9-1. Reservation of Title v Transfer

Reservation of title is an acquisition financing method, sometimes referred to as retention of title. A reservation-of-title right is a non-possessory security right.

---

[116] Lynn M LoPucki and Elizabeth Warren, *Secured Credit: A Systems Approach*, 6th edn (Alphen aan den Rijn, Aspen Publishers, 2009) 158.

[117] UCC, s 9-320(a); Ontario PPSA, s 28(1); Saskatchewan PPSA, s 30(2); New Zealand PPSA, s 53(1); Australian PPSA, s 46(1). See section 4-7-3-2.

[118] An automatic crystallisation clause may provide that crystallisation occurs automatically upon any specified event, eg, creating any subsequent fixed charge. The purpose of such an automatic clause is to crystallise a floating charge before the debtor grants a fixed charge to a competing creditor and thus to preserve the priority of the floating charge as against possible subsequent fixed charges. See Law Commission, 'Registration of Security Rights: Company Charges and Property Other than Land' (Law Com No 164, 2002) [2.44].

[119] Lynn M LoPucki, Arvin I Abraham and Bernd P Delahaye, 'Optimizing English and American Security Rights' (2013) 88 *Notre Dame Law Review* 1785.

Reservation of Title

The secured creditor with a reservation-of-title arrangement reserves ownership title of the collateral, while the debtor (grantor) possesses and uses the collateral. The broad meaning of reservation-of-title arrangements includes sale and repurchase (repo), financial leasing, hire purchase and sale and lease-back:

	Reservation of title	Pledge
Secured creditor	ownership title	possession
Debtor (grantor)	possession	ownership

In a pledge, the pledgee (secured creditor) takes the possession of the collateral, so it is very difficult for the pledgor (debtor) to dispose of the collateral to a third party. If a pledged collateral is disposed of to a third party, the pledge follows the collateral, so the third party would obtain the collateral with the burden of the pledge.

In a reservation-of-title arrangement, since the debtor (grantor) takes the possession of the collateral, the debtor (grantor) might be able to dispose of the collateral to a third party. In such cases, whether a reservation-of-title security right extends to the sale proceeds of the collateral is the issue. It might be said that since the secured creditor with a reservation-of-title arrangement reserves the ownership title of the collateral, the sale proceeds of the collateral should also belong to the secured creditor, as far as the sale proceeds are separated and reasonably identifiable:

	V
	Receivable (V-S) from the sale of the computer to S
	debtor of the receivable (V-S): S
1	transferred to B
2	security right (extension of reservation of title) for T

Let us suppose a case where T sold its computer to V on instalment and for the receivables of the sale price T obtained a reservation-of-title right in the computer and registered this right in the computer under the name of V in the register. The reservation-of-title clause in the sale contract of the computer stipulates that the reservation-of-title right extends to the proceeds of the computer. Later, V sold the computer to S even though V did not have the title since T reserved the title, and S purchased the computer from V on credit. Thus, V obtained a receivable (V-S)[120] for the price of the computer against S. T claims the receivable (V-S) as the proceeds of the computer against S. However, V has already transferred the

---

[120] '(V-S)' indicates that the receivable is V's monetary claim against S, and that V is the creditor and S is the debtor of the receivable.

receivable (V-S) to a third party B and B immediately gave notice of the transfer of the receivable (V-S) to the debtor of the receivable (V-S), ie, S,[121] or registered the transfer of the receivable (V-S) to B under the name of V in the register,[122] before T registers its reservation-of-title security right in the receivable (V-S) under the name of V in the register.

4-9-1-1. English Law

If T had a reservation-of-title clause in the sale contract of the computer, such a clause would not automatically extend to the receivable of the sale price under English law. If the sale contract purported to extend it to the proceeds including receivables, the reservation-of-title right in the receivable would be a charge and hence registrable.[123] If T's reservation-of-title right in the receivable is registrable but not registered, it would not be enforceable against B. With respect to the receivable (V-S), priority between the reservation-of-title seller (T) and the transferee of the receivable (B) is determined by the second limb of *Dearle v Hall*.[124] If B knew of T's prior reservation-of-title right in the receivable (V-S) at the time of the transfer of the receivable (V-S) to B by any method, B cannot have priority over T even if B gave notice of the transfer to the debtor of the receivable (S) earlier than T gave notice of its reservation-of-title right to the debtor (S). If T's reservation-of-title right in the receivable (V-S) is registered in the register of charges at Companies House under the name of V, it would constitute constructive notice to B. Thus, in order for B to have priority over T, B ought to give notice of the transfer of the receivable (V-S) to the debtor (S) before T's reservation-of-title right in the receivable (V-S) is registered in the register of charges at Companies House under the name of V.

4-9-1-2. UCC Article 9 and the PPSAs

UCC Article 9 has created a single, comprehensive security right in movable assets and receivables, unifying numerous and diverse possessory and non-possessory rights in tangible and intangible assets, including transfer-of-title and reservation-of-title arrangements, that existed under state statutes and common law.[125] For many years before the introduction of this UCC right, trade across states and provincial boundaries was hampered by the existence of diverse and highly particularised state regimes for granting security.[126] The idea of unification subsequently spread to other countries such as Canada, New Zealand and Australia.

---

[121] In England, an outright transfer of a receivable of a company is not registrable.
[122] In the US, Canada, New Zealand and Australia.
[123] *E Pfeiffer Weinkellerei-Weineinkauf GmbH & Co v Arbuthnot Factors Ltd* [1987] BCLC 522 (QB), 533, [1988] 1 WLR 150; *Compaq Computer Ltd v Abercorn Group Ltd* [1993] BCLC 602 (Ch).
[124] *Dearle v Hall* (n 80).
[125] UNCITRAL Legislative Guide on Secured Transactions (2007) 23 [62].
[126] ibid 56 [103].

Under UCC Article 9 and the PPSAs of Canada, New Zealand and Australia, a reservation-of-title agreement basically comes within the functional, integrated and comprehensive definition of security rights and thus filing or registration is required for perfection. Thus, priority between the reservation-of-title seller (T) and the transferee of the receivable (B) is determined by the order of UCC Article 9 filing or registration in the PPS registry.

Under UCC Article 9 and the PPSAs, a security right in proceeds is automatically perfected if the security right in the original collateral was perfected.[127] Under UCC Article 9, a security right in proceeds becomes unperfected on the twenty-first day after the security right attaches to the proceeds.[128] Under the Australian PPSA, the security right in the proceeds is temporarily perfected for the period starting at the time the security right in the original collateral attaches to the proceeds and ending at the end of five business days afterwards.[129] It is 10 days in Ontario, 15 days in Saskatchewan in Canada and 10 working days in New Zealand.[130] During these days of the automatic perfection period, priority of the security rights in the proceeds could overlap. In UCC Article 9 or the PPS registry, if T's reservation-of-title right in *the computer* had been registered under the name of V prior to the transfer of the receivable (V-S) to B, and if T registers its security right in the receivable (V-S), ie, the proceeds of the computer within the automatic perfection period, T may prevail over B even though the transfer of *the receivable* (V-S) to B is registered prior to T's security right in the receivable (V-S).

The same rule applies to security rights in receivables, and so priority between a reservation-of-title right and a security right in the receivable is determined by the time order of registration, except for the automatic perfection period.

4-9-1-3. Purchase-Money Security Interest

Under UCC Article 9, a security interest in an asset is a purchase-money security interest to the extent that the asset secures an obligation of an obligor incurred as all or part of the price of that asset or for value given to enable the debtor to acquire rights in or the use of that asset.[131] For example, a financier or lender may lend money to a debtor for the purchase of an asset such as a motor vehicle, new equipment or inventory at the point of sale and acquire a purchase-money security right in that asset.

A purchase-money security right may trump a prior perfected security right under UCC Article 9. With respect to goods other than inventory, a purchase-money security interest in goods other than inventory and its identifiable proceeds has priority over a conflicting security interest in the same goods if the

---

[127] Sepinuck (n 92) 394.
[128] UCC, s 9-103(a) and (b).
[129] Australian PPSA, s 33(2).
[130] Ontario PPSA, s 25(4); Saskatchewan PPSA, s 28(3); New Zealand PPSA, s 47.
[131] UCC, s 9-315(d).

purchase-money security interest is perfected by filing at the UCC filing office within 20 days of the debtor receiving possession of the collateral.[132]

With respect to inventory, a purchase-money security interest in inventory and its identifiable cash proceeds of the inventory has priority over a conflicting security interest in the same inventory to the extent that the identifiable cash proceeds are received on or before the delivery of the inventory to a buyer, if the purchase-money security interest is perfected by filing at the UCC filing office when the debtor receives possession of the inventory.[133]

Let us suppose that a financier F lent money to company V on the security of V's all present and *future* property, and F's security right had been registered. Later, V subsequently acquires an asset (M) with the funds provided by P (not by F) on the security of that asset (M) and P's purchase-money security interest in the asset (M) is registered. F had registered a security right including the asset (M) before P registers a purchase-money security interest in the asset (M).

Under UCC Article 9, the purchase-money lender (P) has priority over any other security rights (of F) in the collateral (M) because it has either supplied the collateral (M) or made advances to enable the debtor to acquire the collateral (M).[134]

However, purchase-money security interests under UCC Article 9 apply only to goods, inventory and livestock.[135] They do not apply to receivables unless they are inventory. Even though it is possible to purchase receivables (which are debts) with the cash borrowed from a bank, using the security of the receivables to obtain the difference between the interest rates, such receivables would not be inventory.

The PPSAs of Canada, New Zealand and Australia also provide for the priority of a purchase-money security right.[136] With respect to collateral other than inventory, a purchase-money security interest in collateral or its proceeds has priority over any other security interest in the same collateral given by the same debtor if the purchase-money security interest in the collateral or its proceeds is perfected by registration within a certain number of days after the debtor obtained possession of the collateral. This is 15 days according to the Ontario PPSA and the Saskatchewan PPSA of Canada, 10 working days according to the New Zealand PPSA and 15 business days according to the Australian PPSA.[137]

With respect to inventory, a purchase-money security interest in inventory or its proceeds has priority over any other security interest in the same inventory given by the same debtor if the purchase-money security interest in the inventory or its

---

[132] ibid s 9-324(a).
[133] ibid s 9-324(b).
[134] ibid s 9-324; LoPucki and Warren (n 116) 519.
[135] UCC, s 9-324.
[136] Ontario PPSA, s 33; Saskatchewan PPSA, s 34; New Zealand PPSA, ss 73–77; Australian PPSA, ss 62–64.
[137] Ontario PPSA, s 33(2); Saskatchewan PPSA, s 34(2); New Zealand PPSA, s 73(1); Australian PPSA, s 62(3).

proceeds is perfected by registration at the time when the debtor obtained possession of the inventory.[138]

However, a non-proceeds security right in a receivable that is given for new value as original collateral overrides a purchase-money security interest in the receivable as proceeds of inventory if the non-proceeds security interest in the receivable is registered prior to the purchase-money security interest in the inventory or its proceeds.[139]

English law has never recognised the priority of such purchase-money security interests,[140] although there are some cases concerning competing claims to an interest in land.[141]

Purchase-money security interest	US	Canada	New Zealand	Australia	England
Collateral other than inventory	20 days	15 days	10 working days	15 business days	✗
Inventory		when the debtor obtained possession of the inventory			✗

4-9-2. Floating Security Rights v Reservation of Title

	V
1	Floating security right over all present and future receivables for F
2	Reservation-of-title right in the inventory for T
3	Receivable from the sale of the inventory to S
	(debtor of the receivable: S)
	Security right (extension of reservation of title) for T

Let us suppose a case where a financier F holds a floating charge (or security right in after-acquired property) over all present and future receivables of company V. F has registered the floating charge (or security right in after-acquired property). Subsequently, T sold its inventory to V and T obtained a reservation-of-title right in the inventory that V possesses. The reservation-of-title clause in the sale contract of the inventory stipulates that the reservation-of-title right extends to the proceeds of the inventory. Later, V sells the inventory to S even though V does not have the title since T reserves the title, and S purchases the inventory from V on credit. Thus, V obtains a receivable for the price of the inventory against

---

[138] Ontario PPSA, s 33(1); Saskatchewan PPSA, s 34(3); New Zealand PPSA, s 74; Australian PPSA, s 62(2).
[139] Saskatchewan PPSA, s 34(6) and (7); New Zealand PPSA, s 75A, as inserted by PPS Amendment Act 2004, s 15; Australian PPSA, s 64(1).
[140] Goode and Gullifer (n 75) 214 [5-62].
[141] *Re Connolly Bros Ltd (No 2)* [1912] 2 Ch 25 (CA).

S. T then claims the receivables as the proceeds of the inventory. Priority between the floating chargee of all present and future receivables (F) and a reservation-of-title supplier (T) claiming the receivable as proceeds in this situation under English law, US law and the PPSAs will be analysed in the following sections.

4-9-2-1. English Floating Charges

In English law, a reservation-of-title right is likely to constitute a registrable charge.[142] If T's reservation-of-title right is registrable but not registered, it is not perfected against a registered floating charge and therefore T's reservation-of-title right does not extend to the receivable as proceeds of the inventory.

On the other hand, if T registered its reservation-of-title right, it extends to the receivable as proceeds of the inventory according to the reservation-of-title agreement. A floating chargee cannot bother T's extension to the receivable based on the reservation-of-title agreement because a floating chargor has the power to dispose of its assets. The second limb of *Dearle v Hall*[143] does not apply to a floating charge. Even if T had notice of the prior floating charge, T's reservation-of-title right trumps the prior floating charge and achieves priority over the prior floating chargee by registration in the register of charges at Companies House.[144]

However, if F's floating charge is equipped with a negative pledge clause with respect to receivables, T's reservation-of-title right does not extend to the receivable as proceeds of the inventory. Negative pledge clauses in floating charges are particulars that must be included in the register.[145] According to the position established in English case law,[146] parties have constructive notice of particulars, which must be and are in fact included in the register. Thus, there would be constructive notice of the negative pledge to subsequent chargees. If notice was given to T of the negative pledge clause, F can assert the negative pledge clause vis-a-vis T and prevent T's reservation-of-title arrangement from extending to the receivables as proceeds of the inventory.

4-9-2-2. Security Rights in After-Acquired Property under UCC Article 9 and the PPSAs

Under UCC Article 9 and the PPSAs, a reservation-of-title right is just another security right, and priority is determined by the order of registration. F's security right in after-acquired receivables prevails over T's reservation-of-title right because the former is registered prior to the latter. Thus, T's reservation-of-title

---

[142] *E Pfeiffer Weinkellerei-Weineinkauf GmbH & Co v Arbuthnot Factors Ltd* (n 123) 533; *Compaq Computer Ltd v Abercorn Group Ltd* (n 123).
[143] *Dearle v Hall* (n 80).
[144] *In re Hamilton's Windsor Ironworks* (n 113); Beale et al (n 85) [14.11] fns 53, 54.
[145] Companies Act 2006 (Amendment of Part 25) Regulations 2013, sched 1, s 859D(2)(c).
[146] *English and Scottish Mercantile Investment Co v Brunton* [1892] 2 QB 700; *Standard Rotary Machine Co Ltd* (1906) 95 LT 829; *Wilson v Kelland* [1910] 2 Ch 306; *G & T Earle Ltd v Hemsworth* (1928) 44 TLR 605; *Siebe Gorman & Co Ltd v Barclays Bank Ltd* [1979] 2 Lloyd's Rep 142, 160.

right does not extend to the receivable against S, unless T purchases the receivable in the ordinary course of V's business.[147]

Once V collects the receivable from S, F's security right in after-acquired receivables extends to the cash V collected from S as proceeds of the receivable; likewise, T's reservation-of-title right extends to the cash thus collected as proceeds of the inventory. Because F's security right is registered prior to T's right, F has priority over T with respect to the collected cash. In any case, T's reservation-of-title right is not protected under UCC Article 9 or the PPSAs.

4-10. Conclusion

Different private international laws in each jurisdiction are commingled in the world. The choice-of-law approach proposed by the UN Receivables Convention could not solve the problem. A unified substantive rule for priority with an international registration system for the transfer of and security rights in receivables is required. One registration in the International Receivables Registry can replace an unlimited number of notifications. The International Receivables Registry would pave the way for circumventing the notification requirement in some jurisdictions where notice of the transfer to the debtor is required in order for the transfer to be perfected against third parties. This function is essential to facilitate the transfer of future receivables and bulk transfers of receivables. In conclusion, registration is the best solution to facilitate international receivables financing. When designing an international registration system for receivables, we need to sophisticatedly deal with technical issues such as the so-called double debtor problem and priority rules for floating charges, reservation of title, purchase-money security interests and proceeds.

---

[147] See section 4-7-3-2.

5

The International Receivables Registry

5-1. Introduction

This chapter tries to find the best solution to limit the scope of application of the International Receivables Registry while facilitating these types of international receivables transactions. In this chapter, transfers of receivables and the granting of security rights in receivables are collectively referred to as transfers.

Section 5-2 explains the reason why this book limits its proposal to establishing an international registration system for transfers of and security rights in receivables only.

Section 5-3-2 compares three approaches to unify national laws on transfers of and security rights in receivables around the world. Section 5-3-3 goes on to identify a workable model in terms of the relationship between the proposed International Receivables Registry Convention and the different national laws in terms of whether the former should prevail over the latter. The issue is whether registration in the International Receivables Registry should be compulsory or optional.

Sections 5-4 to 5-8 look at ways to restrict the scope of application of the proposed International Receivables Registry Convention by requiring certain qualification of the transferors and grantors which are eligible to register transfers of or security rights in their receivables in the International Receivables Registry. Section 5-8-3 proposes that the scope of registration should be limited to a transfer where both the transferor and the transferee (or the grantor and the secured creditor) are legal persons (companies). This is because of the identification issue. Section 5-8-4 also defines the interaction between the proposed International Receivables Registry Convention and the Cape Town Convention.

Section 5-9 discusses the proposed operation of the International Receivables Registry and the rules relating to this. The first issue is which system to adopt: a notice-filing system or a document-filing system. Some jurisdictions have notice-filing systems and other jurisdictions have document-filing systems. Section 5-9-1-1 explains why the International Receivables Registry should adopt a notice-filing system. Section 5-9-1-2 defines required information for the International Receivables Registry.

A serious concern with respect to a notice-filing system exists regarding the abuse of registration by secured creditors or transferees. Section 5-9-2 recommends parties' reciprocal confirmation on registration contents instead of registrar's review.

Section 5-9-3 explains email notification linked to registration in the International Receivables Registry. Section 5-9-4 designs the International Receivables Registrar, which operates the proposed International Receivables Registry Convention with its supervisory authority, taking references from the International Registry of Mobile Assets under the Cape Town Convention. Section 5-9-5 then explains how to search the International Receivables Registry online. It analyses the online operation of the International Receivables Registry in relation to registrant identification and search for registration.

5-2. Scope of the International Receivables Registry

5-2-1. Translation

This book proposes an international registration system focused on transfers of and security rights in receivables only. With respect to national general security rights registry, almost all registries cover both receivables and tangible movable assets.[1] However, this book argues that establishing a general security rights registry at an international level would be impractical because of difficulties in language translation and identification problems.

With respect to security rights, encumbered assets must be identified.[2] Types of tangible movable assets are so unlimited and varied that translation of their descriptions in a single language, ie, English would be very difficult. Descriptions, and their translations, of all types of encumbered items in an international registry would be prohibitively expensive and, even though possible, would still produce uncertainty. It might be possible and plausible to overcome the difficulties in translation only by and among English-speaking states or countries from a similar linguistic family.

5-2-2. Identification

Identification of an encumbered asset is a problem. For example, in Japan, there are two ways to identify tangible movable assets: (i) a detailed description of the asset'[3]

---

[1] There are a few examples of national registration systems that are applicable only to receivables. One example is the filing system of securitisation plans including the transfer of securitised receivables under the Korean ABS Act and Korean MBS Company Act. See section 3-7-6 Qs 1, 3-2 and Qs 1, 3-3. In Japan, the registration system was only for the transfer of receivables from 1998 until the revision of the Japanese Transfer Registration Act in 2005. See section 3-7-7 Qs 1, 2, 3, 4-2.
[2] Many jurisdictions do not acknowledge the legal concept of universal charges where individual assets do not have to be identified.
[3] Japanese Transfer Registration Rules, art 8(1)(i).

or (ii) a brief description of the asset and its location.[4] The first method requires too much detailed information of an individual asset. The second method is for a pool of assets, but it also has a weakness. If the registered assets are moved to another location, the registration becomes invalid.[5] For this reason, in Japan, registration of security rights in movable assets is not used as much as fiduciary transfer of title for security purposes,[6] while registration of security rights in receivables is frequently used.

For this reason, international registries have only been established for specific mobile equipment under the Cape Town Convention. The International Registry of Mobile Assets under the Cape Town Convention is relatively successful. However, such an international registry might not be successful when applied to other types of property. It was relatively simple to establish an international registry for aircraft because there was already a registry for aircraft in every state in accordance with the Convention on International Civil Aviation (hereinafter the 'Chicago Convention').[7] It is true that if there is already a national registry for a certain type of property, it becomes easier to make an international one. In addition, the internet-based International Registry for aircraft uses a drop-down menu bar, provided by aircraft manufacturing companies, to identify the object of security rights.[8] Such an object-specific approach in the International Registry for aircraft enables registration and searches for particular assets to be made very specific.

5-2-3. Separate International Registry for Each Type of Property

To harmonise the laws of security rights in movable assets and receivables around the world, the most suitable approach would be different for each type of asset.

---

[4] ibid art 8(1)(ii).
[5] For example, in Japan, a secured creditor (P) registered his security rights in a pool of assets with a brief description and their current location (X). Then, once the registered assets are moved to another location (Y), the registration identifying the assets by a brief description and their old location (X) is no longer valid. Meanwhile, if another secured creditor (Q) registers security rights in the assets with the new location (Y), only the new registration is valid. As a result, P will lose his security right in the assets, and Q's registration will prevail over P's registration.
[6] Fiduciary transfer of title for security purposes is a kind of acquisition financing. The secured creditor takes the ownership title of the encumbered asset *erga omnes*. However, the grantor and the secured creditor agree between themselves that the grantor still retains the true title ownership of the encumbered asset. Fiduciary transfer of title for security purposes can be perfected by a purely fictitious constructive transfer of possession. Thus, the grantor may retain possession of, and make use of, the encumbered asset.
[7] Signed on 7 December 1944 by 52 states. The Provisional International Civil Aviation Organization functioned from 6 June 1945 until 4 April 1947. By 5 March 1947, the twenty-sixth ratification was received, and the International Civil Aviation Organization (ICAO) came into being on 4 April 1947. In October 1947, ICAO became a specialised agency of the UN linked to the Economic and Social Council (ECOSOC). See: www.icao.int/icaonet/dcs/7300.html.
[8] Answer to Frequently Asked Question No 11 on the International Registry on Mobile Assets website: https://www.internationalregistry.aero/irWeb/showFAQs.do. See also Regulations and Procedures for the International Registry, Regulations, s 5.1.

It is very difficult to find a single method that is applicable to all types of property. For example, the Protocols to the Cape Town Convention set up different rules for each type of mobile equipment: aircraft equipment,[9] railway rolling stock[10] and satellites.[11] Once the international registry for each type of asset such as aircraft, railway rolling stock, satellites, and construction and agricultural equipment could be established, and then it might become feasible to consolidate them into one general international security rights registry. Establishing an international and general security rights registry encompassing all types of personal properties might not be feasible at this stage.

Among other assets, this book focuses on receivables. Currently, there is no international registry for the transfer of receivables. Given the importance of receivables in international finance, harmonising the law regarding the transfer of receivables (outright sale or security rights) is of great practical importance. A receivable could be identified simply by identifying the transferor, the transferee, a list of debtors or a general description of the debtors of the receivables, the amount of monetary obligation and the due date. The concepts of receivables, transferors, transferees, debtors, amounts of monetary obligation and due dates can be easily translated in different languages. Thus, establishing an international registration system for transfers of and security rights in receivables would be feasible.

5-2-4. The International Receivables Registry

This book proposes an international registration system for transfers of and security rights in receivables, which is referred to here as the 'International Receivables Registry'. The International Receivables Registry includes outright transfers of receivables, security transfers of receivables and security rights in receivables in its registration scheme.

This book proposes a set of rules to realise the International Receivables Registry. To explain the details of the proposal, this book drafts a model international convention for the International Receivables Registry, 'The Draft Convention on Priority of Transfers of and Security Rights in Receivables' (hereinafter referred to as the 'proposed International Receivables Registry Convention'). This book includes this as an Appendix.[12]

---

[9] The Convention on International Interests in Mobile Equipment (hereinafter the 'Cape Town Convention') and the Protocol to the Convention on International Interests in Mobile Equipment on Matters Specific to Aircraft Equipment (hereinafter the 'Aircraft Protocol') were adopted jointly in Cape Town on 16 November 2001. The Cape Town Convention entered into force on 1 March 2006.

[10] Luxembourg Protocol to the Convention on International Interests in Mobile Equipment on Matters Specific to Railway Rolling Stock, adopted in Luxembourg on 23 February 2007 (not yet entered into force).

[11] Protocol to the Convention on International Interests in Mobile Equipment on Matters Specific to Space Assets, adopted in Berlin on 9 March 2012 (not yet entered into force).

[12] This is attached at the end of this book as an Appendix. Each article of the proposed International Receivables Registry Convention is drafted with reference to existing international conventions,

Under the proposed International Receivables Registry Convention, the international transfer of receivables would be regulated by a unified legal system with respect to priority and perfection. The International Receivables Registry could help financiers to overcome the obstacles they currently encounter and thus facilitate international transfers of receivables, international project financing and international finance using security rights in receivables. Furthermore, the International Receivables Registry would enable companies to raise finance from a greater range of investors around the world through international receivables financing and to dispose of non-performing loans more easily.

Since under current private international laws, it is not clear which national law on priority among competing transferees should be applied in international transfers of receivables,[13] it could be expected that the parties who wish for certainty of priority would choose to register in the International Receivables Registry. In this book, 'registration in the International Receivables Registry' means registration of a transfer of, or a security right in, a receivable in the International Receivables Registry.

5-2-5. Receivables

Under the proposed International Receivables Registry Convention, 'receivable'[14] does not cover cheques, bonds and other debt securities. Many jurisdictions have their own laws regulating cheques, bonds and debt securities. In most, priority of the right in a cheque, a bond or other debt securities is determined by possession.

Under the proposed International Receivables Registry Convention, 'receivable' does not include bank accounts. This is because when a bank account is transferred, the bank account is controlled by the transferee. In most jurisdictions, priority is determined by the order of control of the bank account, and upon the transferee's control of the bank account, the transfer is perfected against third parties. 'Receivable' includes bank's loan receivables.

5-2-6. Transfer

A 'transfer' is a transaction between the person entitled to the benefit from a contract (the transferor) and a third party to that contract (the transferee), as a result of which the third party becomes entitled to sue the person liable under the contract (the debtor).[15]

---

legislative guides and national laws, including the UN Receivables Convention, the Cape Town Convention and its Regulations and Procedures for the International Registry, the UNCITRAL Model Law on Secured Transactions and the New Zealand PPSA.

[13] See section 4-7-2.
[14] Draft International Receivables Registry Convention, art 1(h). See the Appendix.
[15] Guenter Treitel, *The Law of Contract* (London, Sweet & Maxwell, 2003) 672.

The UN Receivables Convention stipulates that 'transfer' means the transfer by agreement from one person (the transferor) to another person (the transferee) of an interest in the transferor's contractual right to payment of a monetary sum (the receivable) from a third person (the debtor of the receivable).[16] The proposed International Receivables Registry Convention adopts this definition of 'transfer'.[17]

In the transfer of receivables, a debtor may set-off against a transferee the counterclaims that the debtor had against the transferor until notified of the transfer.[18] Notice of the transfer to the debtor of the receivable prevents the debtor from setting-off any claims that the debtor had against the transferor that arise after notice.

By contrast, in a novation, an old agreement is extinguished and a new agreement is created. A novation replaces the old creditor by a new creditor with agreement. A contract which is transferred by novation transfers all duties and obligations of the old creditor to a new creditor. Thus, the debtor cannot set up against the new creditor any set-off available against the old creditor.

5-2-7. Security Rights

In the proposed International Receivables Registry Convention, 'security right' means: (i) a property right in a movable asset that is created by an agreement to secure payment or other performance of an obligation, regardless of whether the parties have denominated it as a security right and regardless of the type of asset, the status of the grantor or secured creditor, or the nature of the secured obligation; and (ii) the right of the transferee under an outright transfer of a receivable by agreement. The term does not include a personal right against a guarantor or other persons liable for the payment of the secured obligation.[19] The proposed International Receivables Registry Convention uses the term 'security right' in receivables.

With respect to security rights, one of the most recent trends is to make a comprehensive registration system which covers every type of security rights. Registration systems in many jurisdictions are not separately provided for each type of security rights. Instead, these countries adopt comprehensive security rights registration systems which cover any type of security rights. For example, UCC Article 9 filing of the US covers any form of security right arrangements. The parties can make special arrangement freely. This trend was initiated from the UCC filing offices of the US. The UNCITRAL Model Law on Secured Transactions

---

[16] UN Receivables Convention, art 2.
[17] Draft International Receivables Registry Convention, art 1(a). See the Appendix.
[18] This is not a mandatory rule, and thus a debtor may voluntarily waive any defences or rights of set-off before or even after being notified of the transfer. Article 31(4) of the Cape Town Convention and art X(3) of its Space Protocol stipulate the obligor's waiver of defences and rights of set-off by agreement in writing.
[19] Draft International Receivables Registry Convention, art 1(j). See the Appendix.

(2016) also recommends this comprehensive, integrated, functional approach.[20] The International Receivables Registry adopts this comprehensive security rights registration system. Thus, any type of security rights is to be registered in the International Receivables Registry in order to be perfected against third parties.

5-2-8. An International Receivables Registry Should Cover Both Transfers and Security Rights

Even though *transfers of receivables* are used more than creating security rights in receivables, an international registration system should cover both transfers of and security rights in receivables due to the following reasons.

In order for the court to determine priority among competing transfers or security rights, it must compare all transfers of and security rights in the receivable. There could be a security right in and a transfer of the same receivable, where a transferor creates a security right in the receivable and later transfers the receivable to a third party, or vice versa. If the secured creditor perfected the security right prior to the transferee, the secured creditor will trump the transferee when the debtor (transferor) defaults.

When a potential transferee purchases a receivable, it must investigate whether there is any prior transfer of or security right in the receivable in order to secure priority over any prior transfer of and security right in the receivable. In order to investigate any prior transfer of and security right in a receivable at once through a registration system and determine clearly and efficiently the priority among competing transfers of and security rights in a receivable, an international registration system should cover both transfers of and security rights in receivables.

5-3. International Receivables Registry Registration

5-3-1. Limitation of Scope of the International Receivables Registry

Let us first think about the most desirable international registration system to facilitate international receivables transactions. If there were one globally unified law which enables transfers of and security rights in receivables to be perfected against third parties once they have been registered with a universal international registration system, receivables could be traded freely internationally without the need for any further domestic perfection and without even paying heed to any domestic perfection rules.

---

[20] UNCITRAL Model Law on Secured Transactions, art 2(kk).

In reality, each state has different national laws for transfers of and security rights in receivables. If the proposed International Receivables Registry Convention would override those national laws with respect to priority and perfection requirements, and if every state would join the proposed International Receivables Registry Convention, it would be the same as the most desirable status where there exists only one universal international registration system, as mentioned above.

However, such a desirable status is impractical to realise for the following reasons: first, practically speaking, it is expected that some states would not join the proposed International Receivables Registry Convention due to various reasons. Thus, the International Receivables Registry would only be applied to the parties in the states that have joined the proposed International Receivables Registry Convention (hereinafter the 'Contracting States').

Second, the International Receivables Registry has to solve the problem of the language barrier. If the International Receivables Registry were to override the perfection requirements of national law, every single transfer of receivables (both international and domestic) in the Contracting States would have to be registered with the International Receivables Registry in order for its priority to be secured. If even purely domestic transfers of and security rights in receivables would have to be registered in the International Receivables Registry, the system would need to provide translation services for those people who cannot speak English, which would raise the cost and ultimately the registration fee. The more states that would join the proposed International Receivables Registry Convention, the higher the costs for translation would be.

Third, if the International Receivables Registry covers every single transfer of and security right in each receivable in the world, the volume of registration in the International Receivables Registry would become too large to manage at a reasonable cost whilst keeping the registration fee at an affordable level.

This book does not reject a system overriding national perfection requirements. However, it emphasises that if we would adopt a system overriding national perfection requirements, the scope of application must be limited in any case in order to solve the practical problems discussed above. Chapter 4 tries to find the best solution to limit the scope of application of the International Receivables Registry while maintaining its merits of facilitating international receivables financing.

With respect to receivables, there are broadly two ways of using receivables for financing: one is a transfer of receivables and the other is creating security rights in receivables, which are exemplified by the following four types of receivables transactions. First, bank loans usually have particular terms or length of maturity. In contrast, depositors may withdraw their savings from a bank at any time. Thus, if all depositors suddenly withdraw their savings from a bank at once, the bank will run out of cash. To mitigate such liquidity risk, a bank may assign its loan receivables to other banks through inter-bank transactions and get an influx of cash. In addition, in order to meet the requirements of the capital adequacy ratio under the Basel III, banks need to dispose of bad loans. Second, a company which does not have sufficient real estate or tangible assets to mortgage for a loan can create security rights in its account receivables and borrow money from banks. Third, a bank may borrow money from central banks with providing security rights in its loan receivables. Fourth, a company may assign its account receivables through factoring and a financial institution may assign its credit card receivables or lease receivables through securitisation in order to disperse the default risk.

5-3-2. Three Approaches to Unify the Laws

A new regime to uniformly cover the world would be the next step in the continued development of international receivables financing. If so, the question becomes which system should be the model. There are three possible suggestions to achieve harmonisation of receivables financing regimes: (1) a compulsory registration system; (2) an optional registration system; and (3) a legislative guide encouraging each state to adopt a relatively unified registration system.

5-3-2-1. *Compulsory Registration*

First, an example of a compulsory registration system is the International Registry of Mobile Assets,[21] established by the Cape Town Convention and its Aircraft Protocol. Once a state signs and ratifies the Cape Town Convention and the Aircraft Protocol, every security right in the subject mobile equipment must be registered in order to have priority. Under this approach, a compulsory registration system prevails over domestic receivables financing regimes.

5-3-2-2. *Optional Registration*

Second, an optional registration system is an alternative international registry that would be added to the existing domestic regimes and allow parties to select it. It is similar to the proposed European security right.[22] Realising that it is much more difficult to unify property laws and security laws than to unify contract laws in the EU, some scholars including Kieninger proposed a European security right. A European security right would be a new security right perfected by registration

---

[21] https://www.internationalregistry.aero/irWeb.
[22] Harry C Sigman and Eva-Maria Kieninger (eds), *Cross-border Security over Tangibles* (Munich, Sellier, 2007) 34. This suggestion was first made by Karl Kreuzer, ‚Europäisches Mobiliarsicherungsrecht oder: Von den Grenzen des Internationalen Privatrechts' in Walter A Stoffel, Paul Volken and Alfred E von Overbeck (eds), *Conflits et harmonisation: mélanges en l'honneur d'Alfred E. von Overbeck à l'occasion de son 65ème anniversaire* (Fribourg, Ed universitaires, 1990) 613 et seq; Eva-Maria Kieninger, *Security Rights in Movable Property* (Cambridge, Cambridge University Press, 2004) 665–72. The European security right could be introduced under a regulation issued pursuant to art 308 of the EC Treaty, which stipulates: 'If action by the Community should prove necessary to attain, in the course of the operation of the common market, one of the objectives of the Community, and this Treaty has not provided the necessary powers, the Council shall, acting unanimously on a proposal from the Commission and after consulting the European Parliament, take the appropriate measures.'

in a European registry, which would be added to the existing domestic security rights regimes. The idea is that a European security right does not change the existing domestic security rights laws of the EU Member States for the time being. This optional system approach is also similar to the registration systems under the Korean Security Registration Act and under the Japanese Transfer Registration Act, in that these special registration systems co-exist with the transfer of receivables regimes under civil codes.[23]

5-3-2-3. Providing Guides and Models

Third, making a legislative guide on receivables financing and encouraging each state to establish a domestic registration system is also an advisable way to harmonise receivables financing regimes around the world. The UNCITRAL Legislative Guide on Secured Transaction (2007) and the UNCITRAL Model Law on Secured Transaction (2016) are good examples. There are other models such as 'Publicity of Security Rights: Guiding Principles for the Development of a Charges Registry' (2004) and 'Publicity of Security Rights: Setting Standards' (2005) of the EBRD, 'Guide to Movables Registries' (2002) of the Asian Development Bank, the Draft Common Frame of Reference (2010),[24] 'Model Registry Regulations under the Model Inter-American Law on Secured Transactions' (October 2009) of the Organization of American States and 'Secured Transactions Systems and Collateral Registries' (January 2010) of the International Finance Corporation (IFC), a member of the World Bank Group. These guides and model laws for registration systems are modelled on the financing statement filing under UCC Article 9 and registration under the PPSAs in Canada and New Zealand. They cover outright transfers of receivables, security transfers of receivables and security rights in receivables.

However, leaving countries to voluntarily revise national laws and establish national registration systems for receivables means that it would take a long time to unify international registration systems in order to facilitate international receivables transactions.

5-3-3. The Relationship between the Proposed International Receivables Registry Convention and National Laws

5-3-3-1. Compulsory or Optional

Establishing an international registration system for transfers of and security rights in receivables is no easy task. Broadly speaking, two models of an international

---

[23] See section 2-4-4-2.
[24] Section 3 of Part 3 (Effectiveness as Against Third Parties) (Registration) of Book IX (Proprietary Security in Movable Assets).

registration system for transfers of and security rights in receivables deserve further discussion. The first model is an international registration system which overrides the perfection requirements of national law, which would result in compulsory registration with the international system.[25] This model would involve issues of practicality that may inhibit its adoption by states around the world. An international registration system designed to override the perfection requirements of national law might probably result in states not adopting the international convention.

The second model is an international registration system equivalent to the perfection requirements of national law, which would result in optional registration with the international system.[26] This model would, however, undermine the utility of the registration system. An international registration system that does not override but is equivalent in its effect to the perfection requirements of national law would be less useful to registrants and searchers because it is up to the parties to choose which system to use, and thus searching the registry does not guarantee that the entire transfers of and security rights in a receivable are recorded in the registry.

In its search for a solution, based on the first model of compulsory system, this book proposes confining the sphere of application using the proposed 'vehicle to the international registration system'.

5-3-3-2. Problems with the Optional Registration System

Establishing an international registration system that does not override the perfection requirements of national law might be a solution. Examples of such a registration system are the Korean Security Registration Act and the Japanese Transfer Registration Act.

Under the Korean and the Japanese Civil Codes, a transfer of a receivable is perfected against third parties only if the transferor gives notice to the debtor by means of a certified document with a fixed date stamp.[27] In Korea and Japan, to circumvent this notification requirement, registration systems have been developed with reference to UCC Article 9. When contemplating the establishment of registration systems, the Korean and Japanese legislators, rather than revising their respective civil codes, which would have entailed costs and caused confusion, adopted alternative optional registration systems that co-exist with existing laws. In Korea, priority is determined by comparing the order in which the debtor received notice of a transfer or a pledge under the Korean Civil Code or in which a security right is registered under the Korean Security Registration Act.[28] In Japan,

---

[25] This is the option set out in section 5-2-1.
[26] This is the option set out in section 5-2-2.
[27] Korean Civil Code, art 450(2); Japanese Civil Code, art 467(2).
[28] Korean Security Registration Act, art 35(3).

priority is determined by comparing the order in which the debtor received notice of a transfer or a pledge under the Japanese Civil Code or in which a transfer or a pledge is registered under the Japanese Transfer Registration Act.[29]

This book reviews the possibility of and rejects the plausibility of establishing an international version of such an alternative optional registration system so as to provide a method of perfecting international transfers of receivables as an alternative to the requirements of national legal systems. Such a system might be able to dispense with the need to give notice of the transfer to debtors of receivables as a condition of priority against third parties.

An optional registration model would provide the parties with optional ways to perfect the transfer of receivables and would enable the parties to a transfer contract to choose whichever of these methods—international registration or the perfection method under their domestic laws—is best suited for them to achieve perfection against third parties.[30] In the event that there are a number of debtors of receivables, most transferors and transferees would naturally choose international registration rather than be forced to give notice of the transfer to all these debtors of receivables. If a transferor might choose the latter, the transferor would have to make sure that every single debtor received notice of the transfer because even one omission could cause the entire transaction to fall apart. An optional registration system would enable the parties to opt for the most efficient way not only for perfecting a transfer of or a security right in a receivable, but also for searching the registration.

However, such an optional registration model could defeat the very objective of setting up an international registration. A potential registrant would have to investigate the applicable national laws to investigate whether there had been perfection under that law, which would have to be treated as though it were a registration with the international registry. In a country with a national registration system, this would involve searching the national register. In countries (such as Germany) without perfection requirements, where a transfer is perfected against third parties upon being made, there is no visibility at all, so that someone intending to register a transfer in the international registry would have absolutely no way of knowing whether there had been a prior transfer domestically.

If the transaction at issue involves one single country, it might be practicable for the parties to check both the registry and enquire of account debtors. If all the parties were in one country—eg, in Germany or in Korea or in Japan—it might be practical to check the International Receivables Registry and the other perfection methods under the applicable national law, ie, national registry or account debtors. However, at an international level, it would be impracticable because the

---

[29] Japanese Transfer Registration Act, art 4(1).
[30] The US system under UCC art 9 may also in some ways be said to be optional between filing and non-filing in some aspects, since there is no obligation to file or not to file. However, if a security right in receivables is not filed, it is not perfected against third parties. Interview with Steven L Schwarcz, Professor, Duke University School of Law, University of Oxford, 26 November 2010.

would-be transferee should check all of the national registries as a potential hidden competing transferee might be in any country. This could defeat the objective of establishing an international registration.

Such an optional registration model could not thus meet the basic requirements for an effective registration system. In the jurisdictions where a transfer or a security right must be registered for perfection against third parties, the basic requirements for an effective registration system are as follows. First, it should enable a searcher to rely with confidence on the absence of an entry in the register. Also, it should enable a registrant to be confident that it will have priority over a later registrant or one who has not registered. Thus, an optional registration model co-existing with national perfection methods would not be desirable for an international registration model.

5-4. The Compulsory Registration System with Limited Scope of Application

According to Goode,[31] in preparing private law conventions in international trade, three limitations on the scope of a project have been found helpful. These limitations are to confine the convention to (1) commercial dealings and (2) cross-border transactions, and (3) to concentrate on a specific type of commercial transaction, selected for its importance in terms of the unit value of the subject matter or the continuity of dealings involving property transfers. The international registration system proposed in this book concentrates on receivables.

This book presents four approaches to confining the scope of application of the proposed International Receivables Registry Convention. The first is to define internationality as between the parties: the transferor, the transferee and the debtor of the receivable. The second is to limit the types of receivable to be registered. The third is to limit the amount of receivables to be registered. The fourth is to limit the parties: the transferor, the transferee or the debtor of the receivable to be registered. These methods to limit the scope of application are analysed in the following subsections.

5-4-1. To Confine the Internationality of the Transfer of Receivables

Confining the application scope of a relevant convention to purely international transactions would considerably reduce pressure on the system, provided the concept of internationality is adequately defined. This means finding ways

---

[31] Roy Goode, 'The Protection of Interests in Movables in Transnational Commercial Law' [1998] *Uniform Law Review* 453, 459–60.

of segregating international transactions to be registered with an international registration system from purely domestic transactions. However, distinguishing international from domestic transfers of receivables is impractical, since they are subject to change and are sometimes commingled.

The UN Receivables Convention applies to transfers of international receivables and international transfers of receivables.[32] If, at the time of conclusion of the original contract, the transferor and the debtor are located in different states, it is an international receivable.[33] If, at the time of conclusion of the transfer contract, the transferor and the transferee are located in different states, it is an international transfer.[34] However, this approach would not be workable for the transfer of receivables.

The following example illustrates this point. A and C are domestic companies, B is a foreign company, and the debtor of the receivable is a domestic company. A has transferred a domestic receivable to a foreign company B. The transfer from A to B is an international transfer and is eligible to be registered in the International Receivables Registry. Subsequently, A transfers the same receivable to C, making C a second transferee. This is not an international transfer and cannot be registered in the International Receivables Registry. C achieves perfection of the transfer under the domestic laws. However, if the International Receivables Registry would override the perfection requirements of national law, the domestic perfection would not be valid. As a result, a domestic company like C must always check the International Receivables Registry before making a transfer even with a domestic company like A. If the International Receivables Registry were designed to override the perfection requirements of national law, domestic transferees would have to check the International Receivables Registry each time in order to secure their priority and furthermore purely domestic transfers would also need to be registered in the International Receivables Registry in order to protect their priority.

The following example will further illustrate this point. A domestic company has transferred its receivables to a foreign company and has registered the transfer in an International Receivables Registry, which overrides the perfection requirements of national law. A potential domestic transferee would first have to check the International Receivables Registry to see whether there was any prior transfer. Furthermore, domestic transferees would also have to register their domestic transfers in the International Receivables Registry in order to protect their priority against any future international transfer. The existence of an International Receivables Registry overriding the perfection requirements of national law would motivate people to register any transfer, whether international or domestic, in the International Receivables Registry, even if the scope of application is limited by the concept of internationality. Thus, confining the scope of application by using the concept of internationality would not be effective, and it would ultimately

---

[32] UN Receivables Convention, art 1(1)(a) (Scope of application).
[33] ibid art 3 (Internationality).
[34] ibid.

result in the situation where all transfers of receivables, whether international or domestic, must be registered in the International Receivables Registry to secure its priority and perfection since a competing transferee may be an international transferee. For this reason, the concept of internationality as defined in the UN Receivables Convention is impractical, and this seems to be one of the reasons why the UN Receivables Convention was not so successful.

5-4-2. To Limit Types of Receivables

Restricting the types of receivables is impractical because there are various types of receivables and where to draw a line is not clear. For example, a convention could limit its scope to credit card receivables or account receivables for sales of goods. However, these types of receivables are often traded domestically. It is difficult to find certain types of receivables which are traded mainly internationally rather than domestically.

If the scope of registration were limited by the types of receivables, it is expected that disputes over the scope of registration would be inevitable for the following reasons. In receivables financing, there are many low-value receivables that are more susceptible to change over time, making them hard to easily identify. By contrast, ships and aircraft are high-value, tangible assets. An aircraft that is registered in the International Registry of Mobile Assets under the Cape Town Convention is highly identifiable. Its manufacturer's serial number, the name of the manufacturer and its model designation are necessary (and sufficient) to identify the aircraft object.[35] Registration in the International Registry of Mobile Assets requires the use of a drop-down menu, provided by the aircraft manufacturing companies, to identify the object of registration.[36] Registrants only need to select and click the appropriate item in the drop-down menu to identify the object. Nevertheless, there is still an argument as to whether an object should be registered in the International Registry or in a domestic registry with respect to the Cape Town Convention and its Aircraft Protocol. This is because there are limitations to the scope of application according to the weight and number of people an aircraft may carry under the Aircraft Protocol.[37] If there is disagreement even with respect to aircraft, it is to be expected that there might be even more disagreement with respect to receivables if the scope were to be restricted to certain types of receivables.

In addition, confining the scope by limiting the types of receivables could give rise to complications of translating the types of receivables. The International Receivables Registry would be set up in English and it could increase transaction

---

[35] Cape Town Convention Aircraft Protocol, art VII.
[36] Answer to Frequently Asked Question No 11 on the International Registry on Mobile Assets website: https://www.internationalregistry.aero/irWeb/showFAQs.do. See also Regulations and Procedures for the International Registry, Regulations, s 5.1.
[37] Cape Town Convention Aircraft Protocol, arts I(2)(e) and I(2)(l).

costs for non-English speaking nationals. If an International Receivables Registry were to provide a translation service, it would increase the registration fee.

5-4-3. To Limit the Value Amount of Receivables

Restricting the scope of registration on the basis of the estimated value of the receivables transaction appears equally impractical. For the purposes of an international registry, the scale of transactions to be registered must be sufficiently large that the parties would be willing to pay additional registration fees. However, there is some difficulty in estimating the value of receivables, which fluctuates over time. The valuation of future receivables is even more challenging. If registration were limited to a certain value, disputes in relation to borderline receivables would be bound to result.

5-4-4. To Limit the Parties to be Registered

Restricting the parties—the transferor, transferee and debtor of the receivable—to be registered in the International Receivables Registry could be a solution for the purpose of limiting the sphere of application. The UNIDROIT Convention on International Factoring (Ottawa, 28 May 1988) limits its sphere of application by defining a 'factor': the Convention applies to the transfer of receivables where the transferee is a factor stipulated in the Convention.[38]

There are basically two methods to index a registry: an asset-based indexed registration system and a grantor-based indexed registration system. An asset-based indexed registration system is only practical for certain types of assets such as land,[39] cars, ships and planes. Registration of these assets may be indexed by a description of the object asset because they have certain defined identity,[40] and therefore searching against a certain object asset shows all transfers of ownership of the asset and all security rights in the asset.

The first issue that arises when designing a new registration system is whether registration should be based on the assets themselves or on the person owning the assets. A registration system for transfers of and security rights in receivables should be a transferor-based registration system. If it were an asset-based registration system, the asset (ie, receivables) would need to be indexed clearly. In order to pinpoint specific receivables, a searcher would input the name of the transferor, the debtors of the receivables, the cause of the receivables, the date of the contract that created the receivables, the date when the receivables would become

---

[38] UNIDROIT Convention on International Factoring, arts 1(1), 1(2) and 2(1).
[39] See section 2-3-1-5.
[40] Lynn M LoPucki and Elizabeth Warren, *Secured Credit: A Systems Approach*, 6th edn (Alphen aan den Rijn, Aspen Publishers, 2009) 296.

due etc. In many cases, the debtors of receivables are too many to be listed in all because receivables financing usually consists of bulk transfers of receivables or security rights in a group of receivables, and therefore only a general description of the debtors of the receivables would be registered in the International Receivables Registry. However, it is technically difficult to identify and specify registered receivables merely by a general description of the debtors of the receivables.[41]

The most precise and definite information by which the International Receivables Registry could be indexed is the name of the transferor (or the grantor). When a third party looks up the International Receivables Registry, he could search against the name of the transferor that he is trading with. For these reasons, this book proposes to limit the sphere of application by restricting the transferor (or the grantor) to be registered. This restriction is discussed in section 5-5.

5-5. Restriction of the Scope of Application of the Proposed International Receivables Registry Convention

5-5-1. The IRT

This book suggests restricting the transferors (or secured creditors) entitled to register transfers (or security rights) in the International Receivables Registry. The proposed International Receivables Registry Convention would apply only to the transfer of receivables where the transferor is a special-purpose company registered with the International Receivables Registrar. Such a special-purpose company will be referred to hereinafter as the 'IRT', which stands for 'International Receivables Trader'. This book invented the idea of an IRT. An IRT is a legal person. Any legal person may register itself as an IRT. Confining the scope of application by using the concept of an IRT makes the application of the International Receivables Registry Convention much more clear and definitive. If the transferor or grantor is an IRT, a potential transferee or secured creditor does not have to check the domestic registers, since the International Receivables Registry prevails over the domestic registers. The proposed International Receivables Registry Convention would exclusively deal with receivables of an IRT. In this book, a 'receivable of an IRT' is referred to as an 'IRT receivable'.

This approach does not distinguish international transfers of receivables from domestic transfers of receivables. Even domestic parties, if the transferor or

---

[41] In fact, it is difficult to identify and specify a receivable even in the filing system under UCC art 9. In particular, a future receivable is much more difficult to specify and identify technically. Even the information on the financing statements only triggers further investigation of the transfer of receivables. The filed information does not actually specify and identify the receivable or group of receivables subject to a security right; rather, the filing focuses on identifying the transferor and the transferee, of whom a potential interested party may ask about the transfer.

grantor is an IRT, would have to register their transfers or security rights in the International Receivables Registry in order to secure their priority. Priority would be determined by the time order of registration in the International Receivables Registry.[42] Under the proposed International Receivables Registry Convention, a registered transfer of or security right in a receivable prevails over an unregistered transfer of or security right in the receivable.[43] An unregistered transfer of or security right in a receivable is not protected against a subsequently registered transfer of or security right in the receivable. This rule induces any transfer or security right of an IRT to be registered in the International Receivables Registry. Thus, the International Receivables Registry is a compulsory registration system. If none of competing transfers is registered, priority is determined by the applicable national law.[44]

The scope of application of the proposed International Receivables Registry Convention would be limited to transfers of receivables of an IRT (that is, the transferor) and security rights in receivables of an IRT (that is, the grantor). In other words, the proposed International Receivables Registry Convention would apply only to cases where the transferor or grantor is an IRT. Accordingly, in order to be registered under the proposed International Receivables Registry Convention, the transferor or the grantor must be an IRT.

	Non-IRT → IRT	IRT → Non-IRT
Transfer	Applicable national law	International Receivables Registry Convention
Security right	Applicable national law	International Receivables Registry Convention

Transfers of receivables *by* an IRT would be governed by the proposed International Receivables Registry Convention. Transfers of receivables *to* an IRT would be governed by the applicable national laws. Security rights in receivables provided *by* an IRT would be governed by the proposed International Receivables Registry Convention. Security rights in receivables provided *to* an IRT would be governed by the applicable national law.

5-5-2. The Transferor or Grantor Needs to be an IRT

The proposed International Receivables Registry Convention applies where the transferor or grantor is an IRT registered as such with the International

---

[42] See section 6-3-1.
[43] Draft International Receivables Registry Convention, art 5(1). See the Appendix.
[44] See section 6-3-1.

Receivables Registrar at the time of the conclusion of the transfer or security right agreement.[45] Transfers of or security rights in IRT receivables must be registered in the International Receivables Registry in order to be perfected against third parties. The International Receivables Registry is indexed by transferor and by grantor.

It does not matter whether the transferee or secured creditor is an IRT or not. The fact that the transferee or secured creditor is situated in a non-Contracting State would not affect the applicability of the proposed International Receivables Registry Convention.[46] If the transferor or grantor is an IRT, the proposed International Receivables Registry Convention would apply regardless of whether the transferee or secured creditor is a foreign party or a domestic party. All transfers (both international and domestic) made by an IRT must be registered in the International Receivables Registry to be perfected against third parties.

The transferee or secured creditor need not be a legal person in a Contracting State. A legal person in either a Contracting State or a non-Contracting State would be able to be registered as a transferee or secured creditor. Thus, any company from any jurisdiction may achieve perfection against third parties by registration in the International Receivables Registry. As a result, even a domestic party must be aware that when it purchases a receivable from, or is granted a security right in a receivable by, an IRT, perfection is not governed by the applicable national laws, but by the proposed International Receivables Registry Convention.

5-5-3. The IRT-Indexed Registry

The International Receivables Registry would be indexed by IRTs, which are transferors and grantors. Under the International Receivables Registry Convention, transferors and grantors of receivables must be IRTs. Therefore, a transferor-indexed registration system for the International Receivables Registry means an IRT-indexed registration system. A third party, who would like to purchase an IRT receivable or to provide a loan to an IRT taking its receivable as security, would check the International Receivables Registry against the IRT to investigate whether there is any prior transfer of or security right in the IRT receivable. If the transferor or grantor is an IRT, the counterparty would only have to investigate the International Receivables Registry and would not have to investigate applicable national laws to see if there has been perfection under that law, thereby avoiding difficulties or issues in connection with choice of laws.

---

[45] The Cape Town Convention also takes this approach as to where the debtor is located, but does not have a system like the 'registered IRT' system. See Cape Town Convention, art 3.

[46] The Cape Town Convention also takes this approach. See ibid art 3(2).

5-6. Registration of an IRT

5-6-1. Public Notification of the List of IRTs

In order to make it absolutely clear that a company is an IRT, a very important prerequisite for an IRT is that it must be registered with the International Receivables Registrar. Registration of an IRT provides public notification. The International Receivables Registrar must publish the list of registered IRTs so that registrants may be aware they are dealing with an IRT. If a company is an IRT, even domestic parties (eg, prospective transferees of the company's receivables) must be aware that the proposed International Receivables Registry Convention could be applied and the application of national laws overridden.

Anyone would be able to investigate whether a company is an IRT in the list provided on the International Receivables Registry website. If the state where a company is registered is a Contracting State of the proposed International Receivables Registry Convention, the company may be an IRT. If the state where a company is registered is not a Contracting State, the company cannot be an IRT. In this book, 'registration of a company as an IRT with the International Receivables Registrar' is referred to as 'IRT registration'.

5-6-2. Two Methods to Use the International Receivables Registry

Where a company (originator) in a Contracting State wishes to assign its receivables to a foreign investment company under the proposed International Receivables Registry Convention, this book envisages two methods: (1) an ordinary company establishes a separate new IRT and transfers its receivables to the new IRT; or (2) an existing ordinary company registers itself as an IRT with the requisite authority.

5-6-2-1. Establishing a Separate IRT

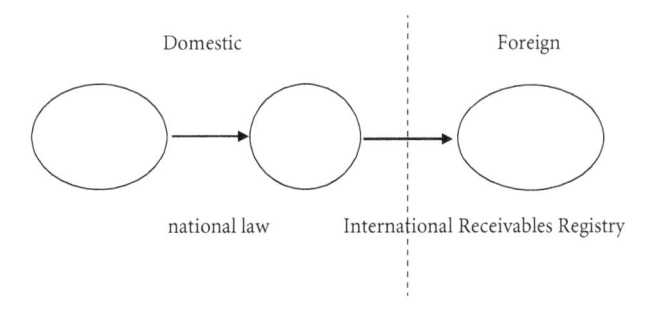

A company may establish a separate new IRT and register it with the International Receivables Registrar to assign its receivables to a foreign company under the proposed International Receivables Registry Convention. Once a company has established an IRT, the company may use the existing registered IRT to assign its receivables under the proposed International Receivables Registry Convention. Then, a company's pre-existing receivables already held by the company prior to the establishment of the IRT will need to be transferred to the IRT as it is a separate legal entity. This transfer to the IRT will be outside the International Receivables Registry system and will be governed by the applicable national laws.

5-6-2-2. Registering Itself as an IRT

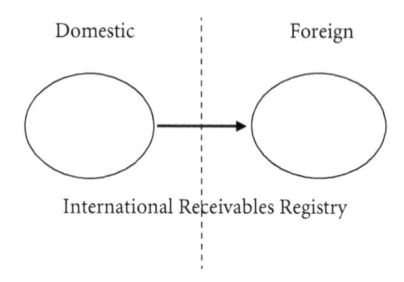

Domestic   Foreign

International Receivables Registry

Alternatively, an ordinary company can register itself as an IRT with the International Receivables Registrar, which will change the status of the company into an IRT. In this way, the IRT is the same legal entity as the company holding the pre-existing interests. Then, the company, after having become an IRT, would be able to assign its receivables to a foreign company by registering the transfer in the International Receivables Registry. Transfers which took place after the IRT registration of the company are governed by the International Receivables Registry Convention, whereas transfers which had already taken place at the time of the IRT registration are governed by the applicable national laws.[47]

The reason why the company might prefer the second approach of registering itself as an IRT to the first approach of establishing a separate IRT is that the second approach does not require the transfer of receivables to the IRT under the applicable national laws.

First, a company wishing to dispose of non-performing loans would register itself as an IRT with the International Receivables Registrar. For instance, an asset management company would register itself as an IRT with the International Receivables Registrar in order to assign non-performing loans to foreign investors under the proposed International Receivables Registry Convention.

Second, a company seeking to borrow funds using its receivables as collateral would register itself as an IRT with the International Receivables Registrar.

---

[47] See section 5-6-4.

To create a floating charge over receivables, a company would register itself as an IRT with the International Receivables Registrar in order to use the International Receivables Registry.

Third, a bank which wishes to borrow money from central banks with providing security rights in its loan receivables would register itself as an IRT with the International Receivables Registrar.

Fourth, a company originating factoring or securitisation would register itself as an IRT with the International Receivables Registrar to transfer its receivables to the factor or the special purpose vehicle (SPV) for securitisation in order to raise finance in international financial markets.

Once a company is registered as an IRT with the International Receivables Registrar, the proposed International Receivables Registry Convention (instead of national laws) would apply to cases where the company transfers its receivables or provides security rights in its receivables.

5-6-3. Pre-existing Security Rights

When a company registers itself as an IRT with the International Receivables Registrar, the treatment of pre-existing security rights in (including security transfers of) the company's receivables is a problem. 'Pre-existing security rights' means in this book the security rights in (and the security transfer of) a company's receivables which are perfected under the applicable national laws prior to the date of the IRT registration. If such pre-existing security rights would be continuously valid, a potential transferee would have to check both the International Receivables Registry and the national perfection methods forever. On the other hand, if pre-existing security rights become invalid all of a sudden upon IRT registration, the pre-existing secured creditor's rights would be unfairly infringed.

Thus, the proposed International Receivables Registry Convention provides the transitional period of one year from the date of the IRT registration of a company, during which period pre-existing secured creditors may perfect or re-perfect their security rights through registration in the International Receivables Registry.[48] This is to avoid a situation in which post-IRT security rights are indefinitely subordinated to pre-existing security rights and to allow pre-existing secured creditors a reasonable time within which to perfect or re-perfect their security rights by registering them in the International Receivables Registry.[49]

If a pre-existing secured creditor registers his pre-existing security rights in the International Receivables Registry within the one-year transitional period, the

---

[48] Draft International Receivables Registry Convention, art 3(4). See the Appendix.
[49] This transitional period functions similarly with the transitional provisions under Cape Town Convention, art 60. See Roy Goode, *Official Commentary on the Convention on International Interests in Mobile Equipment and the Protocol Thereto on Matters Specific to Aircraft Equipment*, revised edn (2008) 289 [4.348]–[4.349].

pre-existing secured creditor can keep and enjoy the priority of the date when the pre-existing security rights were perfected under the applicable national laws, and thus has priority over any post-IRT security rights registered in the International Receivables Registry before the pre-existing security rights are registered in the International Receivables Registry.

After the one-year transitional period, without a pre-existing security right being registered in the International Receivables Registry, a transferee or secured creditor registered in the International Receivables Registry has priority over any other secured creditor subsequently registered in the International Receivables Registry and over any other secured creditor not registered in the International Receivables Registry, even though those secured creditors have been perfected under the applicable national laws.

Let us suppose a case where an ordinary company perfected a security transfer of its receivable for security purposes according to the applicable national domestic laws, and subsequently the company registers itself as an IRT with the International Receivables Registrar and registers a transfer of or security right in the same receivable in the International Receivables Registry. The transfer or security right registered in the International Receivables Registry is subject to the previous security transfer perfected under the applicable national domestic laws and registered in the International Receivables Registry within the one-year transitional period.

5-6-4. Pre-existing Transfers

Let us suppose a case where an ordinary company absolutely transferred its receivable to a third party (not for security purposes) and perfected the absolute transfer of the receivable under the applicable national laws, and subsequently registers itself as an IRT with the International Receivables Registrar. If the company, after becoming an IRT, registers another transfer of or security right in the same receivable in the International Receivables Registry, the registration in the International Receivables Registry is a registration of an ineffective transfer. This is because the receivable has been already absolutely transferred to a third party under the applicable national laws and does not belong to the assets of the company at the time of the registration in the International Receivables Registry. Registration in the International Receivables Registry does not create any enforceable legal right for the transferor company.

As a result, perfection of an absolute transfer of a company's receivable under the applicable national laws prior to the IRT registration of the transferor company prevails over the registration in the International Receivables Registry of a transfer or a security right. However, perfection of a transfer under the applicable national laws after the IRT registration cannot prevail over the registration in the International Receivables Registry of a transfer or a security right.

Thus, this might harm the benefit of the International Receivables Registry—that a potential transferee only has to check the International Receivables Registry if the transferor of a receivable is an IRT—in the following situations where registration in the International Receivables Registry cannot guarantee the perfection as registered. First, where the transferor company has fairly recently registered itself as an IRT with the International Receivables Registrar, potential transferees will have to keep checking national registers etc to check that there are no absolute transfers prior to the IRT registration of the transferor company. Second, where the transferor IRT is itself a transferee from a transferor which is not an IRT, a potential transferee would have to check to make sure that the receivables were properly and effectively transferred to the IRT, ie, that the transfer was properly perfected under the applicable national laws (which might require notice to the debtors).

These problems result from the shortcomings of a transferor (or grantor)-indexed registry. The International Receivables Registry is indexed based on the transferors or grantors (rather than the receivables), and thus it does not show an ownership transfer of a particular receivable. For creation of a receivable, registration is not required. Only transfers of or security rights in receivables can be registered in the International Receivables Registry.[50] As a result, not all receivables of an IRT would be registered in the International Receivables Registry. Thus, searching the International Receivables Registry does not necessarily give a definite answer as to whether the IRT owns the specific receivable in question. A potential transferee may also refer to the financial statement of the IRT, but the financial statement provides only general information of receivables as items among various categories of assets of the IRT.

This book does not suggest a transition period for absolute transfers. In a security transfer, the transferee takes care of the transferred receivables because the transferee should return back the receivables to the transferor when the transferor pays the transferee, and therefore the transferee would not assign the receivables to a third party. However, in an absolute transfer, the transferee would assign the receivables to a third party who might assign the receivables to another third party and so on. After assigning the receivables to a third party, the absolute transferee would no longer take care of the receivables. Thus, it is not reasonable to expect the transferee to register the absolute transfer, which has already been lawfully perfected under the applicable national law, once again in the International Receivables Registry within one year from the IRT registration of the transferor company. For this reason, a transition period requiring registration of absolute transfers in the International Receivables Registry within one year of the IRT registration would not work.

The only way of dealing with this is a sanctions-based approach. The best way to prevent an IRT from assigning and creating a security right in the receivable, which the IRT has already absolutely transferred to a third party or which is not properly and effectively transferred to the IRT and thus the IRT does not own, is

---

[50] It may also record absolute rights where outright transfers of receivables are included. Still, it does not record all of the receivables created.

sanctions for false registration. In the first case where an IRT transfers or creates a security right in the receivable which the IRT has already absolutely transferred to a third party, the IRT is intentional or at least negligent. In the second case where an IRT transfers or creates a security right in the receivable which is not properly and effectively transferred to the IRT, it is the IRT's responsibility to make sure that the receivable has been properly and effectively transferred to the IRT in the first place.

5-6-5. Sanctions for False Registration

5-6-5-1. Fines

The proposed International Receivables Registry Convention imposes severe fines upon an IRT which commits false registration or consent on registration applied by a transferee or a secured creditor.[51] If an IRT intentionally or negligently registers a transfer of or a security right in the receivable that the IRT does not own (eg, which have been already absolutely transferred to a third party) in the International Receivables Registry, or consents to such false registration applied by a transferee or a secured creditor, the IRT will be imposed with a fine of no more than 10 per cent of the amount of the receivables falsely registered. Until the IRT pays the fine to the International Receivables Registrar, any registration filed or applied in connection with the IRT is suspended.[52]

5-6-5-2. Disqualification of the IRT

The proposed International Receivables Registry Convention provides for disqualification of an IRT which commits false registration or consent. If an IRT registers a transfer of or a security right in the receivable that the IRT does not own in the International Receivables Registry, or consents to such false registration applied by a transferee or a secured creditor intentionally or negligently more than three times, the IRT will be disqualified as an IRT and the company thus disqualified cannot be re-qualified as an IRT anymore.[53]

5-6-5-3. Compensatory Damages

In addition, a purported transferee or secured creditor who suffers loss due to such false registration or consent of an IRT can sue the IRT for compensatory damages under the applicable national laws.

On account of these sanctions for false registration or consent, it is expected that an IRT would not assign or create a security right in the receivable which the

---

[51] See section 6-9-2.
[52] Draft International Receivables Registry Convention, art 18(1). See the Appendix.
[53] Draft International Receivables Registry Convention, art 18(2). See the Appendix.

IRT does not own. This would reduce the possibility of there being pre-existing transfers of the receivable and the need to investigate applicable national laws to see whether the receivable has already been transferred to a third party.

5-7. Deregistration of an IRT

For an IRT to recover its ordinary company status and deregister from the list of IRT, the consent of all transferees and secured creditors of the receivables of the IRT that are previously registered in the International Receivables Registry is required. Once a company has been deregistered from the list of IRTs, the status of the company is changed from an IRT back to an ordinary company and thus all transfers of or security rights in the receivables of that company, which have been registered in the International Receivables Registry, shall also be deregistered and therefore lose their priority. Thus, transferees or secured creditors will again have to perfect their transfers or security rights under the applicable national laws in order to keep their priority.

One year before the date of deregistration ('D-date'), prior notice must be registered by the IRT to be deregistered in the International Receivables Registry as follows: 'This company will be deregistered from the list of IRT and the status of this company will be changed into an ordinary company from the D-date, and the proposed International Receivables Registry Convention shall no longer apply to the transfer of or a security right in the receivables of this company from the D-date.' This notice requirement is intended to protect potential transferees or grantors who have relied on the list of IRTs before the IRT is effectively deregistered.

5-8. The Sphere of Application of the Proposed International Receivables Registry Convention

5-8-1. Connecting Factors

The proposed International Receivables Registry Convention would apply to transfers of and security rights in receivables in which the transferor or grantor is an IRT.[54] The fact that the transferor or the grantor is an IRT means that the transferor or grantor is incorporated and registered in a Contracting State.

Where the transferor or grantor is an IRT and the forum state (*lex fori*) in which a legal action is brought is a Contracting State, the proposed International

---

[54] Draft International Receivables Registry Convention, art 2(1). See the Appendix.

Receivables Registry Convention would apply according to Article 2(1) of the proposed Convention.

Where the transferor or grantor is an IRT, the forum state (*lex fori*) is not a Contracting State and the law of the transferor's or grantor's state is the governing law according to the private international law of the forum state (*lex fori*), the court in the forum state (*lex fori*) would apply the proposed International Receivables Registry Convention.

However, where the transferor or grantor is an IRT, the forum state is not a Contracting State, the law of the debtor's state is the governing law according to the private international law of the forum state (*lex fori*) and the debtor of the receivable is situated in a non-Contracting State, the court in the forum state (*lex fori*) might not apply the proposed International Receivables Registry Convention.

5-8-2. Future Receivables

The proposed International Receivables Registry Convention applies to both present and future receivables.[55] Article 2(1) of the proposed International Receivables Registry Convention stipulates: 'This Convention applies to a transfer of and a security right in a receivable, present or future.' The 'present or future' part means that the International Receivables Registry covers future receivables.

Currently, most registration systems around the world cover future receivables. UCC Article 9, the PPSAs of Canada, New Zealand and Australia, the UK Companies Act 2006 and the UNCITRAL Model Law on Secured Transactions require only a general description of the encumbered asset.[56] Thus, it is easy to register a transfer of future receivables even though a debtor of the future receivable is not specified yet.

In Korea, the name and address of the debtor of the receivable are required to be registered.[57] However, if the debtor of the receivable is not specified at the time of registration, it is not required to be registered. Therefore, a transfer of future receivables may be also registered. The Korean Security Registration Act expressly stipulates that it covers future receivables[58] and movable assets which the grantor will get in the future.[59]

In Japan, under the Japanese Transfer Registration Act, it is possible to perfect the transfer of future receivables against unspecified debtors through registration. For future receivables, the debtor's name and address cannot be registered because the debtor of future receivables is not specified at the time of registration, whereas for existing receivables, the debtor's name and address must be registered. Instead,

---

[55] Draft International Receivables Registry Convention, art 2(1). See the Appendix.
[56] See section 2-7-4.
[57] See section 2-7-4-6.
[58] Korean Security Registration Act, art 34(2).
[59] ibid art 3(2).

for future receivables, details of the contract upon which the future receivables will accrue must be registered in order to specify the contract.[60] This may also be quite cumbersome, but Japanese law-makers thought that registration of such details should nonetheless be required to identify future receivables.[61]

5-8-3. A Legal Person (Company)

The proposed International Receivables Registry scheme limits the scope of registrants to a transfer of or a security right in a receivable where both the transferor and the transferee or both the grantor and the secured creditor are legal persons that have company registration numbers in their countries.[62] In the International Receivables Registry, each user would be identified by the country code and the company registration number of its own country. As a result, an IRT can only assign its receivables to a company registered and having a registration number in its country, and must not assign its receivables directly to an individual. If an IRT needs to assign its receivables to an individual, it has to first assign its receivables to an ordinary company and the company may then assign the receivables to an individual.

This book argues that the scope of transferors, transferees, grantors and secured creditors in the International Receivables Registry should be limited to legal persons (companies), and the International Receivables Registry shall not apply to individual natural persons for the following reasons.

The first reason is the language barrier (English capability). On account of cost-effectiveness, an international registration is operated in one language, which would be English. Therefore, users of an international registration need to understand English. However, many natural persons around the world cannot read English and thus cannot use an international registration in English.

The second reason is the problem of identification. Since the International Receivables Registry is a transferor (or grantor)-indexed system, identification of the transferor (or grantor) is important. Furthermore, because registration in the International Receivables Registry is confirmed by mutual reciprocal confirmation of the transferor and the transferee, both the transferor and the transferee must be certified entities and identifiable. Identification of a legal person (company) is clear and convenient. In most countries, there is a registry for companies, and each

---

[60] Transfer of Personal Property and Receivables Registration Regulation, art 9(1)(iii).
[61] During the legislation process, it was discussed whether the debtor's name and address may be additionally registered after a future receivable has actually accrued. However, this idea was not accepted. This was because there was concern about the situation where the debtor registered later might not be the person who the parties intended at first in the contract registered previously. See Katsuhiro Uekaki (植垣勝裕) and Hideki Ogawa (小川秀樹), Q&A on the Japanese Transfer Registration Act (Ichi Mon Ichi Tou Dousan Saiken Jouto Tokurei Hou, 『一問一答・動産・債権譲渡特例法』), 3rd edn (Tokyo, Shouji Houmu (商事法務), 2008) 96–97.
[62] Draft International Receivables Registry Convention, art 2(2). See the Appendix.

company has its registration number in its own country. Transfers of receivables from a company to another company may be registered using the company registration number in order to identify the transferor company and the transferee company.

However, for individuals in many countries, it is very difficult to find a method to accurately identify a natural person and guarantee the accuracy of the identification of an individual. A name is insufficient because there are many cases where different persons have the same name. For example, in the US, where every individual may register his security rights, there are many problems related to the accuracy of names of debtors (grantors).[63] Furthermore, identifying foreigners in English or a translation of a name into English is much more complicated and difficult.

The third reason is to prevent an IRT from hiding its receivables by registering the transfer of the receivables to fictitious people using fake names in the situation of running into bankruptcy.

The fourth reason is that a natural person does not usually use receivables for financing, whereas the purpose of the International Receivables Registry is to facilitate financing using receivables.

In comparison, in Korea, the Korean Security Registration Act applies to security rights where the grantor is a legal person or a natural person—provided, however, the Act applies to a natural person only if the natural person registered his trade name under the Korean Commercial Registration Act.[64] The security right, which is created by a legal person or a natural person who registered his trade name, may be registered under the Korean Security Registration Act. Therefore, the self-employed, farmers, fishermen and livestock raisers may also register their security rights if they registered the trade name. The legal person registration number or the resident registration number of a grantor and a secured creditor must be registered. A foreign legal person can also register its security right as a grantor in Korea.[65] For a foreign legal person that does not have a legal person registration number, the address of its business office or other office located in Korea or, if it does not have any office in Korea, the name of the representative of the foreign legal person and his address must be registered.[66]

In Japan, under the Japanese Transfer Registration Act, the transferor must be a legal person. If a transferor is a natural person, he cannot register his transfer under the Japanese Transfer Registration Act. A legal person registration number or a resident registration number is not required to be registered in Japan. A foreign legal person can also register its transfer as a transferor in Japan.[67]

---

[63] LoPucki and Warren (n 40) 284.
[64] Korean Security Registration Act, art 2(5).
[65] ibid.
[66] ibid art 47(2)(iv); Korean Security Regulation Rule, art 34.
[67] Japanese Transfer Registration Act, art 5(2).

For a foreign legal person, the Japanese Transfer Registration Act stipulates that the address of its business office or other office located in Japan must be registered.[68] Therefore, it might be interpreted that a foreign legal person that does not have any office in Japan cannot register its transfer in Japan.

5-8-4. Interaction with the Cape Town Convention

5-8-4-1. *The Scope of the Cape Town Convention and its Protocols*

There might be overlaps between the proposed International Receivables Registry Convention and the Cape Town Convention because the latter also stipulates the effect, formal requirement and priority of transfers of so-called 'associated rights'.[69] Associated rights include receivables secured by or associated with the object registrable under the Cape Town Convention.[70] These rules apply to aircraft equipment, railway rolling stock and space assets[71] in accordance with the Protocol to the Convention on International Interests in Mobile Equipment on Matters Specific to Aircraft Equipment (hereinafter the 'Aircraft Protocol'),[72] the Luxembourg Protocol to the Convention on International Interests in Mobile Equipment on Matters Specific to Railway Rolling Stock (hereinafter the 'Rail Protocol')[73] and the Protocol to the Convention on International Interests in Mobile Equipment on Matters Specific to Space Assets (hereinafter the 'Space Protocol').[74] Associated rights also include receivables for the repayment of purchase-money loans and the payment of rentals under leases.[75]

5-8-4-2. *Transfer of Associated Receivables*

Let us take the case of an IRT that advances money to a debtor for the debtor's general purposes under a loan agreement, providing for the grant of a security right in an aircraft owned by the debtor to secure the debtor's repayment obligation under the loan agreement.[76] At the time of the conclusion of the agreement on the security right in the aircraft, the debtor was situated in a Contracting State of the Cape Town Convention.[77] The IRT registered its security right in the aircraft in the International Registry of Mobile Assets. Later, the IRT transfers its receivables

---

[68] ibid art 7(2)(iii).
[69] Cape Town Convention, arts 31–37.
[70] ibid art 1(c).
[71] ibid art 2(3).
[72] Adopted in Cape Town on 16 November 2001.
[73] Adopted in Luxembourg on 23 February 2007.
[74] Adopted in Berlin on 9 March 2012.
[75] Goode (n 49) 83 [2.143].
[76] ibid 252 [4.258] Illustration 37.
[77] Cape Town Convention, art 3(1).

under the loan agreement together with the security right in the aircraft, first to A1 and then to A2.

In principle, perfection of the transfer of the receivables by registration in the International Receivables Registry is independent from perfection of the security right in the aircraft by registration in the International Registry of Mobile Assets under the Cape Town Convention. In order to secure priority of the transfer of the receivables, the transfer must be registered in the International Receivables Registry. Furthermore, in order to secure priority of the transfer of the security right in the aircraft, the transfer of the security right in the aircraft must be registered in the International Registry of Mobile Assets.

5-8-4-3. Extension of the Cape Town Convention to the Transfer of Receivables

Nevertheless, if the loan contract between the IRT (the creditor) and the debtor states that the receivables are secured by or associated with the aircraft,[78] and if the IRT receivables under the loan agreement are related to the aircraft,[79] the Cape Town Convention extends its sphere of application to the transfer of receivables.[80]

Let us take the following example. An IRT owns an aircraft and leases the aircraft to an airline company; the lease receivables are secured by the aircraft. At the time of the conclusion of the agreement on the security right in the aircraft, the airline company (the debtor) was situated in a Contracting State of the Cape Town Convention,[81] and the IRT's security right in the aircraft was registered in the International Registry of Mobile Assets. Later, the IRT transfers the lease receivables together with the security right in the aircraft first to one financial institution (F1) and then to another (F2). The priority of transfers of the lease receivables of the aircraft between F1 and F2 is determined by the time order of registration in the International Registry of Mobile Assets according to Article 29 of the Cape Town Convention. In the event of an overlap between the two Conventions applying to such aircraft lease receivables, the proposed International Receivables Registry Convention would not prevail over the Cape Town Convention with respect to priority issues. In case of any conflict in priority, a party that registered in the Cape Town Convention would have priority over another party that registered prior in time in the proposed International Receivables Registry Convention. However, a transferee or secured creditor registered under the proposed International Receivables Registry Convention would be perfected against the insolvency administrator of an IRT from the time of registration in the International Receivables Registry.

---

[78] Cape Town Convention, art 36(1)(a).
[79] ibid art 36(1)(b).
[80] Goode (n 49) 83 [2.143].
[81] Cape Town Convention, art 3(1).

The rationale is that by looking at the contract between the IRT (the creditor) and the airline company (the debtor), a potential transferee can determine whether to search the International Registry of Mobile Assets.[82] In the case of reservation-of-title agreements or financial lease agreements, the receivables necessarily relate to the purchase or lease of the aircraft. Thus, a potential transferee would be in a position to search the International Registry of Mobile Assets.[83]

The likelihood of the proposed International Receivables Registry Convention overlapping with the Cape Town Convention is low. This is because the proposed International Receivables Registry Convention only deals with priority and perfection of transfers of, and security rights in, the receivables of an IRT, and the Cape Town Convention and its Protocols apply only to aircraft equipment, railway rolling stock or space assets.

5-8-5. Contractual Prohibition on the Transfer of Receivables

An IRT must not agree upon contractual prohibition on the transfer of receivables with its debtors. In other words, it is prohibited for an IRT to agree to insert an anti-assignment clause in any contract generating receivables between the IRT and account debtors. Contractual prohibition on the transfer of IRT receivables is ineffective.[84]

If a receivable is transferred to an IRT properly and effectively, the transfer to the IRT itself means that the receivable is transferable and there is no anti-assignment clause in the contract generating the receivable between the transferor and the account debtor.

However, let us suppose a case where there is an anti-assignment clause in the contract generating the receivable between the transferor and the account debtor, and an IRT purchased the receivable without notice of the anti-assignment clause and subsequently transferred the receivable to a third party. Later, if the transfer of the receivable from the transferor to the IRT is invalidated on account of the anti-assignment clause according to the applicable national law in the jurisdiction,[85]

---

[82] Steven L Harris, 'The International Rail Registry' (2007) 12(3) *Uniform Law Review* 531, 544.

[83] Charles W Mooney, Jr, 'Transfers of International Interests in Mobile Equipment and Related Receivables under the UNIDROIT Convention: When Should the Tail Wag the Dog?' (1999) 20(3) *University of Pennsylvania Journal of International Economic Law* 443, 448.

[84] Draft International Receivables Registry Convention, art 20(1). See the Appendix.

[85] Under English Law and under the Dutch Civil Code and the German Civil Code, the transfer of receivables is invalid when there is an anti-assignment clause. However, in *Barbados Trust Co Ltd v Bank of Zambia*, the English Court of Appeal opened an effective way for a party in the position of a transferee to circumvent the block of an anti-assignment clause and sue a debtor joining the creditor (the purported transferor) as a defendant (the so-called *Vandepitte* procedure) if the creditor makes a declaration of trust in favour of the purported transferee. See *Barbados Trust Co Ltd v Bank of Zambia* [2007] EWCA Civ 148, (2007) 9 ITELR 689 (CA); *Vandepitte v Preferred Accident Insurance Corporation of New York* [1933] AC 70 (PC) Under the German Commercial Code (HGB), UCC art 9, the Saskatchewan PPSA, the UN Receivables Convention and the UNIDROIT Convention on International Factoring (Ottawa, 28 May 1988) and according to the French case law, the transfer of

the transfer of the receivable from the IRT to a third party consequently becomes invalid. As a result, the registration of the transfer from the IRT to a third party becomes false registration. A fine will then be imposed upon the IRT. Accordingly, when purchasing a receivable, an IRT must investigate whether there is an anti-assignment clause in the contract generating the receivable. It is the duty of an IRT, and therefore if an IRT fails to find an anti-assignment clause, the IRT is deemed negligent.

Let us suppose another case where there is an anti-assignment clause in the contract generating a receivable between an ordinary company and its account debtor, and later the company registered itself as an IRT with the International Receivables Registrar, and then the company, after having become an IRT, transfers the receivable to a third party. Under the proposed International Receivables Registry Convention, the anti-assignment transfer clause in the contract executed by and between the company and its account debtor becomes ineffective after the company has registered itself as an IRT.[86] Even if there is an anti-assignment clause in the contract executed by and between the company and its account debtor before the IRT registration of the company, the transfer of the receivable of the company after the IRT registration of the company is valid, but the IRT must compensate damages caused by the transfer to the account debtor who relied upon the anti-assignment clause.[87] This is to protect the transferee's trust or expectation that an IRT cannot have an anti-assignment clause. Thus, the transfer of IRT receivables is valid and effective, regardless of whether there is an anti-assignment clause made before the IRT registration of the transferor company.

5-9. The Operation of the International Receivables Registry

5-9-1. A Notice-Filing System

5-9-1-1. Why the Proposed International Receivables Registry Should be a Notice-Filing System

A notice-filing system is suitable for a grantor-based registration system. Since the International Receivables Registry is a grantor-based (transferor-based)

---

receivables is valid in spite of an anti-assignment clause. Under the Korean Civil Code and the Japanese Civil Code, it depends on whether the transferee knew of the anti-assignment clause when the transferee concluded the transfer agreement. If he knew of the anti-assignment clause, the transfer of receivables is invalid. If he did not know of the anti-assignment clause, the transfer of receivables is valid. For more information, see Woo-Jung Jon, 'A Comparative Analysis of the Regulations on Anti-assignment clauses' (University of Oxford, Faculty of Law, MSt dissertation, 2008) 55–68.

[86] Draft International Receivables Registry Convention, art 20(2). See the Appendix.
[87] Draft International Receivables Registry Convention, art 20(3). See the Appendix.

registration system, a notice-filing system is suitable. Let us hypothetically suppose that the International Receivables Registry were a document-filing registration system and required registration of the document of the transaction. The delivery of the application would be burdensome, and the number of documents submitted by registrants would be unmanageably large. Even if the documents could be sent electronically, the storage of such a large amount of data would require significant facilities and high cost. Moreover, if the registrar had to review the documents and issue a certificate confirming that the registered matters meet the registration requirements, it would take time and expense. As for the International Receivables Registry, one Registrar would have to review transaction documents from all over the world, which would be impracticable because of language diversity. This would be inadvisable as it would delay transactions and add to registration fees.

To reduce registration fees, the International Receivables Registry must be a notice-filing system, because it is quick and saves on database storage. In addition, parties prefer a notice-filing system to a document-filing system because they do not like to reveal the details of their transactions. Under a notice-filing system, the registration must indicate the contact information of the relevant parties, such as the grantor and the secured creditor or the transferor and the transferee,[88] so that a potential transferee may contact them and investigate further. The registration process in the International Receivables Registry does not involve human intervention. The International Receivables Registry would not require parties to submit the contract document for a transfer of or a security right in receivables.

5-9-1-2. The Information Required for International Receivables Registry Registration

Having compared the legal systems above, the conclusion is that most require identification of the grantor (debtor) or the transferor, identification of the secured creditor or the transferee, a list or general description of the debtor of the receivable and a general description of the transferred or encumbered asset. In the International Receivables Registry, it must also be registered regardless of whether the registration is for a transfer or a security right.

In Korea and Japan, the cause of registration and the date of the cause must be registered. However, registering the date of the cause would not be necessary for the International Receivables Registry because advance registration is available and priority is determined by the date of registration regardless of the date of the cause.

Under the proposed International Receivables Registry Convention, the following would be required to effect a registration: (1) information identifying the transferor or the grantor; (2) information identifying the transferee or the secured

---

[88] Draft International Receivables Registry Convention, art 13. See the Appendix.

creditor (or, if a holder of a bond is the secured creditor, information identifying the bond); (3) a list or general description of the debtor of the receivable transferred or encumbered; and (4) a general description of the receivable transferred or encumbered, present or future, including the amount of monetary obligation and the due date.[89]

5-9-2. Parties' Reciprocal Confirmation Instead of Registrar's Review

As Goode has said, the parties' reciprocal confirmation of the registration information is 'an important safeguard against improper registration',[90] particularly for an online registration system where no human intervention is involved to review the information registered. In the International Receivables Registry, there would be no division having the authority to review and there would be no human intervention. Thus, the International Receivables Registry would need to devise a way to ensure the authenticity of the registration contents. If the law would require the consent of an IRT—that is, a grantor (or transferor)—in advance of registration, it could prevent the IRT from going through the difficult procedures of cancelling an incorrect registration done by a secured creditor (or transferee) where there is some error with the registration application. For this reason, the proposed International Receivables Registry Convention requires the consent of the IRT for registration of a security right (or transfer) submitted by a secured creditor (or a transferee).

The International Receivables Registry would follow the reciprocal consent system of the Cape Town Convention.[91] Under the proposed International Receivables Registry Convention, a security right in (or a transfer of) receivables may be registered in the International Receivables Registry either by an IRT or a secured creditor (or a transferee). If a security right (or a transfer) is registered by the IRT, the International Receivables Registry system will automatically request the secured creditor (or the transferee) to confirm the registration information entered by the IRT. Conversely, if a security right in (or a transfer of) receivables is registered by the secured creditor (or the transferee), the International Receivables Registry system will automatically request the IRT to confirm the registration information entered by the secured creditor (or the transferee).[92]

Once a party—either the IRT or the secured creditor (or the transferee)—logs on to the website of the International Receivables Registry, completes the electronic forms contained on the website and inserts registration information about a security right in (or a transfer of) receivables, the other party would be automatically

---

[89] Draft International Receivables Registry Convention, art 13. See the Appendix.
[90] Goode (n 49) 207 [4.146].
[91] See section 2-8-2-3-4.
[92] Draft International Receivables Registry Convention, art 14(2). See the Appendix.

notified by email.[93] The other party will be given the opportunity, after logging on to the website, to consent to the registration unilaterally made by one party before the registration becomes searchable on the website. If the other party logs on to the website and confirms the registration, the specific security right in (or the specific transfer of) receivables would be registered immediately. Initiated but not completed registrations will not appear on any search results on the website.[94]

Putting in correct email addresses in the registration is very important because every notice regarding the registration would be sent by email. The consent of the other party would also be initiated by the email automatically sent by the International Receivables Registry operation system.[95] Each user should provide three email addresses for receiving notices, and the registration system should send the notice simultaneously to all three in order to ensure that notice is received.

The process of amendment or discharge of a registration is the same as the application for registration, which requires the parties' reciprocal consent.[96] If there is a mistake in the registration information, the parties may revise the registration in the same manner with both of the parties' consent, but the date of registration will be recorded as of the revised date and time. As a result, though the parties might lose priority, it is their responsibility. As such, making the parties accountable for any mistakes they made under the system, having no official review of the registrar, the system can eliminate the time gap between application and registration, and finally accomplish real-time registration.[97]

5-9-3. Email Notification Linked to International Receivables Registry Registration

Where a transferee who is unfamiliar or unknown to the debtor of the receivable gives notice of the transfer to the debtor, the transferee must present the debtor with evidence of the transfer. International Receivables Registry registration can be good evidence of a transfer (or a security right), since the International Receivables Registry requires reciprocal confirmation of registered information by both the transferor and the transferee (or by both the grantor and the secured creditor).

The proposed International Receivables Registry Convention adopts a similar approach as the Korean Security Registration Act and the Japanese Transfer

---

[93] Draft International Receivables Registry Convention, art 14(2)(a). See the Appendix. The International Receivables Registry would operate under the same principle as the International Registry of Mobile Assets under the Cape Town Convention and its Aircraft Protocol. Each company would be able to sign in to the online International Receivables Registry website and post its receivables transfer records voluntarily.
[94] Draft International Receivables Registry Convention, art 14(4). See the Appendix.
[95] Draft International Receivables Registry Convention, art 14(2). See the Appendix.
[96] Draft International Receivables Registry Convention, art 14. See the Appendix.
[97] The English Law Commission Report also recommended that the 21-day time gap between the transfer and registration should be abolished, and that removing the 21-day period of invisibility can be achieved by the combination of a notice-filing system and an online operation system. Law Commission, *Company Security Rights* (Law Com No 296, Cm 6654, 2005) 4 [1.9], 52 [3.82].

Registration Act. Under these Acts, a secured creditor or a transferee may give notice of the security right or the transfer to the debtor of the receivable by presenting a certificate of registration to the debtor of the receivable. The rationale is that these Registration Acts require both the grantor and the secured creditor[98] or both the transferor and the transferee[99] to apply for registration, which verifies the contents of registration.

Under the proposed International Receivables Registry Convention, a transferee (or secured creditor) may also give notice of the transfer (or security right) to the debtor of the receivable by providing the web address of the relevant registration in the International Receivables Registry, which can evidence the transfer (or the security right).[100] This provision prevails over national laws. Thus, in a Contracting State, even if a transferee (or a secured creditor) is not entitled to give notice of the transfer (or the security right) to the debtor of the receivable under the applicable national laws, a transferee (or a secured creditor) is nonetheless entitled to give such notice to the debtor of the receivable under the proposed International Receivables Registry Convention.

The web address of the relevant registration in the International Receivables Registry can be conveniently provided to the debtor, eg, through email. In order to do this, the transferee (or the secured creditor) needs to ask the transferor (or the grantor) for the email addresses of the debtors of the receivables. The International Receivables Registry can be designed to support email notification by which a transferor or a transferee gives notice of transfers of (or security rights in) receivables to the debtor of the receivable. Once the parties register a transfer of (or a security right in) receivables on the International Receivables Registry website, a transferee (or secured creditor) would be able to give notice of the transfer (or security right) to the debtor of the receivable through an email containing the link to the relevant registration webpage on the International Receivables Registry website. This system is safe from email fraud because the contents of the International Receivables Registry website cannot be altered. Then, clicking the linked web address would lead to the webpage containing the relevant registration in the International Receivables Registry. By simply clicking on the link in the email, the debtor of the receivable could receive notice of the registered transfer of or the registered security right in the receivable on the International Receivables Registry website.

5-9-4. Supervisory Authority and Registry

Under the proposed International Receivables Registry Convention, the International Receivables Registrar would have to be based somewhere. The International Registry of Mobile Assets under the Cape Town Convention and

---

[98] Korean Security Registration Act, art 41(1).
[99] Japanese Transfer Registration Act, art 8(2).
[100] Draft International Receivables Registry Convention, art 15. See the Appendix.

the Aircraft Protocol is the only international registry operating today and is a good example for the supervisory authority and the registrar for the International Receivables Registry. The supervisory authority of the International Registry of Mobile Assets for aircraft objects is the Council of the International Civil Aviation Organization (ICAO), which is a specialised agency of the UN.[101] The ICAO is advised by a Commission of Experts of the Supervisory Authority of the Aircraft Registry (CESAIR).[102] The International Registry of Mobile Assets is located in Dublin, Ireland and the online registration system is operated completely by its IT facilities. The International Registry of Mobile Assets was set up by Aviareto, a joint venture company of SITA SC[103] and the Irish government.[104] SITA SC owns 80 per cent of the shares, while the Irish government owns 20 per cent. The International Registry of Mobile Assets is run by Aviareto pursuant to a five-year contract with ICAO.[105] Aviareto is assisted by the International Registry Advisory Board (IRAB).[106]

The supervisory authority and the International Receivables Registrar would be established as outlined in the proposed International Receivables Registry Convention. It would be desirable if a specialised agency of the UN could be the supervisory authority. The International Receivables Registrar would be operated by an online notice-filing system to reduce registration fees and to make real-time registration 24 hours a day, 365 days a year. The International Receivables Registrar would not require applicants to submit transaction documents. Registration would be operated mainly in English and, if possible, simple legal terminology could be translated into several languages.

The International Registry of Mobile Assets under the Cape Town Convention distinguishes registry user entities from searching persons.[107] Registration is searchable by any member of the public, but access for the purpose of applying, confirming, amending or discharging registrations is tightly controlled. It is restricted to a registry user entity or an administrator of that entity,[108] to be approved as such by the Registrar, 'when the Registrar reasonably concludes: (a) that such entity and administrator are who they claim to be; and (b) on the basis of information submitted, and without undertaking specific legal analysis, that the latter is entitled to act as administrator of the former'.[109] It is the Registrar's job to investigate the identity of registry user entities or administrators of those entities.

---

[101] Goode (n 49) 49 [2.67].
[102] ibid.
[103] SITA SC is an air transport telecommunications company owned by the world's airlines.
[104] Goode (n 49) 117 [3.30].
[105] ibid.
[106] IRAB is set up by Aviareto as Registrar to provide advice to the Registrar on matters relating to the operations of the Registry. See ibid.
[107] Goode (n 49) 119 [3.36].
[108] ibid.
[109] Regulations and Procedures for the International Registry, Regulations, s 4.1.

Following the practice of the International Registry of Mobile Assets, the International Receivables Registrar would also have to investigate the identity of registry users. Registrars at the International Receivables Registry would not review or conduct further scrutiny on the contents of registration applications,[110] but would only check and confirm the identity of registry users. To log in to the International Receivables Registry website, a legal person should have a membership that would require an identification check by the International Receivables Registrar using phone calls etc.

5-9-5. International Receivables Registry Online Search

Having compared the legal systems above, this book proposes that the search systems in the US and under the Cape Town Convention are more appropriate for the International Receivables Registry, while the search systems in the UK and Japan are rather complicated. In the UK, the problem is the 21-day gap between the creation of security rights and registration. In Japan, the problem is that a potential transferee is unable to search the registry online directly. Instead, a potential transferee needs to apply for the issuance of a registration certificate and wait for it. This system would not work for an international registry.

In the International Receivables Registry, any person should be able to search for registration online on the International Receivables Registry website.[111] Applications for registration must be restricted to the legal person whose identification is thoroughly checked and confirmed. After the identification checks, a legal person should pay fees for an ID and password to use the International Receivables Registry, but, other than that, access to the registered information should be free. On this basis, notification of a transfer or a security right through email with the link to the webpage of the relevant registration would be available.[112]

5-10. Conclusion

At an international level, establishing a general security rights registry which covers all movable assets and receivables might not be advisable due to over-leverage and credit expansion problems, and would be impractical because of language translation and identification problems discussed in this chapter. For these reasons, this book focuses on the registration system for transfers of and security rights in receivables.

---

[110] *cf* UNCITRAL Model Law on Secured Transactions, Model Registry Provisions, art 7.
[111] Draft International Receivables Registry Convention, art 19. See the Appendix.
[112] See section 6-9-3.

The registration system may be created as optional or compulsory. Optional registration brings about the situation where a potential transferee needs to check both the International Receivables Registry and national laws and perfection methods, eg, registry or notice to the debtor. The Korean Security Registration Act and the Japanese Transfer Registration Act use optional registration, where either the registration or Civil Code perfection can be chosen. At a single-country level, it might be practicable to check both the registry and enquire of account debtors. However, at an international level, it would be impracticable because a potential transferee should check all of the national registries, since a potential hidden competing transferee might be in any country. This could defeat the object of international registration.

For this reason, the International Receivables Registry is designed to be compulsory registration which prevails over national perfection. However, it imposes limitations on the scope of application, because otherwise all transfers of and security rights in receivables, whether domestic or international, must be registered in the International Receivables Registry, which would become too large to manage at reasonable cost whilst keeping the registration fee at an affordable level.

The proposed International Receivables Registry Convention confines its scope of application by defining the transferor or the grantor and inventing the concept of 'IRT', which stands for 'International Receivables Trader'. The proposed International Receivables Registry Convention applies where the transferor or grantor is an IRT. It also applies to the transfer of receivables where the transferor is an IRT, as well as to security rights in receivables where the grantor is an IRT.

Under the proposed International Receivables Registry Convention, a potential transferee would have to investigate first whether the transferor is an IRT and second whether there is any prior registration against the IRT in the International Receivables Registry. A potential transferee or secured creditor of receivables would first have to investigate whether its counterparty is an IRT or not. Anyone would be able to investigate whether a company is an IRT in the list provided on the International Receivables Registry website. If the state where a company is registered is a Contracting State of the proposed International Receivables Registry Convention, the company may be eligible to become an IRT.

The International Receivables Registry would accelerate international transfers of receivables made by an IRT or between IRTs in different jurisdictions. Insofar as a transferee or a secured creditor is also an IRT, the sequence of transfers or security rights would be automatically traced within the International Receivables Registry system. If a transferee or a secured creditor is not an IRT, the sequence of transfers or security rights cannot be recorded in the International Receivables Registry any further. In that case, one should consult national registries or perfection methods under the applicable national laws. Within national boundaries, the applicable national laws would regulate receivables transactions. Even in that case, the International Receivables Registry would function as a useful bridge to cross national borders as well as to add certainty and efficiency in international receivable financing.

With respect to the contents and effect of registration in the International Receivables Registry, the International Receivables Registry would be in the form of a notice-filing system along the lines of that adopted in UCC Article 9 and the PPSAs. This is because in the International Receivables Registry, there would not be a registrar to review the documents submitted and it would instead be operated automatically online in order to achieve a real-time registration. No human intervention is involved in the process of registration in the International Receivables Registry. For this reason, to increase the authenticity of the registration information, reciprocal confirmation of both a transferor and a transferee (or both a grantor and a secured creditor) regarding the registration information would be required for registration. The contents of registration in the International Receivables Registry should be double-checked by the parties' reciprocal confirmation.

Providing registration web address could be good evidence of proving a transfer of or a security right in IRT receivables, with which a transferee may give notice of the transfer or the security right to the debtor of the receivable. It would facilitate email notification linked to registration in the International Receivables Registry to the debtor of the receivable. A party could give notice of the transfer or the security right to debtors of receivables through emails containing the link to the relevant registration in the International Receivables Registry. As such, debtors of receivables could refer to the relevant registration in the International Receivables Registry by simply clicking the link in the email.

In the International Receivables Registry, a potential transferee could access the registry online in order to check whether a certain receivable has been transferred. Anyone should be able to search the International Receivables Registry online.

6

Priority in the International Receivables Registry

6-1. Introduction

Chapter 6 analyses priority rules with respect to transfers of and security rights in receivables under the proposed International Receivables Registry Convention. Section 6-2 examines perfection in the event of insolvency of the transferor or the grantor. Section 6-3 analyses priority by the time order of registration (section 6-3-1). It also explains that knowledge of an unregistered transfer or security right has nothing to do with priority and perfection in the International Receivables Registry (section 6-3-2), that registration has nothing to do with effectiveness against the debtor of the receivable and that notice to the debtor is required for effectiveness against the debtor (section 6-3-3). Section 6-3 also explains that registration in the International Receivables Registry prevails over notice to the debtor in determining priority between competing transferees, even though the debtor may discharge the debt by paying the transferee who gives notice first (section 6-3-4).

In this chapter, priority rules under the proposed International Receivables Registry Convention in the following four situations are examined. There are four possible combinations of multiple transfers and security rights: double transfers (section 6-3-6); a prior transfer and a subsequent security right (section 6-3-5); a prior security right and a subsequent transfer (section 6-3-6); and double security rights (section 6-3-7).

Furthermore, this chapter solves problems with respect to the double debtor problem, floating charges, reservation of title, preferential creditors, proceeds, bonds and subordination agreements, and proposes recommendable rules for the proposed International Receivables Registry Convention. Section 6-4 solves the double debtor problem. Section 6-5 explains floating security rights under the proposed International Receivables Registry Convention. Section 6-6 explores reservation of title. Section 6-7 explains the ranking of preferential creditors under the proposed International Receivables Registry Convention. Section 6-8 clarifies that a security right registered in the International Receivables Registry covers separated and identifiable proceeds. Section 6-9 shows that the International Receivables Registry could facilitate international bond transactions. Finally, section 6-10 explains the effectiveness of subordination agreements under the proposed International Receivables Registry Convention.

6-2. Perfection

A transfer of and security right in IRT receivables is perfected against third parties by registration in the International Receivables Registry. In the event of an IRT insolvency, a transferee or secured creditor registered in the International Receivables Registry retains priority over the insolvency administrator of the IRT. Registration prior to the commencement of insolvency proceedings against an IRT would perfect the transfer or security right thus registered against the insolvency administrators and other creditors of the IRT. Transferees would have a right in the transferred receivables regardless of the higher priority of preferential creditors such as tax claims and labour claims in accordance with the national insolvency law. This is because upon registration in the International Receivables Registry, the receivables are transferred to the transferee and hence are no longer the property of the IRT.

With respect to a security right in IRT receivables, in the event of an IRT insolvency, secured creditors registered in the International Receivables Registry would be treated as secured creditors under the applicable national laws.

A transfer of (or security right in) IRT receivables which is not registered in the International Receivables Registry is valid between the IRT and the transferee (or between the IRT and the secured creditor), since registration is a perfection requirement for a transfer and a security right, but such transfer is not perfected against third parties, including the insolvency administrator.

6-3. Priority

6-3-1. Priority by Order of Registration

Where the transferor or grantor is an IRT, priority between its transfers, between its security rights or between its transfers and security rights would be governed by the proposed International Receivables Registry Convention and hence determined by the order of registration in the International Receivables Registry. Under the proposed International Receivables Registry Convention, the transfer of (or security right in) a receivable registered in the International Receivables Registry has priority over any other transfer of (or security right in) a receivable subsequently registered in the International Receivables Registry and over any other transfer of (or security right in) a receivable that is not registered in the

International Receivables Registry, even though the transfer (or security right) has been perfected under the applicable national laws.

Registration in the International Receivables Registry would override perfection made under the applicable national laws. Priority under the proposed International Receivables Registry Convention is irrelevant to registration in a national registry. For example, the priority of a foreign investment company could be secured once the transfer is registered in the International Receivables Registry regardless of its domestic perfection. Domestic courts in the Contracting States should accept registration in the International Receivables Registry as perfection for domestic purposes.

An intending transferee or secured creditor could register its transfer or security right in the International Receivables Registry in order to secure priority over any other transfers or security rights, subsequently registered or not registered in the International Receivables Registry. The transfer of an IRT receivable[1] or a security right in an IRT receivable must be registered in the International Receivables Registry in order to secure its priority.

The sanction for failing to do registration is loss of priority against other security right holders. Even if not registered in the International Receivables Registry, a transfer of or a security right in an IRT receivable is still valid under the applicable national laws. If either a transfer or a security right is registered in the International Receivables Registry, it would have priority over the other, notwithstanding the order of perfection under the applicable national laws. The transfer of or a security right in an IRT receivable, once registered in the International Receivables Registry, would have priority over a prior security right if the prior security right was not registered in the International Receivables Registry within a one-year transitional period.[2] Any transfer of or a security right in IRT receivables that is not registered in the International Receivables Registry may not be asserted against a registered transferee or secured creditor.

If there are two security rights not registered in the International Receivables Registry, priority between them is determined by the applicable national laws.

6-3-2. Knowledge of an Unregistered Transfer or Security Right

Knowledge of an unregistered transfer or security right is irrelevant with regard to priority. A registered transfer or security right has priority over an earlier unregistered transfer or security right even if this was known to the registered transferee or secured creditor at the time of registration. This is to encourage transferees and secured creditors to register their transfers of and security rights in receivables as soon as possible. In addition, this is to avoid factual disputes as to whether the

---

[1] In this book, a 'receivable of an IRT' is referred to as an 'IRT receivable'.
[2] See section 5-6-3.

later transferee or secured creditor did or did not know of the earlier unregistered transfer of or security right in a receivable.[3]

6-3-3. Registration has Nothing to do with Effectiveness against the Debtor

Even if a transfer of an IRT receivable is registered in the International Receivables Registry, before the debtor of the receivable receives notice of the transfer, the transferee cannot sue and collect the receivable from the debtor of the receivable, and conversely the debtor may discharge the debt by paying the original creditor (IRT) that is a transferor.

It is notable that registration in the International Receivables Registry is only for perfection against third parties and not for effectiveness against the debtor of the receivable. In order to perfect a transfer of a receivable against the debtor of the receivable, notice of the transfer to the debtor is required in all jurisdictions. Even in jurisdictions with a registration system for the transfer of receivables, registration of a transfer of a receivable or a security right in a receivable in the International Receivables Registry has nothing to do with effectiveness of the transfer or the security right against the debtor of the receivable.

For example, suppose that an IRT ('V') transferred its receivables against D to E and registered the transfer in the International Receivables Registry. The relationship between E and other competing transferees is different from the relationship between E and D. Thus, even if V's transfer to E is registered in the International Receivables Registry, if D does not receive notice of the transfer, D may still discharge the debt by paying V.

This is because a debtor is under no duty to continuously check the register. Registration does not allow a transferee to sue the debtor of the receivable directly. There is no duty for a debtor to check the International Receivables Registry before paying a debt to an IRT. If it is assumed that a transferee could accomplish perfection even against a debtor of a receivable by registration in the International Receivables Registry, a debtor would always have to search the International Receivables Registry before paying a debt to an IRT in order to confirm whom to pay. Checking the International Receivables Registry takes time. If a debtor delays paying off the debt while checking the International Receivables Registry, the debtor would be liable for damages that the IRT suffers from the delay in payment after a due date. Furthermore, consumer debtors of loans for cars or credit card receivables are usually expected to be unaware of registrations in the International Receivables Registry. As such, if the law might require a debtor to check the

---

[3] The Cape Town Convention takes the same approach. See Roy Goode, *Official Commentary on the Convention on International Interests in Mobile Equipment and the Protocol Thereto on Matters Specific to Aircraft Equipment* (revised edn, 2008) 224 [4.183].

International Receivables Registry to determine who should be paid each time a payment is due, it would be unduly harsh on debtors.

6-3-4. Priority between Registration and Notice to the Debtor

In a double transfer situation, there is a problem with respect to the relationship between registration of transfers and giving notice of transfers to the debtors. For instance, a problem involving double transfers occurs where the first transfer of a receivable is registered in the International Receivables Registry and the second transfer of the same receivable is subsequently registered in the International Receivables Registry, but the debtor of the receivable is notified of the second transfer prior to the first transfer and pays the second transferee.

In the case where X transferred his receivable to Y1, and Y1 registered the transfer in the International Receivables Registry (but Y1 did not give notice to the debtor of the receivable) and later X transferred the same receivable to Y2 for the second time and Y2 gave notice to the debtor of the receivable, the debtor of the receivable only has to pay Y2 (who gave notice first) and will be discharged of the receivable.

However, between Y1 and Y2, according to the rule that priority is determined by the time order of registration, Y1 should have priority. Then, whether Y1 can claim against Y2 for unjust enrichment is the issue to be settled. Such a problem occurs because as for receivables, effectiveness against the debtor of the receivable is different from perfection against third parties, which determines priority.[4]

Between the two transfers, the first transferee has priority over the second transferee since priority is determined by the time order of registration in the International Receivables Registry. The second transferee cannot be a bona fide purchaser for value without notice because the second transferee should have checked the International Receivables Registry before the transfer of the receivable if the transferor is an IRT.

In English law, if a prior transfer is an equitable assignment without giving notice to the debtor, since an equitable assignment is not perfected against third parties (even though it is perfected against the insolvency administrator of the IRT), a prior equitable assignment without giving notice to the debtor does not have priority over a subsequent transfer registered in the International Receivables Registry.

Under the proposed International Receivables Registry Convention, a debtor of an IRT need not pay any purported transferee of an IRT receivable without the purported transferee's presenting a registration certificate of the transfer of the IRT receivable in the International Receivables Registry. If the debtor of the

---

[4] As for movable assets, effectiveness is only sole effectiveness against third parties, and there is not any equivalence of effectiveness against the debtor of the receivable.

receivable mistakenly pays the second transferee where the debtor has received notice of the second transfer that is not registered in the International Receivables Registry, the second transferee would have to yield the proceeds collected from the debtor to the first transferee. The first transferee who first registered his transfer can claim for the proceeds that the second transferee has received from the debtor of the receivable. However, this procedure would be burdensome. It is thus recommended that a transferee who has registered his transfer should give notice of the transfer to the debtor of the receivable as soon as available.

6-3-5. Priority between Transfers and Security Rights

6-3-5-1. Prior Security Rights and Subsequent Transfer

Under the International Receivables Registry Convention, priority between transfers of and security rights in an IRT receivable is determined by the time order of registration in the International Receivables Registry.

V (IRT)
security right for A
transferred to B

If in the International Receivables Registry, a security right is registered first and subsequently a transfer is registered, it causes the so-called 'double debtor problem', which was analysed in detail in section 4-7.

6-3-5-2. Prior Transfers and Subsequent Security Rights

V (IRT)
transferred to B
security right for A

Conversely, if a transfer to B is registered first and subsequently a security right for A is registered in the International Receivables Registry, priority between B and A is determined by the time order of registration, and thus B has priority over A.

The transfer to B may be either absolute or by way of security. If the transfer to B is an absolute transfer, the IRT no longer has a right to the transferred receivable and as a consequence cannot create a security right in the receivable for A. In this case, the transfer to B is valid, but the security right of A is invalid.

On the other hand, if the transfer to B is by way of security for less than the full value of the transferred receivable, the IRT may legitimately create a security right for A. Still, B has priority over A.

V (IRT)
security right for A

If the absolute transfer to B, though first in time, is not registered in the International Receivables Registry, then A has priority over the unregistered transferee B: this is an exception to the *nemo dat quod non habet* ('No one gives what he doesn't have') rule, because A has a security right in V's receivable, even though the receivable has already been transferred from V to B.

Let us suppose a case where a company V transferred its receivable to B and perfected the absolute transfer of the receivable to B under the applicable national laws, and later registers itself as an IRT in the International Receivables Registrar. Even though the absolute transfer of the receivable of the company V to B is not registered in the International Receivables Registry, the absolute transfer is valid because it was perfected under the applicable national laws before the IRT registration of the company V.[5] Since the absolute transfer from V to B is valid, the receivable is owned by B from the date when the absolute transfer is perfected under the applicable national laws, and thus V's subsequent creating a security right in the receivable for A is invalid, leading to the result that the registration in the International Receivables Registry of such a security right for A is false registration and thus V (IRT) should be penalised.[6]

6-3-6. Double Transfers of a Receivable of an IRT

6-3-6-1. Double Transfers by an IRT

If an IRT transfers its receivables to a transferee and later to another transferee, priority between the two transfers would be determined by the time order of registration in the International Receivables Registry. The transferee first registered in the International Receivables Registry would be the transferee having priority of the receivable; any subsequent transferee registered in the International Receivables Registry would not. The transferee first registered in the International Receivables Registry would obtain 100 per cent of the right in the receivable; any other transferee subsequently registered in the International Receivables Registry would obtain none.

Before the transfer of an IRT receivable, a potential transferee would check the International Receivables Registry under the IRT. If there is a prior transfer of the receivable registered in the International Receivables Registry under the IRT, the potential transferee would not agree to the transfer of the receivable. As a result, if the transfer of a receivable or a group of receivables is registered in

---

[5] See section 5-6-4.
[6] See section 5-6-5.

the International Receivables Registry under an IRT, no further transfer would be registered for the same receivable or for the same group of receivables under the same IRT.

If more than one transfer of the receivable is mistakenly registered in the International Receivables Registry under an IRT, the transfer that is registered first in time is valid; the other transfers are invalid. Therefore, if the debtor of the receivable receives notice of a second transfer and pays the second transferee, the second transferee must give the proceeds received from the debtor of the receivable to the first transferee that has priority.

6-3-6-2. Double Transfers by an IRT and Subsequent Transfers by the Transferees

Transfers of a receivable may be continued in a chain of transactions. In other words, a transferee of a receivable may assign the transferred receivable to a third party. For example, a receivable may be transferred from V to A and then from A to C. Where V is an IRT, A's priority is determined by the time order of registration in the International Receivables Registry. C succeeds and retains the priority of A. Thus, C's priority is the same as A's priority.

V	A	B
transferred to A	transferred to C	transferred to D
transferred to B		

If two transfers are registered in the International Receivables Registry over the same receivable R of V, the first transfer to A and the second transfer to B, and subsequently A transfers the receivable R to C, and B transfers the receivable R to D, A has priority over B because A's registration is prior in time to B's registration in the International Receivables Registry. As a result, A is the transferee of the receivable R, but B is not the transferee of the receivable R. A can assign the receivable R to C, but B cannot. Therefore, C is a transferee of the receivable R, but D is not, whether or not the transfer from A to C was registered in the International Receivables Registry.

Still, C should perfect the transfer under the applicable national law if A is not an IRT[7] (or register the transfer of the receivable from A to C in the International Receivables Registry if A is an IRT) not to protect itself against other transferees or secured creditors of V, but to secure protection against other transferees or secured creditors of A with respect to the receivable.

It is notable that priority between C and D is not determined by the order of perfection under the applicable national laws, even though A, B, C and D are not

---

[7] If A is not an IRT, the transfer from A to C cannot be registered with the International Receivables Registry.

IRTs. For example, under English law, the transfer of the receivable from A to C and that from B to D can be perfected against third parties by notification of the transfer to the debtor of the receivable.[8] However, priority between C and D is not determined by the time order in which the debtor of the receivable receives notice of the transfer, but instead is determined by the priority between A and B. This is because C and D are not the transferees from the same transferor, while A and B are the competing transferees from the same transferor V.

6-3-6-3. Double Transfers by an IRT and Subsequent Security Rights by the Transferees

The same rule applies where an IRT ('V') transferred its receivable to a transferee and subsequently the transferee creates a security right in the transferred receivable for his creditor. For example, V transferred its receivable R to A and then A creates a security right in the receivable securing a debt to C. Now C has a security right in the receivable R. A's priority is determined by the time order of registration in the International Receivables Registry. C succeeds and retains the priority of A. Thus, the priority of C is the same as the priority of A.

V	A	B
transferred to A	security right for C	security right for D
transferred to B		

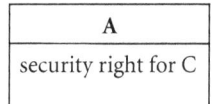

If two transfers are registered in the International Receivables Registry over the same receivable R of V, the first in favour of A and the second in favour of B, and subsequently A created a security right in the receivable for C, and B created a security right in the same receivable R for D, A has priority over B because A's registration is prior in time to B's registration in the International Receivables Registry. As a result, A is the transferee of the receivable, but B is not the transferee of the receivable. A can create a security right in the receivable securing his debt to C up to the value of the receivable, but B cannot create any interest in the receivable for D. Therefore, C has a security right in the receivable and D does not, regardless of whether C's security right in the receivable of A as a grantor was registered or not.

Still, C should perfect its security right under the applicable national law if A is not an IRT[9] (or register its security right in the receivable in the International Receivables Registry if A is an IRT) not to protect itself against other transferees or secured creditors of V, but to secure protection against other transferees or secured creditors of A with respect to the receivable R.

---

[8] *Dearle v Hall* (1828) 3 Russ 1.
[9] If A is not an IRT, C's security right in the receivable of A (A as the grantor and C as the secured creditor) cannot be registered with the International Receivables Registry.

6-3-7. Double Security Rights in a Receivable of an IRT

6-3-7-1. Double Security Rights Created by an IRT

If an IRT creates a security right in a receivable and subsequently creates another security right in the same receivable, priority between the two security rights is determined by the time order of registration in the International Receivables Registry. After satisfying the debt to the first-registered secured creditor from the proceeds of the receivable, the second-registered secured creditor may satisfy its debt from any remainder.

6-3-7-2. Security Rights by an IRT Followed by Transfers of Secured Creditors

A security right in a receivable cannot be transferred to a third party separately from the secured debt for which the security right is intended. However, a security right in a receivable may be transferred to a transferee, following the transfer of the right to the secured debt for which the security right is intended, according to the parties' agreement. Where a debt is secured by a debtor's receivable, if the creditor has transferred the right to the debt to a transferee, the transferee will have the right to the debt as well as the security right in the receivable securing the debt according to the parties' agreement. This involves two transfers: first, the transfer of the secured debt and, second, the transfer of the security right in the receivable.

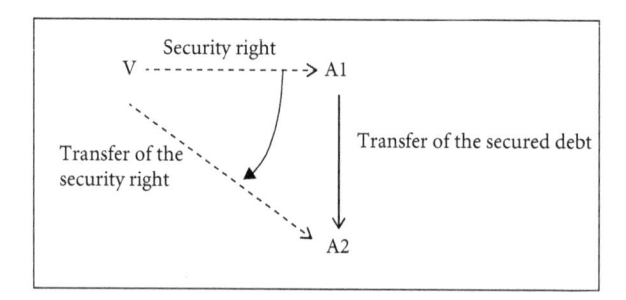

```
                  Security right
        V ------------------> A1

 Transfer of the                Transfer of the secured debt
 security right
                         ↓
                         A2
```

Let us take the following example. An IRT ('V') has a receivable against its account debtor, and V owes a debt to A1. V provides a security right in its receivable for A1 and registers A1's security right in the receivable in the International Receivables Registry. There are two receivables: the receivable and the secured debt. Subsequently, A1 transfers the secured debt to transferee A2 together with the security right in the receivable securing the debt. The transfer of the secured debt from A1 to A2 cannot be registered in the International Receivables Registry if A1 is not an IRT.[10] Nevertheless, the transfer of the security right in the receivable can be

---

[10] The transfer of the secured debt from A1 to A2 is perfected under the applicable national laws if A1 is not an IRT.

registered in the International Receivables Registry by and under the name of V. Under the proposed International Receivables Registry Convention, the transfer of a registered security right can be registered in the International Receivables Registry.[11] If more than one transferee claims that the security right registered in the International Receivables Registry was transferred to itself, priority between the competing transferees is determined by the order of registration of the transfer of the security right in the International Receivables Registry.[12]

With respect to V's other potential transferees or secured creditors, A2 can assert the priority of A1's security right registered in the International Receivables Registry if A2 can effectively prove the fact that A1 transferred the security right to A2. Registration of the transfer of the security right from A1 to A2 can evidence this fact.

6-3-7-3. Double Security Rights Created by an IRT Followed by Transfers of Secured Creditors

V
security right for A1 → transferred to A2
security right for B1 → transferred to B2

If two security rights are registered in the International Receivables Registry over an IRT receivable R in favour of A1 and B1, respectively, and A1 transfers its right to the secured debt (owed by V to A1) to A2 together with the security right in the receivable R, and B1 transfers its right to the secured debt (owed by V to B1) to B2 together with the security right in the same receivable R, A2's security right in the receivable R has priority over B2's security right in the receivable R, whether or not A2's security right was registered in the International Receivables Registry.

Under the proposed International Receivables Registry Convention, the transferred security right retains its original priority, ie, the transferee of a security right retains the transferor's priority.[13] The Cape Town Convention also stipulates that each transferee enjoys the same priority as its transferor.[14] Thus, the priority of A2's security right is determined by the time order of registration of A1's security right in the International Receivables Registry. A2 retains A1's priority once A1's security right has been registered in the International Receivables Registry.

In the case given above, A1's security right in the receivable R has priority over B1's security right in it, since A1's interest was registered in the International Receivables Registry prior to B1's, ie, B1's security right is subordinated to A1's. Since the transferred security right retains its original priority, the transferee of a

---

[11] Draft International Receivables Registry Convention, art 8(1). See the Appendix.
[12] The Cape Town Convention follows the same logic (art 35).
[13] Draft International Receivables Registry Convention, art 8(2). See the Appendix.
[14] Cape Town Convention, art 31(1)(b). See Goode (n 3) 81 [2.141].

security right retains the transferor's priority. As a result, A2's security right in the receivable has priority over B2's so that B2's security right is subordinated to A2's.

Moreover, A2 should perfect the transfer of the secured debt from A1 to A2 in accordance with the applicable national laws if A1 is not an IRT (or if A1 is an IRT, A2 should register the transfer of the secured debt from A1 to A2 in the International Receivables Registry) in order to secure protection against any of A1's potential transferees, to whom A1 might assign the right to the secured debt owed by V together with the security right in the receivable.

The same rule applies where a security right in a receivable is transferred to a third party by legal or contractual subrogation. For example, the person who discharges the debt owed by a debtor instead of the debtor itself takes over the security right securing the debt held by the creditor.

6-3-7-4. Security Right Created by an IRT and Subsequent Security Right by the Secured Creditor

Under the International Receivables Registry Convention, it is not possible to create a security right in a security right in a receivable.

6-4. The Double Debtor Problem

6-4-1. Security Rights and Subsequent Transfers

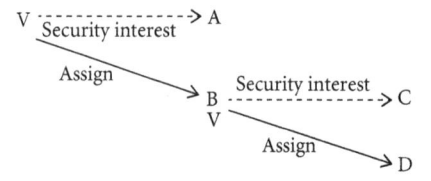

Let us imagine a case where an IRT ('V') provides a security right in its receivable R to A and registers the security right under the name of V in the International Receivables Registry. Subsequently, V transfers the receivable R to B and registers the transfer under the name of V in the International Receivables Registry. A's security right in the receivable R has priority over B's right to the receivable R since A's security right was registered in the International Receivables Registry prior in time to B's transfer. B should have checked the International Receivables Registry before concluding the transfer because V is an IRT, and therefore B knew or should have known that A's security right was attached to the receivable R. Thus, B's right to the receivable R is subject to A's security right.

If the security right in the receivable R continues to be perfected even after the receivable R is transferred to a third party B, the transferee B of the receivable

R might take the receivable R subject to the security right of another creditor A previously registered under the name of V in the International Receivables Registry.

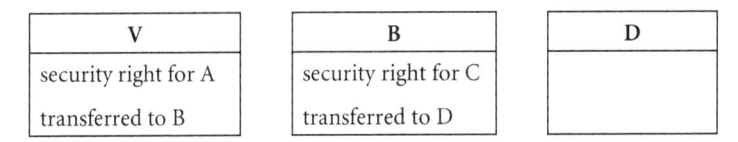

V	B	D
security right for A transferred to B	security right for C transferred to D	

A problem arises where B transfers the receivable R to D. According to the *nemo dat quod non habet* rule that a transferee cannot obtain more rights than the transferor had, D would obtain the receivable subject to A's security right just as B did. If B is not an IRT, the transfer from B to D is perfected under the applicable national domestic laws, and therefore D would not need to check the International Receivables Registry. If B provided a security right in the receivable R for C, the priority between C and D would be determined by the applicable national domestic laws, and C would be protected against D if C had completed the perfection of the security right under the applicable national domestic law. The following question then arises: how can D know that the receivable R is subject to A's security right registered under the name of V in the International Receivables Registry? Such a problem is referred to as 'double debtor problem', since there are two debtors—an old debtor (V) and a new debtor (B)—creating security rights in the same receivable R. Whether D or A should be protected is a problem.[15]

These problems have their origin in the transferor (or grantor)-based registration system. The International Receivables Registry is indexed by the IRT. In comparison, the International Registry of Mobile Assets under the Cape Town Convention and its Aircraft Protocol does not face such problems, since it is an asset-based registration system in which each aircraft or other mobile asset is indexed separately.[16] Thus, a potential buyer of an aircraft can see all records of security rights in a specific aircraft and check whether there is any prior security right in the aircraft by searching the Registry against the aircraft.[17]

If a security right in an IRT receivable registered in the International Receivables Registry might become unperfected after the IRT receivable is transferred to a third party, the validity of a security right would be invalidated and terminated by any subsequent registration of transfer of the IRT receivable. Then the security right in the IRT receivable could not be protected.

---

[15] This is the double debtor problem, about which there is considerable literature in the US and in the PPSA jurisdictions. See Jonathan C Lipson (ed), *Forms under Revised Article 9* (Chicago, American Bar Association, 2002) 37–39; Gerard McCormack, *Secured Credit under English and American Law* (Cambridge, Cambridge University Press, 2004) 159–61.

[16] Goode (n 3) 50 [2.70].

[17] Ronald C Cuming, 'The International Registry for Interests in Aircraft: An Overview of its Structure' [2006] *Uniform Law Review* 45, 45–46.

242   *Priority in the International Receivables Registry*

The question is how far the security right in the IRT receivable registered in the International Receivables Registry should continue to be perfected after the IRT receivable is transferred again and again to third parties away from the IRT and the International Receivables Registry. There are four options to solve the double debtor problem: the first option is that B and subsequently D take the receivable free of A's security right (Solution I). The second option is that B takes the receivable subject to A's security right, but subsequently D takes the receivable free of A's security right (Solution II). This requires a potential transferee to check the registry with respect to his transferor. The third option is that B and subsequently D take the receivable subject to A's security right (Solution III). The fourth option is that B takes the receivable free of A's security right, but subsequently D takes the receivable subject to A's security right (Solution IV). Solution III and Solution IV require a potential transferee to check the registry with respect to his transferor and the former transferor if his transferor purchased the receivable from the former transferor. See Table 6.1. Section 6-4 presents the solution of the proposed International Receivables Registry Convention.

Table 6.1: The double debtor problem

	A's security right	C's security right	D
Solution I	free of	free of	authority given by A and C
Solution II	free of	subject to	bona fide purchaser change of jurisdiction IRT → non-IRT → non-IRT non-IRT → IRT → IRT
Solution III	subject to	subject to	*nemo dat quod non habet* rule IRT → IRT → non-IRT
Solution IV	subject to	free of	buyer in the ordinary course of seller's business

6-4-2. International Receivables Registry Jurisdiction

6-4-2-1. IRT → IRT → Non-IRT

V	B (IRT)	D
security right for A transferred to B (IRT)	security right for C transferred to D	

The proposed International Receivables Registry Convention takes Solution III mentioned above for the case where an IRT transfers its receivable to another

IRT and the second IRT transfers the receivable to a non-IRT entity. Solution III requires a potential transferee D to investigate the International Receivables Registry against not only the transferor but also the transferor of the transferor.

If the transferor of the transferor is also an IRT, it would not obstruct receivable transactions. If V is also an IRT and thus the transfer from V to B is registered in the International Receivables Registry, it would be automatically linked to B's registration by the International Receivables Registry system. Then a potential transferee D could easily investigate any security rights created by V. If B is an IRT, D would have to check the International Receivables Registry under B and furthermore follow the link to V that would be automatically signposted by the International Receivables Registry system. For this reason, D should have known or knew of A's security right. D would take the receivable subject to anything registered in the International Receivables Registry under B and V.

The proposed International Receivables Registry Convention creates a special worldwide jurisdiction where an IRT transfers its receivables or provides a security right in its receivables. An IRT may trade receivables with other IRTs, but if an IRT transfers its receivables or provides a security right in its receivables to a non-IRT entity, the subsequent transactions of the non-IRT entity are outside the jurisdiction of the proposed International Receivables Registry Convention.

Under the proposed International Receivables Registry Convention, if a security right in an IRT receivable created by an IRT is registered in the International Receivables Registry, the security right continues to be perfected even after the receivable is transferred to another IRT as far as it is continuously transferred to IRTs and the sequence of transfers is automatically traced by the International Receivables Registry system.[18] However, if the receivable is transferred to a non-IRT entity, the security right in the receivable registered in the International Receivables Registry becomes unperfected unless it is re-perfected under the national law of the state where the non-IRT entity is located.[19]

6-4-2-2. IRT → Non-IRT → Non-IRT

V	B	D
security right for A transferred to B	security right for C transferred to D	

If an IRT transfers its receivable to a non-IRT entity and the non-IRT entity transfers the receivable to a third party, the third party takes the receivable free of any security rights registered in the International Receivables Registry. If the transferor (B) is not an IRT, a potential transferee or secured creditor (D) only has to search the national registry against the direct counterparty (B) or enquire of

---

[18] Draft International Receivables Registry Convention, art 16(1). See the Appendix.
[19] Draft International Receivables Registry Convention, art 16(2). See the Appendix.

the account debtor as to whether it has received notice of any prior transfer of the receivable, but does not have to check the International Receivables Registry against the transferor of the transferor (V). If the transferor is not an IRT, a potential transferee has no obligation to check the International Receivables Registry. The purpose of the International Receivables Registry is to facilitate international receivables financing. Accordingly, the proposed International Receivables Registry Convention would narrowly impose an obligation to check the International Receivables Registry only to the extent necessary, as imposing such an obligation could slow down international transactions of receivables. As a result, registration in the International Receivables Registry of a security right in a receivable might lose its effectiveness after two consecutive transfers of the receivable.

Let us suppose a case where neither B nor D is an IRT. When B purchases the receivable from V, B must check the International Receivables Registry. The proposed International Receivables Registry Convention applies to V's transfer to B. However, the proposed International Receivables Registry Convention does not require D to check the International Receivables Registry because B is not an IRT. The transfer from B to D is governed by the applicable national laws and therefore D must check the national registry or enquire of the account debtor. If D, in purchasing the receivable from B, were required to check the International Receivables Registry against V as well as the national registry or the account debtor, it would hamper receivable transactions. For this reason, under the proposed International Receivables Registry Convention, D is not required to check the International Receivables Registry. Therefore, D should obtain the receivable free of A's security right.

Where a receivable is transferred across national borders, the same problem occurs as in interstate transfers of receivables within the US. Let us take the case where secured creditor A registers its charge over a receivable of X in the Company Charge Register in the UK and subsequently the chargor X transfers the receivable to a third party B, and B then transfers the receivable to an American company D. Later, D transfers the receivable to an American company E and registers the transfer under UCC Article 9. How can E know that the receivable is subject to A's charge?

In this regard, the proposed International Receivables Registry Convention follows Solution II mentioned above. As a result, registration in the International Receivables Registry of a security right in a receivable would lose its effectiveness after two consecutive transfers of the receivable. The proposed International Receivables Registry Convention for its part seeks to minimise uncertainty, and registration in the International Receivables Registry does not provide a grace period equivalent to the grace period of one year provided under UCC Article 9 or the temporary perfection period provided under the PPSAs.[20]

---

[20] See section 4-7-4.

6-4-2-3. Non-IRT → IRT → Non-IRT

The same rule of following Solution II applies to the case where a non-IRT entity transfers its receivable to an IRT and the IRT transfers the receivable to another non-IRT entity. This is because if a potential transferee has to investigate national registry as well as the International Receivables Registry, it would hamper receivable transactions.

V (non-IRT)	B (IRT)	D
security right for A	security right for C	
transferred to B	transferred to D	

Let us suppose a case where V is a non-IRT entity and B is an IRT. Under the proposed International Receivables Registry Convention, if a potential transferee D is to purchase an IRT receivable, it must check the International Receivables Registry before making a transaction. Consequently, D would purchase the receivable subject to C's security right. However, although D must check the International Receivables Registry before purchasing the receivable from B, D has no obligation to check the national registry where A's security right is registered under V or enquire of the account debtor of V. Thus, D should obtain the receivable free of A's security right. In this regard, the proposed International Receivables Registry Convention takes Solution II mentioned above.

If the state in which A's security right is registered is a Contracting State and the law of the state provides for a temporary perfection period, it might be declared by the state as a 'non-consensual right' that has priority over a security right registered in the International Receivables Registry according to Article 10 of the proposed International Receivables Registry Convention.

6-4-3. The Secured Creditor's Rights in Proceeds

If D takes the receivable free of A's security right, A should seek the sale proceeds of the receivable that B obtains from D. A is a secured creditor of V. If V transfers the receivable to B, A retains the security right in that receivable as well as in the sale proceeds which V obtained from B for consideration of the receivable.[21] If B transfers the receivable to D, A no longer owns the security right in that receivable, but only in the sale proceeds which B obtains from D for consideration of the receivable. If V transfers the receivable to B and then B transfers it to D, secured creditor A has two options: claiming the security right in the sale proceeds of the receivable that V obtains from B or, alternatively, claiming the security right in the

---

[21] UCC, s 9-315(a)(2); Ontario PPSA, s 25(1)(b); Saskatchewan PPSA, s 28(1)(b); New Zealand PPSA, s 45(1)(b); Australian PPSA, s 32(1)(b).

sale proceeds of the receivable that B obtains from D, but only for one satisfaction of the debt which V owes A.[22]

In order to alert a secured creditor to the fact that its security right might become ineffective after two consecutive transfers, the proposed International Receivables Registry Convention requires the consent of previously registered secured creditors for the registration of the transfer of a receivable.

6-4-4. The Consent of Secured Creditors to a Transfer to a Non-IRT

Under the proposed International Receivables Registry Convention, to register a transfer of a receivable to a non-IRT entity, the transferor (an IRT) or the transferee must obtain the consent of all prior secured creditors registered in the International Receivables Registry who hold security rights (except floating security rights) in the receivable including the secured creditors of the former IRT transferors, by whom the receivable is transferred to the transferor (IRT).[23] Thus, if B is not an IRT, to register the transfer of the receivable from V to B in the International Receivables Registry, the consent of A is required.

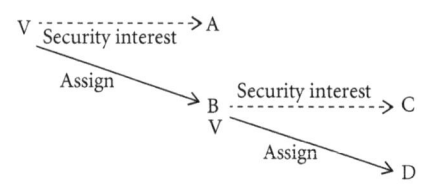

```
V ---------------> A
   Security interest
    Assign
          ↘         Security interest
             B ------------------> C
             V
              ↘ Assign
                      ↘ D
```

If B is an IRT, in order to register the transfer of the receivable from B to D (a non-IRT) in the International Receivables Registry, the consent of A and C is required. The International Receivables Registry system would automatically indicate not only all prior secured creditors of the latest IRT transferor, which have security interests in the receivable (such as C), but also all prior secured creditors of all previous former IRT transferors, which have security interests in the receivable (such as A), as far as they are registered in the International Receivables Registry.

Such consent does not constitute authorisation for the IRT to assign its receivables free of the security right;[24] rather, it is consent to assign the receivables subject to the security right that is required for registration of a transfer in the International Receivables Registry. Where an IRT or its transferee registers a transfer

---

[22] See section 6-3-1.
[23] Draft International Receivables Registry Convention, art 17. See the Appendix.
[24] To assign a receivable free of the security right, the secured creditor's authorisation to waive its security right is needed.

made to a non-IRT entity, the consent of all previously registered secured creditors is required.[25]

While being asked to consent to the registration of the transfer of the receivable, the previously secured creditor would naturally be notified of the transfer and accordingly know that it needs to ask the IRT: (i) to separate the sale proceeds from the other assets of the IRT; or (ii) to give notice of the prior security right to the account debtor of the receivable. The security right would extend to the sale proceeds and follow the transfer, so that a subsequent transferee obtains the receivable subject to its security right. The secured creditor has a choice as to whether to enforce against the sale proceeds or the receivable transferred.

First, the secured creditor can ask the IRT to separate the sale proceeds from its other assets, for example, to open a blocked bank account into which the proceeds are deposited, since for a security right to extend to the proceeds, the proceeds must be separated and identifiable. Under the proposed International Receivables Registry Convention, if the proceeds are separated and identifiable, even if the IRT obtains the sale proceeds from the transferee, the IRT may not spend the proceeds, but must retain them until the due date of the debt. If the IRT becomes insolvent, the sale proceeds are separated from its insolvency assets so that the secured creditor can be satisfied before other creditors.[26]

Second, a previously secured creditor can give notice of its security right to the account debtor of the receivable and, if the IRT defaults, collect the receivable directly from the account debtor and satisfy the debt which the IRT owes to the secured creditor.[27]

6-5. Floating Security Rights of the International Receivables Registry

6-5-1. The Fixed Charge and the Floating Charge

6-5-1-1. *The Characteristics of Receivables*

There is a problem relating to security rights over receivables. In the normal business of a company, receivables continually change into cash as account debtors pay

---

[25] Draft International Receivables Registry Convention, art 17. See the Appendix.
[26] See section 6-8-4.
[27] In English law, priority is determined by the time order in which the debtor is notified of the transfer or the security right under the *Dearle v Hall* rule. Thus, in England, a secured creditor should have given notice of its security right to the account debtor of the receivable before the transferee did in order to collect the receivable directly from the account debtor at the default of the transferor (grantor). In the US, under UCC art 9, priority is determined by the order of filing of the transfer or the security right, and even if the debtor of the receivable pays the transferee who gave notice first, the transferee should return the proceeds to the secured creditor who filed its security right first, since priority between the secured creditor and the transferee is determined by the order of filing.

up. Payment by the account debtors cancels the receivable and the total amount of receivables subject to the security right gradually decreases. For example, in a case where a security right over a receivable does not cover its proceeds, the due date of the receivable is prior to the due date of the debt secured by the security right over the receivable, and the account debtor of the receivable pays the receivable before the due date of the debt secured by the security right over the receivable, the security right over the receivable becomes of no value. In this sense, a security right over a receivable without its proceeds is a very weak one.

6-5-1-2. The Practice of Financial Institutions

Broadly speaking, there are two different practices of receivables financing depending on the types of financial institution involved. On the one hand, receivables financiers, who advance against outright transfers or fixed charges, do require the proceeds as a means of repayment. They would use the normal 'security right' in a receivable, including its proceeds under the proposed International Receivables Registry Convention.

On the other hand, most banks are interested in the outstanding receivables, and the security right is usually over a stream of receivables. They have little interest in the proceeds until enforcement and are happy to let the borrower (grantor) have access to them. They would use the 'floating security right' over all present and future receivables under the proposed International Receivables Registry Convention.

To reflect the practices of financial institutions, the proposed International Receivables Registry Convention provides two types of security right over IRT receivables. First, a security right in a receivable may extend to the proceeds of the receivable. Second, a decrease in the value or amount of receivables subject to a security right over time could be supplemented by future receivables in addition to the proceeds. An IRT could create a floating security right over all its present and future receivables.

6-5-1-3. Security Rights

For the first type of security right over a receivable discussed above, the proceeds must be separated and reasonably identifiable from any other property owned by the IRT. Since the proceeds of a receivable are usually in cash (a receivable being a monetary claim) and it is easy for cash to become commingled with the IRT's other property, it would be advisable for the creditor to require separation of the proceeds.

6-5-2. Two Types of Security Rights over Receivables in the International Receivables Registry

Under the proposed International Receivables Registry Convention, one way of solving the problem of dwindling amounts of receivables subject to a security right is to create a floating security right over all present and future receivables. A floating security right over all present and future receivables is referred to as a 'floating security right' under the proposed International Receivables Registry Convention,[28] and this term will also be used in this book.

A floating security right over all present and future receivables covers the proceeds of receivables (both proceeds of collection and proceeds of sale, including cash or bank deposits) as far as they are held by the IRT for the benefit of the secured creditor separately and are reasonably identifiable from the other assets of the IRT. Although the floating charge covers the proceeds, this is not necessarily particularly valuable for the chargee, since the chargor has the right to dispose of the proceeds freely. However, this will vary to some extent depending on what form the proceeds take.

6-5-3. Floating Security Right v Subsequent Transfer

Under the proposed International Receivables Registry Convention, a floating security right over all present and future receivables of an IRT is subordinated to the subsequent transfer of a specified receivable of the IRT.[29] Let us suppose that a floating security right were not subordinated to a subsequent transfer of a specific receivable—in the case where a floating security right was registered and subsequently the transfer of a specific receivable was registered, the transferee of the specific receivable would take the receivable subject to the previously registered floating security right. If so, once a floating security right was registered, receivables transactions would be discouraged. Also, the parties in a floating security right intend the grantor to be able to dispose of secured assets in the ordinary course of its business. For these reasons, the proposed International Receivables Registry Convention provides that the transfer of a specified receivable prevails over a previously registered floating security right.

6-5-4. Floating Security Right v Subsequent Security Right

In principle, a floating security right under the proposed International Receivables Registry Convention follows English law on floating charges, in that a floating security right over all present and future receivables registered in the International Receivables Registry is subordinated to a subsequent security right in a specified receivable (which is similar to a fixed charge in English law).

In addition, in the case of a floating security right, a negative pledge clause or an automatic crystallisation clause in the agreement on the floating security right must be registered in the International Receivables Registry in order to be effective

---

[28] Draft International Receivables Registry Convention, art 9. See the Appendix.
[29] Draft International Receivables Registry Convention, art 9(1). See the Appendix.

vis-a-vis third parties.[30] If a floating security right is registered with a negative pledge, it prevails over subsequent security rights, but can be overcome by a subsequent transfer.

6-5-5. Crystallisation

If a floating security right over all present and future receivables of an IRT is registered in the International Receivables Registry, upon the debtor's default, the floating security right is crystallised into a security right in all the receivables that the IRT has outstanding at the time of the crystallisation, and those receivables would then be the object of liquidation subject to any prior transfers of specified receivables or any prior security rights in specified receivables (if there is no negative pledge).

6-6. Reservation of Title

6-6-1. Reservation of Title v Transfer

Let us suppose a case where T obtained a reservation-of-title right in company V's inventory. The reservation-of-title clause in the contract of sale in relation to the inventory stipulates that the reservation-of-title right extends to the proceeds of the inventory. Later, V sells the inventory to S and obtains a receivable for the price of the inventory against S. T claims the receivable as the proceeds of the inventory. However, V has transferred the receivable to a third party B and immediately registered the transfer of the receivable before T registers its reservation-of-title right.

Where the transferor or grantor is an IRT, such extension to the proceeds would not be acknowledged unless registered in the International Receivables Registry, since priority of transfers of or security rights in an IRT receivable is determined by the time order of registration in the International Receivables Registry. The problem is that a reservation-of-title right in a tangible movable asset cannot be registered in the International Receivables Registry. As a result, a reservation-of-title right would not automatically extend to receivables against S that are sales proceeds of the inventory subject to the reservation-of-title arrangement. A security right in the receivables should be registered in the International Receivables Registry separately. In conclusion, B would have priority over T with respect to the receivable against S if its transfer to B were registered in the International Receivables Registry. Instead, T's reservation-of-title right would extend to the cash proceeds that B paid V for consideration of the receivable. If T registered its

---

[30] Draft International Receivables Registry Convention, art 9(2). See the Appendix.

security right, priority between B and T would be determined by the time order of registration in the International Receivables Registry.

The security right in proceeds, which is automatically and continues to be perfected for five to 20 days according to UCC Article 9 and the PPSAs of Canada, New Zealand and Australia, may be declared by the Contracting State as a 'non-consensual right' that has priority over a security right registered in the International Receivables Registry according to Article 10 of the proposed International Receivables Registry Convention. In the Contracting State where the security right in proceeds for an automatic perfection period is declared to be a 'non-consensual right', if T registers its security right in the receivable in the International Receivables Registry within the automatic perfection period, T may prevail over B even if B registered the transfer prior in time to T. Thus, when B purchases a receivable from a sale of an asset, B needs to check whether there is any security right in the asset against V in the national registry, eg, the UCC Article 9 or PPS registry. After the lapse of the automatic perfection period, automatic perfection loses its effectiveness, and priority is determined by the time order of registration in the International Receivables Registry.

6-6-2. Floating Security Right v Reservation of Title

The proposed International Receivables Registry Convention adopted the English law approach in that the IRT providing a floating security right to a creditor is entitled to dispose of its receivables without the consent of the creditor holding a floating security right. Thus, any security right (including reservation of title) subsequently registered in the International Receivables Registry prevails over a floating security right registered in the International Receivables Registry, unless a negative pledge clause is registered with the floating security right.

6-6-3. Purchase-Money Security Interests

The International Receivables Registry would not acknowledge the exception for purchase-money security interests[31] to the rule that priority is determined by the time order of registration. In the International Receivables Registry, a purchase-money security interest does not have priority over other prior transfers or security rights. In the International Receivables Registry, priority is determined by the time order of registration regardless of whether it is a purchase-money security interest.[32]

---

[31] See section 4-9-1-3.
[32] See Draft International Receivables Registry Convention, art 5. See the Appendix.

6-7. Preferential Creditors

In terms of preferential creditors, the extent to which a floating security right registered in the International Receivables Registry should be subordinated to preferential creditors in the event of the insolvency of an IRT is a matter for the applicable national insolvency law. Such an insolvency and bankruptcy issue should be left up to national laws. The International Receivables Registry serves to determine priority among competing transferees or secured creditors with respect to receivables of an IRT, but not among preferential creditors, which are regulated by the legislation of sovereign nations.

The proposed International Receivables Registry Convention follows the solution provided by the Cape Town Convention,[33] in that a Contracting State may declare the list of categories of non-consensual rights or interests which have priority over a security right or a floating security right registered with the International Receivables Registry, whether in or outside insolvency proceedings.[34] A non-consensual right or interest has priority over a security right or a floating security right registered with the International Receivables Registry if the former is of a category covered by the declaration deposited and publicised prior in time to the registration of the security right or the floating security right.[35]

6-8. Proceeds

6-8-1. Proceeds from the Collection and Sale of Receivables

There are two important kinds of proceeds in the context of a security right in a receivable: (1) the proceeds of a receivable which the account debtor of a receivable pays an IRT; and (2) the proceeds from sale which a transferee of a receivable pays the IRT that transferred the receivable to the transferee. Under the proposed International Receivables Registry Convention, a security right and a floating security right in an IRT receivable registered in the International Receivables Registry extends to the proceeds from collection as well as the proceeds from sale.

In security transfers of receivables, even if the transferor (or grantor) collects the proceeds from the account debtor of the receivable, it collects it as a trustee

---

[33] Cape Town Convention, art 39. Under art 39(3) of the Cape Town Convention, any non-consensual right or interest, eg, state liens for unpaid taxes do not have priority over an international interest registered in the International Registry of Mobile Assets unless it is of a category covered by a declaration deposited prior to the registration of the international interest. See Goode (n 3) 256–60 [4.264]–[4.276].

[34] Draft International Receivables Registry Convention, art 10(1). See the Appendix.

[35] Draft International Receivables Registry Convention, art 10(3). See the Appendix.

of the transferee (or secured creditor) and thus the proceeds collected are separated from the transferor's (or the grantor's) other property. Under the proposed International Receivables Registry Convention, even though proceeds are paid to the transferor (IRT), insofar as the proceeds are separated upon the transferee's instruction and reasonably identifiable from the other assets of the IRT, the transferee has priority over the paid proceeds.[36] This is intended to facilitate practices such as securitisation and undisclosed invoice discounting, where payments are usually channelled into a blocked bank account held by the transferor, separately from the transferor's other assets, on behalf of the transferee.[37]

6-8-2. Proceeds Separated and Reasonably Identifiable

Registration of a security right in a receivable in the International Receivables Registry does not extend to the proceeds of the receivable unless these proceeds are separated and reasonably identifiable from the other assets of the IRT. In order for a security right over a receivable to cover its proceeds, the proceeds must be identifiable. They are identifiable if the IRT holds them separately under instructions from the secured creditor for the latter's benefit or in a blocked bank account containing only proceeds.

6-8-3. Dual Security Rights in a Transferred Receivable and Proceeds from Sale

Upon collection of the proceeds by the creditor from the debtor of the receivable, the receivable is satisfied and therefore terminated. Notwithstanding the foregoing, where an IRT (V) transfers its receivable R, to which a security right (of A) attaches, to another IRT (B), if the security right (of A) in the receivable is registered in the International Receivables Registry, the security right (of A) continues to be perfected after the receivable is transferred to another IRT (B), and the transferee IRT (B) would thus take the receivable subject to the security right (of A). Consequently, the secured creditor (A) would have dual security rights: one in the receivable R that has been transferred to the transferee (B) as well as one in the sales proceeds that the grantor and transferor (V) obtained from the transferee (B) for consideration of the receivable R.[38]

---

[36] Draft International Receivables Registry Convention, art 7. See the Appendix.
[37] Explanatory Note by the UNCITRAL Secretariat on the United Nations Convention on the Transfer of Receivables in International Trade (UNCITRAL 2004), 42, www.uncitral.org/pdf/english/texts/payments/receivables/ctc-transfer-convention-e.pdf.
[38] See section 6-4-3.

254 *Priority in the International Receivables Registry*

6-8-4. The Proposed International Receivables Registry Rules on Proceeds

Under the proposed International Receivables Registry Convention, the transferee has the same right as the secured creditor in the proceeds collected by the transferor. With respect to the transferee's right over the proceeds and the security right in the proceeds, the proposed International Receivables Registry Convention, following the approach of the UN Receivables Convention,[39] stipulates that once proceeds are received by the IRT, the right of the transferee to those proceeds has priority over the right of a competing claimant, including the insolvency administrator if the IRT has received the proceeds under instructions from the transferee and if the proceeds are held by the IRT for the benefit of the transferee separately and are reasonably identifiable from the assets of the IRT.[40]

6-9. Bonds

6-9-1. Debt Represented by Bonds

The transfer of the right to a debt represented by a bond may not be registered in the International Receivables Registry because the transfer of the right to a debt represented by a bond should be regulated by the applicable national laws on bonds, under which whoever holds the bond has the right to the debt. Thus, bonds are expressly excluded in the proposed International Receivables Registry Convention.

However, a debt represented by a bond may be secured by the assets (eg, receivables) of the bond issuer. Such security rights in the bond issuer's receivables can be registered in the International Receivables Registry. This could function as a covered bond secured by the bond issuer's receivables.

Where an IRT issues bonds, the IRT is a debtor (bond issuer) and the bond holder is a creditor. The security right in IRT receivables securing the debt represented by a bond can be registered in the International Receivables Registry. Thus, the International Receivables Registry could help to facilitate international trading of bonds secured by the bond issuer's receivables.

6-9-2. Covered Bonds

Sovereign bonds represent a large portion of international capital movements. However, since it is difficult to execute insolvency proceedings against a

---

[39] UN Receivables Convention, art 24(2).
[40] Draft International Receivables Registry Convention, art 7. See the Appendix.

sovereign state, creditors of sovereign bonds often cannot collect even the principal.[41] For this reason, after the global financial crisis in 2008, covered bond markets have grown noticeably. A covered bond is a corporate bond with a security right in a cover pool of assets of the covered bond issuer. In the event of the insolvency of the covered bond issuer, the covered bond holder may request the covered bond issuer to redeem the covered bond itself as well as execute the security right in the cover pool of the bond issuer's assets. The difference between a covered bond and an asset-backed securitisation is that in a covered bond, an originator itself issues cover bonds, whereas in an asset-backed securitisation, an originator transfers its assets to an SPV and the SPV issues securities. The main point is that in a covered bond, there is redress against the cover pool of assets of the covered bond issuer.

Covered bonds are covered under specific regulations in specific countries. According to the EU Capital Requirement Directive,[42] classes of assets that are eligible as collateral for covered bonds are limited to mortgage loans (commercial and residential), senior MBS issued by securitisation entities, loans secured by ships etc. It seems that the reason why the scope of assets that are eligible as collateral for covered bonds is limited is that in many of the EU Member States, there are no developed registration systems for collaterals of other types of assets than those eligible thereunder. Mortgages are registered in the real estate registry. Ship mortgages are registered in the ship registry. If there were to be a registration system for the transfer of and security right in receivables, it is expected that receivables could also be eligible as collateral for covered bonds.

6-9-3. Security Rights in the Bond Issuer's Receivables

Where an IRT issues a covered bond secured by its receivables, under the proposed International Receivables Registry Convention, there could be three ways to protect the bond holder's security right in the IRT receivables.

First, where an IRT issues a bond and the bond is backed by a receivable of the IRT, the 'holder' of the bond could be registered as a secured creditor holding a security right in the receivables of the IRT (the bond issuer) in the International Receivables Registry with the information identifying the bond itself instead of identifying the bond holder. A bond could be identified by the issuer and its serial number, the type of the bond, the terms of the bond, its interest rate etc.[43] The 'holder' of the bond could have priority from the date of the registration.

---

[41] For example, in 2010, investors in Greek sovereign bonds suffered huge losses.
[42] Adopted by the European Council on 7 June 2006 and published in the Official Journal (OJ) of the European Union on 30 June 2006 (L177) under reference Directive 2006/48/EC and 2006/49/EC. For the UK covered bond market, the UK government introduced the Regulated Covered Bond Regulations 2008 in March 2008, and the FSA supervises Regulated Covered Bond programmes. See www.fsa.gov.uk/fsaregister/use/other_registers/rcb_register/qanda.
[43] Draft International Receivables Registry Convention, art 13(b). See the Appendix.

While the bond is traded in markets, whoever purchases the bond would be the 'holder' of the bond and could assert the priority of its security right in the receivables of the IRT (the bond issuer) upon showing the bond.

Second, if a bond issue is secured and the security is held by a trustee, the trustee may be registered as a secured creditor holding the security right in the receivables of the IRT (the bond issuer) in the International Receivables Registry.

Third, if an initial bond holder is registered as a secured creditor holding the security right in the receivables of the IRT (the bond issuer) in the International Receivables Registry with information identifying the bond holder, the subsequent purchaser of the bond that is secured by the security right in the receivables of the IRT (the bond issuer) may retain the priority of the initial bond holder by showing the bond and the contract evidencing the sale of the bond by the initial bond holder registered in the International Receivables Registry to the subsequent purchaser. This is because a transferred security right retains its original priority and the priority of the transferee is the same as the priority of its transferor.

Where an IRT issued a bond, once the security right in the IRT receivables securing the debt represented by a bond is registered in the International Receivables Registry, a bond holder may request the IRT to redeem the bond itself as well as execute the security right in the IRT receivables registered in the International Receivables Registry in the event of the default of the IRT.

6-10. Subordination Agreements

With respect to subordination agreements, the proposed International Receivables Registry Convention would directly adopt the approach of the UN Receivables Convention and the Cape Town Convention. The priority of competing security rights under the proposed International Receivables Registry Convention may be varied by a subordination agreement between secured creditors.[44] Secured creditors may negotiate and relinquish priority in favour of a subordinate claimant where commercial considerations so warrant.[45] A registered secured creditor may agree to be subordinated to a subsequently registered secured creditor or a prior or subsequent unregistered secured creditor.[46] A secured creditor in whose favour a subordination has been made should register the subordination in the International Receivables Registry, otherwise it would not bind a transferee of the subordinated security right.[47] When subordinating priority in favour of future

---

[44] See Cape Town Convention, art 29(5).
[45] Explanatory Note (n 37) 42.
[46] Goode (n 3) 69 [2.111].
[47] ibid 69 [2.112].

transferees, it can be effected unilaterally, for example, by means of an undertaking of the first-ranking transferee to the transferor, empowering the transferor to make a second transfer ranking first in priority.[48]

6-11. Conclusion

Under the proposed International Receivables Registry Convention, the priority of transfers of and security rights in IRT receivables is determined by the time order of registration in the International Receivables Registry. With respect to the double debtor problem, under the proposed International Receivables Registry Convention, if an IRT transfers its receivable to a non-IRT entity and the non-IRT entity thereafter transfers the receivable to a third party, the third party takes the receivable free of any security rights registered in the International Receivables Registry. Thus, a potential transferee or secured creditor only has to investigate the International Receivables Registry against the direct counterparty IRT and does not have to search against the transferor of the transferor. If the transferor is not an IRT, a potential transferee has no obligation to check the International Receivables Registry before purchasing the receivable. As a result, registration in the International Receivables Registry of a security right might lose its effectiveness after two consecutive transfers of the receivable.

For the protection of secured creditors registered in the International Receivables Registry, to assign an IRT receivable to a non-IRT entity, the International Receivables Registry requires the consent of all prior secured creditors registered in the International Receivables Registry, who hold security rights in the receivable including the secured creditors of the former IRT transferors. The International Receivables Registry system would automatically indicate not only all prior secured creditors of the latest IRT transferor, which have security interests in the receivable, but also all prior secured creditors of all previous former IRT transferors, which have security interests in the receivable, as far as they are registered in the International Receivables Registry. However, in order to assign an IRT receivable to another IRT, the consent of prior secured creditors is not required and the security rights registered in the International Receivables Registry would be protected within the International Receivables Registry.

With respect to reservation of title, the automatic perfection period in some jurisdictions might produce uncertainty with respect to the priority rule of registration, but it is a relatively short period. A Contracting State may declare this as a 'non-consensual right' that has priority over a security right registered in the International Receivables Registry under Article 10 of the proposed International

---

[48] Explanatory Note (n 37) 43.

Receivables Registry Convention. The categories of preferential creditors who have super-priority may also be determined and declared by the Contracting State.

A registered floating security right equipped with a negative pledge clause prevails over subsequently registered security rights, but not over a subsequently registered transfer. A security right (including a floating security right) covers the proceeds of the receivables if they are separated and reasonably identifiable. The priority of competing security rights under the proposed International Receivables Registry Convention may be varied by a subordination agreement between the secured creditors.

A bond holder may also be registered in the International Receivables Registry as a secured creditor with information identifying the bond itself, so that whoever purchases the bond can assert the priority of the security right in the receivables of the IRT (the bond issuer) upon presenting the bond.

7

Conclusion

This book first analysed the need for an international registration system for transfers of and security rights in receivables, compared the registration systems for movable assets and receivables of each jurisdiction, and then proposed establishing the International Receivables Registry. Furthermore, it has presented a proper model for the International Receivables Registry. The Cape Town Convention was established as the first example of an international registration system for mobile equipment such as aircraft. This demonstrates that an international registration system for transfers of and security rights in receivables is also possible. The UN Receivables Convention is a move towards establishing international registration systems. The UN Receivables Convention sets forth in its Annex alternative priority rules based on registration for the states to choose.

Establishing an international registration system is desirable for several reasons. A general security rights registry has many benefits. It enables companies to raise more funds by using their movable assets and receivables as collateral. For investors, a registration system for security rights provides financial information about companies and the basis for further *ex ante* investigation before entering into transactions. After concluding a security rights agreement, it provides an *ex post* mechanism for secured creditors to prove, as an evidentiary matter, the existence of their security rights and the time when the security rights were registered by the order of which priority is determined. Under the proposed International Receivables Registry Convention, priority would be determined by the time order of registration in the International Receivables Registry.

Another advantage of a general security rights registry is that it can meet the economic demands for non-possessory security rights in tangible movable assets. For tangible movable assets, non-possessory security rights are needed for a company to use its equipment, machines and inventory as collateral. These advantages of a general security rights registry also apply to an international registration system for transfers of and security rights in receivables.

At an international level, establishing a general security rights registry that covers all types of movable assets and receivables might not be advisable due to over-leverage and credit expansion problems, and it would be impractical because of language translation and identification problems. For these reasons, this book has focused on the registration system for transfers of and security rights in receivables only.

The International Receivables Registry has the following merits. The International Receivables Registry would remove the barriers to cross-border transfers of receivables. The International Receivables Registry could definitely facilitate international receivables financing using future receivables and bulk receivables. It could also help receivables financing to cross national borders, so that entrepreneurs could raise funds from a greater range of investors in global capital markets. This would ultimately result in the efficient distribution of capital at a global level. The International Receivables Registry would also facilitate international project financing, which is very important, especially during a financial crisis. Since every company and every financial institution is influenced by a financial crisis and cash-flow is frozen during a financial crisis, an influx of foreign capital is necessary.

However, legal systems around the world vary widely in terms of how they deal with priority and perfection of transfers of and security rights in receivables and choice-of-law rules in private international laws. This legal variety makes it difficult for financiers to conduct their international receivables financing business. Under such circumstances, in order to facilitate international receivables financing, this book proposes the International Receivables Registry Convention. Under the proposed International Receivables Registry Convention, international transfers of receivables would be regulated by a unified legal system with respect to priority and perfection. The proposed International Receivables Registry Convention could help financiers to overcome the obstacles they currently encounter. The International Receivables Registry would enable companies to raise finance from a greater range of investors around the world through international receivables financing and to dispose of non-performing loans more easily.

In receivable financing, it is impractical for financiers to enquire of the account debtors whether they have received notice of any prior transfer of or security right in the receivables they owe before each transaction and to give notice to the account debtors after the transaction. One registration in the International Receivables Registry would replace an unlimited number of notifications.

The International Receivables Registry would pave the way for circumventing the notification requirement in some jurisdictions where notice of the transfer to the debtor is required for perfection against third parties, including the insolvency administrator. This function is essential to facilitate the transfer of future receivables and bulk transfers of receivables. Giving notice of the transfer to all account debtors is impossible in the transfer of future receivables and impractical in bulk transfers of receivables because it is too time-consuming and costly.

The registration system may be created as optional or compulsory. An optional registration scheme might bring about a situation where a potential transferee needs to check both the International Receivables Registry and national laws for the applicable perfection methods, eg, registry or notice to the debtor. Within a country, it might be feasible to check both the registry and enquire of account debtors. However, at an international level, this would be impracticable because a potential transferee would have to check all of the national registries since a potential hidden competing transferee might be in any country. This would defeat the object of international registration.

For this reason, the International Receivables Registry is designed as a compulsory registration scheme which prevails over national perfection. However, the International Receivables Registry needs to be limited in the scope of its application, because otherwise all transfers of and security rights in receivables, whether domestic or international, must be registered in the International Receivables Registry, which would make it too large to manage at a reasonable cost whilst keeping the registration fee at an affordable level. Accordingly, the proposed International Receivables Registry Convention confines its scope of application by defining the transferor or the grantor that is eligible for registration in the International Receivables Registry and, in this regard, inventing the concept of 'IRT', which stands for "International Receivables Trader'. The proposed International Receivables Registry Convention applies where the transferor or the grantor is an IRT.

Under the proposed International Receivables Registry Convention, the priority of transfers of and security rights in IRT receivables is determined by the time order of registration in the International Receivables Registry. With respect to the double debtor problem, under the proposed International Receivables Registry Convention, if an IRT transfers its receivable to a non-IRT entity and the non-IRT entity transfers the receivable to a third party, the third party takes the receivable free of any security rights registered in the International Receivables Registry.

Thus, a potential transferee or a potential secured creditor only has to investigate the International Receivables Registry against the direct counterparty IRT and does not have to search against the previous transferor who is the transferor of the transferor. If the transferor is not an IRT, a potential transferee has no obligation to check the International Receivables Registry before purchasing the receivable. As a result, registration in the International Receivables Registry of a security right might lose its effectiveness after two consecutive transfers of a receivable.

For the protection of secured creditors registered in the International Receivables Registry, in order to assign an IRT receivable to a non-IRT entity, the International Receivables Registry requires the consent of all prior secured creditors registered in the International Receivables Registry who hold security rights in the receivable, including the secured creditors of the former IRT transferors. However, in order to assign an IRT receivable to another IRT, the consent of prior secured creditors is not required.

The automatic perfection period in some jurisdictions might produce uncertainty with respect to the priority rule of registration, but it is a relatively short period. A Contracting State of the proposed International Receivables Registry Convention may declare this as a 'non-consensual right' under Article 10 of the proposed International Receivables Registry Convention. The categories of preferential creditors who have super-priority may also be determined and declared by the Contracting State.

A registered floating security right equipped with a negative pledge clause prevails over subsequently registered security rights, but not over a subsequently registered transfer. A security right (including a floating security right) covers the proceeds of the receivables if they are separated and reasonably identifiable. The priority of competing security rights under the proposed International Receivables Registry Convention may be varied by a subordination agreement between secured creditors.

With respect to the contents and effect of registration in the International Receivables Registry, the International Receivables Registry would be in the form of a notice-filing system along the lines of that adopted in UCC Article 9 and the PPSAs. This is because in the International Receivables Registry, there would not be a registrar to review the documents submitted and it would instead be operated automatically online in order to realise a real time registration. Furthermore, since there would not be any human intervention in the process of registration in the International Receivables Registry, to increase the authenticity of the registration information, reciprocal confirmation of both a transferor and a transferee (or both a grantor and a secured creditor) would be required for registration as is the case under the Cape Town Convention.

Under the proposed International Receivables Registry Convention, a party could give notice of the transfer to debtors of receivables through emails containing a link to the relevant registration on the International Receivables Registry webpage on the International Receivables Registry website. Debtors could refer to the relevant registration in the International Receivables Registry by simply clicking and following the link in the email.

The proposed International Receivables Registry Convention would be a receivables version of the Cape Town Convention. Priority would be determined by the time order of registration in the International Receivables Registry. Operationally, it would be an automatic online registration system operating 24 hours a day, 365 days a year like the International Registry of Mobile Assets under the Cape Town Convention. It is expected and hoped that the proposed International Receivables Registry Convention could be ratified by many states.

APPENDIX: DRAFT CONVENTION ON PRIORITY OF TRANSFERS OF, AND SECURITY RIGHTS IN, RECEIVABLES ('DRAFT INTERNATIONAL RECEIVABLES REGISTRY CONVENTION')

Article 1 (Definitions)

In this Convention, except where the context requires otherwise, the following terms have the meanings set out below:

(a) 'Transfer' means the transfer by agreement from one person (transferor) to another person (transferee) of an interest in the transferor's contractual right to payment of a monetary sum (receivable) from a third person (the debtor of the receivable).[1]

(b) 'Consenting party' is a party whose consent is required in accordance with Article 8(2) of this Convention in order for a registration, amendment or discharge to become effective (in a transfer of a receivable, if an IRT is a registering party, a consenting party is a transferee, and if a transferee is a registering party, a consenting party is an IRT; in a security right in a receivable, if an IRT is a registering party, a consenting party is a secured creditor, and if a secured creditor is a registering party, a consenting party is an IRT).[2]

(c) 'Floating security right' is a security right over all present and future receivables subject to change in quantity and value while the IRT is allowed to dispose of its receivables, and becomes crystallised into a security right in all the receivables that the IRT has outstanding at the time of the crystallisation.

(d) 'Grantor' means: (i) a person that creates a security right to secure either its own obligation or that of another person; (ii) a buyer or other transferee of an encumbered asset that acquires its rights subject to a security right; and (iii) a transferor under an outright transfer of a receivable by agreement.[3]

---

[1] *cf* UN Receivables Convention, art 2.
[2] *cf* Regulations and Procedures for the International Registry, Regulations, s 2.1.7.
[3] *cf* UNCITRAL Model Law on Secured Transactions, art 2(o).

(e) 'Insolvency administrator' means a person or body, including one appointed on an interim basis, authorised in insolvency proceedings to administer the reorganisation or the liquidation of the insolvency estate.[4]
(f) 'International Receivables Registry' means the international registration system for transfers of and security rights in receivables established for the purposes of this Convention.[5]
(g) 'Execution creditor' means a creditor, under the national laws of a Contracting State, who has obtained a judgment or provisional court order against the transferor or the grantor.[6]
(h) 'Receivable' means a right to payment of a monetary obligation, excluding a right to payment evidenced by a negotiable instrument, a right to payment of funds credited to a bank account and a right to payment under a non-intermediated security.[7]
(i) 'Registering party' is a party who completes the electronic forms with the relevant information required for registration in accordance with Article 8(1) of this Convention (in a transfer of a receivable, either an IRT or a transferee is a registering party and, in a security right in a receivable, either an IRT or a secured creditor is a registering party).[8]
(j) 'Security right' means: (i) a property right in a movable asset that is created by an agreement to secure payment or other performance of an obligation, regardless of whether the parties have denominated it as a security right, and regardless of the type of asset, the status of the grantor or secured creditor, or the nature of the secured obligation; and (ii) the right of the transferee under an outright transfer of a receivable by agreement.[9]
(k) 'International Receivables Trader' is a special purpose company registered with the International Receivables Registrar in order to use the International Receivables Registry. 'IRT' is the abbreviation of 'International Receivables Trader'.
(l) An 'IRT receivable' is a receivable of an IRT.
(m) 'IRT registration' is registration of a company as an IRT with the International Receivables Registrar.

Article 2 (Sphere of Application)

(1) This Convention applies to transfers of and security rights in receivables, present or future, in which the transferor or grantor is an IRT.

---

[4] *cf* UNCITRAL Legislative Guide on Secured Transactions, Terminology.
[5] cf Cape Town Convention, art 1(p).
[6] cf UNCITRAL Legislative Guide on Secured Transactions, Recommendation 84.
[7] cf UNCITRAL Model Law on Secured Transactions, art 2(dd).
[8] cf Regulations and Procedures for the International Registry, Regulations, s 2.1.9.
[9] cf UNCITRAL Model Law on Secured Transactions, art 2(kk).

(2) An IRT may assign its receivables or provide security rights in its receivables to legal persons that have company registration numbers in their states.

Article 3 (Registration of the IRT)

(1) A company may be created as an IRT by the registration with the International Receivables Registrar.
(2) An existing company may register itself as an IRT with the International Receivables Registrar and become an IRT from the time of the registration.
(3) The International Receivables Registrar must publish the list of registered IRTs.
(4) This Convention does not apply to a pre-existing security right, which retains the priority it enjoyed under the applicable national law prior to the date of the IRT registration of a company for one year from the date of the IRT registration. After this one year, this Convention will become applicable, for the purpose of determining priority, including the protection of any existing priority, to pre-existing security rights.[10]

Article 4 (Deregistration of the IRT)

(1) An IRT may recover its ordinary company status by deregistering itself from the International Receivables Registrar.
(2) In order to deregister an IRT, the consent of all transferees and secured creditors of the receivables of the IRT, previously registered with the International Receivables Registry, is required.
(3) One year before the date of deregistration ('D-date'), prior notice must be registered with the International Receivables Registry as follows: 'this company will be deregistered from the list of IRT and the status of this company will be changed into an ordinary company from the D-date, and this Convention shall not apply to transfers of or security rights in the receivables of this company from the D-date'.

Article 5 (Priority)

(1) A registered transfer of or security right in a receivable has priority over any other transfer of or security right in the receivable subsequently registered

---

[10] cf Cape Town Convention, art 60.

and over an unregistered transfer of or security right in the receivable, even if the registered transferee or secured creditor has notice of the prior transfer or security right.

(2) Priority between competing transfers or security rights is determined by the time order of registration of the transfer or security right in the International Receivables Registry (as defined in Article 11).

Article 6 (Perfection)

(1) Upon registration of a transfer of a receivable or a security right in a receivable in the International Receivables Registry, the transfer or the security right is perfected against the insolvency administrator of the transferor or the grantor, if the registration information becomes searchable in accordance with Article 9 of this Convention prior to the time when the court adjudicates insolvency of the transferor or the grantor.

(2) Upon registration of a transfer of a receivable or a security right in a receivable in the International Receivables Registry, the transfer or the security right is perfected against an execution creditor of the transferor or the grantor, if the registration information becomes searchable in accordance with Article 9 of this Convention prior to time when the execution creditor takes the steps necessary to acquire rights in the receivable by reason of a judgment or provisional court order.

(3) If a transfer of or security right in a receivable of an IRT is not registered in the International Receivables Registry, the transfer or security right cannot be asserted in the insolvency of the IRT.

Article 7 (Proceeds)

If proceeds are received by the IRT, the right of the transferee or the secured creditor in those proceeds has priority over the right of a competing claimant including the insolvency administrator in those proceeds to the same extent as the transferee's right or the secured creditor's security right had priority over the right in the transferred or encumbered receivable of that claimant if:

(a) the IRT has received the proceeds under instructions from the transferee or the secured creditor to hold the proceeds for the benefit of the transferee or the secured creditor; and

(b) the proceeds are held by the IRT for the benefit of the transferee or the secured creditor separately and are reasonably identifiable from the assets of the IRT, such as in the case of a blocked bank account containing only proceeds.

Article 8 (Transfer of a Security Right)

(1) A transferee of a security right that has been registered in the International Receivables Registry can register the transfer of the security right in the International Receivables Registry.
(2) The transferred security right retains its original priority.
(3) Priority between competing transferees of a security right that has been registered in the International Receivables Registry is determined by the time order of registration of the transfer of the security right in the International Receivables Registry.

Article 9 (Floating Security Right)

(1) A floating security right over all present and future receivables is subordinated to a subsequent transfer of or security right in a specific receivable. It includes proceeds of receivables that are held by the IRT for the benefit of the secured creditor separately and are reasonably identifiable from the other assets of the IRT.
(2) In the case of a floating security right, the following items must be registered in the International Receivables Registry:
    (i) whether there is a negative pledge clause in the agreement of the floating security right;
    (ii) whether there is an automatic crystallisation clause in the agreement of the floating security right.

Article 10 (Rights Having Priority without Registration)

(1) A Contracting State may declare those categories of non-consensual right or interest which have priority over a security right or a floating security right registered in the International Receivables Registry, whether in or outside insolvency proceedings.
(2) A declaration made under the preceding paragraph may be expressed to cover categories that are created after the deposit of that declaration.

(3) A non-consensual right or interest has priority over a security right or a floating security right registered in the International Receivables Registry if and only if the former is of a category covered by a declaration deposited prior to the registration of the security right or the floating security right.
(4) Notwithstanding the preceding paragraph, a Contracting State may, at the time of ratification, acceptance, approval of, or accession to the Protocol, declare that a right or interest of a category covered by a declaration made under paragraph 1 shall have priority over a security right or a floating security right registered prior to the date of such ratification, acceptance, approval or accession.

Article 11 (International Receivables Registry)

An International Receivables Registry shall be established for registrations of transfers of receivables and security rights in receivables.[11]

Article 12 (The Supervisory Authority and the Registrar)[12]

(1) There shall be a Supervisory Authority.
(2) The Supervisory Authority shall:
   (a) establish or provide for the establishment of the International Receivables Registry;
   (b) appoint and dismiss the Registrar;
   (c) supervise the Registrar and the operation of the International Receivables Registry;
   (d) after consultation with the Contracting States, make or approve the regulation for the operation of the International Receivables Registry;
   (e) establish administrative procedures through which complaints concerning the operation of the International Receivables Registry can be made to the Supervisory Authority.
(3) The Supervisory Authority shall own all proprietary rights in the databases and archives of the International Receivables Registry.

---

[11] *cf* Cape Town Convention, art 16(1).
[12] *cf* ibid art 17.

(4) The Registrar shall ensure the efficient operation of the International Receivables Registry and perform the functions transferred to it by this Convention and the regulation.

Article 13 (Information Required to Effect Registration)[13]

The information required to effect the registration of a transfer of a receivable or a security right in a receivable is:

(a) the name, the location, the email address, the telephone number, the fax number, the contact person and the company registration number registered in the state of the transferor or the grantor;
(b) the name, the location, the email address, the telephone number, the fax number, the contact person and the company registration number in its state of the transferee or the secured creditor (or, if a holder of a bond is the secured creditor, the issuer of the bond, the type of the bond, its serial number, the terms of the bond and its interest rate);
(c) a list or general description of the debtor of the receivable transferred or encumbered; and
(d) a general description of the receivable transferred or encumbered, present or future, including the amount of monetary obligation and the due date.

Article 14 (Registration, Amendment and Discharge)

(1) To effect, amend or discharge a registration, a registering party shall complete the electronic forms contained on the website with the relevant information required by Article 13 of this Convention.[14]
(2) A consenting party shall be electronically requested to consent thereto prior to that registration, amendment or discharge becoming searchable. Once a registering party has entered registration, amendment or discharge information on the website and has digitally signed it, a consenting party:
(a) will be notified thereof by electronic mail; and

---

[13] *cf* New Zealand PPSA, s 142(1).
[14] *cf* Regulations and Procedures for the International Registry, Procedures, s 12.1.

(b) shall be given the opportunity to consent thereto, through the website, for a period of 36 hours.

In the event that a consenting party fails to give its consent within the 36-hour period, the registration, amendment or discharge will be automatically aborted.[15]

(3) Upon receipt of the consent of a consenting party, the Registrar shall automatically issue a confirmation thereof by email to the registering party and the consenting party, provided that the email addresses of the parties have previously been provided.[16]

(4) Initiated, but not completed, registrations, amendments or discharges shall not appear on any search results.[17]

(5) Rectification of any error or inaccuracy in a registration, once searchable, may only be effected through an amended registration.[18]

Article 15 (Transferees Entitled to Give Notice to the Debtor)

A transferee or secured creditor is entitled to give notice of the transfer or security right registered in the International Receivables Registry to the debtor of the receivable with providing the web address of the relevant registration in the International Receivables Registry.

Article 16 (International Receivables Registry Jurisdiction)

(1) If a security right in an IRT receivable created by an IRT is registered in the International Receivables Registry, the security right continues to be perfected after the receivable is transferred to another IRT as far as it is continuously transferred to IRTs and the sequence of transfers is automatically traced by the International Receivables Registry system.

---

[15] cf ibid s 12.2.
[16] cf ibid s 12.3.
[17] cf ibid s 12.7.
[18] cf ibid s 12.6.

(2) If a receivable of an IRT is transferred to a non-IRT entity, the security right in the receivable registered in the International Receivables Registry becomes unperfected unless it is re-perfected under the national law of the state where the transferee is located.

Article 17 (Consent of Secured Creditors to Transfer to a Non-IRT)

To register a transfer of a receivable to a non-IRT entity in the International Receivables Registry under an IRT, the transferor (IRT) or a transferee must obtain the consent of all prior secured creditors registered in the International Receivables Registry, who hold security rights (except floating security rights) in the receivable, including the secured creditors of the former IRT transferors, by whom the receivable is transferred to the transferor (IRT).

Article 18 (Sanction for False Registration)

(1) If an IRT intentionally or negligently registers a transfer of the receivable which the IRT does not own or a security right in the receivable which the IRT does not own in the International Receivables Registry, or consents to such false registration applied by a transferee or a secured creditor, the IRT will be imposed with a fine no more than 10% of the amount of the receivables falsely registered. Until the IRT pays the fine to the International Receivables Registrar, registration with respect to the IRT is suspended.
(2) If an IRT commits false registration or consent described in the preceding paragraph intentionally or negligently more than three times, the IRT will be disqualified as an IRT and cannot be re-qualified as an IRT anymore.

Article 19 (Search)

Upon the consent of a consenting party to the information inputted by a registering party in accordance with Article 14 of this Convention, the registration information becomes searchable by any person on the website of the International Receivables Registry. Searches of the International Receivables Registry may be performed against a transferor of a receivable or a grantor of a receivable.

Article 20 (Contractual Prohibition on Transfers of Receivables)

(1) Contractual prohibition on the transfer of receivables of an IRT is not effective.
(2) Contractual prohibition on the transfer of receivables agreed upon between a company and its account debtor becomes ineffective after the company registers itself as an IRT with the International Receivables Registrar.
(3) Even if there is an anti-assignment clause made by a company and its account debtor before the IRT registration of the company, the transfer of the receivable of the company after the IRT registration of the company is valid, but the IRT must compensate the account debtor who relied upon the anti-assignment clause for damages due to the transfer.

BIBLIOGRAPHY

Books

Australian Attorney-General's Department, *Personal Property Securities Discussion Paper 2: Extinguishment, Priorities, Conflict of Laws, Enforcement, Insolvency* (March 2007).

Basedow, J, Baum, H and Nishitani, Y (eds), *Japanese and European Private International Law in Comparative Perspective* (Tubingen, Mohr Siebeck, 2008).

Beale, H, Bridge, M, Gullifer, L and Lomnicka, E, *The Law of Personal Property Security* (Oxford, Oxford University Press, 2007).

Bridge, M, Gullifer L, McMeel, G and Worthington, S, *The Law of Personal Property* (London, Sweet & Maxwell, 2013).

Cui, J, *Contract Law*, 3rd edn (Beijing, Law Press China, 2004).

Cooke, E, *The New Law of Land Registration* (Oxford, Hart Publishing, 2003).

Dickson, M, Rosener, W and Storm, P (eds), *Security on Movable Property and Receivables in Europe* (London, ESC Publishing, 1988).

Draft Common Frame of Reference (DCFR) Full Edition, Volume 2, Book III (Munich, Sellier, 2009).

Draft Common Frame of Reference (DCFR) Full Edition, Volume 6, Book IX (Munich, Sellier, 2009).

Draft Common Frame of Reference (DCFR) Outline Edition (Munich, Sellier, 2009).

Fawcett, J, Carruthers, J and North, P, *Private International Law*, 14th edn (Oxford, Oxford University Press, 2008).

Fenton, R, *Garrow & Fenton's Law of Personal Property in New Zealand: Volume 2. Personal Property Securities*, 7th edn (London, LexisNexis, 2010).

Fleisig, H and Peña, N, *Guatemala: How Problems in the Framework for Secured Transactions Limit Access to Credit* (Washington DC, Center for the Economic Analysis of Law, 1998).

——. *Nicaragua: How Problems in the Framework for Secured Transactions Limit Access to Credit* (Washington DC, Center for the Economic Analysis of Law, 1998).

Fleisig, H, Safavian, M and Peña, N, *Reforming Collateral Laws to Expand Access to Finance* (New York, World Bank, 2006).

Getzler, J and Payne, J (eds), *Company Charges: Spectrum and Beyond* (Oxford, Oxford University Press, 2006).

Goode, R, *Official Commentary on the Convention on International Interests in Mobile Equipment and the Protocol thereto on Matters Specific to Aircraft Equipment*, revised edition (UNIDROIT, 2008).

Goode, R and Gullifer, L, *Goode on Legal Problems of Credit and Security*, 4th edn (London, Sweet & Maxwell, 2008).

Goode, R and McKendrick, E, *Goode on Commercial Law*, 4th edn (London, Penguin Books, 2010).

Gullifer, L and Payne, J, *Corporate Finance Law: Principles and Policy* (Oxford, Hart Publishing, 2011).

Han, S, *Contract Law General Principles* (Beijing, Law Press China, 2004).

The International Comparative Legal Guide to: Securitisation 2005 (London, Global Legal Group, 2005).
The International Comparative Legal Guide to: Securitisation 2007 (London, Global Legal Group, 2007).
Johnston, W (ed), *Security over Receivables: An International Handbook* (Oxford, Oxford University Press, 2008).
Kieninger, E (ed), *Security Rights in Movable Property in European Private Law* (Cambrudge, Cambridge University Press, 2004).
Lipson, J (ed), *Forms under Revised Article 9* (Chicago, American Bar Association, 2002).
LoPucki, L and Warren, E, *Secured Credit: A Systems Approach*, 6th edn (Alphen aan den Rijn, Aspen Publishers, 2009).
Marshall, OR, *Transfer of Choses in Action* (London, Pitman, 1950).
McCormack, G, *Secured Credit under English and American Law* (Cambridge, Cambridge University Press, 2004).
Mehren, A (ed), *International Encyclopedia of Comparative Law*, Volume 7, Chapter 13 (Tubingen, Möhr, 1992).
Mises, L, *Interventionism: An Economic Analysis* (Indianapolis, Liberty Fund, 2011).
Oditah, F, *Legal Aspects of Receivables Financing* (London, Sweet & Maxwell, 1991).
Parry, R, Ayliffe, J, Shivji, S, Anderson, H and Trower, W, *Transaction Avoidance in Insolvencies*, 2nd edn (Oxford, Oxford University Press, 2011).
Röver, J, *Secured Lending in Eastern Europe: Comparative Law of Secured Transactions and the EBRD Model Law* (Oxford, Oxford University Press, 2007).
Sepinuck, S (ed), *Practice under Article 9 of the Uniform Commercial Code*, 2nd edn (Chicago, ABA UCC Committee, 2008).
Shen, J, *Research on the Transfer of Rights Focused on Transfer Notice* (Beijing, Law Press China, 2008).
Sigman, H and Kieninger, E (eds), *Cross-border Security over Receivables* (Munich, Sellier, 2009).
Smith, R, *Property Law* (London, Longman, 2003).
Tolhurst, G, *The Transfer of Contractual Rights* (Oxford, Hart Publishing, 2006).
Treitel, GH, *The Law of Contract* (London, Sweet & Maxwell, 2003).
——. *An Outline of the Law of Contract*, 6th edn (Oxford, Oxford University Press, 2005).
Uchida T, *Civil Code III Credit General and Security Right*, 3rd edn (Tokyo, University of Tokyo Press, 2006).
Uekaki, K and Ogawa, H, *Semi-official Guide (Ichi Mon Ichi Tou Dousan Saiken Jouto Tokurei Hou)*, 3rd edn (Tokyo, Shouji Houmu, 2008).
Weber, H, *Kreditsicherungsrecht*, 8th edn (Munich, CH Beck, 2006).
Welser, R, *Koziol-Welser Bürgerliches Recht Band II* (Vienna, Manz, 2007).
Wood, P, *Principles of International Insolvency* (London, Sweet & Maxwell, 2007).
——. *Law and Practice of International Finance, University Edition* (London, Sweet & Maxwell, 2008).

Articles/Chapters

Aleknaitė, L, 'Why the Fruits of Capital Markets are Less Accessible in Civil Law Jurisdictions or How France and Germany Try to Benefit from Asset Securitisation' (2007) 5 *DePaul Business & Commercial Law Journal* 191.

Bazinas, SV, 'The Work of UNCITRAL on Security Rights: An Overview' [2010] *Uniform Law Review* 315.
Bebchuk, L and Fried, J, 'The Uneasy Case for the Priority of Secured Claims in Bankruptcy', (1996) 105 *Yale Law Journal* 857.
Cuming, R, 'The International Registry for Interests in Aircraft: An Overview of its Structure' [2006] *Uniform Law Review* 14.
Derham, R, 'Recent Issues in Relation to Set-Off' (1994) 68 *Australian Law Journal* 331.
Fenton, R, 'Notice to the Debtor in Statutory Assignment: New Zealand Developments' (2008) 5 *Conveyancer and Property Lawyer* 392.
Finch, S, 'Canada' in W Johnston (ed), *Security over Receivables: An International Handbook* (Oxford, Oxford University Press, 2008).
Fox, D, 'Relativity of Title at Law and in Equity' (2006) 65 *CLJ* 330.
Getzler, J, 'The Role of Security over Future and Circulating Capital: Evidence from the British Economy circa 1850–1920' in J Getzler and J Payne (eds), *Company Charges: Spectrum and Beyond* (Oxford, Oxford University Press, 2006).
Goode, R, 'The Protection of Interests in Movables in Transnational Commercial Law' [1998] *Uniform Law Review* 453.
Gordon, J and Muller, C, 'Confronting Financial Crisis: Dodd-Frank's Dangers and the Case for a Systemic Emergency Insurance Fund' (2011) 28 *Yale Journal on Regulation* 151.
Gullifer, L, 'What Should We Do about Financial Collateral?' (2012) 65 *Current Legal Problems* 377.
Haag, H and Peglow, O, 'Germany' in W Johnston (ed), *Security over Receivables: An International Handbook* (Oxford, Oxford University Press, 2008).
Harris, S, 'The International Rail Registry' (2007) 12(3) *Uniform Law Review* 531.
Hubert, O, 'France' in W Johnston (ed), *Security over Receivables: An International Handbook* (Oxford, Oxford University Press, 2008).
Kieninger, M, 'General Principles on the Law Applicable to the Transfer of Receivables in Europe' in J Basedow, H Baum and Y Nishitani (eds), *Japanese and European Private International Law in Comparative Perspective* (Tubingen, Mohr Siebeck, 2008).
Kim, JH, 'Organisation and Contents of the Draft of the Act Concerning Security Rights in Movable Assets, Receivables, etc.' (2009) 58(11) *Lawyers Association Journal* 5.
Kötz, H, 'Rights of Third Parties. Third Party Beneficiaries and Transfer' in A Mehren (ed), *International Encyclopedia of Comparative Law*, Volume 7, Chapter 13 (Tubingen, Möhr, 1992).
Leavy, J, 'France' in H Sigman and M Kieninger (eds), *Cross-border Security over Receivables* (Munich, Sellier, 2009).
Lee, C, 'Study on Development and Evolving Process of Securitisation Laws in Korea' (2005) 18(2) *Commercial Case Study (SangSaPanRyeYeonGu)* 208.
Lee, M, 'Securitisation in Korea' (2002) 2(1) *Journal of Korean Law* 116.
Lipson, J, 'Secrets and Liens: The End of Notice in Commercial Finance Law' (2005) 21 *Emory Bankruptcy Developments Journal* 421.
LoPucki, L, 'The Unsecured Creditor's Bargain' (1994) 80 *Virginia Law Review* 1887.
LoPucki, L, Abraham, A and Delahaye, B, 'Optimizing English and American Security Rights' (2013) 88 *Notre Dame Law Review* 1785.
Mooney, Jr, C, 'The Mystery and Myth of Ostensible Ownership and Article 9 Filing: A Critique of Proposals to Extend Filing Requirements to Leases' (1988) 39 *Alabama Law Review* 683.

——. 'Relationship between the Prospective UNIDROIT International Registry, Revised Uniform Commercial Code Article 9 and National Civil Aviation Registries' [1999] *Uniform Law Review* 335.

——. 'Transfers of International Interests in Mobile Equipment and Related Receivables under the UNIDROIT Convention: When Should the Tail Wag the Dog?' (1999) 20(3) *University of Pennsylvania Journal of International Economic Law* 443.

Pennington, RR, 'The Genesis of the Floating Charge' (1960) 23 *Modern Law Review* 630.

Rakob, JK, 'Germany' in H Sigman and M Kieninger (eds), *Cross-border Security over Receivables* (Munich, Sellier, 2009).

Rank, W, 'The Netherlands' in W Johnston (ed), *Security over Receivables: An International Handbook* (Oxford, Oxford University Press, 2008).

Roff, E, 'New York' in W Johnston (ed), *Security over Receivables: An International Handbook* (Oxford, Oxford University Press, 2008).

Rudden B, 'Economic Theory v Property Law: The *Numerus Clausus* Problem' in J Eekelaar and J Bell (eds), *Oxford Essays in Jurisprudence* (Oxford, Clarendon Press, 1987).

Salomons, A, 'Deformalisation of Transfer Law and the Position of the Debtor in European Property Law' (2007) 15 *European Review of Private Law* 639.

Schwarcz, S, 'The Universal Language of International Securitization' (2002) 12 *Duke Journal of Comparative & International Law* 285.

——. 'Securitisation Post-Enron' (2004) 25 *Cardozo Law Review* 1539, 1540.

Sigman, H, 'Security in Movables in the United States—Uniform Commercial Code Article 9: A Basis for Comparison', in M Kieninger (ed), *Security Rights in Movable Property in European Private Law* (Cambridge, Cambridge University Press, 2004).

Thiele, A, 'Dutch Securitisations: A Step Forward' (2005) *In-House Lawyer* 30.

Timmerman, S and Veder, M, 'The Netherlands' in H Sigman and M Kieninger M (eds), *Cross-border Security over Receivables* (Munich, Sellier, 2009).

Vermylen, M, 'Belgium' in W Johnston (ed), *Security over Receivables: An International Handbook* (Oxford, Oxford University Press, 2008).

Yarnell, M and May, R, 'New Zealand' in W Johnston (ed), *Security over Receivables: An International Handbook* (Oxford, Oxford University Press, 2008).

Zhang, X, 'Notification: Effectiveness Requirement of the Transfer of Rights' (2005) 7 *Legal Science Monthly* 97.

INDEX

After-acquired property
  priority 179–80
  and reservation of title 186–7
Anti-assignment clauses
  Draft International Receivables Registry
    Convention 272
    IRT receivables 219–20
    text of Art 20 272
  governing law 154
  validity 219
Australia
  after-acquired property
    priority 179–80
    and reservation of title 186–7
  classification of jurisdiction 99
  comparative analysis of perfection and
    priority
    answers to six common questions 108–9
    case study 71–2
    preliminary answers to the six common
      questions 73–4
    six common questions 72–3
  governing law 156
  information requirements for
    registration 20, 54–5
  negative pledges 179–80
  perfection 108
  Personal Property Security Acts (PPSAs) 20
  potential transferee checkpoints 109
  priority 109
  purchase-money security interests 185
  reservation of title
    comprehensive security right 182–3
    purchase-money security interest 183–5
  terminology of security rights 5
Austria
  classification of jurisdiction 100
  comparative analysis of perfection and
    priority
    answers to six common questions 135–6
    case study 71–2
    preliminary answers to the six common
      questions 73–4
    six common questions 72–3
  governing law 157
  perfection 135–6
  potential transferee checkpoints 136
  priority 136

Belgium
  classification of jurisdiction 100
  comparative analysis of perfection and
    priority
    answers to six common questions
      119–20
    case study 71–2
    preliminary answers to the six common
      questions 73–4
    six common questions 72–3
  governing law 157
  perfection 119
  potential transferee checkpoints 120
  priority 120
Block discounting
  bulk transfers of receivables 164
  potential transferee checkpoints 72
  receivables financing 7
  receivables financing structure 3, 9
Bonds
  covered bonds 254–5
  debts represented by 254
  security rights 255–6
Bordereau 84–6

Canada
  after-acquired property
    priority 179–80
    and reservation of title 186–7
  classification of jurisdiction 99
  comparative analysis of perfection and
    priority
    answers to six common questions 105–6
    case study 71–2
    preliminary answers to the six common
      questions 73–4
    six common questions 72–3
  governing law 156
  negative pledges 179–80
  perfection 105
  Personal Property Security Acts (PPSAs) 20
  potential transferee checkpoints 106
  priority 106
  purchase-money security interests 185
  reservation of title
    comprehensive security right 182–3
    purchase-money security interest 183–5
  terminology of security rights 5

Index

Cape Town Convention
  consent before registration 64–5
  efforts at harmonisation 41
  interaction with Draft International Receivables Registry Convention
    extension to transfer of receivables 218–19
    overlap of scope 217
    transfers of associated receivables 217–18
  searches 68
China
  classification of jurisdiction 100
  comparative analysis of perfection and priority
    answers to six common questions 127–31
    case study 71–2
    preliminary answers to the six common questions 73–4
    six common questions 72–3
  governing law 157
  Japanese and Korean systems compared 36
  perfection 127–30
  pledges
    movable assets 26–7
    receivables 27–8
  potential transferee checkpoints 131
  priority 130–1
Compensatory damages
  anti-assignment clauses 220
  contractual prohibitions on transfers 272
  delay in payment by debtor 232
  false registrations 212–13
  necessity of registration 169
  potential transferees without publicity 167
  time of creation doctrine 83–4
Conflict of laws *see* **Governing law**
Consenting parties
  Cape Town Convention 64–5
  defined 263
  double-debtor problem 246–7
  safeguards against improper registration 57
  three general approaches
    authorisation by grantor before registration 59–62
    compulsory notice to grantor 58–9
    consent before registration 62–5
Contractual prohibitions *see* **Anti-assignment clauses**
Convention on International Interests in Mobile Equipment *see* **Cape Town Convention**
Creditors *see* **Execution creditors**; **Preferential creditors**; **Secured creditors**
Crystallisation
  effect on set-offs 81
  English floating charges 179

International Receivables Registry (proposed) 250
negative pledges 249–50

Damages *see* **Compensatory damages**
Debtor-indexed registration systems
  double-debtor problem
    changes of jurisdiction 177–8
    English law 173–5
    systemic weakness 170–3
    Uniform Commercial Code (UCC) 175–8
  England 17–18
  no publicity
    possible solutions 165–6
    underlying problems 167–8
  problems of notification
    bulk transfers 164–5
    future receivables 164
    growing problem 163–4
  registration
    necessity 168–70
    possible solutions 165–6
Deregistration of IRTs
  Draft International Receivables Registry Convention 265
  procedure 213
Discounting *see* **Block discounting**
Document-filing systems
  see also **Notice-filing systems**
  applicability to proposed IRR 221
  impracticalities 57
  Korea 56
  need to replace 19
  notice-filing systems compared 47–8
  safeguards against improper registration 57
Domestic registration systems
  Australia
    information requirements for registration 20, 54–5
    Personal Property Security Acts (PPSAs) 20
  China
    mortgages 25–6
    pledges 26–8
  England
    authorisation by grantor before registration 62
    debtor-indexed registration system 17–18
    information requirements for registration 52–3, 56
    non-possessory security rights 14–15
    publicity problems 15–16
    registration as *ex ante* method 16
    registration system for company charges 16–17
    searches 65–6
  France 24, 28
  functions 1

Index

Germany
  fiduciary transfers of title 23–4
  numerus clausus principle 22–3
  special registers 24
Japan
  consent before registration 62–3
  information requirements for registration 53–4, 56
  Japanese Transfer Registration Act 30–2
  optional registration 28–9
  searches 66–7
  Special Act for the Transfer of Receivables 30
  Specified Claims Act 29–30
Korea
  Asset-Backed Securitisation Act 32–3
  authorisation by grantor before registration 62
  information requirements for registration 53, 56
  Korean Security Registration Act 33–6
  MBS Company Act 33
  optional registration 28–9
New Zealand
  information requirements for registration 52, 54–5
  Personal Property Security Acts (PPSAs) 20
Personal Property Security Acts (PPSAs) 20
Uniform Commercial Code (UCC)
  historical background 18–19
  notice-filing system 19
Double-debtor problem
  changes of jurisdiction 177–8
  English law
    bona fide purchasers without notice 174–5
    nemo dat quod non habet rule 173–4
  International Receivables Registry (proposed)
    consent of secured creditors to transfers 246–7
    jurisdiction 242–5
    secured creditors rights in proceeds 245–6
    security rights and subsequent transfers 240–2
  systemic weakness 170–3
  Uniform Commercial Code (UCC)
    buyers in ordinary course of business 176–7
    taking subject to perfected security 175–6
Double security rights
  IRT receivables
    created by an IRT 238
    created by an IRT followed by transfers 239–40
    Draft International Receivables Registry Convention 240
    followed by transfers 238–9

Double transfers
  function of publicity 13
  IRT receivables
    creation of subsequent security rights 237
    double transfers by IRT 235–6
    and subsequent transfer by transferees 236–7
  necessity of registration 169
  problem with no publicity 167
  time of creation doctrine 83–4
Draft Common Frame of Reference (DCFR)
  consent before registration 63–4
  efforts at harmonisation 39–40
Draft International Receivables Registry Convention *see also* **International Receivables Registry (proposed)**
  anti-assignment clauses
    IRT receivables 219–20
    text of Art 20 272
  consent of secured creditors 271
  contractual prohibitions on transfers 272
  definitions 263–4
  deregistration of IRTs 265
  double security rights 240
  false registrations 271
  floating security rights 267
  information required to effect registration 269
  interaction with Cape Town Convention
    extension to transfer of receivables 218–19
    overlap of scope 217
    transfers of associated receivables 217–18
  International Receivables Registry (proposed) 268
  jurisdiction 270
  notice to debtors 270
  perfection 266
  priority 265, 267
  proceeds 266
  registration, amendment and discharge 269
  registration of IRTs 265
  searches 271
  sphere of application 264
    companies 215–17
    connecting factors 213–14
    future receivables 214–15
  supervisory authority and the registrar 268
  transfers of security rights 267

EBRD Model Law on Secured Transactions
  contents 37–8
  efforts at harmonisation 36
  Guide to Movables Registries 197
England
  authorisation by grantor before registration 62
  classification of jurisdiction 100–1

280 Index

comparative analysis of perfection and priority
  answers to six common questions 120–6
  case study 71–2
  preliminary answers to the six common questions 73–4
  six common questions 72–3
debtor-indexed registration systems 17–18
double-debtor problem
  bona fide purchasers without notice 174–5
  nemo dat quod non habet rule 173–4
floating security rights
  floating charges 178–9
  and reservation of title 186
governing law 157
information requirements for registration 52–3, 56
non-possessory security rights
  long legal history 14–15
  publicity problems 15–16
perfection
  against insolvency trustee 92–3
  security rights 120–1
potential transferee checkpoints 126
priority
  equitable assignments 122–3
  security rights 125–6
  statutory assignments 123–4
  time order of notice 121
purchase-money security interests 185
registration as *ex ante* method 16
registration system for company charges 16–17
reservation of title 182
searches 65–6
terminology of security rights 5
EU Directive on Financial Collateral Arrangements
financial collateral
  credit claims 147
  publicity 147
implementation 148–50
perfection 148
priority 148
scope of application 146–7
Execution creditors
Australia 108
defined 168
England 120
Germany 83
Hong Kong 142–3
Korea and Japan 75
necessity of registration 168
New Zealand 107
perfection requirements 88, 91, 93–4
problems of notification 164

Factoring
bulk transfers of receivables 164
meaning and scope 4
potential transferee checkpoints 72
receivables financing 7
False registrations
Draft International Receivables Registry Convention 271
International Receivables Traders (IRTs)
  compensatory damages 212–13
  disqualification of IRT 212
  fines 212
Fiduciary transfers of title
Germany 23–4
identification of encumbered assets 190
Japan 30–2
Korea 35
Filing systems *see* **Document-filing systems; Notice-filing systems**
Floating security rights
defined 263
double-debtor problem 170
Draft International Receivables Registry Convention 267
International Receivables Registry (proposed)
  crystallisation 250
  fixed and floating charges 247–8
  versus reservation of title 251
  subsequent security rights 249–50
  subsequent transfers 249
  two types of security rights 248–9
priority
  after-acquired property 179–80
  English floating charges 178–9
  negative pledges 180
  and reservation of title 185–7
France
classification of jurisdiction 100
comparative analysis of perfection and priority
  answers to six common questions 114–19
  case study 71–2
  preliminary answers to the six common questions 73–4
  six common questions 72–3
general security rights registry 28
governing law 157
perfection 114–17
potential transferee checkpoints 118–19
priority 117–18
special registers 24
terminology of security rights 5
Future receivables
Chinese Japanese and Korean systems compared 36
Draft International Receivables Registry Convention 214–15, 263

floating security rights   185, 248
France   116
function of publicity   13
Germany   132
governing law   153
Japan   54, 56
Netherlands   137
problems of notification   164
proposed IRR   260
Un Receivables Convention   41
valuation challenges   203

Germany
classification of jurisdiction   100
comparative analysis of perfection and priority
    answers to six common questions   131–4
    case study   71–2
    preliminary answers to the six common questions   73–4
    six common questions   72–3
fiduciary transfers of title   23–4
governing law   157
numerus clausus principle   22–3
perfection   131–3
potential transferee checkpoints   134
priority   133–4
special registers   24
terminology of security rights   5

Governing law
concluding remarks   187
insolvency   154
international Receivables Trader   205
perfection   159–62
potential transferee checkpoints   162
priority
    private international laws   156–9
    Rome I Regulation   155–6
relationship between competing transferees   154–5
relationship between transferor and debtor   153–4
relationship between transferor and transferee   153
triangular relationship of transfers   152–3
Un Receivables Convention   163

Hong Kong
classification of jurisdiction   100–1
perfection   142–3
potential transferee checkpoints   146
priority   143–6

Information centres   102–3
Insolvency administrators
defined   264

double-debtor problem
    consent of secured creditors to transfers   246–7
    rights in proceeds   245–6
governing law   154
perfection   72
perfection against administrator
    terminology   89–90
    as transferee   90–1
    as trustee   92–4
preferential creditors under proposed IRR
    concluding remarks   258
    general principles   252
    perfection   230
procedures of grantor   94–6
receivables financing   7
secured creditors
    disadvantages of international system   46
    double security rights   238–40
    Draft International Receivables Registry Convention   271
    perfection   72
    purpose of publicity   14
    reservation of title   181
International conventions
see also **Draft International Receivables Registry Convention**
Cape Town Convention   41
    consent before registration   64–5
    efforts at harmonisation   41
    interaction with Draft International Receivables Registry Convention   217–19
    searches   68
Rome I Regulation
    priority   155–6
    relationship between transferor and transferee   153
Rome II Regulation
    relationship between competing transferees   155
    relationship between transferor and transferee   153
UN Convention on the Transfer of Receivables
    governing law   163
    overview   40–1
International Receivables Registry (proposed)
see also **Draft International Receivables Registry Convention**; **International registration system**
benefits   8–9
compulsory registration
    limitations on scope   200
    purely international transactions   200–2
    restrictions on parties   203–4
    types of receivables   202–3
    value of receivables   203

concluding remarks 259–62
coverage of both transfers and security rights 194
deregistration of IRTs 213
double-debtor problem
  consent of secured creditors to transfers 246–7
  jurisdiction 242–5
  secured creditors rights in proceeds 245–6
  security rights and subsequent transfers 240–2
Draft International Receivables Registry Convention 268
false registrations
  compensatory damages 212–13
  disqualification of IRT 212
  fines 212
floating security rights
  crystallisation 250
  fixed and floating charges 247–8
  versus reservation of title 251
  subsequent security rights 249–50
  subsequent transfers 249
  two types of security rights 248–9
general conclusions 226–8
identification of encumbered assets 189–90
new set of rules 191–2
notice-filing system
  information requirements for registration 221–2
  notice by email 223–4
  underlying rationale 220–1
online searches 226
overview 188–9
parties' reciprocal confirmation of information 222–3
perfection
  general principles 230
  overview 229–30
preferential creditors 217
priority
  bonds 254–6
  double-debtor problem 240–7
  double security rights 238–40
  double transfers 235–7
  effectiveness against debtor 232–3
  floating security rights 247–50
  knowledge irrelevant 231–2
  by order of registration 230–1
  overview 229–30
  prior security rights and subsequent transfers 234
  prior transfers and subsequent security rights 234–5
  between registration and notice 233–4
  reservation of title 250–1
  subordination agreements 256–7

registration
  compulsory registration 196
  legislative guide for domestic systems 197
  optional registration 196–7
  scope of registry 194–6
registration of IRTs
  methods to use Registry 207–9
  pre-existing transfers 210–12
  public notification 207
  treatment of pre-existing security rights 209–10
relationship with national laws
  problems with optional registration 198–200
  two alternative approaches 197–8
reservation of title
  versus floating security rights 251
  purchase-money security interests 251
  versus transfers 250–1
restrictions on scope of application
  indexing by IRTs 206
  international Receivables Trader 204–5
  where transferor or grantor is IRT 205–6
separate registry for different assets 190–1
supervisory authority 224–6
terminology
  receivables 192
  security rights in receivables 193–4
  transfers of receivables 192–3
  translation difficulties 189
International Receivables Traders (IRTs)
defined 264
deregistration
  Draft International Receivables Registry Convention 265
  procedure 213
disqualification 212
registration
  Draft International Receivables Registry Convention 265
  methods to use Registry 207–9
  pre-existing transfers 210–12
  public notification 207
  treatment of pre-existing security rights 209–10
restrictions on scope of proposed Registry
  basic approach 204–5
  indexing by IRTs 206
  where transferor or grantor is IRT 205–6
International registration system
see also **International Receivables Registry (proposed)**
advantages
  analysis 46–7
  benefits of common law jurisdiction 42–3
  movable assets as security 42
  World Bank Report 43–5

disadvantages
    analysis   46–7
    over-leverage   45–6
    treatment of unsecured creditors   46
functions   1–2
international conventions
    Cape Town Convention   41
    UN Convention on the Transfer of
        Receivables   40–1
soft law approaches
    Draft Common Frame of Reference
        (DCFR)   39–40
    EBRD Model Law on Secured
        Transactions   37–8
    OAS Model Inter-American Law on
        Secured Transactions   38–9
    UNCITRAL Model Law on Secured
        Transactions   39
IRT receivables
    anti-assignment clauses   219–20
    defined   264
    double security rights
        created by an IRT   238
        created by an IRT followed by
            transfers   239–40
        Draft International Receivables Registry
            Convention   240
        followed by transfers   238–9
    double transfers
        creation of subsequent security rights   237
        double transfers by IRT   235–6
        and subsequent transfer by
            transferees   236–7

Japan
    Chinese and Korean systems compared   36
    classification of jurisdiction   99
    comparative analysis of perfection and
        priority
        answers to six common questions
            112–14
        case study   71–2
        preliminary answers to the six common
            questions   73–4
        six common questions   72–3
    consent before registration   62–3
    governing law   156
    information requirements for
        registration   53–4, 56
    Japanese Transfer Registration Act   30–2
    optional registration   28–9
    perfection   112–14
    potential transferee checkpoints   114
    priority   112–14
    searches   66–7
    Special Act for the Transfer of
        Receivables   30
    Specified Claims Act   29–30

Jurisdiction
    classification   99–102
    double-debtor problem   177–8, 242–5
    Draft International Receivables Registry
        Convention   270

Korea
    Asset-Backed Securitisation Act   32–3
    authorisation by grantor before
        registration   62
    Chinese and Japanese systems compared   36
    classification of jurisdiction   99
    comparative analysis of perfection and
        priority
        answers to six common questions
            109–12
        case study   71–2
        preliminary answers to the six common
            questions   73–4
        six common questions   72–3
    governing law   156
    information requirements for
        registration   53, 56
    MBS Company Act   33
    new form of security right   111
    optional registration   28–9
    perfection   109–10
    pledges   111
    potential transferee checkpoints   112
    priority   111–12

Mortgages
    benefits of registration   47
    China   25–6, 129
    Chinese Japanese and Korean systems
        compared   36
    covered bonds   255
    English law   6, 15–17
    Korea   33, 110
    numerus clausus principle   22–3
    pledges compared   22

Negative pledges   180, 249–50
***Nemo dat quod non habet* rule**   173–4
Netherlands
    classification of jurisdiction   100
    comparative analysis of perfection and
        priority
        answers to six common questions
            136–8
        case study   71–2
        preliminary answers to the six common
            questions   73–4
        six common questions   72–3
    governing law   157
    perfection   136–8
    potential transferee checkpoints   138
    priority   138

New Zealand
  after-acquired property
    priority 179–80
    and reservation of title 186–7
  classification of jurisdiction 99
  comparative analysis of perfection and priority
    answers to six common questions 106–8
    case study 71–2
    preliminary answers to the six common questions 73–4
    six common questions 72–3
  governing law 156
  information requirements for registration 52, 54–5
  negative pledges 179–80
  perfection 106–7
  perfection against insolvency trustee 93–4
  Personal Property Security Acts (PPSAs) 20
  potential transferee checkpoints 108
  priority 107–8
  purchase-money security interests 185
  reservation of title
    comprehensive security right 182–3
    purchase-money security interest 183–5
  terminology of security rights 5
Notice-filing systems
  see also **Document-filing systems**
  advance registration 50–1
  document-filing systems compared 47–8
  effect of registration 48–9
  International Receivables Registry (proposed)
    information requirements for registration 221–2
    notice by email 223–4
    underlying rationale 220–1
  priority
    entitlement to give notice 77–9
    perfection against debtor 80
    set-offs 80–1
    time order of notice 75
  safeguards against improper registration 57
  Uniform Commercial Code (UCC) 19
Numerus clausus principle
  obstacle to registration 20–1
  publicity 21–2

OAS Model Inter-American Law on Secured Transactions 38–9
Online searches 226

Perfection
  see also **Priority**
  comparative analysis
    answers to six common questions 103–46
    case study 71–2
    preliminary answers to the six common questions 73–4
    six common questions 72–3
  comparative requirements 88–9
  concluding remarks 150–1
  defined 70–1
  Draft International Receivables Registry Convention 266
  EU Directive on Financial Collateral Arrangements 148
  governing law 159–62
  insolvency administrators
    terminology 89–90
    as transferee 90–1
    as trustee 92–4
  insolvency procedures of grantor 94–6
  International Receivables Registry (proposed)
    general principles 230
    overview 229–30
  need for publicity
    four methods of publicity 12
    two main functions 13–14
  notice of transfer 80
  security rights in receivables
    checkpoints 96–9
    classification of jurisdiction 99–102
    against insolvency administrators 89–90
    insolvency administrators as transferees 90–1
    insolvency administrators as trustees 92–4
    insolvency procedures of grantor 94–6
    overview 86–8
    priority requirements 88–9
Personal Property Security Acts (PPSAs)
  adoption in Commonwealth countries 20
  after-acquired property
    priority 179–80
    and reservation of title 186–7
  negative pledges 179–80
  reservation of title
    comprehensive security right 183–5
    purchase-money security interest 183–5
  terminology of security rights 5
Pledges
  China
    movable assets 26–7
    receivables 27–8
  Chinese Japanese and Korean systems compared 36
  floating security rights 180
  France 117
  Korea 111
  mortgages compared 22
  negative pledges 180, 249–50
  numerus clausus principle 22–3

Index

Preferential creditors
Korea   33
priority in proposed IRR
  concluding remarks   258
  general principles   252
  perfection   230
secured creditors   23

Priority
see also **Perfection**
check points
  potential transferees   98–9
  between transfers and security
    rights   96–7
classification of jurisdictions   99–102
comparative analysis
  answers to six common questions
    103–46
  case study   71–2
  preliminary answers to the six common
    questions   73–4
  six common questions   72–3
concluding remarks   150–1
Draft International Receivables Registry
  Convention   265, 267
EU Directive on Financial Collateral
  Arrangements   148
floating security rights
  after-acquired property   179–80
  English floating charges   178–9
  negative pledges   180
  and reservation of title   185–7
governing law
  private international laws   156–9
  Rome I Regulation   155–6
International Receivables Registry (proposed)
  bonds   254–6
  double-debtor problem   240–7
  double security rights   238–40
  double transfers   235–7
  effectiveness against debtor   232–3
  floating security rights   247–50
  knowledge irrelevant   231–2
  by order of registration   230–1
  overview   229–30
  prior security rights and subsequent
    transfers   234
  prior transfers and subsequent security
    rights   234–5
  between registration and notice   233–4
  reservation of title   250–1
  subordination agreements   256–7
registration   81–2
reservation of title
  English law   182
  and floating security rights   185–7
  overview   180–2
  Uniform Commercial Code
    (UCC)   182–5

time of creation doctrine
  conclusion of transfer contract   82–4
  delivery of transfer deed   84–6
transfers of receivables
  checkpoints   96–9
  classification of jurisdiction   99–102
  notification   75–81
  registration   81–2
  time of creation doctrine   82–6
  transfers vis-a-vis third parties   75
transfers vis-a-vis third parties
  entitlement to give notice   77–9
  overview   75
  perfection against debtor   80
  set-offs   80–1
  time order of notice   75–7

Proceeds
from collection and sale of receivables
  252–3
double-debtor problem   245–6
Draft International Receivables Registry
  Convention   254, 265, 266
dual security rights   253
secured creditors rights   245
separated and reasonably identifiable   253

Publicity
debtor-indexed registration systems
  possible solutions   165–6
  underlying problems   167–8
EU Directive on Financial Collateral
  Arrangements   147
four methods of publicity   12
information centres   102–3
IRT receivables   207
non-possessory security rights in
  England   15–16
numerus clausus principle   21–2
two main functions
  evidence   14
  provision of information to
    public   13

Purchase-money security interests
Cape Town Convention   217
double-debtor problem   170
International Receivables Registry
  (proposed)   251
reservation of title   183–5

Receivables
see also **IRT receivables**
Chinese registry of pledges   27–8
defined   1, 264
factoring   4
financing   7
future receivables
  Draft International Receivables Registry
    Convention   214–15
  problems of notification   164

286　Index

International Receivables Registry
　(proposed)　192
securitisation　3
Registration *see* **Debtor-indexed registration systems; Domestic registration systems; International registration system; Notice-filing systems** see **International Receivables Registry (proposed)**
Research methods　9–10
Reservation of title
　Chinese Japanese and Korean systems compared　36
　double-debtor problem　170
　English law　182
　and floating security rights　185–7
　International Receivables Registry (proposed)
　　versus floating security rights　251
　　purchase-money security interests　251
　　versus transfers　250–1
　overview　180–2
　Personal Property Security Acts (PPSAs)
　　comprehensive security right　183–5
　　purchase-money security interest　183–5
　Uniform Commercial Code (UCC)
　　comprehensive security right　182–3
　　purchase-money security interest　183–5
Rome I Regulation
　priority　155–6
　relationship between transferor and transferee　153
Rome II Regulation
　relationship between competing transferees　155
　relationship between transferor and transferee　153

Searches
　differing approaches
　　Cape Town Convention　68
　　England　65–6
　　Japan　66–7
　　Uniform Commercial Code (UCC)　66
　Draft International Receivables Registry Convention　271
　International Receivables Registry (proposed)　226
Secured creditors
　disadvantages of international system　46
　double-debtor problem
　　consent of secured creditors to transfers　246–7
　　rights in proceeds　245–6
　double security rights　238–40
　Draft International Receivables Registry Convention　271
　perfection　72
　purpose of publicity　14
　reservation of title　181

Securitisation
　bulk transfers of receivables　164
　China　128–9
　France　114–17
　Germany　132
　Korea　32–3
　potential transferee checkpoints　72
　receivables generally　3
Security rights in receivables
　balance sheet accounting　7–8
　benefits　4–5
　comparative analysis of perfection and priority
　　answers to the six common questions　103–46
　　case study　71–2
　　perfection defined　70–1
　　six common questions　72–3
　　table of preliminary answers　73–4
　defined　264
　double security rights
　　created by an IRT　238
　　created by an IRT followed by transfers　239–40
　　Draft International Receivables Registry Convention　240
　　followed by transfers　238–9
　International Receivables Registry (proposed)
　　coverage of both transfers and security rights　194
　　terminology　193–4
　international terminology　5
　outright sales compared　86
　perfection
　　checkpoints　96–9
　　classification of jurisdiction　99–102
　　against insolvency administrators　89–90
　　insolvency administrators as transferees　90–1
　　insolvency administrators as trustees　92–4
　　insolvency procedures of grantor　94–6
　　overview　86–8
　　priority requirements　88–9
　priority in proposed IRR
　　prior security rights and subsequent transfers　234
　　prior transfers and subsequent security rights　234–5
Set-offs　80–1
Singapore
　classification of jurisdiction　100–1
　perfection　138–8, 138–9
　potential transferee checkpoints　142
　priority　139–42
Soft law
　Draft Common Frame of Reference (DCFR)　39–40

EBRD Model Law on Secured
    Transactions 36
OAS Model Inter-American Law on Secured
    Transactions 38–9
problems of over-leverage 45
UNCITRAL Model Law on Secured
    Transactions 39
Subordination agreements
  effectiveness under proposed IRR 230
  priority 256–7, 262
Supervisory authority 224–6, 268

Terminology
  Draft International Receivables Registry
      Convention 263–4
  insolvency administrators 89–90
  International Receivables Registry (proposed)
      receivables 192
      security rights in receivables 193–4
      transfers of receivables 192–3
      translation difficulties 189
  international terminology of receivables 5
Third parties
  see also **Publicity**
  information centres 102–3
  perfection 70–1
  priority of transfers
      entitlement to give notice 77–9
      overview 75
      perfection against debtor 80
      set-offs 80–1
      time order of notice 75
Time of creation doctrine
  conclusion of transfer contract 82–4
  delivery of transfer deed 84–6
Transfers of receivables
  comparative analysis of perfection and
      priority
      answers to the six common
          questions 103–46
      case study 71–2
      perfection defined 70–1
      six common questions 72–3
      table of preliminary answers 73–4
  double transfers
      creation of subsequent security
          rights 237
      double transfers by IRT 235–6
      function of publicity 13
      necessity of registration 169
      problem with no publicity 167
      and subsequent transfer by
          transferees 236–7
      time of creation doctrine 83–4
  Draft International Receivables Registry
      Convention 267
  governing law
      insolvency 154

  relationship between competing
      transferees 154–5
  relationship between transferor and
      debtor 153–4
  relationship between transferor and
      transferee 153
  triangular relationship 152–3
  importance 1
  International Receivables Registry (proposed)
      coverage of both transfers and security
          rights 194
      terminology 192–3
  international transfers of receivables 2–3
  meaning and scope 6–7
  priority
      checkpoints 96–9
      classification of jurisdiction 99–102
      notification 75–81
      registration 81–2
      time of creation doctrine 82–6
      transfers vis-a-vis third parties 75
  priority in proposed IRR
      prior security rights and subsequent
          transfers 234
      prior transfers and subsequent security
          rights 234–5

UN Convention on the Transfer of Receivables
  governing law 163
  overview 40–1
**UNCITRAL Model Law on Secured
    Transactions**
  advance registration of notice-filing 50–1
  authorisation by grantor before
      registration 61–2
  efforts at harmonisation 39
  information requirements for
      registration 20, 54–5
Uniform Commercial Code (UCC)
  advance registration of notice-filing 50–1
  after acquired property
      priority 179–80
  after-acquired property
      and reservation of title 186–7
  authorisation by grantor before
      registration 59–61
  classification of jurisdiction 99
  double-debtor problem
      buyers in ordinary course of
          business 176–7
      taking subject to perfected
          security 175–6
  governing law 156
  historical background 18–19
  information requirements for
      registration 51, 54–5
  perfection 103–4
  potential transferee checkpoints 105

priority 104–5
purchase-money security interests 185
reservation of title
  comprehensive security right 182–3
  and floating security rights 186–7
  purchase-money security interest 183–5
searches 66
terminology of security rights 5
United States *see* **Uniform Commercial Code (UCC)**

World Bank Report 43–5

Ingram Content Group UK Ltd.
Milton Keynes UK
UKHW021025040423
419614UK00005B/228